Regional Cultures, Economies, and Creativity

Drawing on Australian and comparative case studies, this volume reconceptualises non-metropolitan creative economies through the 'qualities of place'.

This book examines the agricultural and gastronomic cultures surrounding 'native' foods, coastal sculpture festivals, universities and regional communities, wine in regional Australia and Canada, the creative systems of the Hunter Valley, musicians in 'outback' settings, Fab Labs as alternatives to clusters, cinema and the cultivation of 'authentic' landscapes, and tensions between the 'representational' and 'non-representational' in the cultural economies of the Blue Mountains. What emerges is a picture of rural and regional places as more than the 'other' of metropolitan creative cities. Place itself is shown to embody affordances, unique institutional structures and the invisible threads that 'hold communities together'.

If, in the wake of the publication of Florida's *Rise of the Creative Class*, creative industries models tended to emphasise 'big cities' and the spatial-cum-cultural imaginaries of the 'Global North', recent research and policy discourses – especially, in the Australian context – have paid greater attention to 'small cities', rural and remote creativity. This collection will be of interest to scholars, students and practitioners in creative industries, urban and regional studies, sociology, geography and cultural planning.

Ariella Van Luyn is a lecturer in writing at the University of New England, Armidale. Her research interests include practice-led research, historical fiction, community narratives and regional creativity.

Eduardo de la Fuente is an adjunct fellow in the School of Humanities and Social Inquiry at the University of Wollongong. His research interests include culture, economy, creativity and place.

Routledge Advances in Sociology

Globalization, Modernity and the Rise of Religious Fundamentalism
The Challenge of Religious Resurgence against the "End of History" (A Dialectical Kaleidoscopic Analysis)
Dimitrios Methenitis

Urban Environments for Healthy Ageing
A Global Perspective
Edited by Anna Lane

Conflict and the Social Bond
Peace in Modern Societies
Michalis Lianos

Boundaries of European Social Citizenship
EU Citizens' Transnational Social Security in Regulations, Discourses and Experiences
Edited by Anna Amelina, Emma Carmel, Ann Runfors and Elisabeth Scheibelhofer

Cultures, Citizenship and Human Rights
Edited by Rosemarie Buikema, Antoine Buyse and Antonius Robben

Regional Cultures, Economies, and Creativity
Innovating Through Place in Australia and Beyond
Edited by Ariella Van Luyn and Eduardo de la Fuente

Care, Power, Information
For the Love of BluesCollarship in the Age of Digital Culture, Bioeconomy, and (Post-)Trumpism
Alexander I. Stingl

For more information about this series, please visit: www.routledge.com/Routledge-Advances-in-Sociology/book-series/SE0511

Regional Cultures, Economies, and Creativity

Innovating Through Place in Australia and Beyond

Edited by Ariella Van Luyn and Eduardo de la Fuente

LONDON AND NEW YORK

First published 2020
by Routledge
2 Park Square, Milton Park, Abingdon, Oxon OX14 4RN

and by Routledge
52 Vanderbilt Avenue, New York, NY 10017

Routledge is an imprint of the Taylor & Francis Group, an informa business

© 2020 selection and editorial matter, Ariella Van Luyn and Eduardo de la Fuente; individual chapters, the contributors

The right of Ariella Van Luyn and Eduardo de la Fuente to be identified as the authors of the editorial material, and of the authors for their individual chapters, has been asserted in accordance with sections 77 and 78 of the Copyright, Designs and Patents Act 1988.

All rights reserved. No part of this book may be reprinted or reproduced or utilised in any form or by any electronic, mechanical, or other means, now known or hereafter invented, including photocopying and recording, or in any information storage or retrieval system, without permission in writing from the publishers.

Trademark notice: Product or corporate names may be trademarks or registered trademarks, and are used only for identification and explanation without intent to infringe.

British Library Cataloguing-in-Publication Data
A catalogue record for this book is available from the British Library

Library of Congress Cataloging-in-Publication Data
Names: Van Luyn, Ariella, editor. | Fuente, Eduardo de la, editor.
Title: Regional cultures, economies, and creativity : innovating through
    place in Australia and beyond / [edited by] Ariella Van Luyn and Eduardo
    de la Fuente.
Description: London ; New York, NY : Routledge/Taylor & Francis
    Group, 2020. | Series: Routledge advances in sociology ; 272 | Includes
    bibliographical references and index.
Identifiers: LCCN 2019039390 (print) | LCCN 2019039391 (ebook) |
    ISBN 9781138310674 (hbk) | ISBN 9780429459290 (ebk)
Subjects: LCSH: Australia—Civilization. | Cultural landscapes—Australia. |
    Culture and tourism—Australia. | Culture—Economic aspects—Australia. |
    Regionalism—Australia. | Creation (Literary, artistic, etc.)—Australia. |
    Australia—Intellectual life—Economic aspects.
Classification: LCC DU107 .R44 2020 (print) | LCC DU107 (ebook) |
    DDC 338/.0640994—dc23
LC record available at https://lccn.loc.gov/2019039390
LC ebook record available at https://lccn.loc.gov/2019039391

ISBN: 978-1-138-31067-4 (hbk)
ISBN: 978-0-429-45929-0 (ebk)

Typeset in Bembo
by Apex CoVantage, LLC

Contents

List of contributors	viii
Acknowledgements	xv

Introduction: Problematising regional creativity and innovation in Australia and beyond: landscapes, economies, identities, imaginaries   1
EDUARDO DE LA FUENTE AND ARIELLA VAN LUYN

SECTION 1
Landscapes, tastescapes and sensescapes: Creatively responding to place   19

1 **Fruit forward? Wine regions as geographies of innovation in Australia and Canada**   21
JULIE MCINTYRE, DONNA SENESE AND JOHN S. HULL

2 **There's no taste like home: Histories of native food on the changing tastescape of the Northern Rivers**   45
ADELE WESSEL

3 **Terraform and Terra Firma: Transnational economies of image, landscape and location in screen production in Queensland**   67
ALLISON CRAVEN

4 **Landscape as tension: The Blue Mountains and cultural economies of place**   82
EDUARDO DE LA FUENTE

vi *Contents*

5 **Deck-chair innovation: Innovation within arm's reach for regional Australian architecture: A little of what we found when we rode the Grand Section across Australia's girth in 2017** 102

BOBBIE BAYLEY AND OWEN KELLY, INSPIRED BY
AND CO-AUTHORED WITH JOHN ROBERTS

SECTION 2
Placing knowledge and innovation economies: Regional universities, ecosystems and Fab Labs 119

6 **The troubling third tier: Small cities, small universities and an ambivalent knowledge economy** 121

TARA BRABAZON

7 **Locating knowledge in Australian cities: The Knowledge City Index** 142

LAWRENCE PRATCHETT, MICHAEL JAMES WALSH,
RICHARD HU AND SAJEDA TULI

8 **Universities and regional creative economies** 159

DONNA HANCOX, TERRY FLEW, SASHA MACKAY AND YI WANG

9 **The role of Fab Labs and Living Labs for economic development of regional Australia** 174

ANA BILANDZIC, MARCUS FOTH AND GREG HEARN

SECTION 3
Regional creative industries and their potentials: Case studies and comparative perspectives 199

10 **The Hunter Region: A creative system at work** 201

PHILLIP MCINTYRE, SUSAN KERRIGAN, EVELYN KING
AND CLAIRE WILLIAMS

11 **"Anything that's not in London": Regions, mobility and spatial politics in contemporary visual art** 223

EMMA COFFIELD

12 **Sculptural coastlines: Site-specific artworks, beachscapes, and regional identities** 244

ELIZABETH ELLISON AND MICHELLE THOMPSON

Contents vii

13 One piece blokes: On being a performing musician in regional Queensland 259

ANDY BENNETT, DAVID CASHMAN AND NATALIE LEWANDOWSKI

14 Positive deviance: Stories of regional social innovations from the *Big Stories, Small Towns* project 270

MARTIN POTTER

Index 287

Contributors

Bobbie Bayley (BDes Arch) and her research partner Owen Kelly are architectural practitioners, academics and overlanders. Their unprecedented study of Australia's inland architecture has positioned them at the forefront of arid and semi-arid design thinking. Their continued research focuses on designing specifically for Australia, questioning the mongrel-esque buildings of Australia's architectural heritage. Their work has been recognised and awarded by the Australian Institute of Architects. Bobbie grew up in the Hunter Valley, NSW. She studied at the University of Newcastle, NSW. She has worked widely in Nepal, Regional Australia, the USA and Peru. Bobbie has won several prestigious scholarships including the Byera Hadley Travelling Scholarship. Engagement is at the core of her approach. After spending a year living in a $5.5m^2$ footprint, Bobbie is interested in how much building we actually need.

Andy Bennett is Professor of Cultural Sociology in the School of Humanities, Languages and Social Science at Griffith University. He has written and edited numerous books including *Popular Music and Youth Culture*, *Music, Style and Aging* and *Music Scenes* (co-edited with Richard A. Peterson). He is a faculty fellow of the Yale Centre for Cultural Sociology, an international research fellow of the Finnish Youth Research Network, a founding member of the Consortium for Youth, Generations and Culture and a founding member of the Regional Music Research Group.

Ana Bilandzic is a PhD candidate with the Urban Informatics Research Group at QUT Design Lab, Brisbane, Australia. Her research is on social and spatial precursors for innovation in innovation hubs. She aims to unpack these precursors by investigating hubs that have a focus on social innovation in the peri-urban area of Brisbane. Her research is motivated by the increasing number of innovation spaces around the world as well as an early study conducted in collaboration with her colleagues discovering users' needs for diversity in such spaces.

Tara Brabazon is the Dean of Graduate Research and the Professor of Cultural Studies at Flinders University in Australia. She is the author of 18 books including *The University of Google, City Imaging, Digital Dieting* and *Trump Studies*. She has won six teaching awards, has written over 200 refereed articles and chapters and is a columnist for the *Times Higher Education*.

David Cashman is an educator, researcher, musician and advocate for the Australian music industry. He has designed degree programs in the creative industries and lectured in contemporary music, jazz, art music and music technology. As a researcher, his area of research interest is live music performance and industry, particularly in regional areas and in tourism, and the performance practice thereof. He has worked with and consulted for peak industry bodies and local and state governments.

Emma Coffield is an early career academic fellow at Newcastle University, UK, where she works in the School of Arts and Cultures. Emma leads the Art Museum and Gallery Studies MA and contributes to a wide range of teaching. Her interdisciplinary research focuses on artist-run initiatives, the everyday experiences of creative practitioners, identity, inequality, spatial politics and employability in the cultural and creative industries. A co-authored book, *Art Museum and Gallery Studies: The Basics*, was published with Prof Rhiannon Mason and Alistair Robinson in 2018.

Allison Craven is Associate Professor of Screen Studies and English at James Cook University, Townsville, Australia. She publishes on Australian cinema and has written extensively on film and cinema in Queensland, including her book, *Finding Queensland in Australian Cinema: Poetics and Screen Geographies* (2016). She also publishes on transnational fairytale, gender and culture and is the author of *Fairy Tale Interrupted: Feminism, Masculinity, Wonder Cinema* (2017).

Eduardo de la Fuente is an adjunct fellow in the School of Humanities and Social Inquiry, University of Wollongong and a faculty fellow of the Yale Center for Cultural Sociology. His work deals with the topics of culture, economy, creativity and place; he is currently developing a line of theoretical and empirical inquiry he has labelled "textural sociology," a topic on which he recently published a programmatic essay in *The Sociological Review*. Eduardo's interest in the textures of social and cultural, economic and spatial life has recently focused upon topics such as the role of "glossiness" in producing a sense of cosmopolitan modernity, changing attitudes to Brutalist architecture and to the material and affective qualities of concrete, how music and sound are used to constitute atmospheres of domesticity/homeliness and the role played by landscape within (particularly) regional creative and cultural economies.

Elizabeth Ellison is a senior lecturer in creative industries at Central Queensland University, Noosa, Australia. She researches Australian writing, film and television, with a special interest in the Australian beach. Her PhD explored representations of the Australian beach in literature and film, and

x *Contributors*

she continues to publish in this area, including the upcoming edited collection *Writing the Australian Beach: Global Site, Local Idea* (with Donna Lee Brien).

Terry Flew is Professor of Communication and Creative Industries in the Creative Industries Faculty at the Queensland University of Technology, Brisbane, Australia. He is the author of 11 books, including *Understanding Global Media* (2018), *Politics, Media and Democracy in Australia* (2017), *Media Economics* (2015) and *Global Creative Industries* (2013). He has been an executive board member of the International Communications Association (ICA) since 2013 and served as ICA president in 2019–2020. He has been a chief investigator on seven Australian Research Council (ARC) grants and has led an ARC Discovery Project on Digital Platform Governance and the Future of Media Policy from 2019–2021. In 2011–12, Professor Flew chaired the Australian Law Reform Commission Review of the National Media Classification Scheme.

Marcus Foth is Professor of Urban Informatics in the QUT Design Lab, Creative Industries Faculty, at Queensland University of Technology. His transdisciplinary work is at the international forefront of human–computer interaction research and development with a focus on smart cities, community engagement, media architecture, internet studies, ubiquitous computing and sustainability. Professor Foth founded the Urban Informatics Research Lab in 2006 and the QUT Design Lab in 2016. Ahead of their time and before the term "smart cities" became popular, Foth pioneered a new field of study and practice: urban informatics examines people creating, applying and using information and communication technology and data in cities and urban environments.

Donna Hancox is the Associate Director of the Creative Lab at Queensland University of Technology. Her research is focussed on transformative creative practice and social impact, particularly the role of stories and creative technology in amplifying marginalised voices. In the past two years she has led research projects working with refugee and asylum-seeker communities around the notions of belonging and inclusion that deployed arts-led methods for data collection and large-scale digital storytelling projects in regional and remote Australia. Currently Dr Hancox is a chief investigator on the 2018 ARC Linkage project *The Role of the Creative Arts in Regional Australia: A Social Impact Model*. She has published extensively in international journals and edited collections in her field and was a Leverhulme Visiting Fellow at Bath Spa University in 2013. In 2017, she was awarded a Smithsonian Research Fellowship to collaborate with the Cooper Hewitt National Design Museum in New York City.

Greg Hearn is Research Professor and Director of Commercial Research and Development in the Creative Industries Faculty. His research has examined the evolution of creative systems from economic social and cultural perspectives. Most recently he has examined creative work and careers, including a study of 20 creative regional hotspots across Australia.

Richard Hu is an urban planner and designer and is Professor at Canberra Business School, University of Canberra. Richard has cross-national academic and professional experiences in Australia, China and America and has undertaken many significant urban projects there. Currently, Richard provides research and consulting services for Australian federal, state and local governments and the business sectors to inform planning and policy making for competitive and sustainable Australian cities and regions.

John Hull is an associate professor in the Faculty of Adventure, Culinary Arts and Tourism, Thompson Rivers University, Canada, in the Tourism Management Department. He is also affiliated with Harz University of Applied Sciences in Germany and the New Zealand Tourism Research Institute at AUT University, New Zealand. Dr Hull researches in economic geography focused on themes of mountain and polar tourism as well as food/wine and health/wellness tourism.

Owen Kelly (MA) and his research partner Bobbie Bayley are architectural practitioners, academics and overlanders. Their unprecedented study of Australia's inland architecture has positioned them at the forefront of arid and semi-arid design thinking. Their continued research focuses on designing specifically for Australia, questioning the mongrel-esque buildings of Australia's architectural heritage. Their work has been recognised and awarded by the Australian Institute of Architects. Kelly was raised in the Blue Mountains and studied at Newcastle, NSW. Owen continues his involvement with Healthabitat after instigating the Healthabitat Nepal Sanitation Studios in 2013. He has worked in Regional Australia and Nepal. He believes architecture should think about place, people and buildings, in that order.

Susan Kerrigan is an associate professor at the University of Newcastle, Australia. She is a screen production scholar who specialises in creative practice research methodologies. She was co-investigator on the Filmmaking Research Network grant, funded by the UK's Arts and Humanities Research Council, and has held an Australian Research Council Grant investigating the creative industries. Susan has professionally produced and directed Australian television programs, including *Play School*.

Evelyn King is a freelance writer with an interest in the role of the creative and knowledge industries in urban regeneration and the potential of local government in supporting the growth of sustainable jobs in the sector. With a background in education, PR and the development of cultural and heritage tourism, her most recent roles have been in urban revitalisation, smart cities and innovation ecosystems.

Natalie Lewandowski graduated with a PhD in 2015, through Macquarie University, on Australian and New Zealand film soundtrack personnel.

xii *Contributors*

Natalie has lectured in screen sound, media copyright and Australian contemporary art and has published articles on soundtrack personnel, sound in contemporary Australian film, music supervision and science fiction. Her recent research projects include an edited volume on music, health and well-being; regional live music scenes; music in the animated film series *Toy Story*; and labour studies in the Australian and New Zealand film soundtrack industries.

Sasha Mackay is a research associate in the Creative Industries Faculty at the Queensland University of Technology, Brisbane, Australia. She is a former creative producer at social impact arts organisation Creative Regions, where she designed and led oral history and digital storytelling projects with and for regional communities. Sasha's PhD, awarded in 2015, investigated life narrative as a form of participation in public service media and the profound challenges and exciting opportunities that arise when institutions such as the Australian Broadcasting Corporation invite audiences to be content-creators and storytellers. Her research areas include participatory arts, digital storytelling and public service media.

Julie McIntyre is a senior lecturer in history at the University of Newcastle, Australia. She directs the Wine Studies Research Network in UON's Centre for 21st Century Humanities. Dr McIntyre is an associate editor of the *Journal of Wine Research* (UK) and an executive committee member of the Australian NZ Environmental History Network. She is the 2018 State Library of New South Wales Merewether Fellow and a 2019 Fulbright Scholar at University of California, Davis.

Phillip McIntyre is an associate professor and scholar who researches creativity and the creative industries. He has four books on this topic to his credit and been the recipient of Australian Research Council grants investigating these ideas. He is also a songwriter, musician, producer and audio engineer. He has managed various musical groups dealing with promoters, record companies and distribution labels, worked as a music journalist and made a number of music videos and documentaries. His band's recordings are currently available on iTunes, Spotify, Pandora and other online streaming and subscription services.

Martin Potter creates and researches participatory media. He is a multi-award winning producer of documentaries and participatory media projects including *Big Stories, Small Towns*. He has worked internationally with UN agencies, international NGOs and broadcasters across East Africa, South and South East Asia and Australia. He works with Deakin University and is a member of the Alfred Deakin Institute for Citizenship and Globalisation, investigator with the Centre of Excellence for Australian Biodiversity and Heritage (www.epicaustralia.org.au) and board member of Engage Media, a not-for-profit Video for Change organisation focusing on creating social change through the distribution of human rights and environmental video.

Lawrence Pratchett is Pro-Vice Chancellor at the University of Canberra. He was previously Professor of Local Democracy and Head of the Department of Public Policy at De Montfort University in the United Kingdom and co-founder of its Local Governance Research Unit. His research background spans multiple publications in the area of local and community governance, with a particular emphasis on citizen participation and new forms of democratic engagement. He has also been an expert advisor to the Council of Europe and undertook a number of research projects for the UK Government. His more recent research interests have focused on understanding the changing nature of work and the local significance of global trends towards the knowledge economy.

Donna Senese is an associate professor of geography at the University of British Columbia, Okanagan Campus. Dr. Senese is a member of UBC's Centre for Environmental Impact Assessment and is Founding Director of the Sonnino Working Group in Tuscany, Italy, an international trans-disciplinary research and writing collective that shares Donna's international curricular and research interests in rural sustainability, including the role of tourism, wine and local food in driving resilience.

Michelle Thompson is a lecturer in tourism at Central Queensland University, Cairns, Australia. She has a PhD from James Cook University (2015), where her research examined the development of tourism in agricultural regions. Her research interests focus on regional tourism development, specifically agri-tourism, food and wine tourism, remote area tourism and cultural tourism. Michelle continues to teach int CQU's Master of Sustainable Tourism Management program and is writing a book on tourism in agricultural regions.

Sajeda Tuli is a Fulbright scholar at the Institute for Governance and Policy Analysis at the University of Canberra. She is a qualified urban planner who is passionate about working on Australian cities and their future directions. She has worked extensively with both public and private institutions on urban analytics, including cities' economic development, migration, benchmarking and index development, spatial analysis, environmental issues and strategic policies. Her research interests include the knowledge economy, smart cities and innovation, knowledge precincts and social equity and talent movement.

Ariella Van Luyn is a Lecturer in writing at the University of New England, Australia. She is the author of a novel, *Treading Air*, and several short stories published in magazines including *Island*, *Southerly* and *Overland*. Her research interests include creative writing, practice-led research, community narratives and creativity in regional communities.

Michael James Walsh is an assistant professor in the Faculty of Business, Government and Law at the University of Canberra. His research interests include the sociology of interaction, the writings of Erving Goffman, cultural sociology, technology and music sociology. A chief dimension of his research explores the reception of communication technologies as they relate to and impact on social interaction. Michael's publications have appeared in journals such as *New Media & Society*, *Symbolic Interaction* and *Information, Communication and Society*.

Yi Wang is a PhD student and sessional academic in the Digital Media Research Centre in the Creative Industries Faculty at the Queensland University of Technology, Brisbane, Australia. Her doctoral research investigates the knowledge exchange and innovation in creative industries between Shenzhen and Brisbane through the university-industry-government networks. Her main research interest centres on how knowledge transfer contributes to the open innovation in creative sectors within the city context.

Claire Williams is a freelance researcher, writer and editor whose most recent publications have been in the areas of empathy and communication in healthcare, as well as creative industries. She has taught communications and librarianship at the university level and, as Faculty Director Creative Industries at Hunter TAFE, she managed programs in fine art, music, digital media, fashion, performing arts and design. Claire is active in community theatre and has worked professionally as an actor with a number of theatre companies as well as in film and television, including voiceover work. Claire has held committee and board positions in both the visual and performing arts and is currently President of Newcastle Theatre Company.

Adele Wessel is Associate Professor of History at Southern Cross University. Her research is in the field of food studies and she is editor of *Locale: Pacific Journal of Regional Food Studies* and founding member of the Regional Food Network. Adele has published widely on food production and cookbooks.

Acknowledgements

As befits the theme of creativity and innovation in the regions, this book began as a rather ill-defined exercise in 'intellectual play'. In 2016, the editors were fortunate to receive a Research Infrastructure Block Grant (RIBG) from their then employer, James Cook University in North Queensland, on the promise that they would be dismantling institutional and disciplinary 'silos'. The very generous sum of $46,000 was given by the Division of Tropical Environments and Societies to facilitate cross-disciplinary research and to engage community and industry. The project was entitled "North Queensland Regional Innovation Lab". The thirteen-member team (the grant application included twelve but soon enough we became thirteen) consisted of Eduardo de la Fuente (Lead Applicant), Ian Atkinson, Margaret Atkinson, David King, Lisa Law, Connar McShane, Trina Myers, Stephen Naylor, Martin Potter, Warwick Powell, Anne Swinbourne and Ariella Van Luyn. The disciplines ranged from sociology and creative writing to psychology, planning and IT; these researchers were financially supported by the Research Office; the Office of Academic Registrar (indeed, at the time, the Registrar himself was part of the team); the College of Arts, Society and Education; the College of Business, Law and Governance; the College of Healthcare Sciences; and the College of Science and Engineering. The thirteenth person to join our merry group was the Deputy Vice-Chancellor in charge of the Division of Tropical Environments and Societies, Iain Gordon, who has previously run the James Hutton Institute in the United Kingdom, and who, in joining our playful group, was someone who clearly enjoyed interdisciplinarity and the kinds of synergies we were aiming for.

In the first twelve months, we hosted three evening salons at a local bar called Heritage Exchange for North Queensland community members, civic and industry leaders, on the themes of 'Townsville's Futures'; 'Food Futures'; and 'City and Landscaping Futures'. Taking the form of 15-minute panel discussion followed by 45 minutes of open-mic discussion (with food and one free drink provided), these sessions were genuinely dialogical and helped to overcome the sense that the university was a Brutalist 'bunker' marooned some 17 kilometres from the town centre. The team also hosted workshops on tourism, events and social media for local industry in collaboration with QUT and participated in that year's Townsville *Festival of Ideas*, where amongst other things 'design

xvi *Acknowledgements*

thinking' and 'co-creation' workshops were run on what Townsville might look like in terms of urban design and spatial layout.

In a sense, then, *Regional Cultures, Economies and Creativity: Innovating Through Place* was not only conceived during the period of the initial RIBG grant: it is the belated payment of a debt of gratitude to our fellow players and to Deputy DVC, Professor Gordon, in particular. Without the support, encouragement and ideas that they exchanged with us during 2016–17, we would not have had the courage or necessary sensibility to undertake this project. We are also pleased that people who contributed to "North Queensland Regional Innovation Lab" events other than ourselves, such as Allison Craven, Terry Flew and Martin Potter, were also able to contribute chapters.

The journey in question would not have been possible without our publisher Routledge and the folks in the Sociology section of that rather large operation, in particular. The project began when Emily Briggs, Editor for Sociology at Routledge, contacted one of the editors (Eduardo) to meet up at a conference as she was soliciting new book projects. The planned meeting in Vienna didn't take place in July of 2016 due to travel itineraries, but a Skype call with both editors soon followed, and Emily has been unrelenting in her support for the edited collection ever since. We thank her for understanding the value of a social science discussion of creative economies that advocates for a more place-sensitive approach and also for taking a 'punt' on a book primarily focused on Australian case studies. The same goes to Senior Editorial Assistant Elena Chui (who has now moved to Oxford University Press) and her wonderful and patient replacement, Lakshita Joshi.

Ariella Van Luyn would like to thank James Cook University, and particularly Bradley Smith in the Division of Research and Innovation, for the ongoing support of cross-disciplinary, practice-led and action research. My colleagues at the University of New England (UNE) have been unendingly supportive and patient while I attempted to balance teaching, admin and engagement alongside pulling together the strands of this collection. My move to UNE brought me into contact with the very best horizontal mentor ever, Dr Beck Wise, who has taught me to see creativity and the discipline of writing in new, visionary and complex ways. I would also like to thank the authors in this collection for their care and attention, particularly in the last push towards the end – I have learnt so much from reading these chapters and watching their progress.

Eduardo de la Fuente would like to acknowledge the resources and support given to him as an Adjunct Fellow at the School of Humanities and Social Inquiry since mid-2018 and his longstanding affiliation with the Yale Center for Cultural Sociology (despite the fact that these days he is a very wayward member of the 'cultural sociological' club). But more than anything he would like to thank the love and support given to him by those close to him. In the final stretch his mother texted him almost daily to ask, "Have you finished that book yet?" His 4-year old son Alejandro showed patience way beyond his years and occasionally even fed himself so 'trains of thought' would not be broken. On the night, Eduardo finally put his pen down (metaphorically

Acknowledgements   xvii

speaking) and yelled out 'finished', Alejandro came running in and excitedly asked, "Can I read it?" He and the Tenterfield Terrier 'Magic' also insisted on going for either a walk or to the 'doggy park' every afternoon – which, when you live somewhere as beautiful as the Blue Mountains, is a 'no brainer'; unless of course, you are busy writing a book. And, to our family's main bread winner, who commutes by train daily so that I get to live the life of 'peri-metropolitan creative-cum-knowledge worker', Dani Clark, thank you for all your love, support, understanding and forbearance of discussions of esoteric things like place and "nonrepresentational landscape theory". I promise my cooking repertoire will expand now that I have got this beautiful little monkey off my back!

Introduction

Problematising regional creativity and innovation in Australia and beyond: landscapes, economies, identities, imaginaries

Eduardo de la Fuente and Ariella Van Luyn

The city-regional binary that underpins many academic, policy and media discourses elides the complexity of creative work and industries in the regions. As David Bell and Mark Jayne (2010: 209) point out, the last decade or so has seen the "fostering, celebrating, maintaining and measuring of 'The Creative City' across a range of policy and academic publication[s], conferences and workshops", an agenda that emerged in parallel with strategies designed to "achieve post-industrial growth and cultural vitality" in cities and regions "throughout Europe, Australia, Canada, Singapore, the USA, New Zealand, and more recently in Africa, China and Latin America". But, as leading scholars in the application of concepts of the "creative economy" to "small cities" (Bell and Jayne 2006) and the "countryside" (Bell and Jayne 2010: 209), Bell and Jayne are all too aware that the "academic research and policy intervention" has predominantly tended to "focus on certain forms of urban activity, labelling these as essential to the working of the creative economy, and as necessary preconditions for fostering creativity". On the basis of exemplars that overwhelming focus on "creative cities", cultural geographer Allen Scott (2010: 14) emphasised "agglomeration" and "path dependencies", Harvard Business School's Michael Porter (1990) highlighted "clusters", and celebrity academic author Richard Florida (2002: 249) promoted his famous Three Ts of Technology, Talent and Tolerance, claiming that a "place must have all three" in order to "attract creative people, generate innovation and stimulate economic growth" (Florida 2002: 249). Note, however, that the discussion of place has tended to involve formulations regarding what generic factors are required rather than what intrinsic or unique qualities creative economies thrive upon.

Furthermore, in a country like Australia, geographically distinct because of the vast distances between metropolitan clusters, such imposed limitations may lead to overlooking the resilience of both individual creative agents and regional economies and innovation. Indeed, these narratives of lack undercut more complex ways of imagining and nurturing regions and elide structural dimensions of urban and regional disparity. As Chris Gibson and Natasha Klocker (2005: 95) argue, policy that defines regions as problematic because they "lack" creativity do not acknowledge the actual causes of such disparity, such as "uneven distribution of resources [and] capitalist modes of production".

2   *Eduardo de la Fuente and Ariella Van Luyn*

Narratives of regional lack are also tied to coloniser narratives of emptiness, mobilised to justify settler occupation of the land in Australia. Richie Howitt (2002: 233) argues that "Australians' geographical imaginations have been profoundly affected by frontier metaphors", including "old-style colonial metaphors of empty spaces" (Howitt 2002: 234). Howitt (2002) has long since called for a challenge to these metaphors; there are compelling reasons why such frameworks for understanding place, economy and creativity should be resisted.

Further, as Ban van Heur (2010: 189) suggests, the state of knowledge in the creative economy research and policy agenda is often "divorced from the actual complexity of cultural life in concrete cities around the world and the ways in which these life-worlds shape processes of economic valorization". The major problem here is that "policy makers lack substantive empirical data on the cities [and regions] in which they have to implement their policies" (van Heur 2010: 189). Rather – what economic geographer Jamie Peck (2002) famously termed "fast policy" – it highlights how under neoliberal, global capitalism, policy frameworks travel across spaces and places with a high degree of velocity and suffer from a tendency towards imitation. Others have also suggested that creative economy paradigms and "fast policy" travel in the embodied form of celebrity "theorists" and consultants such as Florida and Landry (Gibson and Klocker 2004: 427).

This trifecta of "metropolitan creative industries imaginary", "fast policy" and celebrity authors/consultants has created bias in creative industries research. For example, on the basis of a search of ISI Web of Knowledge of the early period of academic research (1992–2009), using terms such as "creative industries", "cultural industries", "creative economy" and "cultural economy", van Heur (2010: 189) found the largest number of articles were "either theoretical contributions or discuss[ions of] empirical data without explicit geographical reference"; closely followed by articles covering "countries in general" and then articles which discussed major global metropolises such as "London", "Los Angeles/Hollywood", "New York City", "Paris" and the "city-state of Singapore". No doubt, a more up-to-date search might have thrown up recent creative city "hot spots" such as Portland, Oregon, and Austin, Texas, in the USA or Shanghai or Beijing in China. Indeed, consummate with the country's rise to global economic and political superpower, Chinese cities and regions have become the focal point for new creative industries research and policy analysis (Keane 2013; Rong and O'Connor 2018).

Regardless, both the tenor and empirical biases of creative industries research have tended to reproduce what some commentators have termed "metropolitan creative industries imaginaries" and led to policy which "often" resorts to the "facile use of the generic vocabulary of creative industries" (van Heur 2010: 190). The latter includes "concepts such as 'creative class', 'clusters', 'learning and innovation', 'knowledge wave' and 'cool places' . . . becom[ing] mantras" (Gibson and Klocker 2004: 428). In many respects, creativity and innovation policy is the very epitome of what Peck (2002: 344) has termed "off-the shelf program[s]".

Introduction 3

However, there are two important countervailing trends to the generic nature of creative economy research. Both, directly or indirectly, inform the essays in this collection: firstly, the move to study the "cultural economy of small cities" (Jayne et al. 2010), and, secondly, the fact that an important "exception" to the metropolitan bias of creative industries research has been research on Australia. As one scholar has observed, research on Australian creative economies has not only focused on "Adelaide, Brisbane, Sydney and Melbourne, but also on smaller cities such as Darwin, Hobart, Tamworth, and Wollongong" (van Heur 2010: 189). Australian scholarship has also led the way in dispelling the myth that cultural and economic value is not created in "suburban" and "peri-metropolitan" contexts (Collis, Freebody and Flew 2013; Flew 2012a; Gibson 2016). Further, through the writings of Sue Luckman (2012), Australian research has also made important contributions to understandings of how spatial designators such as "remote", "regional" and "rural" operate in the field of cultural economies. However, rather than exemplifying some kind of scholarly "nativism" or "nationalism" that highlights the "exceptionalism" of Australia's region, the nation's research on the creative industries has been sophisticated and often comparative. Thus, even when focusing on rural and remote case studies, Australian studies of creative industries still keep an eye on international and transnational field sites, working to unpick regional-metropolitan binaries. Thus, for example, Luckman's (2012: 3) exploration of how "place is an actor in cultural work, above and beyond the organizational economies and synergies of creative cities, clusters and densities", is transnational in its choice of fieldwork sites. Synergies have also existed between British and Australian scholarship, policy and practice in the aforementioned field of "small city" creative industries research (Jayne et al. 2010); at the level of national government policy, "the mid-1990s release of the Australian Keating Government's *Creative Nation* document . . . influenced the subsequent Blair government's DCMS (Department of Culture, Media and Sport) framework for the development of Britain's creative industries" (Luckman 2012: 11). Furthermore, the decentering of the "metropolitan imaginary" is quite advanced in the case of United Kingdom creative industries research, where "despite the obvious dominance of London . . . research" has also been "published on Birmingham, Bristol, Glasgow, Hastings, Newcastle, Sheffield, Swansea, and York" (van Heur 2010: 190). Aptly, the present collection contains a chapter, Emma Coffield's "'Anything That's Not London': Regions, Mobility and Spatial Politics in Contemporary Visual Arts" (Chapter 11), detailing fieldwork undertaken in the northern United Kingdom city of Durham. This continues to foster the types of synergies and dialogues already happening between Australian and United Kingdom creative economy researchers. Coffield's work clearly demonstrates the ways that unravelling regional-metropolitan binaries offers a more inclusive framework for understanding creativity and draws attention to structural barriers to participation in the arts.

Likewise signalling a more inclusive vision of what constitutes creativity in Australia, this collection includes two chapters by teams of scholars working

4 *Eduardo de la Fuente and Ariella Van Luyn*

at the Queensland University of Technology (QUT); QUT has been an academic research, policy and pedagogy leader in the Australian higher education context with respect to creative industries. They were first to move to re-label (not without controversy) their entire Humanities, Creative Arts and Social Science disciplines under the rubric of "creative industries". QUT also importantly housed the ARC Centre of Excellence in Creative Industries and Innovation between 2005 and 2013; during this period it was home to important creative industries researchers such as Stuart Cunningham (2006, 2013), Terry Flew (2012b), John Hartley (Hartley et al. 2013), Justin O'Connor (Kong and O'Connor 2009), Jason Potts (Hartley and Potts 2014) and leading expert on the Chinese creative industries, Michael Keane (2013). In more recent times, the focus on creative industries has evolved into a research agenda also encompassing social media, geolocative media and urban informatics (Burgess and Green 2018; Foth et al. 2014), as well as extending the creative industries model via the notion of the "embedded" or non-creative industries creative worker (Hearn et al. 2014). It is therefore appropriate that for this volume, one of the QUT contributions – Terry Flew, Donna Hancox, Sasha Mackay and Yi Wang's "Universities and Regional Creative Economies" (Chapter 8) – is about how universities can play a role in fostering and sustaining regional arts (i.e. the traditional cultural industries), whereas the second – Ana Bilandzic, Marcus Foth and Greg Hearn's "The Role of Fab Labs for Economic Development in Regional Australia" – is a comparison of Fab Labs or "informal" collaboration-innovation spaces in three regional Queensland contexts (i.e. the innovation ecologies associated with startups, makerspaces and technology micro-entrepreneurs).

In the move to theorise the complex intersections of culture-economy-space in non-metropolitan settings, and their fleshing out through qualitative case studies, one of the major Australian contributions has come from the "Wollongong School of Cultural Geography". The latter has involved a group of academic researchers and PhD students within the geography program at the University of Wollongong associated with the Australian Centre for Cultures, Environments, Society and Spaces (ACCESS), which has as one of its three core themes "Reworking Cities and Economies". The Wollongong contribution to creative industries research has covered wide-ranging topics and dealt with the important issue of whether creative industry discourse and planning is compatible with places that diverge from the post-Fordist/post-industrial "script" of dispensing with manufacturing (Gibson, Carr and Warren 2012), as well as why the "geographies of making" provide important insights into the links between embodiment, skilled dwelling and place (Carr and Gibson 2017).

Having the city of Wollongong and the Illawarra region as a ready-made "laboratory" (somewhat in the vein of the Chicago School of Urban Research a century earlier) seems to have given many of the academic outputs produced by these researchers their distinctive sensibility. Indeed, in one of their analyses of the history and recent spatial dynamics of the local creative industries, entitled "Creative Small Cities: Rethinking the Creative Economy in Place",

Gordon Waitt and Chris Gibson (2009) offer what might be considered an exemplary piece of analysis, if not quasi-manifesto, of how to do place-sensitive creative industry research. Early in the essay, the authors state their aim is to pay "attention to the significance of place" in discussions of "urban regeneration, deindustrialisation and the creative cities model". In their study of the regional Australian city of Wollongong and the Illawarra region, the researchers have documented how moves to revitalise regions can encounter opposing processes including a sense of loss or disassociated processes of gentrification and glamorisation of peripheral areas of the region. Cultural planning, as well as studies of creativity, therefore face the reality that place is a complex material and symbolic thing, and that, when it comes to fostering creative economies, place shapes creatives and creative processes as much as creatives and creative outputs shape place.

Furthermore, Luckman (2012: 1) suggests that once we add "the lens of 'good' and 'bad' work" – as in "people attempting to live lives well-lived" – then the categories of rural, regional and remote creative and cultural work also become a question of creative and cultural practitioners "seeking to create physical, economic and emotional space for [such work] while negotiating the multiple contingencies of place". The emphasis here is on the "affective relationship to rural and regional places at the heart of creative work"; as well as the "environmental affordances of place", which Luckman (2012: 3) suggests are "an important part of the 'soft infrastructure' enabling creativity for many cultural workers".

The conceptual and practical significance of recognising place-specific "environmental affordances" is not to be underestimated. Focusing on some of the motives underpinning why creatives move to rural, regional and remote locations, Ross Gibson (2015a) broadens cultural assets to include phenomena such as weather, light and landforms, suggesting that a region's infrastructure does not merely come in the shape of fast-speed Internet or the number of cultural venues or creative industries training institutions a place has to offer. Place offers all kinds of subjective, ambient and spatio-temporal qualities that are not neatly captured by measures of "hard infrastructure". Creative practitioners, and to some extent all living beings, are drawn to the kinds of "lived experience" and the rhythms of life that place offers.

To the extent that place nourishes with the conditions for sustaining and thriving in life, it is clear why some theorists of creativity have labelled the link between creative processes and place as "ecological" – as in the *ecologies of creativity* (Howkins 2009). The ecologies that creativity scholars analyse can range from structural conditions that resemble Porter's "clusters", or Pierre Bourdieu's (1993; see also Pratt 2004) "fields", through to writings that focus on the phenomenological-cum-sensory characteristics of place (Seamon 1979). For scholars interested in considerations such as materiality and affect, the latter end of the place/ecology spectrum is more important (Ingold 2000). Thus, in *Locating Cultural Work*, Luckman (2012: 23) suggests "an affective relationship to place and landscape persists in the lives of cultural workers, notably those

6 *Eduardo de la Fuente and Ariella Van Luyn*

outside of urban locales". It is not just climate or landscape per se that constituted an affordance for creatives. It was the way that such natural or physical features of place combined with social and cultural practices and meaning-making that made "embodied and environmental affordances, dispositions and habits" important (Luckman 2012: 33).

A lack of regional place-sensitivity comes at a significant cost. One is purely empirical. As one collection on Australian regional creative places puts it, the non-metropolitan offers as case studies a "range of locales from remote [inland] . . . to 'tree-change' havens and regions living in the aftermath of old-pastoral economies . . . to seaside enclaves and post-industrial urban outlands" (Gibson 2015b: 7–8). The editors of *Creative Communities: Regional Inclusion and the Arts* lend this diversity of spatial experience an interesting temporal dimension when they suggest the issue of creativity in/and regional communities needs to confront both existences that involve a "close association with the land, and familial connections that frequently span multiple generations", as well as regional identities marked by "communities in terminal decline" and the "phenomenon of fly-in fly-out workers" (McDonald and Mason 2015: 1). The editors also suggest that "what differentiates creative practice in regional centres is its role in the formation and maintenance of inclusive communities" (McDonald and Mason, 2015: 1). This formulation is a substantive advance on Florida's earlier (2002) equation of place with amenity and richness (or lack thereof) of experience. However, "inclusive communities", like "lifestyle amenity", can become a marketing and/or bureaucratic formula.

Yet the crucial thing is how place comes to embody things that are more difficult to reify, like culture or identity or everyday practices. In situating the essays in *By-Roads and Hidden Treasures*, Ross Gibson (2015b: 11) alludes to "scales of value that evade the measure of demographics and economics", although the forms of capital and assets generated may very well lead to successful demographic outcomes (i.e. they may stall or even reverse population decline) or to economic growth (i.e. they may generate employment or lead to investment in sustainable businesses). But neither demography nor economics are what are primarily driving these exercises in place-attachment and place-maintenance. Gibson (2015b: 11) suggests that, first and foremost, the scales of value embedded in the culture and everyday practices of the regions he and his ARC team studied evinced an "awareness of the value of commitment, relationship, care and intimacy in regions that are not blessed with metropolitan proximity to influence and decision-making". The import of place qualities therefore comes from "an urge to care for a place lovingly by monitoring all its present needs and imagining a wide range of future options and an investment in the real value of emotion and imagination" (Gibson 2015b: 11). Gibson (2015b: 12) suggests that the real value of emotion and imagination is to express – through culture, ritual and practice – "the great value regional people give to and draw from the *connective* work they do, connective to fellow inhabitants but also to the distinctive characteristics – animal, vegetable, mineral, meteorological – of a place". Furthermore, what links research to creative

Introduction 7

practice, and planning to everyday community ritual, is the need to *bear witness* to the special qualities of place:

> to catch the rich and special sounds and smells, the rhythms and closely felt textures, the particular qualities and rituals . . . [that allow place] to survive all the contingencies and exigencies that are so often pushed upon it from outside and far away.
>
> (Gibson 2015b: 12)

Given the felt need to bear witness to the special qualities of place, including its sounds and smells, rhythms and closely felt textures, it is appropriate that the present volume starts with a discussion of wine and terroir/heritage, ideas about native food in colonial/settler societies, landscapes as experienced in visual culture and through embodied forms of dwelling, and what architecture might learn about place and senses of place from the vantage point of the architect-cum-cyclist-as-ethnographer. While the chapters in this section, titled "Landscapes, Tastescapes and Sensescapes: Creatively Responding to Place", deal with varied topics and come from a range of disciplines, they all address the ways that the distinct qualities of regional geographies inform innovative modes of placemaking and creative practices.

Julie McIntyre, Donna Senese and John Hull's chapter "Fruit forward: Wine Regions as Geographies of Innovation in Australia and Canada" compares wine production in the Hunter Valley, Australia, and Okanagan Valley, Canada. These regions share a similar history of coloniser agriculture and reliance on landscape and tastescape for not just wine production but also wine tourism. However, in recent years, the two regions have taken vastly different approaches to sustaining the industry. While the Hunter Valley promotes the heritage value of settlers' uninterrupted history of wine production, Okanagan Valley actively promotes sustainable, organic wine production through the slow food movement. This comparison allows the authors to understand how regional innovation responds to the distinct qualities of landscape and also to suggest how sustainable agribusinesses might better react to drastic changes in the landscape such as climate change.

Adele Wessel's "There's No Taste Like Home: Histories of Food in the Changing Landscape of the Northern Rivers Region" draws on the history of native food production and consumption in the Northern Rivers region of Australia to argue that, following Bill Gammage and Bruce Pascoe, Indigenous people's cultivation of native food has been elided from national historical narratives, as well as to document the ways that native plants have been at once ignored, consumed and exported by the area's colonisers. Wessell introduces the notion of "tastescape" as transnational, suggesting that white colonisers imposed a tastescape of "home" on the Northern Rivers landscape, which drove the often violent and destructive cultivation of land and attitudes to native food evidenced in the cookbooks of the era. The chapter's discussion of contemporary tastescapes, referring to Indigenous and non-Indigenous chefs

8   *Eduardo de la Fuente and Ariella Van Luyn*

who use native foods in cooking, analyses how contemporary consumption of native foods does not yet redress or acknowledge earlier colonial attitudes and are driven by economy rather than ethics. Together, these chapters suggest the complex ways the aesthetics of the everyday, and the distinct cultural, historical, geographical and economic qualities of the region, inform diverse modes of innovative placemaking.

Allison Craven's "Terraform and Terra Firma: Transnational Economies of Image, Landscape and Location in Screen Production in Queensland" uses two case studies from regional Queensland, Australia – Winton and Tropical North Queensland as rendered in the Gold Coast's studios – to compare the ways regional landscapes are represented in the films that use these locations as a backdrop as part of the state's burgeoning film production industry. Given the complex ways that film visualises landscape, Craven contrasts an emerging aesthetic dichotomy in the Queensland film industry and its use of regional landscapes between what she terms *terraform* and *terra firma*. If *terraforming* is a form of cultural production created through the convergent blend of studio and location production and digital engineering that results in images that are, paradoxically, both generic of the "tropics" and unique to the specific film's copyright, then *terra firming* is an aesthetic evidenced in the use of the spectacular arid landscapes that surround the inland town of Winton as a backdrop to stories that are not necessarily local. With respect to the latter, Craven shows that in cultivating the film-friendliness of their town, the residents and local council of Winton have generated an annual film festival, expanding Winton's existing cultural infrastructure and elevating the town's place in national culture.

Craven's contrast between the filmic representation of tropical and arid landscapes via the aesthetics of *terraform* and *terra firma* is followed by Eduardo de la Fuente's discussion of a very different landscape and its visual–cum–material expressions: namely, the sandstone escarpments to the west of Sydney known as the Blue Mountains. While Aboriginal groups have had a connection with the Blue Mountains stretching back tens of thousands of years, settler society has made much of the 1813 crossing by explorers and its subsequent development as a site of leisure, tourism and nature appreciation. In "Landscape as Tension: The Blue Mountains and Cultural Economies of Place", de la Fuente, like Craven, looks at processes of aesthetic and social construction of landscape, as well as the cultural economic consequences that flow from constructing "the Mountains" (as Sydneysiders know them) as either something to be looked at or something to immerse oneself in. De la Fuente outlines how approaches to the Blue Mountains landscape have echoed debates in landscape studies regarding the "representational" and the "non-representational". The more provocative aspect of de la Fuente's argument is that, in a place where landscape is so ubiquitous, these contrasting landscape modalities have "practical" as well as "theoretical" application and have either directly or indirectly shaped the cultural economies of the Blue Mountains. The author suggests we might want to see the cultural economy of landscape-as-representation as underpinning "mass tourism" and its visual iconography, whereas the cultural economy of

Introduction 9

landscape-as-nonrepresentation sustains the boutique economy of "elevated sensory experiences" and the "economics of singularity" (Karpik 2010).

Rounding out the section on regionality as landscape, tastescape and sens-escape and what this might be mean for creative responses to place is an experimental piece of research and writing by recent architecture postgraduate students Bobbie Bayley and Owen Kelly (inspired by and co-authored with their academic mentor John Roberts). In their chapter "Deck-Chair Innovation: Innovation within Arm's Reach for Regional Australian Architecture: A Little of What We Found When We Rode the Grand Section across Australia's Girth in 2017", Bayley and Kelly drew on postgraduate work that was awarded the 2019 Australian Institute of Architects Student Prize for the Advancement of Architecture. Bayley and Kelly's playful chapter suggests that, in the era of the aforementioned "fast policy" and a "FIFO workforce", their bicycle-centred epistemology and ethos of community engagement slow things down and allows the sensory and environmental factors that operate within place more of an opportunity to come to the fore. Their slow methodology registers climatic and other affordances, as well as examples of shelter/dwellings that seem ill-suited to the places in which they find themselves. Secondly, the hypothesis of "Deck-chair innovation" is that it is in "non-urban" or "regional" Australia – where climatic and other conditions can be unforgiving – that we obtain a more immediate sense of the impacts of place on building, design and materials. In an age of computational modelling and starchitects like Frank Gehry, it seems likely that place will be erased and design will become less and less regional. To counter the erasure of place, Bayley and Kelly follow in the footsteps of architectural pioneers and mavericks who have espoused the value of "experience amplifiers" and the types of knowledges of place that can only be wrought through embodied, kinetic activity.

The next section of this edited collection poses arguably the greatest challenge for a place-sensitive approach to creativity and the regions. It deals with the role knowledge plays in regional innovation and creative economies. Unlike notions of creativity garnered from the production of goods associated with landscapes, tastescapes and sensescapes, all of which suggest some connection to *genius loci* or the particularities of place, in the case of knowledge and knowledge goods we seem to pass from the "particular" to the "universal", from the "localised" to the "free-floating". Mathematics, science, computational logic and technology would appear to be the same whether one is in Wagga Wagga or London, Longreach or New York. But, as these chapters demonstrate, knowledge and knowledge goods, including the capacity for knowledge innovation, make different kinds of contributions to regional growth.

"Placing Knowledge and Innovation Economies: Regional Universities, Ecosystems and Fab Labs" features four chapters that tackle the opportunities and obstacles present in regional knowledge and innovation economies. In their own way, each of the chapters critically engages with the promises and limitations that the knowledge and creative economies throw up for the regions; regional universities are one of the key institutions explored. Thus,

10 *Eduardo de la Fuente and Ariella Van Luyn*

Tara Brabazon's "The Troubling Third Tier: Small Cities, Small Universities and an Ambivalent Knowledge Economy" compellingly posits that universities in "third-tier cities" are at once understudied and present both benefits and dilemmas for regional economies. The early section of the chapter provides a relational model of cities as tiers and a framework for understanding regional and urban development and decline. Continuing the ideas Brabazon posits in *Unique Urbanity? Rethinking Third Tier Cities, Denegation, Regeneration and Mobility* (Brabazon 2015), this chapter offers a call for small city innovation to be grounded in a staged strategic model that emphasises the city's history; the present environment; an exploration of the similarities and differences with other third-tier cities around the world; and a city modelling that takes and transforms strategies that operated well in one location. The discussion of universities highlights the tensions at the heart of "third-tier city" adoption of knowledge economy strategies. While the universities offer regional economies employment opportunities, economic stability and sites of knowledge exchange, these same universities suffer from harmful stereotypes, the invisibility of their contribution and the problem of retaining staff and students in the area where the university is located.

Lawrence Prachett, Michael Walsh, Richard Hu and Sajeda Tuli's chapter "Locating Knowledge in Australian Cities" challenges the tendency to untether knowledge from place in much discussion of digital innovation and knowledge economies. Rather, they argue, work and social life are mediated by online interactions and geographical realities. From this framework, they investigate the ability of regions to nurture knowledge economies and attract talented workers, given that the future of the work is likely to be one based in the information, knowledge or service sectors. The authors ambitiously develop a "Knowledge City Index" of 25 Australian cities, which positions knowledge across two core domains: knowledge capital (the existing knowledge infrastructure of a region) and knowledge economy (the knowledge activity that is related to a particular region and its relationship to regional prosperity). These domains are broken down into further statistical measures: *knowledge capital* includes knowledge capacity (focusing on the educational qualification of residents), knowledge mobility (the number of migrant workers in knowledge-intensive industries) and digital access (the physical infrastructure that underpins knowledge access). *Knowledge economy* constitutes measures of knowledge industries (the importance of the knowledge base in the local economy), income (the value that knowledge contributes to the economy) and smart work (the number of workers who work from home). This statistical framework allows the authors to compare the knowledge strengths and weaknesses of a number of regions in Australia. The authors conclude that knowledge economies are concentrated in particular geographical locations and that the future of regions lies in their capacity to attract knowledge workers to live and work. This chapter can profitably be read alongside one of its authors other recent publications – Edward Blakeley and Richard Hu's (2019) *Crafting Innovative Places for Australia's Knowledge Economy* – which suggests that cities and communities are in the process of rediscovering the significance of places, and with this rediscovery comes the opportunity for the co-designing of "where" innovation will and ought to take place.

Donna Hancox, Terry Flew, Sasha Mackay and Yi Wang's chapter "Universities and Regional Creative Economies" uses three case studies of regional universities to reflect on the role universities can play in regional creative industries. This chapter applies the "Triple Helix" framework (following Etzkowitz 2003) of university–industry–government to the regional arts sector, suggesting, like Prachett et al. that knowledge exchange is central for the development of regional economies. The chapter then presents three case studies: Writing the Digital Futures, a partnership between the Queensland University of Technology, Arts Queensland and a range of regional and remote communities focusing on digital skills in the writing and publishing industry; the Regional Arts Services Network, a partnership between Central Queensland University, State Government and regional arts organisations to coordinate the delivery of arts programs; and Creative Regions, a partnership between Central Queensland University and a regionally-based arts production company. Together, these three case studies offer models for how universities might promote regional resilience by partnering with government and industry to foster knowledge exchange, arts service delivery and evaluation of arts.

Ana Bilandzic, Marcus Foth and Greg Hearn's "The Role of Fab Labs and Living Labs for Economic Development of Regional Australia" focuses not on individual agents within a system but on the spaces necessary to foster innovation and creativity. This chapter provides a case study of three regional Queensland "Casual Creative Environments", otherwise known as fab(rication) labs or living labs. The chapter proposes that, given assumptions regarding how economic innovation is driven by urban agglomeration and associated factors, such as the presence of skilled human capital, Fab Labs may be able to play a similar or comparable role in smaller regional centres. The chapter suggests that regional Fab Labs are based on welcoming informal learning environments as a mode of fostering innovation and concludes with policy recommendations for supporting regional Casual Creative Environments.

The third and final section of this edited collection is entitled "Regional Creative Industries and their Potentialities: Case Studies and Comparative Perspectives". This section of the book contains five chapters that cover case studies on regional creative industries within Australia and beyond. Here, the stated aim of the volume to consider creative practices beyond the metropolitan urban imaginaries of the global North – to which Australia, as an advanced economy, socio-culturally if not geographically belongs. The case studies are diverse in terms of regions covered and also the range of creative practices/systems of creativity covered.

Philip McIntyre and Susan Kerrigan's "The Hunter Region: A Place Where Creative Systems in Action and Innovation Ecosystems Intersect" offers an Australian counterpoint to Coffield's United Kingdom case study: that of the Hunter region in New South Wales, Australia. McIntyre and Kerrigan draw

12 *Eduardo de la Fuente and Ariella Van Luyn*

on in-depth interviews, participation observation and statistical analysis of creatives in the region. They use a "creative systems approach" that synthesises concepts in the work of Pierre Bourdieu and Mihaly Csikszentmihalyi and which is capable of accounting for both individual artists and the wider social and cultural context in which they operate. Here, creative work happens in the interplay between individual agents, who possess the necessary *habitus* or cultural, social, symbolic and economic capital, and the "fields" of symbolic and cultural production in which such agents operate. The authors use this framework to map the organisation of the creative industries in the Hunter region and the range of creatives whom are pushed to working innovatively within this system. The diverse examples used, some outside the usual categories of the creative arts (but certainly within the broader remit of the DCMS definition of "creative industries"), point to possible ways in which creative workers in the regions can respond to the pressures and possibilities offered by technology and globalisation.

We are very pleased that in this volume we have had the good fortune to have authors whose contributions place the discussion of Australian regional or non-metropolitan creative industries in international context. Thus, Emma Coffield's "'Anything That's Not in London': Regions, Mobility and Spatial Politics in Contemporary Visual Art" presents an important contribution that challenges linear histories of contemporary art that elide the importance of the regions to contemporary practice and which – like the previously outlined research of the Wollongong School of Cultural Geography – situates creative and cultural work within disadvantaged and much maligned spatial imaginaries. The small town of Durham is located just south of Newcastle-upon-Tyne and therefore, despite its university and medieval cathedral and town centre, is spatially and aesthetically positioned within what the British refer to as "The North" (Ehland 2007). But Coffield pays attention to the "in-between" status of Durham's geographical and cultural location and sees some advantages, as well as disadvantages, in the town's creative scene, which, in some respects, is neither local nor global "enough" to be worthy of attention. Through an analysis of qualitative data gathered in a UK Arts and Humanities Research Council project on artist-run initiatives, she documents the resilience of regional arts workers given the stereotypes of artists needing to live either in thriving cities or areas known for their natural beauty. Coffield also charts developments in UK creative industries research that is moving beyond the metropolitan creative industries scripts critiqued earlier. Coffield's research seems to suggest that the liminality of regionality, not to mention other advantages like cheaper living, mean that there is room for cultural experimentation in the regions – without necessarily having to succumb to "ruralist" stereotypes of traditionalism.

Liz Ellison and Michelle Thompson's "Sculptural coastlines: Site-specific artworks and regional identities" usefully analyses three regional beach sculpture festivals along the Queensland coastline in Currumbin, Noosa and Townsville. These are all sites where Australian beachscapes and tourism intersect; this provides the festivals with much of their rationale. The authors draw on an analysis of the festivals' programming and aesthetics, as well as a spatial analysis of the sites and their curation, to understand how these sculpture festivals "stage" the beach and the interactions between viewer and artwork. The chapter argues that such beachside sculpture mobilises various national mythologies of the Australia beach as an egalitarian space that invites public engagement. Unlike museums, beaches are places which are more often associated with leisure than (high) culture. Their ability to mobilise public engagement and tourism visitation accounts for the appeal of such outdoor sculpture festivals to local regional councils. Planning authorities also see them as regional forms of place-making, and councils often seek to capitalise on this quality in their place branding. Yet, the authors argue, the seaside festival is in danger of suffering from the copycat-cum-cookie-cutter problem. Thus, the authors tell us, there are water-scapes and associated sculpture festivals – such as the "Floating Land" festival at Noosa – that are calling out for curatorial innovation and for sculptures and public interactions that better respond to the distinctive and dramatic spatial qualities of the Noosa regional waterscapes. Again, what is at issue is whether or not creative economy thinking and policy is doing full justice to the qualities and aesthetic potentials of place.

Moving to the music industry, Andy Bennett, David Cashman and Natalie Lewandowski's "One Piece Blokes: On Being a Performing Musician in Regional Queensland" draws on 42 interviews with musicians in Central Queensland, Australia, to document why musicians are draw to the regions and strikingly posits that in "small remote towns there is a dearth of musicians, whereas in regional urban areas such as Mackay, there is a dearth of musical opportunities", challenging homogenous notions of the regions. The chapter also argues regional musicians must contend with impediments such as lack of educational opportunities and a culture of pub venues demanding cover music. In Central Queensland, while a number of festivals exist, these are not enough to sustain regional musicians' careers. Yet, high-profile acts continue to emerge from the region, and there is demand for both performances and opportunities to perform. While regional musicians in Central Queensland face difficulties in accessing industry knowledge, smaller audiences and demanding logistics, they rely on touring and portfolio careers to overcome these challenges.

In the last chapter in this section and the book, Martin Potter's "Positive Deviance: Stories of Regional Social Innovators from the *Big Stories, Small Towns* Project" uses the case study of a series of documentary films and photos made in a collaboration between the author, other filmmakers and the Lepo Lorun Weavers Collective as part of the storytelling project, *Big Stories, Small Towns*. The notion of "positive deviance" is used to frame both a way of designing the filmmaking approach and also to analyse the collective itself. Recasting the negative implications of the word "deviancy", Potter adopts the notion of positive deviancy to mean successful behaviours and strategies that allow people to find better solutions to problems despite having no specialist knowledge (Zeitlin 1991); positive deviancy can occur at both an individual and

14 *Eduardo de la Fuente and Ariella Van Luyn*

organisational and community level – a form of creativity and innovation. The chapter's account of the film on the Lepo Lorun Weavers Collective in Flores, Indonesia, demonstrates that films and photographs are both a process of enacting positive deviancy, as well as one of showcasing or "re-mediating" it. The films made about the Lepo Lorun collective suggest both the ways organisations and individuals can engage in innovation to enrich identity in a regional South East Asian place and the ways the act of filmmaking aids in this process.

Conclusion

What emerges most strikingly from the chapters in this collection is that – despite suggestions that globalisation and digitisation deemphasise place – the historical, cultural, economic and geographical qualities of place matter to innovators and creatives. However, notions of place cannot be understood simply. As chapters such as "'Anything's That's Not in London'" and "One Piece Blokes" suggest, the metropolitan-regional binary, and associated stereotypes of regions as "nowhere" or devoid of creative industries, reinforce power structures invested in the notion that metropolitan centres are the only locations where important acts or creativity or innovation can happen. Indeed, threaded throughout previous accounts of regional creativity is a sense of culturally impoverished but affordable regions. Such accounts also elide the rich pre-settler history of the Australian landscape. The accounts in this collection complicate this narrative.

As "Locating Knowledge in Australian Cities" suggests, regions cannot be understood as homogenous but rather as having strikingly different capacities to nurture innovation and economic growth through knowledge economies. Yet, as Coffield points out, and which is reinforced by interviews in chapters such as "The Hunter Region: A Place Where Creative Systems in Action and Innovation Ecosystems Intersect" and "One Piece Blokes", regional locations have a significant impact on the level of professionalism or semi-professionalism of artists. Regional artists face structural difficulties including accessing education, communities of practice and recognition of their work.

Indeed – as the strong focus on knowledge economies in this collection demonstrates – knowledge systems and regional locations' capacity to sustain them seem to be key drivers in the resilience of regions. Universities in regional locations, particularly third-tier cities, as Brabazon and Hancox et al. point out, have much work to do in fostering partnerships with community and government, retaining staff and students in regional areas and making their contributions to knowledge exchange visible. These opportunities are still underutilised; further investigation of models for universities' role in regional knowledge economies and innovation is required.

However, what these accounts of resilient artists (Coffield, Cashman), creative agents (McIntyre) and mavericks and "positive deviancy" (Potter) in the regions suggest is that how regions are perceived and articulated – as well as the impact of historical, geographical and socioeconomic imperative – shape

Introduction 15

how artists, arts workers and innovators experience place. Yet through artistic practices such as visual art (Coffield, Ellison and Thompson), music (Cashman), filmmaking (Potter), publishing, radio and television (McIntyre and Kerrigan), as well as new perceptions of what constitutes creativity – where acts such as walking and foraging inform the re-visioning of place (de la Fuente) and tastescapes (Wessel; McIntrye, Senese and Hull) constitute experiences of place as much as landscapes – regional identities are also evolving. Such practices, through tourism (de la Fuente, Ellison and Thompson), enrich regional economies. The regions also seem to, at least in this collection, invite a slowing down – a "deck-chair innovation" (Bayley and Owens) – and an interest in ethical and sustainable modes of consumption that seek to redress environment degradation and historical violence, even if much of this work is still ahead (McIntrye, Senese and Hull; Wessel).

In summary, this edited collection uses several Australian and a few international or comparative case studies to examine how discussions of regional creativity and innovation can be enhanced through an understanding of the qualities and meanings associated with "place". In the context of globalisation, increased connectivity and socio-economic processes such as de-industrialisation and technological disruption, it is all the more evident that place is neither static nor completely malleable. Place has its own "textures" (Adams, Hoelscher and Till 2001) and conditions the kind of symbolic, sensory, imaginative and material resources that can be mobilised by cities and regions, individuals and collectives, and formal and informal organisations when attempting to create themselves anew. While the notion of creative regions and regional innovation has started to receive increasing attention, especially in the Australian context, the field arguably has some way to go in conceptualising the non-metropolitan, the peripheral, the rural and the types of creative and innovative activities taking place in small regional towns. This book aims to contribute to this ongoing and important discussion.

References

Adams, P. C., Hoelscher, S., and Till, K. E. 2001. "Place in Context: Rethinking Humanist Geographies." Pp. xiii–xxxiii in *Textures of Place: Exploring Humanist Geographies,* edited by Adams, P. C., Hoelscher, S., and Till, K. E. Minneapolis: University of Minnesota Press.

Bell, D., and Jayne, M. (eds.). 2006. *Small Cities: Urban Experience Beyond the Metropolis.* London: Routledge.

Bell, D., and Jayne, M. 2010. "The Creative Countryside: Policy and Practice in the UK Rural Cultural Economy." *Journal of Rural Studies* 26: 209–218.

Blakeley, R., and Hu, R. 2019. *Crafting Innovative Places for Australia's Knowledge Economy.* London: Palgrave Macmillan.

Bourdieu, P. 1993. *Fields of Cultural Production.* Cambridge: Polity Press.

Brabazon, T. 2015. *Unique Urbanity? Rethinking Third Tier Cities, Degeneration and Mobility.* Singapore: Springer.

Burgess, J., and Green, J. 2018. *YouTube: Online Video and Participatory Culture* (2nd ed.). Cambridge: Polity Press.

16 *Eduardo de la Fuente and Ariella Van Luyn*

Carr, C., and Gibson, C. 2017. "Animating Geographies of Making: Embodied Slow Scholarship for Participant-Researchers of Maker Cultures and Material Work." *Geography Compass* 11(6): 1–10.

Collis, C., Freebody, S., and Flew, T. 2013. "Seeing the Outer Suburbs: Addressing the Urban Bias in Creative Place Thinking." *Regional Studies* 47(2): 1–13.

Cunningham, S. 2006. *What Price a Creative Economy?* Platform Papers. Strawberry Hills, NSW: Currency House.

Cunningham, S. 2013. *Hidden Innovation: Policy, Industry and the Creative Sector.* Brisbane: University of Queensland Press.

Ehland, C. (ed.). 2007. *Thinking Northern: Textures of Identity in the North of England.* Amsterdam: Rodopi.

Etzkowitz, H. 2003. "Innovation in Innovation: The Triple Helix of University-Industry-Government Relations." *Social Science Information* 42(3): 293–337.

Flew, T. 2012a. "Creative Suburbia: Rethinking Urban Cultural Policy." *International Journal of Cultural Studies* 15(3): 231–246.

Flew, T. 2012b. *The Creative Industries: Culture and Policy.* London: Sage.

Florida, R. 2002. *The Rise of the Creative Class.* New York: Basic Books.

Foth, M., Rittenbruch, M., Robinson, R., and Viller, S. (eds.). 2014. *Street Computing: Urban Informatics and City Interfaces.* London: Routledge.

Gibson, C., Carr, C., and Warren, A. T. 2012. "A Country That Makes Things?" *Australian Geographer* 43(2): 109–113.

Gibson, C., and Klocker, N. 2004. "Academic Publishing as 'Creative' Industry, and Recent Discourses of 'Creative Economies': Some Critical Reflections." *Area* 36(4): 423–434.

Gibson, C., and Klocker, N. 2005. "The 'Cultural Turn' in Australian Regional Economic Development Discourse: Neoliberalising Creativity?" *Geographical Research* 43(1): 93–102.

Gibson, M. 2016. "Creative and Attenuated Sociality: Creative Communities in Suburban and Peri-Urban Australia." Pp. 49–61 in *Creative Communities: Regional Inclusion & the Arts,* edited by McDonald, J., and Mason, R. Bristol: Intellect.

Gibson, R. 2015a. "Preface" Pp. 1–6 in *By-Roads and Hidden Treasures,* edited by Ashton, P., Gibson, C., and Gibson, R. Perth: University of Western Australia Press.

Gibson, R. 2015b. "Orientation: Remote, Intimate, Lovely." Pp. 7–15 in *By-Roads and Hidden Treasures,* edited by Ashton, P., Gibson, C., and Gibson, R. Perth: University of Western Australia Press.

Hartley, J., and Potts, J. 2014. *Cultural Science: A Natural History of Stories, Demes, Knowledge and Innovation.* London: Bloomsbury.

Hartley, J., Potts, J., Cunningham, S., Flew, T., Keane, M., and Banks, J. 2013. *Key Concepts in Creative Industries.* London: Sage.

Hearn, G., Bridgstock, R., Goldsmith, B., and Rodgers, J. (eds.). 2014. *Creative Work Beyond the Creative Industries: Innovation, Employment and Education.* London: Edward Elgar.

Howitt, R. 2002. "Frontiers, Borders, Edges: Liminal Challenges to the Hegemony of Exclusion." *Australian Geographical Studies* 39(2): 233–245.

Howkins, J. 2009. *Creative Ecologies.* St Lucia, QLD: University of Queensland Press.

Ingold, T. 2000. *The Perception of the Environment.* London and New York: Routledge.

Jayne, M., Gibson, C., Waitt, G., and Bell, D. 2010. "The Cultural Economy of Small Cities." *Geography Compass* 4(9): 1408–1417.

Karpik, L. 2010. *Valuing the Unique.* Princeton, NJ: Princeton University Press.

Keane, M. 2013. *The Creative Industries in China: Art, Design and Media.* Cambridge: Polity Press.

Kong, L., and O'Connor, J. 2009. *Creative Economies, Creative Cities: Asian-European Perspectives.* Dordrecht: Springer.

Luckman, S. 2012. *Locating Cultural Work: The Politics and Poetics of Rural, Regional and Remote Creativity*. London: Palgrave Macmillan.

McDonald, J., and Mason, R. (Eds). 2015. *Creative Communities: Regional Inclusion and the Arts*. Chicago: University of Chicago Press.

Peck, J. 2002. "Political Economies of Scale: Fast Policy, Interscalar Relations, and Neoliberal Workfare." *Economic Geography* 78(3): 331–360.

Porter, M. 1990. *The Competitive Advantage of Nations*. New York: Free Press.

Pratt, A. 2004. "The Cultural Economy: A Call for a Spatialized 'Production of Culture' Perspective." *International Journal of Cultural Studies* 7: 117–128.

Rong, Y., and O'Connor, J. 2018. *The Cultural Industries in Shanghai: Policy and Planning Inside a Global City*. London: Intellect.

Scott, A. J. 2010. "The Cultural Economy of Landscape and Prospects of Peripheral Development in the Twenty-First Century: The Case of the English Lake District." *European Planning Studies* 18(10): 1568–1589.

Seamon, D. 1979. *A Geography of the Lifeworld*. London: Croom Helm.

van Heur, B. 2010. "Small Cities and the Geographical Biases of Creative Industries Research and Policy." *Journal of Policy Research in Tourism, Leisure and Tourism* 2(2): 189–192.

Waitt, G., and Gibson, C. 2009. "Creative Small Cities: Rethinking the Creative Economy in Place." *Urban Studies* 46(5–6): 1223–1246.

Zeitlin, M. 1991. "Positive Deviance in Nutrition." *Nutrition Review* 49(9): 259–268.

Section 1

Landscapes, tastescapes and sensescapes

Creatively responding to place

1 Fruit forward?

Wine regions as geographies of innovation in Australia and Canada

Julie McIntyre, Donna Senese and John S. Hull

Introduction

The Australian-led globalisation of mass-produced white grape wine from the 1990s is credited with boosting regional Australian economies (Anderson, Giesecke and Valenzuela 2010: 9). Looking outward from Australia, the ripple effect of this global boom in wine production, consumption, export and tourism has been unprecedented. Indeed, by the early 2000s, wine production, more than any other food crop, proved to be economically regenerative in agricultural regions in many parts of the world (Mattiacci and Zampi 2004). The globalisation of wine consumption over the past generation has gained pace through the affordability and transportability of mass-produced wine branded for nations rather than regions. At the same time, regionally branded wine and wine tourism offers a localist taste of place: a counterpoint to the homogeneous sensory experience of mass-produced comestibles, including wine. Contemporary consumer interest in products of specified origin is a hallmark of middle class consumer pushback in the present global consumerist age. This practice is evident in the locavore movement of reducing the distance that food is transported (Blake, Mellor and Crane 2010) and in privileging gastronomic products of specific provenance. The new global consumer obsession with wine (both mass-produced and provenanced for geographical origin) means that European literature on wine appreciation since ancient times has been joined in the past decade by a multidisciplinary scholarship on wine production, trade and consumption (McIntyre and Germov 2017). More attention is required, however, to the "cultural reconversion" (cited in Mattiacci and Zampi 2004: 768) in which businesses in agricultural regions outside of traditional European wine-producing countries have responded to, and driven, new habits of wine drinking and wine tourism connected with fine food and accommodation.

In this chapter we consider the emergence of the Hunter Valley, New South Wales, Australia and Okanagan Valley, British Columbia, Canada: two successful specialised contemporary clusters of premium wine entrepreneurship within picturesque rural settings. The Hunter and the Okanagan wine regions are based in agricultural districts within nations established as British settler societies from the late eighteenth century. Winegrowing began in the Hunter in 1828 as a small part of wider agricultural enterprise and has continued since as a resilient

22   *J. McIntyre, D. Senese and J. S. Hull*

feature of the wider regional economy due to family business innovation and networks (McIntyre and Germov 2013; Grimstad, Waterhouse and Burgess 2019). Wine grapes were first planted in the established agricultural landscape of the Okanagan Valley in the 1920s and, like the Hunter, experienced exponential growth from the 1960s following the relaxation of temperance strictures and a rise in consumer interest in food and wine (Senese, Wilson and Momer 2012). Both the Hunter and Okanagan wine regions exist within large rural valleys containing other industries. Each of these larger valleys are delineated by varying levels of government as economic and social units for the purpose of allocating resources. Although there are historical and physical differences between the Hunter and Okanagan wine regions, the success of wine production and tourism in each place is definitional of the spaces of which they are part and is integral to the economies and societies of these regional geographies.

Our contribution to the literature on regional creativity is paying attention to "wine regions", which depend on visitor fantasies of pleasure, escape and worthiness within broader "regions" as bounded geographies that are quantified economically and socially by the state for administrative purposes. Our comparative case study of the Hunter and Okanagan Valleys is located theoretically at the intersection of regional historical geography and wine studies, a partial subset of food studies that is also treated separately from food in the humanities and social sciences (McIntyre and Germov 2017). We are concerned with how wine cluster entrepreneurs within the wider geography of each region have leveraged their community capital over time to successfully configure their "wine regions". Community capital includes the natural landscapes, built environments, human knowledge and social forms that are drawn upon as part of a community's or rural region's product offering (George, Mair and Reid 2009). Natural landscape is the core factor in the community capital of the wine regions of the Hunter and the Okanagan Valleys.

Natural landscapes, natural endowments

The basic environmental requirements to grow wine grape vines are appropriate soils and favourable conditions of climate and weather, including sufficient water at peak growing times. So called non-premium wines, sold for less than AUD$5/litre, are produced from large-scale plantation-style vineyards in locations where there is little risk to investors. These wines cost consumers little and require scant specialist knowledge from drinkers. Vineyards and wineries producing non-premium products are neither landscaped with tourism in mind nor served by facilities for visitor wine tastings, shopping, meals or accommodation. Premium wines require additional investment in vineyard management and wine manufacture to capitalise on geographical provenance connected with the development of distinctive sensory profiles in the wine. For example, grapes may be hand-picked to make premium wines rather than the less expensive and far more prevalent practice of machine harvesting. This carefully handled fruit may then be fermented, processed and stored in a manner that concentrates certain recognisable flavours that vary from year to year

Fruit forward? 23

because each growing season is different. Wine grape vineyards in attractive rural surrounds may be curated to appeal visually to tourists seeking to taste good wine and food in picturesque places connected with the products they are consuming. Companion plants such as roses may be grown. Signage may be designed to appear rustic rather than instrumental. Perhaps surprisingly, a touristic "wine region" does not need working vineyards and wineries, only cellar doors and facilities for wine tasting and dining, shopping and other activities. Nevertheless, wines from visitable places are viewed as a valuable part of the touristic experience, as well as assuring some diversity of income for regional producers. In this chapter we are concerned with the past, present and future of the wine regions of the Hunter and the Okanagan Valleys as natural landscapes with sustained wine productiveness and scenic beauty.

What are the characteristics of the wider geographies that host the Hunter and Okanagan wine regions? The Hunter Valley (Figure 1.1) – an assemblage of valleys emanating from the Hunter River – contains some of Australia's more recent geological formations, dating from approximately 380 million years ago. The Hunter is on the eastern coast of the continent, forming the north-eastern portion of the wider Sydney Basin. The long and broad coastal lowland of the Hunter Valley totals three million hectares and is bounded to the south, west and north by spurs of the Great Dividing Range and to the east by the Pacific coastline. The region is divided by the Hunter-Mooki Tectonic Fault Thrust system separating the Williams and Paterson river valleys (to the Upper Allyn River and Barrington Tops) in the northeast from hills and plains at lower altitude. The naturalised vegetation of the Paterson and Gresford districts is more green and lush in appearance than the remainder. The north-eastern portion is geologically Carboniferous, composed of rocks dating to 360 million to 300 million years ago, compared with the more erodible Permian rocks of the central lowlands – estimated to have been formed 299 to 251 million years ago (McManus et al. 2000). The other waterways of the region are the Goulburn River in the Upper Hunter to the west, Wollombi Brook in the south-east or Lower Hunter and the Karuah River flowing into Port Stephens in the north0east of the wider valley.

There are basalt soils in the upper-western district, and otherwise the soil types are defined as texture-contrast, with topsoil varying from clay to sand and coal deposits. Seismic activity revealed coal deposits that led to the Hunter Valley's central role in Australian coal extraction and export from the region's large harbour at Newcastle at the mouth of the Hunter River. Away from the riverbank alluvium are red clay, white sand and some black soils. Due to the greater accessibility to the meeting point of the Carboniferous and Permian sections of the wider Hunter Valley by riverways, many early vineyards were located there until growers determined the unsuitability for vineyards of the flood plains and the wet eucalypt Carboniferous districts (McManus et al. 2000). The climate is maritime in the contemporary wine subregions of Pokolbin, Broke-Fordwich, Wollombi, Mount View and Lovedale near the township of Cessnock in the Lower Hunter (benefiting from cooling oceanic breezes). These subregions also receive inconvenient summer rains and sometimes hail during the grape-ripening season. The Upper Hunter, further westward, is less susceptible to climatic

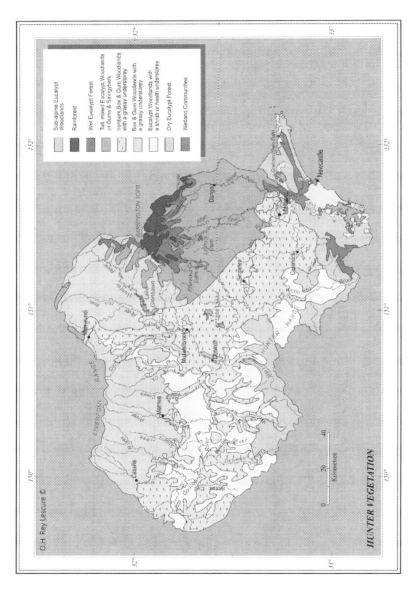

Figure 1.1 Naturalised Hunter Valley vegetation. Most contemporary vineyards lie in the mid-section of the wider geographical region traditionally possessing eucalypt woodlands, distant from natural water sources and receiving summer rain.

Source: McManus et al. 2000

variability. It is a two-hour drive by motor car north-west from Sydney – the state's largest city and international tourist gateway – to Pokolbin at the centre of the touristic Hunter wine region.

The Okanagan Valley (Figure 1.2) is approximately a third of the size of the Hunter Valley and located in the southern interior of British Columbia in the

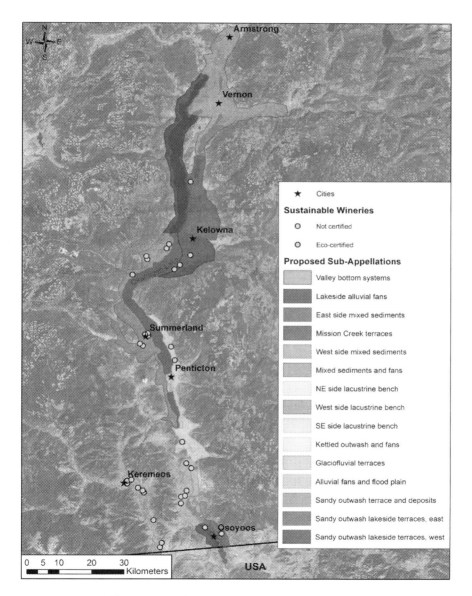

Figure 1.2 Sustainable wineries and proposed sub-appellations in the Okanagan.
Source: Pederson and Senese (2017)

Dry Interior Plateau of the province (Senese, Wilson and Momer 2012). The valley was formed during the Pleistocene glacial period 9,000 years ago and is 250 km in length and 20 km wide, containing numerous large lakes providing a moderating effect during the growing season (Marsh 2006). The valley is physically located between the Cascade Mountains to the west and the Monashee Mountains to the east, which provide a protective rain shield that results in a dry, continental climate with over 2000 hours of sunlight a year (Belliveau, Smit and Bradshaw 2006; Marsh 2006; McGillivray 2011). Physiographically, the area is a rolling upland, typical of the province's Interior Plateau. Extensive kame and outwash terraces and an assortment of other glacial and alluvial features hold generally well-drained soils that dominate the lower elevations of the valley. As the northern point of the great arid zone that extends southward into the United States to the Sonoran Desert, precipitation varies somewhat south to north and upslope. The regional values range generally between 300 and 400 mm per year on the agriculturally viable lands, with the higher amounts in the north. Variations in temperature also range over this space, with the highest values in the south of the region (Senese, Wilson and Momer 2012). The soil, topography and hot, sunny climate historically has served as the basis for growth of a diversified agricultural economy in the region. It is a four-hour drive from Vancouver – the largest proximal international Canadian city – to the Okanagan Valley.

Histories of settler agriculture, viticulture and gastronomic tourism: Hunter Valley

From the outset of settler incursions into Awabakal, Worimi, Biripi, Wonnarua, Darkinjung and Kamilaroi countries in the early nineteenth century, the Hunter Valley was considered by British officials and settler capitalists to be one of the most ideal parts of the colony of New South Wales for European-style farming and grazing. The Hunter's coal mining industry and thoroughbred horse breeding businesses are also vital primary industries, and some non-wine grape agriculture remains but is a much smaller concern than in the past. These other land uses are not tied to tourism in the same manner as wine production.

Logging of native forest trees began in the region in the 1810s with convict timber-getters radiating outward from a small settlement at Newcastle Harbour. Coal mining also began at Newcastle at this time, leading – over the subsequent century – to the formation of townships based around the pitheads of mines. A small band of former convicts (emancipists) encouraged into the Paterson River district from 1811 showed the potential for farming, although this class of smallholders did not plant wine grapes. The first joint stock venture in the colony, the Australian Agricultural Company, trialled sheep and cattle grazing and some winegrowing. When the British colonial office began to encourage settler capitalists from Britain to take possession of 2000-acre land grants in the colony from 1821, the allocated portions of land fronting the major rivers of the Hunter Valley were rapidly privatised. By 1825, all river frontage had

Fruit forward? 27

been claimed by wealthy settlers on the proviso that they invest in "improvement" through cropping and/or grazing on their properties and build houses, outbuildings and fences (McIntyre and Germov 2018a). These activities greatly disrupted Aboriginal locals. Some settlers valued Aboriginal people as guides and labourers (Dunn 2017). Even so, by the mid-1880s the regional Aboriginal population had declined appreciably, was disconnected from winegrowing properties in the Hunter (McIntyre and Germov 2018a) and was unacknowledged as participants in other agricultural industries in the region.

From 1828 to 1846 as many as a dozen settler capitalists, and the Australian Agricultural Company, made some attempt to grow wine grapes and make wine as part of their incipient cropping and grazing. In 1846 James King shipped the first six barrels of wine from the Hunter to Sydney. Just as agricultural innovation in eighteenth-century Britain and France required access to "land, labour, capital, technology, and agricultural organisation" (Sexauer 1976: 492–493), Hunter winegrowing did not begin to flourish until the formalisation of a viticultural group in 1847. Significantly, the dozen or so winegrowers who inaugurated the Hunter River Vineyard Association (HRVA) maintained connections to the Hunter Agricultural Society, as monoculture was not profitable. From 1849 the HRVA supported the immigration of experienced vineyard workers, winemakers and coopers from southwestern German wine regions. The association lobbied for favourable export terms for wine in barrels from the Hunter to Sydney and onto Britain even before export quantities of wine were produced in the region. The determination of individuals in the HRVA to create a "wine region" in imitation of reputable European wine districts is clear from this period. Thanks to the reporting of HRVA meetings by the local *Maitland Mercury* newspaper, and the republication of these stories across the continent and in Britain, the Hunter gain a reputation for producing wine out of proportion to the small quantity of product actually flowing from the region (McIntyre and Germov 2018a). Although little Hunter wine was sold commercially until the 1860s, expectations of visiting a vineyard landscape and drinking Hunter wine quickened in the latter half of the nineteenth century, fostered too by the success of the region's red and white wines of several varieties in colonial and international exhibitions. The region's concentration on Semillon (called Shepherd's Riesling in the Hunter for many years) and Shiraz grapes for wine began in this period.

There were two reasons the HRVA stopped meeting in 1876. Family and social networks of the two previous generations were disrupted by failed succession planning and other factors, and land reforms to encourage smallhold farming permitted the entry of a new wave of grape growers and winemakers at Pokolbin, which was more suited to grapes than the earlier settled areas. By the 1870s Hunter winegrowers benefited too from increased transport efficiency as they were connected by rail (rather than coastal steamer and poor roads) to the metropolitan market hub of Sydney (McIntyre and Germov 2018a).

From the 1860s to 1880s other environmental and economic forces fostered Hunter wine production. In Europe, an outbreak of the North American vine disease powdery mildew, which prevents healthy vine leaf and fruit growth, was followed by a massive plague of the (also) North American vine-feeding wood louse phylloxera. The resulting destruction of two-thirds of centuries-old winelands spurred the first wave of wine globalisation (Simpson 2011) just as wealthy countries such as Britain sought to increase wine imports. When wine merchants in Europe's Old World could not fill domestic or export orders, they turned elsewhere. The French colony of Algeria, for example, provided a significant quantity of new wine supplies, as did South Africa and Australia, to a much lesser extent.

Powdery mildew and phylloxera also affected the New World wine countries. Mildews are readily treated with chemical spray. Phylloxera may be curtailed only by planting European wine grape varieties onto rootstock of North American non-wine grape vines. The Hunter did not suffer from phylloxera as did some other New South Wales wine regions. The Hunter, as a quality rather than quantity wine region, also did not produce much wine to contribute to changing international trade demands. Even so, Hunter wines were known to be blended in London and sold back to Australia as French wines that had long been popular among the Australian colonies' modest settler middle class. Luxury French wines gained new Australian customers during the eastern colonial gold rushes. In an environment of increasing demand for wine, Hunter producers thrived, and winegrowing became a dominant form of regional land use, alongside cattle grazing for dairy and beef, some grain crops and poultry farming (McIntyre and Germov 2018a), until the turn of the twentieth century.

Hunter wine dominated the very small domestic market for wine in New South Wales until 1901. In that year, constitutional federation of the British colonies of Australia led to new intercolonial trade agreements and an influx of wine from the substantially larger wine-producing colony of South Australia. Hunter company Lindeman & Sons responded to this new intranational competition by redirecting products from the Sydney market to London. Lindeman's had emerged in the late nineteenth century from vineyards and wineries owned by Henry Lindeman in the Hunter and the south of New South Wales to be the major wine distribution company in New South Wales. The company's growth was fostered by astute succession planning as Henry's sons managed different elements of the business: vineyards, winemaking and wine sales (McIntyre and Germov 2018b).

Federation and the threat of wines flooding from South Australia to Sydney provided the imperative for a new generation of viticultural organisation to ensure the economic sustainability of the Hunter wine region. In 1901, after a generation without such a group in the Hunter, the Pokolbin and District Vinegrowers Association (PDVGA) was inaugurated with more than twenty members. This association emerged from existing family, social and professional networks and immediately exerted influence to tighten federal government regulations on correct labelling of wine to prevent fraudsters trading on the Hunter's long-established reputation. The PDVGA met annually until the late 1920s when membership fell away as grape growers and others further along the supply chain left the industry because of strict wartime restrictions on alcohol licencing (that continued into peacetime), new pest problems and economic downturn (McIntyre and Germov 2018a).

In New South Wales and most other Australian states, it was illegal from the late 1910s to 1955 to serve wine after 6 pm in restaurants, clubs, wine shops or public houses (or "pubs", the main retailers of beer). For two generations, convivial night-time wine-drinking culture was confined to private homes. In 1924, downy mildew struck Hunter vineyards, requiring costly regimes of preventative spraying of grape vines. The 1930s depression lowered the economic viability of a luxury crop such as wine grapes. Hunter winegrowers received little government support from the 1920s through to the 1950s. In the 1920s, the New South Wales viticultural expert ceased visiting the Hunter, expressing greater interest in the longevity of irrigated winegrowing districts in the southwest of the state. This disinterested viticultural expert appears to have advised the economists, whose 1931 *Report on the Wine Industry in Australia* stated that, due to the unfavourable growing conditions for wine grapes in the Hunter, and a poor market for quality table wines (containing approximately 15%alcohol by volume, or less), "it appears doubtful whether this area can continue in production" (Gunn and Gollan 1931: 10). The Overseas Wine Marketing Board, established as a result of the Gunn and Gollan report, excluded the Hunter from its executive committee and broader remit. Hunter wine was considered too fine and delicate to fortify with grape spirit for export at a time when the report recommended export, particularly to Britain, as a way of mitigating a dull domestic market for wine.

Between the 1930s and 1959, the Hunter winegrowing community contracted sharply to ten vineyards, with total acreage of about 200 hectares (the lowest acreage since the 1860s), and four wineries. In this period key community representatives – especially from the Tulloch family and Maurice O'Shea at Mount Pleasant – advocated for the region and their business in Sydney and Newcastle newspapers. They worked with Sydney restauranteurs to invite small groups of aficionados to the region for rustic winery meals. O'Shea formed a partnership with the family firm of McWilliam from Griffith, in the state's southwest, to sustain his vineyard and winery. Tulloch and O'Shea each purchased grapes from other growers (McIntyre and Germov 2018a).

From the mid-1950s, the fortunes of winegrowers nationally began gradually to turn. New electricity-powered refrigeration and filtration technologies allowed greater control over the types of wine made in the Hunter, and, despite little demand among the region's mainly working classes, export to Sydney and elsewhere rapidly returned to, and surpassed, pre-temperance levels. In New South Wales and other states, from 1955, licenced premises such as restaurants and clubs were permitted to again serve wine in the evenings. A fine dining culture began to re-emerge, led in part by post-war Italian immigrants accustomed to wine-friendly dining. New social and sexual freedoms for women from the 1960s, and a rise in the advertising of wine to women, contributed to a revolution in drinking culture. More people owned motor cars as a new professional

30   *J. McIntyre, D. Senese and J. S. Hull*

class emerged due to post-war industrialisation. Grape harvest festivals were staged in Cessnock every second year from 1963, drawing large crowds each year for a celebration that combined agricultural show-style entertainment with wine education. From 1965, Hunter wine grape acreages were recharged through an influx of investment from corporations with no prior experience in wine production. By the late 1970s as much as a third of the white wine consumed in Australia was made by Lindeman's, which now sourced grapes from all over the continent to make these wines (McIntyre and Germov 2018b).

1972 saw the inauguration of a new Hunter Valley Vineyard Association (HVVA) with more than 100 members, later changing its name to the Hunter Wine Industry Association (HWIA). The HWIA ensured the quality of regional wines through competitive tasting and a shared regional vision for tourism. The association lobbied local, state and federal governments for the facilities required to foster visitation. These included road construction, planning laws to allow "cellar door" development and prevent non-touristic construction antithetical to maintaining a picturesque landscape, licencing laws plus promotion of the region in Sydney and internationally. From 1973, the association revised the Cessnock Festival into the Hunter Vintage Festival. Upper Hunter vine plantings began to boom. Entrepreneurial producers ran bus tours of tourists from Newcastle to the Upper as well as Lower Hunter, converting working-class beer drinkers to wine. In the 1980s, the HVVA forced the introduction of air pollution controls at a local aluminium smelter to protect the pristine qualities of Pokolbin in the Lower Hunter (McIntyre and Germov 2018a).

The HVVA's success as a professional network overseeing regional branding lay in its base in family and social networks from earlier times (McIntyre and Germov 2013). The reconversion of the region to Hunter Wine Country by the late 1990s is encapsulated in geographer Phillip O'Neill's description of the Hunter as primarily a "gastronomic landscape" (O'Neill 2000: 158). This depended largely on access to an engineered water supply. In the Upper Hunter, water is readily pumped directly from the Hunter River. In the Lower Hunter, traditionally dry-land farmed, a Private Irrigation District (PID) was established in the 1990s by key members of the HVWIA to provide a co-operatively funded pipeline from the Hunter River. This allowed drip-irrigation of vineyards to maintain their grape yields and visual beauty as well as the development of watered lawns at sites such as Hunter Valley Gardens, a popular family destination. Then, even before the Global Financial Crisis of 2008, Hunter regional wine production collapsed, particularly in the Upper Hunter, when the Australian dollar was close to parity with the American dollar, leading to a fall in export income. This shock consolidated the region's wine tourism as more viable than wine export.

In 2013, the HWIA merged with the region's tourism body to form the Hunter Valley Wine & Tourism Association (HVWTA) with a mission to increase promotion of the wine landscape for nuptials, rock concerts and family getaway holidays (Hunter ValleyWineTourismAssociation Prospectus 2013). This strategy has succeeded in assuring that there are today 150 wine firms in the region (Hunter Wine Country 2018). Yet the Hunter Valley is one of sixty-five wine regions in Australia spread across the southern portion of the continent from New South Wales, Victoria and Tasmania in the east to South Australia, in the southern central part of the country, and the south-west of Western Australia (Wine Australia 2017). And the Hunter produces less than 3% of the total Australian grape crush (NSW Wine Industry Association 2018). By contrast, the Hunter is New South Wales' second most visited location after Sydney, receiving a fifth of all tourists, and the Hunter is the most visited wine region by international travellers, attracting 65.7% of visitors who spend close to four out of five of their wine tourism nights in the Hunter (Destination NSW 2017). In 2017, annual direct and indirect regional value of wine tourism was estimated at AUD$185 million versus AUD$143 million (or $8.40/litre) for wine, indicating the extent to which tourism has eclipsed productive value from the fruit of the vine (Gillespie and Clarke 2017). The Hunter is Australia's largest regional economy and accounts for 28% of New South Wales' domestic product from a highly diverse economic base (NSW Department of Planning 2019). Local and state governments share the HVWTA vision for tourism as the economic basis of the region's wine landscape (Destination NSW 2018). The Hunter wine sector in 2017 contributed AUD$502 million to the regional economy(Gillespie and Clarke 2017).

Histories of settler agriculture, viticulture and gastronomic tourism: Okanagan Valley

Regional histories of settler agriculture in the Hunter and Okanagan Valleys share similar evolutionary paths in terms of their cluster development of community capital tied to natural and cultural environments. Agriculture has played a significant role among the Syilx/Okanagan Nation, the original people of the territory, and continues to play a significant role economically in Okanagan Valley, promoting the growth and identity of the region since the beginning of European settlement (City of Kelowna 2018). In 1859, Father Charles Pandosy, a French Catholic missionary, planted the first apple seedlings in the Okanagan. By 1900, there were more than a million fruit trees growing in the valley (Central Okanagan Economic Profile for Agriculture 2017). The communities of Vernon, Kelowna and Penticton in the region were small villages in a sparsely settled valley with a combined resident population of 1,663 residents in 1908 (Statistics Canada 2018; Central Okanagan Economic Profile for Agriculture 2017; McGillivray 2011). At this time, the valley was recognised for its farming potential, with cattle ranching, grain growing and the tree fruit industry dominating the sector (Senese, Wilson and Momer 2012). By 1910, Kelowna was gaining fame as the Orchard City serving Canadian and Commonwealth markets. The region boasted four co-ops and dozens of packinghouses (Canadian Encyclopedia 2018). In 1914, the Government of Canada established the Dominion Experimental Farm in Summerland to support the further growth of the agricultural industry in the province. The growth of agriculture led to increased infrastructure development. The Okanagan River was channelised in the early twentieth century for agricultural and hydroelectric development, to protect residents from flooding and to support a period of rapid urbanisation as the population of the region grew to approximately 12,000 residents by 1921 (Statistics Canada 2018; Okanagan Basin Water Board 2018). During this time period, the valley was relatively isolated (Wagner 2008). However, large investments in transport infrastructure in the valley assisted in increasing the movement of people and agricultural products. With completion of the transcontinental Canadian Pacific Railway in the mid-1880s, and the construction of a rail spur from this line south to the north end of Okanagan Lake in 1892, the regional economy began to change (Senese, Wilson and Momer 2012). By 1893, CPR's new transport connection was extended south to Kelowna and Penticton with the launch of the *Aberdeen* steamboat on Okanagan Lake. Steamboats became a lifeline to emerging settlements, determining the location of many town sites along the lake as people and merchants settled near boat landings. Between 1904 and 1914, the shift to intensive agriculture took on more momentum as tens of thousands of acres of grazing land, hay flats and grain fields became 5–40-acre orchard lots, supplied with gravity-fed irrigation water and planted to orchards.

In only half a generation, the area's landscape turned from brown to green and took on the look and feel of a well-manicured and bucolic agricultural landscape (Dendy 1976; Wilson 1989; Senese, Wilson and Momer 2012). In 1910, Penticton was selected as the headquarters for the new Kettle Valley Railway, the rail line that would link the transportation of the coast to the wealth of the Kootenays. The arrival of the railway brought jobs, and the town's population more than doubled by the time the line was finished in 1915. The railway provided fast and efficient transportation for local products, boosting the tree fruit industry by opening up distant markets to Okanagan fruit. The KVR also allowed tourists to visit an area that had long been isolated from the rest of the province, increasing the accessibility of the Okanagan as a tourist destination (City of Penticton 2018). By the latter half of the 1920s, commercial-scale grape growing began when J. W. Hughes planted roughly 125 acres of grapes in the Kelowna area and in 1939 added another seventy-five acres (Agriculture Canada 1984: 2). His market for this early production capacity was both the fresh fruit market and an emerging wine enterprise that began with Growers Wines in Victoria in the 1920s and with Domestic Wine and By-products Ltd in 1932 in the Okanagan (Senese, Wilson and Momer 2012). By 1957, the population of the Okanagan Valley had more than doubled to well over 30,000 residents (Statistics Canada 2018). At the time, there were thirty-six agricultural cooperative societies, twenty independent shippers and five grower shippers in the Okanagan whose products were sold internationally through BC Tree Fruits, reinforcing the importance of the agricultural economy to the region (Central Okanagan Economic Profile for Agriculture 2017).

With few exceptions, the first century of wine production all over North America followed the migration patterns of European settlers and clergy

Fruit forward? 33

members. For most of those first 100 years of production, the wine industry in North America remained small, geographically isolated and relatively insignificant in its contribution to rural landscapes, economies or cultures. Growth of the Canadian wine industry, in particular, remained slow and steady throughout the period 1960–1990, largely based on the popularity of sweet and fortified wines that could be produced by lambrusco varieties grown in southern Ontario, Quebec and British Columbia. An explosion of the wine industry in Canada took place in the 1990s as part of the new global wine boom, and this unprecedented growth continues today.

In British Columbia, wine industry growth has had an increasing imprint on the rural landscape in terms of region building through provenanced products. The speed and spatial extent of winery growth in British Columbia is most pronounced in the Okanagan Valley of the province where wine has come to dominate agricultural production and tourism industry growth. The process that has most influenced region building is intertwined with a more widespread, globalised redefinition of rural space for the consumption of metropolitan consumers. The British Columbian region saw this same post-war era of new urban wealth and mobility to rural areas where tourists aimed to taste, as well as view, rurality through wine experiences.

The residual character of rural areas is understood as not only based on the retention of older ways of life but also the scenic values and recreational opportunities of the countryside that attract visitors from urban areas (George et al. 2009; OECD 1994). Researchers (George et al. 2009: 19) point out that the intensification of travel to rural areas, in Canada and elsewhere, is the product of a number of important changes, including the growth of disposable income and leisure time, changes to transportation networks and technologies and such forces as "nostalgia" and "escapism" that engender a powerful attraction to rural experiences, especially for urban dwellers. Viniculture, viticulture and local culinary industries provide products central to postproduction rural spaces: a leisure landscape suitable for a highly mobile metropolitan population and a cultural commodity in the form of localised epicurean products. When localised, both products satisfy the market demands of an aging baby boom and emerging millennial consumer markets. In the Okanagan, as in the Hunter, the adaptive capacity of these industries has been catalysed by community capital built through the alignment of the wine, culinary and tourism industries, which has in turn helped to refine a place-based reputation. A number of public and private agency actors, including ad hoc and grassroots organisations, have contributed to the provenance of this region by driving key policy and plans to guide definitions of the Okanagan as a unique wine and culinary region.

After the 1960s, the Okanagan tourism and wine sectors grew and diversified. Tourism expanded from mainly a summer activity centred on lake-based recreation to a year-round industry with four distinct seasons, with the development of golf courses and the opening of ski resorts at Crystal Mountain, Mt Baldy and Silverstar in the 1960s and Big White in the 1970s (McGillivray 2011). During the 1960s and 1970s, the number of acres for grape production was supported by increasing liberal trade laws and federal government support for Canadian grape growers. The establishment of the Grape Marketing Board in 1970 successfully pushed a requirement that British Columbia wineries use as much as 81% of the grapes grown in the province (McGuire 1993). Between 1964 and 1974, grape acreage increased from less than 1,000 acres to almost 3,000 acres, driven by consumer trends that saw domestic wine sales in British Columbia triple (Nichol 1983; BC Wine Institute 2012; Senese, Wilson and Momer 2012). The dry climate and the four distinct seasons, along with the low land and housing prices and easy access from the Lower Mainland, resulted in the first interests in the region as a retirement destination. With the passage of the Free Trade Agreement between Canada and the USA in 1989, new varieties of grape production and new rules permitting the sale of wine from farms helped to promote a wine tourism industry in the region. At this time, other industries, including mining and forestry, also expanded in the region, increasing employment and the population base (McGillivray 2011).

By the twenty-first century, the Okanagan was recognised as having one of the most beautiful winescapes in Canada and was promoted as a region of mountains, forests and vines (Aspler 2013: 13). As in the Hunter, the scenic natural environment, agricultural heritage and recreational amenities have produced a valuable tourism economy centred on the wine industry and local rural aesthetic (Senese, Wilson and Momer 2012; Hull 2016). The region is recognised for its wine and culinary tourism, outdoor adventure, cultural heritage and wellness experiences (TOTA 2012). The Thompson Okanagan Tourism Association (TOTA), the regional Destination Marketing Organisation (DMO), reports that the region welcomes over 3.5 million visitors annually, generating CAD$1.7 billion to the regional economy and employing approximately 15,000 residents. The majority of visitors are from the Vancouver metropolitan region of the Lower Mainland of British Columbia (64%) and the metropolitan regions (Calgary, Edmonton) of Alberta (17%) with other Canadians representing (2%) of the overall market. Internationally, visitors are mainly from the USA, UK, Germany, Netherlands and Australia and comprise 17% of the total market. The BC Wine Institute (BCWI 2016) reports that, as of 2016, there are more than 350 licensed wineries in the province and that every year they attract one million tourists to taste wine; the industry generates an economic impact of CAD$2.8 billion annually. In 2015, the Okanagan Valley was named one of the ten best wine destinations in the world by Wine Enthusiast Magazine (BCWI 2016). The new BC Wine Institute Wine and Food Tourism Strategy aims not only to increase revenues and direct sales from wine tourists but also is committed to partnering with regional DMOs to produce wine and food tourism marketing initiatives (BCWI 2016).

The Thompson Okanagan Tourism Association is integral to regional innovation. The ten-year strategy of the regional destination management organisation, *Embracing our potential, 2012–2022*, has been recognised internationally by the World Travel and Tourism Council's Tourism For Tomorrow Awards 2018 for its commitment to responsible and sustainable tourism focused on

Fruit forward? 35

three pillars of responsibility: environment, economic and social (TOTA 2018). TOTA has also signed an agreement with the Biosphere International and the Responsible Tourism Institute in Spain as part of its efforts to complete a Regional Sustainable Tourism Certification defined by inclusive and sustainable growth; social inclusiveness, employment and poverty reduction; resource efficiency environmental protection and climate change; cultural values, diversity and heritage; and mutual understanding, peace and security (Biosphere Tourism 2018).

Most forms of rural tourism, and in particular rural tourism in wine regions, represent a merging of perhaps two of the most influential yet contradictory features of modern life. Not only are the forces of economic, social, cultural, environmental and political change working to redefine rural spaces the world over, but broad global transformations in consumption and transportation patterns are reshaping leisure behaviour and travel (George et al. 2009: 14). Consumer and rural tourism market demands for hyper-localised production of product and place are dependent on regional branding that allows for a simultaneous sense of collectivity and differentiation in wine territories (Patchell 2008). Amalgamation of local wine production and tourism that capitalises on lifestyle values, a sense of community and ecological stewardship is paramount to the Okanagan in the social construction of its locality.

Leverage of natural landscapes for tourism: Hunter Valley heritage protection versus Okanagan eco-certification

The histories of the Hunter and Okanagan wine regions have shaped different approaches to contemporary cultural reconversion to achieve economic sustainability. The endurance of the Hunter as Australia's oldest continuously producing wine region is credited to the continuous existence and co-operation of extant family wine businesses with continuous operation dating from the nineteenth century. These families are the Tyrrell, Drayton and Tulloch families (McIntyre et al. 2013; Grimstad, Waterhouse and Burgess 2019) and, since the mid-twentieth century, families such as the McWilliams and McGuigans. Although these family firms have not shared infrastructure, except in times of strife, and are industry competitors, their members traditionally co-operate to ensure the adaptability of the wine region. This is evident in the co-operative stance in the Australian Research Council Industry Linkage Project (2014–2018) undertaken by a team at the University of Newcastle including one of this chapter's authors, the Hunter Valley Wine and Tourism Association and Newcastle Museum. The project, called "Vines, Wine & Identity: the Hunter Valley NSW and Changing Australian Taste", produced a suite of public-facing as well as scholarly outputs. These include the monograph *Hunter Wine: A History* (McIntyre and Germov 2018a) and a major exhibition of the region's cultural heritage at Newcastle Museum, titled *Vines, Wine Identity* (4 August 2018 to 31 January 2019). A new oral history series, recorded audio-visually and available online, presents the memories of key members of the Hunter wine community, including labourers, women wine company owners and the wives of male wine business operators who are often absent from personality-driven marketing that treats winemakers as new folkloric heroes. Significantly, *Hunter Wine* has underpinned the Hunter Valley Heritage Vineyards Study (Johnston 2019) conducted on behalf of the HVWTA, with support from the NSW Office of Environment and Heritage. This study recommends formal state government heritage listing for historic vineyards in the Pokolbin and Broke-Fordwich winescape to protect against competing land use from extractive industries and urban sprawl. The HVWTA is seeking national as well as state heritage listing to scale up recognition of the region's historical capital.

The current state of adaptive change in Okanagan Valley is a different story. There is increasing pressure everywhere for wine industries to shift towards more sustainable modes of production and consumption in order to remain a defensible use of land and resources (Point, Tyedmers and Naugler 2012). Firms in the Okanagan Valley are far more responsive to this pressure than in the Hunter Valley. Among the most significant benefits of organic and biodynamic practices in wine production is the expression *terroir* to develop a more unique wine and geographical identity (Provost and Pedneault 2016). The synergy of terroir and the benefits of sustainable and organic production have driven wine regions such as the Okanagan to identify regionally as sustainable. In 2017, a number of open-ended interviews were conducted with wine industry stakeholders in the Okanagan who practice some form of environmental sustainability in their vinicultural and viticultural processes to better understand the obstacles and benefits of using various forms of eco-certification. In the Okanagan, approximately 25% of vineyards are eco-certified, and more are in transition. Eco-certification comes in a number of forms and include those that are organic, biodynamic, or with equivalent viticulture and viniculture processes, and are regulated and certified by a formally recognised certification organisation. Our research found that the practice of ecologically sound viticulture has been largely grassroots, where many more wine producers practice eco-friendly viniculture but do not receive certification. There are various reasons for not certifying as organic or sustainable among winery stakeholders relating to the desire for flexibility in response to changing environmental conditions and the costs of eco-certification, which are beyond what small producers can bear. While these results are similar to those found by Magali A. Delmas, Olivier Gergaud and Jinghui Lim in 2016, in 2017 the desire to regionalise sustainability practices across the appellation and specifically within sub-appellations was apparent among those interviewed in the Okanagan. The ability to label wines as eco-friendly or sustainable to a market with an interest and desire to consume sustainable wine was also universal among stakeholders in the Okanagan.

Organic Okanagan is a grassroots movement among consumers and producers in the local viticultural community. Members of the movement envision a transition of the entire Okanagan Valley food and wine system to 100% organic by the year 2020. The Okanagan Organic declaration identifies the pristine Okanagan Valley as a northernmost semi-desert viticulture region, with the least number of pests of any commercial fruit growing region in the world, making it the easiest to achieve organic transition, an ideal agricultural and residential region to demonstrate a model of returning to living in harmony with nature.

(Organic Okanagan 2016)

In order to include the valley comprehensively, Organic Okanagan declares three cornerstones of the movement: protection of the natural environment and aboriginal stewardship, water resource protection and economic sustainability through regional identification.

Drawing from the natural environment that surrounds the viticultural region and the thousands of years of aboriginal history, Organic Okanagan declares:

the Okanagan Valley is surrounded by mountainous wilderness for hundreds of kilometres in every direction, a unique agricultural oasis. This highly vulnerable and delicate eco-system has been historically protected by the original stewards, the Okanagan indigenous peoples. We declare that this precious valley deserves to be honoured and protected for all generations to come.

(Organic Okanagan 2016)

With regard to water protection:

Okanagan Lake supplies a vast portion of the region's drinking water. It is one of the world's easiest lakes to stifle with its lake retention time, or total turnover time of 52.8 year. Toxic farming chemicals now draining into the lake at unprecedented rates threaten its vitality and health.

(Organic Okanagan 2016)

With an eye towards economic sustainability, Organic Okanagan suggests economic success through regional organic identification:

the economic rewards and sustainability of growing organic are now proven positive, thanks in great part to worldwide enthusiasm. Statistics are showing vast market share leaps in the consumption of organic foods and beverages and organic farms are now demonstrating that organic practices are cost effective. Organic wine is the single fastest growing segment of the wine industry and the fledgling, yet already famous Okanagan wines will become a model for the world, a windfall opportunity for everyone in the valley to flourish. Tourism and all businesses will boom, representing abundance that is our natural heritage.

(Organic Okanagan 2016)

The Okanagan Bioregion Food System Design and Study project was set in motion in 2018 by a team of local university researchers in southern British

Columbia led by the Institute for Sustainable Agriculture at Kwantlan Polytechnic University. The project now involves partner researchers at the University of British Columbia and Okanagan College to study the potential to increase food production and processing for local markets in the Okanagan and Similkameen regions. The multi-year, public–private partnered study also looks at the impacts of local food production on food security, the economy, the environment and policy gaps that hinder local food systems. The objective of the study is to bring forth data-driven information regarding the food production, resource utilisation, environmental stewardship and economic potentials of a more regionally focused food. The Bioregion Food System Design and Study considers, and builds upon, existing food system planning and other related work to identify "a region of local and sustainable agriculture" (OBFSP 2018). Reflective of the community capital that has driven grassroots movement towards a region identified as sustainable, the project involves a large and varied number of community groups all advocating for sustainable local food systems. Participating grassroots organisations include the Central Okanagan Food Policy Council, South Okanagan Similkameen Conservation Partnership, Similkameen Okanagan Organic Producers Association and the North Okanagan Food Advocacy group. As a signature of the growing importance of the local food movement, a wide chorus of local government and industry organisations have joined the Okanagan Bioregion Food System project to identify the provenance of the local food system. Industry partners include the Real Estate Foundation of BC and the Regional Districts of Okanagan-Similkameen (RDOS), Central (RDCO), and North Okanagan (RDNO), the Okanagan Nation Alliance (ONA), the First Nations Okanagan Basin Water Board (OBWB) and the Central Okanagan Food Policy Council (OBFSP 2018).

The main tenets of the Slow Food Movement for fair, local, quality food production have been used successfully to brand regions where gastronomic production and tourism are central to local economies. It is not by coincidence that some of the most successful gastronomic tourism destinations are located in wine regions with a history of wine and food valorisation championed by the Slow Food Movement (Senese et al. 2017). The Thompson Okanagan Slow Food convivium was certified in 2012, three years after the town of Naramata became just the second certified Slow City or *Cittaslow*, in North America. Like Naramata, all six Cittaslow-certified cities in North America are in important wine-producing regions. Discover Naramata, the local tourism organisation, pursued Cittaslow accreditation on behalf of local community members, tourism operators and the twenty-six wineries located in the small town. The main goal of Cittaslow is to promote the philosophy of the Slow Food Movement and apply the concept of eco-gastronomy to everyday life (Lowry and Lee 2011). Since 2009, Naramata has developed a strong geographically indicated terroir brand in synergy with Cittaslow and the increasing production value of its wineries. Here, the Naramata Bench Winery Association has worked with Discover Naramata to develop the terroir brand that promotes health, wellness and tradition built out of the cultural capital of the wine and agricultural industries and the natural capital of the environmental setting (Senese et al. 2017). The Naramata Bench stands out as a cohesive place in a tourism region known for a particular combination of attractions, wine and culinary tourism, outdoor adventure and wellness experiences (Hull 2016). The region works to reflect the concepts of eco-gastronomy and continues to influence lifestyle-based mobilities of the Slow Food movement and a reputation for excellent fresh produce and local wines (Discover Naramata 2018).

The cumulative effort of the Naramata community to establish a place-based reputation built on the synergy of terroir and the slow movement will be acknowledged in 2019, when Naramata will become only the third certi-fied sub-appellation in British Columbia (BCWI 2018). In 2018, a series of open-ended interviews was conducted with stakeholders in the food and wine industries in Naramata to explore the impacts of Cittaslow accreditation on resilience, adaptive capacity and innovation in the community. Overwhelm-ingly, the results of the interviews indicated that Cittaslow had a positive effect on the social, economic and environmental fabric of the community, largely by promoting community cohesion as it facilitates farmer–consumer interac-tion and creative ways to respond to changing economies and environment. Respondents note the impact of shared local food on a growing sense of pride and identity and increased engagement of people with a shared set of values and goals. According to many of those interviewed, Cittaslow had also acted as a conduit for creativity and innovation in the community, as the valorisation of local food and wine inspired people to be engaged as active participants in their local food system. Community members felt empowered to create new, more ecologically friendly and socially responsible ways to produce, process and consume food. Finally, Cittaslow is also seen by respondents as a support to entrepreneurs, or "innovators for change" (Cradock-Henry 2017), who are identifying new ways to manage change in the community through the promo-tion of locally identified food. Here, the production value of slow gastronomy also captures the political and ethical discourse of sustainable values based in territory, landscape and culture (UNWTO 2016) that has defined a shared sense of place in the region.

The Hunter Valley Wine & Tourism Association does not foreground eco-logical protection. Of the 150 wine businesses in the region, the Australian Wine Research Institute's Entwine site lists three accredited vineyards and two wineries with only one property, Margan, appearing on both lists (AWRI 2019). Entwine accreditation requires payment and does not reflect organic or biodynamic accreditation. There are four wine firms in the Hunter trading as organic or biodynamic, and three are listed on the region's tourism website. Firms in the small Lovedale subregion of the Hunter, where there are no his-toric families, employ environmentally sustainable tourism practices, primarily in their accommodation facilities (Grimstad 2011). The Hunter's apparent eva-sion of a region-wide environmental policy is not unusual in Australia, where only South Australia's McLaren Vale wine region has a whole-of-region model for ecologically sustainable wine production (Santiago-Brown 2014; Skinner

2015). Key historic firms in the Hunter wine region position themselves as "custodians" of the region through historic depth of tradition rather than ecological practices (Grimstad, Waterhouse and Burgess 2019).

In conclusion, the Okanagan wine region does not have the Hunter's deep vinicultural heritage, and the Hunter does not have the Okanagan's region-wide appetite for practicing and promoting ecological protection of its wine landscape. Wine regions as commodity communities have creative yet highly localised responses to change, even when they share global economic conditions. The promotion to tourists of regional worthiness, along with pleasure and escapism, has proved to be contingent on whether the producer community is attached, or not, to tradition.

Some final remarks on adaptation to climate change

Rurality and visitation are the present basis of the economic viability of the Hunter and Okanagan wine regions within their wider regional geographies. What of future shocks that may profoundly and irreversibly alter the natural landscapes upon which these economic communities depend? Premium wine-growing, as regional practice, is at serious risk due to climate change (Mozell and Thach 2014). Despite their demonstrated agility and acumen in cultural reconversion, the Hunter and the Okanagan are vulnerable to the environmental changes brought by global warming. The increasing number of forest fires in the Okanagan region over the last decade has been particularly hazardous, destroying over 235 homes in 2003 and forcing the evacuation of thousands of residents in the Kelowna area in 2009 (McGillivray 2011). A provincial state of emergency in British Columbia in 2018 threatened the region, requiring policy-makers to address the increasing impacts of global climate change. Hunter wine-growers, for their part, have not lost vineyards and wineries to bushfires since 1968. There is another reason that there is not the same urgency for a Hunter wine community response to climate change as there is for the Okanagan community. In the past five years, the Hunter has experienced not one but two of the best wine-grape vintage years since 1965, due to lower damaging rainfall at harvest and reduced problems with mildew affecting leaf and grape growth. Hunter growers are climate-proofing their viticulture practices by changing to grape varieties better suited to drier and warmer conditions (Grimstad, Waterhouse and Burgess 2019). But is this enough? Wine production is no longer the economic boon it once was compared with tourism, and global warming means greater instability and unpredictability of climate and weather for travellers. The Hunter's best hope of future economic vitality is, like Okanagan, continued protectiveness of the natural landscape that hosts both vineyards and visitors.

References

Agriculture Canada. 1984. *Atlas of Suitable Grape Growing Locations in the Okanagan and Similkameen Valleys, British Columbia*. Canada: Agriculture Canada.

Anderson, K., Giesecke, J., and Valenzuela, E. 2010. "How Would Global Trade Liberalization Affect Rural and Regional Incomes in Australia?" *Australian Journal of Agricultural and Resource Economics* 54(4): 389–406.

Aspler, T. 2013. *Canadian Wineries*. Richmond Hill, ON, Canada: Firefly Books.

Australian Wine Research Institute. 2019. "Entwine Member Register." Retrieved June 11, 2019 (https://online.entwineaustralia.com.au/entwine/registrylist.php).

BC Wine Institute. 2012. "Market Analysis Report." Retrieved December 15, 2018 (https://www2.gov.bc.ca/assets/gov/farming-natural-resources-and-industry/agriculture-and-seafood/statistics/exports/global_export_market_bcwine_industry.pdf).

BC Wine Institute. 2016. "Winery Touring Guide." Retrieved December 20, 2018 (http://s3-nln-documents.s3.amazonaws.com/1462906322.483a509e12baa366a953436a17ff54ad.pdf).

BC Wine Institute. 2018. "Annual Report." Retrieved January 5, 2019 (https://winebc.com/industry/wp-content/uploads/sites/2/2018/07/BCWI-Annual-Report-2018.pdf).

Belliveau, S., Smit, B., and Bradshaw, B. 2006. "Multiple Exposures and Dynamic Vulnerability: Evidence from the Grape Industry in the Okanagan Valley, Canada." *Global Environmental Change* 16(4): 364–378.

Biosphere Tourism. 2018. "Home Page." Retrieved January 15, 2019 (www.biospheretourism.com/en).

Blake, M., Mellor, J., and Crane, L. 2010. "Buying Local Food: Shopping Practices, Place, and Consumption Networks in Defining Food as 'Local'." *Annals of the Association of American Geographers* 100(2): 409–426.

Canadian Encyclopedia. 2018. "Historica Canada." Retrieved December 10, 2018 (www.thecanadianencyclopedia.ca/en/article/historica-canada).

Central Okanagan Economic Profile for Agriculture. 2017. "Agricultural Profile." Retrieved December 5, 2018 (www.investkelowna.com/application/files/8715/0006/6559/2017_Agricultural_Profile_-_FINAL.pdf).

City of Kelowna. 2018. "Heritage Driving Tour Brochure." Retrieved November 28, 2018 (www.kelowna.ca/sites/files/1/docs/community/heritage_driving_tour_brochure.pdf).

City of Penticton. 2018. "About Penticon." Retrieved December 15, 2018 (www.penticton.ca/EN/main/community/about-penticton/our-history.html).

Cradock-Henry, N. A. 2017. "New Zealand Kiwifruit Growers' Vulnerability to Climate and Other Stressors." *Regional Environmental Change* 17(1): 245–259.

Dechent, S., and Sadler, P. 2010. "Geographical Indications in the Wine Industry." *The Wine Industry* 12: 3–9.

Delmas, M. A., Gergaud, O., and Lim, J. 2016. "Does Organic Wine Taste Better? An Analysis of Experts' Ratings." *Journal of Wine Economics* 11(3): 329–354.

Dendy, D. R. B. 1976. *One Huge Orchard*. B.A. Graduating Essay, University of Victoria, Victoria British Columbia.

Destination NSW. 2017. "Wine Tourism to NSW." Retrieved October 15, 2018 (www.destinationnsw.com.au/wp-content/uploads/2018/05/wine-tourism-to-nsw-ye-dec-2017.pdf?x15361).

Destination NSW. 2018. "NSW Food and Wine Tourism Action Plan." Retrieved June 11, 2019 (www.destinationnsw.com.au/wp-content/uploads/2018/11/nsw-food-and-wine-tourism-strategy-and-action-plan-2018-2022.pdf?x15361).

Discover Naramata. 2018. "Home Page." Retrieved December 3, 2018 (https://discovernaramata.com/).

Dunn, M. 2017. "In the 'Contact Zone': Aboriginal Workers in Colonial Newcastle and Its Hinterland." *Journal of Australian Colonial History* 19: 43.

George, E. W., Mair, H., and Reid, D. G. 2009. *Rural Tourism Development: Localism and Cultural Change*. Bristol, UK: Channel View Publications.

Gillespie, R., and Clarke, M. 2017. "Economic Contribution of the Hunter Valley Wine Sector to the Hunter Valley Economy." Retrieved June 11, 2019 (https://hvwta.engage menthub.com.au/economic-report).

Grimstad, S. 2011. "Developing a Framework for Examining Business-Driven Sustainability Initiatives with Relevance to Wine Tourism Clusters." *International Journal of Wine Business Research* 23(1): 62–82.

Grimstad, S., Waterhouse, J., and Burgess, J. In press. "'Creating a Little Bit of La Dolce Vita'. Explaining Resilience and Transformation in the Hunter Valley Wine Region, NSW, Australia." *International Journal of Globalization and Small Business* (Accepted for Publication March 14, 2019).

Gunn, J., and Gollan, R. M. 1931. *Report on the Wine Industry of Australia*. Canberra: Government Printer.

Hull, J. S. 2016. "Wellness Tourism Experiences in Mountain Regions: The Case of Sparkling Hill Resort, Canada." Pp. 25–35 in *Mountain Tourism: Experiences, Communities, Environments and Sustainable Futures*, edited by Richins, H., and Hull, J. S. Wallingford: CABI.

Hunter Valley Wine and Tourism Association Prospectus. 2013. "Hunter Valley Wine Country." Retrieved October 15, 2018 (https://issuu.com/huntervalleywinecountry/docs/hvwta).

Hunter Valley Wine Country. 2018. "Cellar Door Tasting." Retrieved October 15, 2018 (www.winecountry.com.au/wine/cellar-door-tasting).

Johnston, S. 2019. "Hunter Valley Heritage Vineyards Strategic Study." Prepared for the Hunter Valley Wine and Tourism Association with support from the NSW Office of Environment and Heritage (www.maitlandmercury.com.au/story/5585154/how-100000-and-one-decade-old-idea-could-safeguard-wine-country-history/).

Lowry, L., and Lee, M. 2011. "CittaSlow, Slow Cities, Slow Food: Searching for a Model for the Development of Slow Tourism." *42nd Annual Conference Proceedings: Seeing the Forest and the Trees – Big Picture Research in a Detail-driven World*.

Marsh, J. 2006. "Okanagan Valley." Retrieved November 3, 2018 (www. thecanadianencyclo pedia. ca/en/article/okanagan-valley/# h3_jump_0, accessed 3 November 2018).

Mattiacci, A., and Zampi, V. 2004. "Brunello di Montalcino: How a Typical Wine Could Revive a Poor Country-Village." *British Food Journal* 106(10/11): 767–778.

McGillivray, B. 2011. *Geography of British Columbia: People and Landscapes in Transition*. Vancouver, BC, Canada: UBC Press.

McGuire, D. W. 1993. "The Political Economy of the Grape and Wine Industry in British Columbia and the Impact of the Free Trade Agreement." *Okanagan University College, Department of Economics, Canada, Kelowna British Columbia*.

McIntyre, J., and Germov, J. 2013. "Drinking History: Enjoying Wine in Early Colonial New South Wales." Pp. 120–142 in *Eat History: Food and Drink in Australia and Beyond*, edited by Eriksson, S., Hastie, M., and Roberts, S. Melbourne: Cambridge Scholarly Publishers.

McIntyre, J., and Germov, J. 2017. "The Changing Global Taste for Wine: An Historical Sociological Perspective." Pp. 202–218 in *The Social Appetite: Sociology of Food*, edited by Germov, J., and Williams, L. Melbourne: Oxford University Press.

McIntyre, J., and Germov, J. 2018a. *Hunter Wine: A History*. Sydney: NewSouth.

McIntyre, J., and Germov, J. 2018b. "'Who Wants to be a Millionaire?' I Do: Postwar Australian Wine, Gendered Culture and Class." *Journal of Australian Studies* 42(1): 65–84.

McManus, P., O'Neill, P., Loughran, R., and Lescure, O. R. (eds.). 2000. *Journeys: The Making of the Hunter Region*. Sydney: Allen & Unwin.

Mozell, M. R., and Thach, L. 2014. "The Impact of Climate Change on the Global Wine Industry: Challenges & Solutions." *Wine Economics and Policy* 3(2): 81–89.

Nichol, A. E. 1983. *Wine and Vines of British Columbia*. Vancouver: Bottesini Press.

NSW Department of Planning. 2019. "Hunter Regional Plan." Retrieved June 4, 2019 (www.planning.nsw.gov.au/Plans-for-your-area/Regional-Plans/Hunter/Hunter-regional-plan/The-leading-regional-economy-in-Australia/).

NSW Wine Industry Association. 2018. "Hunter Valley." Retrieved October 15, 2018 (www.nswwine.com.au/hunter-valley/).

OBFSP. 2018. "Okanagan Food." Retrieved January 16, 2019 (www.okanaganfood.com/).

OECD. 1994. "Tourism." Retrieved December 12, 2018 (www.oecd.org/industry/tourism/2755218.pdf).

Okanagan Basin Water Board. 2013. "History." Retrieved December 12, 2018 (www.obwb.ca/overview/history/).

O'Neill, P. 2000. "The Gastronomic Landscape." Pp. 158–178 in *Journeys: The Making of the Hunter Region*, edited by McManus, P., O'Neill, P., Loughran, R., and Lescure, O. R. Sydney: Allen & Unwin.

Organic Okanagan. 2016. "Home Page." Retrieved December 15, 2018 (http://organicokanagan.com/).

Patchell, J. 2008. "Collectivity and Differentiation: A Tale of Two Wine Territories." *Environment and Planning A* 40(10): 2364–2383.

Pederson, S., and Senese, D. 2017. "Eco Certification as a Step Towards Social Ecological Resilience in the Okanagan Wine Industry." *Wine and Culinary Tourism Futures Conference*, Kelowna British Columbia, October.

Point, E., Tyedmers, P., and Naugler, C. 2012. "Life Cycle Environmental Impacts of Wine Production and Consumption in Nova Scotia, Canada." *Journal of Cleaner Production* 27: 11–20.

Provost, C., and Pedneault, K. 2016. "The Organic Vineyard as a Balanced Ecosystem: Improved Organic Grape Management and Impacts on Wine Quality." *Scientia Horticulturae* 208: 43–56.

Santiago-Brown, I. 2014. *Sustainability Assessment in Winegrowing*. PhD Thesis, Agriculture, Food and Wine, University of Adelaide.

Senese, D. M., Randelli, F., Hull, J. S., and Myles, C. C. 2017. "Drinking in the Good Life: Drinking in the good life: Tourism Mobilities and the Slow Movement in Wine Country." Pp. 214–231 in *Slow Tourism, Food and Cities: Pace and the Search for the 'Good Life'*, edited by Clancy, M. London: Routledge.

Senese, D. M., Wilson, W., and Momer, B. 2012. "The Okanagan Wine Region of British Columbia, Canada." Pp. 81–91 in *The Geography of Wine*, edited by Dougherty, P. H. Dordrecht: Springer.

Sexauer, B. 1976. "English and French Agriculture in the Late Eighteenth Century." *Agricultural History* 50(3): 491–505.

Simpson, J. 2011. *Creating Wine: The Emergence of a World Industry, 1840–1914*. Princeton: Princeton University Press.

Skinner, W. 2015. *Fermenting Place: Wine Production and Terroir in McLaren Vale, South Australia*. PhD Thesis, Anthropology, University of Adelaide.

Statistics Canada. 2018. "Census." Retrieved December 10, 2018 (www.bac-lac.gc.ca/eng/census/Pages/census.aspx).

TOTA. 2012. "Regional Strategy." Retrieved January 16, 2019 (https://totabc.org/resources/regional-strategy/).

TOTA. 2018. "Home Page." Retrieved January 20, 2019 (https://totabc.org/).

UNWTO. 2016. "Gastronomy Report." Retrieved January 17, 2019 (http://cf.cdn.unwto.org/sites/all/files/pdf/gastronomy_report_web.pdf).

Wagner, J. R. 2008. "Landscape Aesthetics, Water, and Settler Colonialism in the Okanagan Valley of British Columbia." *Journal of Ecological Anthropology* 12(1): 22–38.

Wilson, K. W. 1989. *Irrigating the Okanagan*. MA Thesis. University of British Columbia, Vancouver, BC.

Wine and Culinary Tourism Futures Conference. 2017. "Home Page." Retrieved November 25, 2018 (http://wineandculinarytourismfutures.ca/).

Wine Australia. 2017. "Australian Wine Regions." Retrieved October 15, 2018 (www.wineaustralia.com/getmedia/9da8ba52-21da-46e8-b27e-3521d362b1c3/Australian-Wine-Regions.pdf).

2 There's no taste like home

Histories of native food on the changing tastescape of the Northern Rivers

Adele Wessel

Introduction

Settler Australians brought with them a series of expectations and desires from their homelands that patterned how they sought to interact with the lands that they farmed. The capacity of people to respond to opportunities was in turn fundamentally conditioned by the land (here I mean to evoke land as a bundle of relationships both human and non-human), and the efforts of farmers iteratively transformed the ecology in a co-adaptive process that continues to this day. The emigres from the British Isles had left behind a land of forests, with four seasons and a climate that supported the agricultural practices that fashioned their diet. They came to a sub-tropical rainforest with diverse food resources intent on the introduction of species established in world trade. Land clearing for food production compromised native food sources, and introduced species settled into sometimes uneasy relations in the local ecology. It was not until the 1970s and 1980s that a commercial interest and taste for the native foods of the Northern Rivers expanded, but this has a much longer and more complex history. The establishment of the macadamia industry and the harvesting of lemon myrtle, aniseed myrtle, Davidson's plum, riberry, native mint, wild limes, warrigal greens, Dorrigo pepper and finger limes signals new trends in how the land is used and, conversely, a continuation of colonial relations and land use patterns.

This chapter will draw on biographies of land, cookbooks and historical records to trace the history and commodification of native foods in the Northern Rivers of New South Wales. While a number of scholars have contributed to an understanding of early culinary experimentation and consumption of native foods (Santich 2011; Bannerman 2006; Craw 2012; Singley 2012, 2017), a regional history provides a lens through which to observe responses to specific foods, the local effects of the global food system and the operations of colonialism in agricultural practice. The food imported by colonists into Australia reaffirmed cultural and historical bonds and sustained a shared sense of identity to create a tastescape that was familiar to them. However, the conventional representation of colonial distaste for native foods is both simplistic and misleading. Moreover, as Charlotte Craw points out, it elevates contemporary interest as a means of rejecting the colonial attitudes of the past relations with Indigenous people and the land, a distinction she disputes and suggests is insufficient to address this history (2012). At a local level it is possible to explore this history through attitudes to indigenous flora and fauna without drawing an artificial boundary between contemporary food culture and colonial attitudes.

The Northern Rivers extends from the Queensland border in the north, south to Glenreagh and west to Woodenbong and Tabulum. Bundjalung Country is defined by features of the land, from the Logan River and Allora in Queensland to the mouth of the Clarence River at Illuka and inland to the ranges east of Tenterfield. It is a sub-tropical environment of green hills, sweeping floodplains, rainforest remnants and beaches. The caldera of rich volcanic soil that nurtures much of the region was deposited over twenty-five million years ago by a now long extinct volcano, Wollumbin or 'Cloud Catcher' (also named Mount Warning by Cook).

Food production was both the motivation for settlement of the area and the grounds on which Aboriginal people were dispossessed of their land. At the time of white settlement in the North Coast, the most significant aspect of the world economy was the cultivation of new land in order to provide the European market with food. Henry Rous, who explored the river system in the 1820s, was commissioned to find fertile lands suitable for settlement in the midst of a prolonged drought. Food production was the motivation for this expansion and the justification for the seizure of land from Indigenous people, which they defined as 'unoccupied' by virtue of erasing the history of cultivation. In this way, Australian agricultural history has been premised on a process of exclusion and forgetting, and the devaluing and misrepresentation of native foods has been part of this historiography. In *Dark Emu Black Seeds: Agriculture or Accident* (2014), Bruce Pascoe argues for a reconsideration of the naming of pre-colonial Aboriginal Australians as 'hunter-gatherers', using the records and diaries of Australian explorers to rebut the colonial myths that have worked to justify dispossession. He builds a compelling case for arguing that Indigenous food-production systems and land management have been grossly undervalued, and for acknowledging Aboriginal histories of land management prior to colonialism as a pathway to more equality.

Inscribed on the land and in written documents, oral traditions and cooking practices is a long history of Aboriginal agriculture. Rural landscapes, like the Northern Rivers, integrate historical, ethnographic and architectural information about food and the cultural dynamics and politics of the choices we make over time. As in Europe, Bill Gammage tells us,

> land was managed at a local level. Detailed local knowledge was crucial. Each family cared for its own ground, and knew not merely which species fire or no fire might affect, but which individual plant and animal, and their totem and Dreaming links. They knew every yard intimately, and knew well the ground of neighbours and clansmen, sharing larger scale

management or assuming responsibility for nearby ground if circumstance required.

(2011: 3)

The historical elements that contribute to identities of place have largely divided between Indigenous and colonial experiences and disconnected the past and present. Deep local histories, on the other hand, of both place and the non-human species that inhabit it can inform an alternative understanding of the effects of transnational systems, economies and the interplay between nature and culture.

The Landed Histories Project uses biographies of land to explore the local effects of the global food system, foregrounding land and relationships mediated through the land as core to Australian history both past and present (Landed Histories Collective). At the heart of this project is an attempt to bring to light histories of land and the experience of farmers, their agency in the food system and the constraints and potential available within that. While that general question has been explored (see for example Kneafsey et al. 2008), what makes our own methodology unique is the concurrent examination of a number of farms, from the period of colonisation of the region, to try and understand the motivations behind farmers' engagement with particular sorts of production practices and a deeper understanding of the land they live on and how that has shaped their lives, the surrounding communities and their encounters with other institutions, people and ideas. This paper focusses on the history and fate of native foods, drawing on the biographies of land coming out of the Landed Histories project, cookbooks and historical records to trace the genesis and consequences of different ways of seeing Australian foods in place. Food cultures emerge from, and are lived in, place and particular ecologies and are understood through specific cultural and socioeconomic conditions which have the capacity to shape, limit and frame the possible food cultures that flourish upon them.

Local food cultures

The introduction of European landholding patterns and philosophy is central to understanding the complex interactions of people with the land, and thus the transformation of the region, one parcel at a time. Gammage (2011) explains that a key difference between how European and Aboriginal farmers managed land was the scale of the enterprise. Clans could spread resources over larger areas, providing for adverse seasons, and had allies, sometimes hundreds of kilometres away, who could trade or give refuge. "They were thus ruled less by nature's whims, not more, than farmers" (Gammage 2011: 3–4). Goori families travelled from Casino, Lismore and as far south as the Clarence to the Blackall Range in Southern Queensland when bunya trees were fruiting, staying between one and three months (Hoff 2006). Guests were bound by a strict

48   *Adele Wessel*

code of etiquette. Seasonal holidays to the coast along well-established corridors for oysters and other seafoods were also common. Middens extending along the coastline demonstrate the extent and length of this migration. Massacres that followed settlement around the Bunya Mountains deterred visitors and interrupted the gatherings. A number of historians have argued that the mass poisoning of sixty Aboriginal people at Kilcoy Station in 1842 led to an agreed strategy to oppose European settlement planned at the bunya gatherings (Laurie 1959 Kerkhove 2014; Connors 2015). Arthur Laurie had described this as the "Black War in Queensland" as early as 1959. If Europeans had kept to their own country, as Turrbal Elder Dalaipi explained to Tom Petrie, they would not have killed them:

> This (killing of whites) is nothing. . . . What a number were poisoned at Kilcoy! . . . They stole our ground where we used to get food, and when we got hungry and took a bit of flour or killed a bullock to eat, they shot us or poisoned us! Why did the white man not stop in his own country, and not come here to hunt us about like a lot of kangaroo?
>
> (Petrie 1904, cited in Kerkhove 2014: 52)

The tri-annual gathering (or annual for local groups) acted to establish and maintain bonds that Leichhardt had identified as "the united tribes" (Darragh and Fensham, cited in Kerkhove 2014: 41).

Settlers recalled communities also meeting for seasonal fishing harvests. James Ainsworth, a cedar cutter at Ballina in the late 1840s remembered,

> the blacks in the month of September flocked to the beaches for salmon fishing. This was a very fine eating fish resembling a small jewy in shape, and while the brief season of a month lasted Binghi's larder was overflowing.
>
> (Hoff 2006:155)

Conditioned by food supplies, each clan had a small territory, moving from one established camp site to the next. John McFarlane recorded his personal observations of the Clarence River District, noting that Aboriginal people were "located in the midst of plenty":

> Food in abundance was attainable without toil and with little energy . . . the scrubs abounded with paddymelons, bandicoots, opossums, snakes, lizards, grubs, turkeys, pigeons and yams. The open country was plentifully supplied with kangaroos and wallabies. The swamps provided an endless variety of game including ducks, geese, swans and coots. The rivers and creeks were teeming with fish.
>
> (1980: 14)

McFarlane explained that traditionally Aboriginal people on the floodplain established camps of about fifty people which shifted every "couple of weeks" but "seldom more than a mile" (1980: 15). Oxley and Rous had described structures of between thirty and forty feet long, housing a number of local people; however, Bundjalung people became more mobile as a result of European settlement rather than this being a continuation of a traditional way of life.

The characterisation of the abundance of food, however, also serves to diminish the industry of Aboriginal people and deny agricultural innovation. Bruce Pascoe recounts the observations of James Kirby, one of the first two Europeans in Wait Wati Country near Swan Hill, of a man fishing on a weir built across the river constructed to control the movement of fish: "I have often heard of the indolence of the blacks and soon came to the conclusion after watching a blackfellow fish in such a lazy way, that what I had heard was perfectly true" (Pascoe 2018: 4). Such depictions have denied Aboriginal achievement, but they also reinforce the image of Aboriginal people as hunters and gatherers. The justification for assumption of dominion over Australia by England was fundamentally rooted in an apparent absence of cultivation, and thus, according to English political philosophy, an absence of Aboriginal land owners (see Banner 2005; Borch 2001; Connor 2005).

Though not universal or entirely evenly felt throughout Australia, the imposition of English land and property law in the Northern Rivers created a political and economic geography that produced a landscape of smallholder family farms, and it was this landscape through which settlers made their lives. These were lives that were very much affected by global political and economic forces, drawing Bundjalung people into those systems as well, and both cultures were certainly most immediately effected by the ecological contexts in which people found themselves.

Early reports of the agricultural potential of the Northern Rivers were very optimistic. Oliver Fry, Commissioner of Crown Lands for the Border Police District of the Clarence, in his report to John Dunmore Lang, claimed

> that there is a sufficiency of land of the most astonishingly fertile nature, in the valley of the Richmond, to afford ample scope for the entire surplus population of Britain, even without infringing to any injurious extent upon the rights of the Squatter.
>
> (Fry in Lang 1847: 54)

The squatters who arrived on the Richmond and the Tweed in the 1840s and 1850s, preceded by the cedar getters, heralded a violent and complex process of dispossession and accommodation with the Aboriginal owners. Squatters began the process that would fence Aboriginal people out of their traditional country and compromise animal resources and seasonal movement. Strategies to sustain food resources, harvesting appropriately, landscape manipulation and cultivation and restrictions on hunting were some of the ways that land was actively used and managed by Aboriginal owners, who did not assume, as the people who came to the country did, that it would be always productive. As Bundjalung Elder Thelma James explained, "Each one of us has a totem. It can be an animal or a tree. We can't eat it and we have to take care of it to make sure it will always be with us" (Southern Cross University Annual Lecture, Lismore Regional Gallery, October 2018). The large pastoral properties with their sparse populations of newcomers enabled some level of dual occupation between the traditional owners and the squatters in different pockets of the region. Rodney Harrison has explained that many Aboriginal people would assist in land clearing and form an integral part of the pastoral industry in New South Wales (2004: 20). Moreover, the grazing practices of squatters did not require wholesale land clearing (McFarlane 1980). While co-existence may have been possible, access to food would still be an issue, and resistance to invasion was met with violence. A number of massacres in the region can be traced to attempts to eradicate this and reprisals for taking livestock. Prior to the massacre of twenty-three Gumbaynggnir people from poisoned flour given as compensation for working at Kangaroo Creek in the Clarence Valley, station owner Thomas Coutts was reported to have a poor relationship with Aboriginal people around his station. Tomkinson, another hut-keeper stationed about ten miles from the head station, reported that

> Mr Coutts was very unfriendly towards the Blacks before the time above-mentioned. . . . They were not allowed to be about the Head Station before that – I have often heard Mr Coutts complain of the Blacks having killed his cattle, and say that they deserved shooting – Moses Jones told me Mr Coutts had lost a pistol by going out after the Blacks. . . . Before this period none of them would go near the Head Station.
>
> (cited in Lydon 1996: 156)

Coutts was arrested and brought to Sydney but discharged due to lack of evidence (Ryan et al. 2018). The testimony of Aboriginal people was inadmissible. Residents voted overwhelmingly not to change the current name of the village from Coutts Crossing in 2018 (Harper and Bali 2018).

It was ultimately the breakup of the large squatting runs into the small farming blocks of two to three hundred acres from the late 1800s that accomplished Aboriginal exclusion from the region and brought radical environmental change. The Robertson Land Acts, introduced in 1861, opened up the whole leasehold area of the colony of New South Wales to selection and sale. Selectors could purchase between 40 and 3,240 acres of Crown Land, including that held on pastoral lease, at £1 per acre with a £10 deposit and were required to reside on the land and to make 'improvements' that could include fencing and land clearing. Soil erosion followed the tree felling undertaken to increase grasslands for livestock grazing. Closer settlement, driven by the land selection acts of the 1860s and the Crown Lands Acts of the 1880s, came late to the Far North Coast because of the difficult terrain and distance from Sydney. However, once established, the region came closer than other regions of New South Wales to the ideal Robertson intended the legislation to promote of the small-scale, yeoman farmer, breaking up the power of squatters. 'Improving' the

There's no taste like home 51

land provided a moral justification to colonialism and reinforced the myth of an absence of agriculture. "I am one of those who think this fine country never was intended to be occupied by a nomad race who made no use of it", wrote a Queensland squatter at mid-century, "except going from place to place and living only on the wild animals and small roots of the earth, and never in any way cultivating one single inch of ground" (cited in Waterhouse 2004). While supporters of the Selection Acts drew on the ideology of creating civilisation through agriculture, the arguments were mostly pragmatic, connected to the equitable settlement of the land and the efficiency of small-scale agriculture (Waterhouse 2004), but the effect was to deny that the land was previously occupied and managed by Aboriginal people.

To accomplish this social and economic imagining of the countryside, the myth of terra incognita – land unknown and unowned – was sustained from the frontier era. It further required wholesale clearing of the forests, where the piecemeal encroachment of the earlier timber getters was overtaken by the slash-and-burn techniques of the new farmers 'improving' their land as demanded by their lease. The 'Big Scrub' and the absence of grasses for pasturing livestock in the many parts of the Northern Rivers had created a barrier to early settlement. The clearing of the 'Big Scrub' rainforest was almost complete by the early 1900s (Ryan and Smith 2006). A series of reservations made in 1858 also removed vast tracts of potential agricultural land from pastoral lease. The alienation of Crown Land through free selection proceeded rapidly throughout the 1870s and 1880s with little conflict, the interests of the pastoralists and the first settlers being both mutually exclusive in terms of the land considered best for cultivation and aligned, accelerating the dispossession of Aboriginal people and limiting their land and economy after this period.

The transformation of the land in the interests of agricultural and pastoral production was underpinned by productivist notions of 'use' from the outset, with the emphasis on items of importance to trade. Part of the heritage of local towns are the plans drawn up by Frederick Septimus Peppercorne, a licensed surveyor who arrived on the Richmond in 1855. In the *Magazine of Science and Art*, written in 1858, he described the banks of the rivers and streams as comprising

> some of the richest land in the colony and little apprehension need to entertained of their affording abundant returns for the labour that may be bestowed on the cultivation of maize, tobacco, cotton, the sugar-cane, the coffee plant and other plants indigenous to tropical regions.
>
> (cited in Potts 2005: 13)

When the surveyor Greaves came to the Clarence to lay out the town of Maclean in 1862, his party camped for several weeks, and he said "the aboriginals [were] very friendly, so much so that I lent them my shotgun and they kept us supplied with pigeons, brush turkeys and ducks as well as plentiful supplies of fish" (cited in McSwan 1992: 5). Land reforms were based on "a

52 *Adele Wessel*

long-held English tenet that a 'civilised' society was settled and agricultural, while an 'uncivilised' culture was characterised by nomadic herding and hunting" (Waterhouse 2006). Clearly the consumption of native foods was less at issue than turning the land to a profit based on food commodities.

Despite the increasingly exuberant promotion of the area within the colony of New South Wales and in Britain, it was a hard place to farm. While the fertility and water availability of much of the Richmond/Tweed catchment meant that the small family farming community could endure, the combination of distance from the market hub of Sydney and the challenging terrain of rivers, forest, swamps and mountains meant a relatively poor subsistence life for most. Many farming families started as tenant farmers. Other smaller settlers, not in a position to lay out money for clearing and technology. would also wait years to get any return on their efforts. Across the Northern Rivers, this flow of migration was seen to hinge on the suffocation from Sydney of its 'North Coast brethren', a sentiment that would echo throughout the following decades of the spectre of city arrogance over country folk. "Why is this area, the most prospective in the Commonwealth, not developing?" demanded W. Ager in 1919 in the newspaper *The Voice of the North*. Answering his own question, he claimed that Sydney was "strangulating this area . . . the country gets the promises, the city gets the money" (8).

Farmers sustained themselves often in semi-subsistence lifestyles, growing much of their own food but supplementing this with wild-caught food. Adam Smith reviewed historical and anecdotal records of the Clarence River floodplain for the purpose of framing management and restoration practices there, but his work also documents the use of waterbirds as food on the Clarence River floodplain (2011). Only the Pacific black duck was traded, being sent to Sydney, but other species were hunted for personal consumption:

> The Purple Swamphen *Porphyrio porphyrio* was favoured for the making of 'Redbill Soup' a clear and very tasty soup (Terry Harrison, pers. comm.). Latham's Snipe were said to taste like quail and presented hunters with a challenge due to their unexpected, rapid and erratic flight (Roy Bowling pers. Comm.). The hunting of Magpie Geese is well before living memory; however, anecdotes relate the use of muzzle-loading shotguns. Roy Bowling related how his father would go out on a Friday night 'to get a goose for Sunday dinner'.
>
> (Smith 2011: 796)

The loss of waterbirds, however, has not been due to hunting for food, but loss of habitat, through drainage for flood mitigation. By 1969, about 60% of waterbird habitat had been destroyed on the Far North Coast of New South Wales (Goodrick in Smith 2011: 804). Nevertheless, the passage of the Birds Protection Act in New South Wales in 1881 included a closed season for specified native birds as well (Stubbs 2001). The black swan, considered game in the first bill, was omitted from the schedule of birds protected, despite an argument

There's no taste like home   53

for them being ornamental in the Amending Bill in 1893, because "in some parts of the colony" it was "a necessary article of food to persons in poor circumstances, and it would be seriously wrong to deprive them of this article of diet" (in Stubbs 2001: 33–34). Emus, however, were included for protection, therefore also depriving Aboriginal people of this food source.

Waterbirds were an obvious food source for white farmers, bearing a degree of familiarity to the European food species also consumed. The high status and regularity of meat in the diet encouraged the consumption of other native fauna, although this was prepared in familiar ways, following the "flavor principle" used by Rozin and Rozin to explain the introduction of new ingredients by using traditional methods (1981). New ingredients were adapted to fit in with familiar culinary expectations in a new setting. In the first book of recipes published in Australia, *The English and Australian Cookery Book*, which appeared in 1864, Edward Abbott often drew on native and exotic ingredients to produce very familiar dishes using English methods and principles, such as kangaroo stuffed with beef suet, bread crumbs, parsley, shallots, marjoram, thyme, nutmeg, pepper, salt, cayenne and egg. *Mrs Beeton's Cookery Book and Household Guide*, published in 11892, gave a selection of "Australian" recipes: Kangaroo Tail Soup (prepared like ox tail soup), Roast Wallaby (which was compared to hare), and Parrot Pie ("not unlike one made of pigeons"). Black swan was roasted or boiled. In her *Recollections of a Visit to the Australian Colonies in 1856–7*, Emma Macpherson visited the northern area of the state and provided a substantial account of everyday life there and preparation of opossum, witchetty grubs, snakes and bunya nuts. She also prepared native meats using European methods:

> The kangaroo rabbit I had dressed the next day, roasted and stuffed, in hare fashion, and very nice it proved, by no means inferior to our European rabbit. Another small variety of the kangaroo tribe, the 'Rock Wallaby', bears a very close resemblance to the hare; indeed when dressed in the same way and eaten with currant jelly, it would be by no means easy to distinguish them apart.

> (Macpherson 1860: 48)

Likewise, native fruits from the region were prepared by settlers in ways that made them palatable to European tastes. Fish and game appeared in cookbooks and recipes for forageable nuts and berries and fruit, like bunya nuts, riberries and Davidson's plum were found in community cookbooks throughout the twentieth century, (often 'tried and tested' contributions from home cooks), which suggest that they were being used. As Sarah Black has noted, however,

> traditional Aboriginal foodways made vanishingly few appearances in the community cookbooks of the period to 1980, apart from occasional influences evident in the foodways of remote bush areas. In the pre–war era certain indigenous ingredients appeared, for example game such as kangaroo,

54   *Adele Wessel*

> local fish such as barracouta, emu eggs and fruits such as rosellas. This was a recognised element of settler foodways from pioneer days. . . . These indigenous foodstuffs were, however, generally treated in Anglo-Saxon ways which showed negligible adaptation to native foodways . . . it appears that ideas of 'native' cuisine in colonial and twentieth-century Australia were largely restricted to such British-influenced food as roasted wildlife, native fruit jellies or baked goods, and damper baked in the ashes.
>
> (2010: 300)

Riberry was one of the first fruits consumed by early colonists as jam or cordials (Rural Industries R&D Corporation). Davidson's plum was used for jam and jelly, as well as wine. During World War II, lemon myrtle was used in a soft drink to flavour lemonade, although the potential use for commercial production was promoted as early as 1889. As Colin Bannerman has explained, native foods were exploited from the earliest days of white occupation for survival as well as comfort, but also for experimentation. Mina Rawson encouraged people to experiment and "try everything", advising in her *Antipodean Cookery Book* (1895: 54): "Whatever the blacks eat the whites may safely try". By the 1950s, references to native foods had disappeared from cookbooks, local supplements no longer being necessary as food production and the attendant infrastructure for the processing, storage and distribution of exotic foods expanded (Bannerman 2006: 20). As European agriculture expanded into Aboriginal land, the reproduction of native foods was reduced. Understorey shrubs as well as larger trees suffered from land clearance. One of the implications of the lack of acknowledgement of Aboriginal cultivation was the lack of attention paid to knowledge about reproduction and how to reduce the impact of consumption. Believing native foods to be all 'wild-harvested' in an 'unmanaged' ecosystem is underpinned by the separation of nature and culture and ignores thousands of years of human habitation. The designation of wilderness, as Callicott reminds us, enabled colonists to see the land as essentially empty of human beings and thus available for occupancy to "make over into a landscape like the one they left behind" (2000: 24).

The agricultural industry began in the 1860s, with maize and sugar cane being the main cash crops (Stubbs 2007: 37). However, when the dairy industry expanded into the region in the 1870s, it quickly became the dominant concern. Dairying was envisaged by the governments of George Dibbs and George Reid as a partial remedy to the 1890s Depression (Wilkinson 1999: 2). The movement of dairy farmers from the south of the state had started in the 1880s, and the slump in the sugar industry at the same time caused many local growers to turn to dairying. As early as 1897, Richmond River butter was exported to the British market. The replacement of the Big Scrub with dairy farms throughout the area was almost complete at the turn of the century. By the early 1900s, despite Aboriginal people, agriculturalists, forest preservationists and timber-getters all maintaining active interests in the land, dairying was responsible for much of the wealth in the area and the flourishing of the small interconnecting towns spread across the region. Religious, commercial, educational, transport and health services gradually improved throughout this period, but the population struggled with isolation, flooding and then worsening market conditions as the 1920s came to a close. The seeds for diversification were sown at this stage. The 1930s began with a wave of Italian immigrants, who took up cash vegetable cropping and banana farming (Ryan 1999: 122). A particularly famous local recipe around town was the spaghetti sauce that Americo Melchior's grandmother used to make. He learned its secrets when he was six, just a few years after arriving from Italy in 1950, and continued to make the sauce for the Italo Club in North Lismore. "My grandmother was a wonderful cook. . . . Everyone knew about her sauce, and spending so much time with her, I picked it up at a young age", he says (Fittal 2013). Americo Melchior's family employed Aboriginal workers on their farm, which was located close to a self-managed Aboriginal settlement called Cubawee, and he recalls his grandmother using kangaroo meat in the family spaghetti sauce (2011).

The post-war boom of the 1950s and 1960s signalled the beginning of the downturn of the dairy industry along with other rural sectors, as oversupply, international competition and mechanisation began to impact profitability and decrease employment opportunities (Kijas 2003: 29). While these traditional sectors declined and serious population concerns emerged, the importance of coastal land use to the region increased in two important and contradictory ways. Firstly, the mining of zircon and rutile from beach sands, which had started in the 1930s, continued amidst concerns over the destruction of the shoreline (Stubbs 2007: 50–51). Secondly, post-war affluence brought tourism into the reach of the broad population of Australia, bringing new visitors to the region and creating the possibility of a profitable tourism industry from the beautiful natural landscape that had typically been sidelined by concerns with growing primary industries (Ryan and Smith 2001: 124–126).

The real population recovery came with the arrival of the 'alternatives' from 1973 for the Aquarius festival, who often stayed on, taking up the land around Nimbin left by dairy farmers. New communal living and land-ownership arrangements emerged, often fostered by a 'rediscovery' of the land as a source of meaning and spirituality (Irvine 2003: 66), which led to a range of different land-use strategies, with attendant diversity in food production and consumption (Page 2010). Many of the concerns over forest conservation and coastal devastation, which had previously attracted only very limited concern in the context of the forestry and agricultural industries, now found political expression through the newcomers in the region (making up the largest alternative community in the country) and in the context of emerging international awareness of the importance of environmental preservation.

In the 1980s, the counter-cultural, counter-urban overlaying of alternatives into the community was further complicated. New arrivals were running from the cities as much as toward the Northern Rivers (Offord 2003). Throughout the 1980s and 1990s, young unemployed people, driven by cost pressures in capital cities and increasing disadvantage, moved to the region seeking a

56   *Adele Wessel*

better quality of life. Retirees and professionals similarly sought a "lifestyle" change (Wilson 2003), bringing regional agriculture under increasing pressure for competition for land from non-agricultural uses. This gives potential for conflict between those who just want to live in a rural setting and those who want to make a living from it. Land-use conflicts specific to agricultural land in the Northern Rivers include population pressures, resulting in residential encroachment onto farmland, increasing land-use conflicts between farming and non-farming neighbours (most visible in complaints about noise and smells) and increasing land prices that makes it difficult for farmers to purchase additional land or young land-less farmers to commit to agriculture (see Tweed Shire Council 2011: 13). Although the experiences of these more recent arrivals have not been characterised by such an intimate relationship with the land as the previous waves, their presence is an important contribution to a complicated contemporary land-use picture, of which just some elements are expanding five-acre blocks' into the landscape (often in the most fertile farmland) and attendant conflicts over development, infrastructure and sustainability; a market for quality locally grown sustainable and/or ethical foods; and the emergence of luxury food cultures especially around the iconic town of Byron Bay.

At the same time, it is important to recognise that conventional agriculture retains a significant presence in the region. In some cases there is a clear-cut division between conventional farming and alternative food systems: eco-farming (organics, permaculture, etc.) versus conventional; agri-business versus community food security; and so on. However, in many cases, well-established farms are shifting their land towards more sustainable practices, not necessarily as part of an alternative politics, but as a consequence of experiencing difficulties around the increased costs and decreased benefits of conventional inputs. As in the earlier history of the region, new people, ideas, economic and political conditions, and experiences on the ground have led to changing land-use practices. Although crops have been diversified since the 1930s, one of the most prominent shifts in food production since the dairy industry began to decline has been the increased cultivation of cash crops based on the region's subtropical location (macadamia nuts, lemon myrtle and finger limes being the most recognisable). As well, artisanal producers, often associated with luxury and local food cultures, have become more prominent in conventional industries such as cheese making.

Native foods: distinguishing consumption from production

The role of capital in the development of agriculture in the Northern Rivers clearly separates production from consumption. The early history of the region shows the effect of land clearing: food production compromised native food sources, and introduced species settled into sometimes uneasy relations in the Australian ecology. Settler Australians came into the region with expectations and desires that patterned how they sought to interact with the lands that they

There's no taste like home   57

farmed. As importantly, the constraints of their role and relation to the empire and to the market impinged on people and their efforts across the history of the region. Though there was nothing so simple as that suggested by the phrase 'market demand', shifting markets and demands for particular products constantly buffeted the smallholders of the Northern Rivers as they struggled to reproduce themselves through simple commodity production and/or wage labour. The capacity of people to respond to opportunities were, in turn, fundamentally conditioned by the land and the impact of their own use.

At the time of settlement, the British Isles were no longer self-sufficient in food production and relied on other territories for their raw materials and fertile lands. As Eric Holt-Giménez explains, "By the end of the nineteenth century, mercantilism, colonialism, and industrialisation had all combined in a new form of global capitalism that spread powerfully, if unevenly, around the earth" (2017: 32). This was the food regime that dominated the settlement of the Northern Rivers. British investment in Australia was directed to the production and transport of raw materials and foods for the imperial market. The industrialisation of food was a critical phase in the transformation of food systems at the end of the nineteenth century, when production, processing and distribution were undergoing dramatic change, and this had a profound impact on the settlement and land use of the Northern Rivers. Developments in preservation and refrigeration and decreased transit times marked the period and shaped the landscape. A butter factory was opened near Wollongbar in the heart of the Big Scrub in 1889. Only a few months after it began operations, the railway line connecting Lismore, Bangalow, Byron Bay, Mullumbimby and Murwillumbah opened, giving dairy farmers in the area direct access to markets and the port facilities at Byron Bay. The replacement of the Big Scrub with dairy farms throughout the area was almost complete by the end of the century.

Imperial interest in native foods was reduced to novelty or to demonstrate colonial prowess, curbing production in favour of items already established on the world market. Although native foods featured in the international expositions, such as the 1855 Paris Exposition Universelle (Santich 2011: 71), the business of exhibitions essentially conformed to the requirements of an industrial, commercial, material culture, as did that of farms. The first exposition, in London's Crystal Palace in 1851, placed emphasis on material culture and celebrated colonial appropriation of raw materials. The South Australian Gallery at the Melbourne International Exhibition in 1888 for example, included two tableaux: one representing the "noble savage in his native state", and the other "the civilised man in the act of driving the savage out" (*Popular Guide* 1888: 116). The material progress made since taking possession of the land was represented graphically in wheat fields. Examples of dinners held by Acclimatisation Societies offering native delicacies or menus that featured kangaroos at home shows the complexity of the relationship between European settlers and native foods (Singley 2012: 37), but these were also intended, as Charlotte Craw explains, as a means of "enacting and displaying the reach of the British Empire" (2012a: 17) rather than expanding markets.

58 *Adele Wessel*

Conversely, the *consumption* of native foods on the North Coast was widespread. While emphasis has been placed on the *exchange value* of food, as a consequence of its significance to changing land-use patterns, other sources record the taste for native foods in the region. James Ainsworth, the publican at Ballina, reminisced in 1922 about the "splendid bread" made from nut flour "eagerly sought after by the whites when rations ran short" (1987: 44). Fresh meat was a luxury for all first settlers, but the *Town and Country Journal* advised in 1881:

> Nearly all the creek water in the scrub land, which is beautifully clear, contains fish, comprising eels, cod, bream, lobster, perch etc. The bush abounds in game, including the scrub turkey, green and bronze wing pigeon, parrots, ducks, plover, quail, and others of different varieties, sufficient to tempt the appetite of even a dying man, so there need not be any occasion for the selector to disarrange his digestive organs by earing damper and corned beef only, if he can muster a fishing line and flowing-piece.
> ("A Trip to the Richmond District II", 27 August 1881, p. 26).

Bundjalung clans had a varied diet of berries, seeds and fruit, and the same journal described native fruits for the settlers, including citrus. By 1935, S. W. Jackson was already reporting the destruction of finger lime, or gulalung, due to the advance of agriculture (6 November, p. 30), although he remarked on its use by locals for jam and pickles.

Despite their enjoyment of native foods, settlers were not cultivating the plants or using local knowledge to ensure their sustainability. An early arrival to Lismore, James Wotherspoon, praised the finger lime as making an excellent drink with sugar added. He lamented its near extinction in 1936: "Knowing the lime to be so plentiful then I can scarcely imagine it becoming most extinct in so short a time, as I seldom see a bush now". Many of the plants were destroyed not for food but to make handles on tools used to break stones for roads. As an understory shrub or tree, natural distribution of the finger lime in sub-tropical rainforests from the Richmond River to Mount Tambourine was limited by land clearing. All finger lime currently traded in Australia is cultivated. Similarly, the local species of Davidson's plum is now classified as endangered, and a permit is required to pick and/or sell material from these plants, but it was widely enjoyed in the early settlement period. A review of *The Useful Native Plants of Australia* in 1889 was surprised that a "common fruit" such as Davidson's plum was omitted (*Queenslander* 452). In 1904, it was praised as making a "splendid acid drink, and a very good preserve" (Johnstone, p. 21). The pleasure of its taste did not encourage conservation.

Macadamia nuts are an exception to the division described between consumption of native plants and the production of commercial crops. It was both eaten as a 'bush nut' and used in experiments in commercial production began in the nineteenth century. As early as 1867, macadamia nuts were being grown and distributed from the Botanical Gardens (*Queenslander* 11). By this time the nut was already well known "to timber-getters, to the natives, and others. . . . Of

There's no taste like home   59

the quality of the fruit we can speak in the highest terms". Indeed the history of macadamia nuts demonstrates the influence of the market on land use and the relationship between ecological change and taste. Although von Mueller described and named the nut tree in 1857, it was another hundred years before Australian farmers got seriously involved in the industry and only after the potential of the nut was indicated by successful planting in Hawaii after it had been imported in the 1880s.

The first commercial orchard of macadamia trees, however, was planted in the early 1880s twelve kilometres southeast of Lismore. Besides the development of a small boutique industry in Australia during the late nineteenth and early twentieth centuries, macadamia was extensively planted as a commercial crop in Hawaii from the 1920s, and it is only recently that Australia became the world's major producer of macadamia nuts. As a writer in the *Sunday Times* pointed out in 1905, "Possibly when America begins to export them to Australia we will begin to appreciate them". There were repeated calls to cultivate the crop commercially, dating from the late nineteenth century and recorded in the *Agricultural Gazette* as well as newspapers. At least part of the problem might have been the confusion about the nuts created by the name, variously called bush nuts, bopple or bauple nuts, Queensland nuts, Mullumbimby nuts and Australian nuts by the nut society who first met in 1930 to promote the crop. Aboriginal names include gyndl, jindilli, boombera and bauple. Macadamia, on the other hand, was the American trade name from the beginning. North Coast macadamia production expanded rapidly in the early 1970s. Industry processing is centred in northern New South Wales (NSW). While it might be ironic, given that the crop is native to the area, management of impacts on the environment, especially erosion control, is a big challenge in the region. The Australian Native Food Industry (rebranded in 2017 as Australian Native Food and Botanicals) did not start on the North Coast until around the late 1980s, which provides some indication of the inception of commercial production. A growing interest in local food as a product of concern for the environment and consumer demand has been used to partly explain a renewed appreciation of native foods in Australia more generally. However, as Charlotte Craw explains in relation to packaged foods with native ingredients, notions of local are frequently conflated with the national "Australian native ingredients" with indefinite provenance (2012a: 4). Added to this, attachments to the local have also been critiqued for their essentialism and romanticisation, neglecting attention to relationships between the local and global in political and economic terms (Ferguson, Kijas and Wessell 2017: 15). Indigenous food sources are diverse across different locations and seasons. The origins of ingredients and their connections with Indigenous Australian cultures and places are often omitted, marginalising Indigenous knowledges and conceptions of place.

Chefs have also played a role in driving demand for native foods and stimulating interest, but emphasis on the role of Indigenous communities and their knowledge and relationship to native food can still be lacking. Australian-born non-Indigenous chefs have been slower in taking up native foods. Scottish born

60 *Adele Wessel*

chef Jock Zonfrillo was awarded the Basque Culinary World Prize in 2018 for his work as a champion of Native Australian foods and long-term supporter of many Indigenous communities. Zonfrillo started the Orana Foundation to support farming projects in Indigenous communities to help make products scalable. The 'Noma effect', the influence of Rene Redzepi's Australian season in 2016, saw local growers struggling to meet supply (O'Neill 2016). Native ingredients in gourmet cuisine does not make them any more accessible to Aboriginal communities. Support for Indigenous people to create their own businesses, facilitate access to their own cultural food and recognise the knowledge and customs associated with growing and preparing native foods remains an issue. Lawyer Terri Janke has proposed the recognition of Indigenous knowledge in the commercialisation of native foods, calling for protection of Indigenous cultural and intellectual property rights and to share in the benefits from the use of Indigenous heritage (Janke and Kearney 2018).

Chefs can play an important role in changing how we eat and making food preparation and ingredients accessible. The contribution of Aboriginal chefs like Dale Chapman to the growing Indigenous food movement should be acknowledged for the work they do to encourage native foods to be an everyday part of the diet (Fredericks and Stoter 2013). For Bundjalung chef Clayton Donovan, more education is needed about native foods to introduce native foods in the TAFE system and back into high schools to increase common knowledge. "The rest of us in the industry keep on pushing and now we've got a lot of different chefs and different people outside the industry that have come into the native food industry", he said. "But the grand scheme of things, I think we're still behind" (Honan and McCarthy 2017). Mark Olive (Bundjalung chef aka 'Black Olive'), a cousin and mentor to Donovan, has been promoting native foods for more than thirty years. He explains, "we've slowly progressed to a stage where Aboriginal ingredients are commercially produced and people are aware of it. But other countries often embrace what Australia grows more than we do" (Papas 2018). It is a very slow progression in the context of the history of native foods in Australia over tens of thousands of years and early settlers' consumption.

Pragmatic and economic factors have shaped the value of food and conditioned land use and production through which the land was possessed and occupied, dispossessing Aboriginal people from their country and exposing both the land and farmers to the vagaries of the market. In the development of the contemporary tastescape, the availability of foodstuffs familiar to settlers, knowledge of harvesting and preparation and cultural contact and respect all have an important role to play, as well as cultural taste and the local ecology. But these factors are inherently unstable. Growing other native foods is still not the main income of most contemporary growers. From original 'wild'-harvested crops, the industry has transitioned to managed crops, which offer both domestic and export potential. The core plants being harvested are lemon myrtle, aniseed myrtle, Davidson's plum, riberry, native mint, wild limes, warrigal greens, Dorrigo pepper and finger limes. In the 1990s, lemon myrtle was promoted as an alternative food crop to beef cattle farmers to diversify due to low cattle prices. Over a million trees have since been established in NSW and Queensland, but some have since been removed. Lemon myrtle is still a 'new crop' with high risks, as the crop is not known anywhere else in the world, and in the Northern Rivers you are as likely to find it as an ingredient in cosmetics as in food. Attractive prices for Davidson's plums in the past were governed by limited supply, but currently farmers experience a glut of produce. Tens of thousands of trees have been planted in the past ten years.

The history of native foods in the Northern Rivers, as in other parts of the country, is intimately connected with the market. From the outset the region was intended for food production. The gastronomic landscape created is a transnational one, shaped by tastes not internal to the place but linked elsewhere in a series of interconnecting cultures, ideas, histories and so on, which English geographer Doreen Massey argues construct places beyond the place where people live. Like other traditions, food does not have to be "place-bound" (1995). Our tastes and the market, however, do shape the landscape at a local level for those regions involved in agricultural production. For this reason, our consumption is also an agricultural act. Food is not merely an agricultural product, and the landscape is shaped by consumption *and* production. Wendell Berry argues that:

> Eating ends the annual drama of the food economy that begins with planting and birth. Most eaters, however, are no longer aware that this is true. They think of food as an agricultural product, perhaps, but they do not think of themselves as participants in agriculture. They think of themselves as 'consumers'. If they think beyond that, they recognise that they are passive consumers.
>
> (2009)

Berry advocates reclaiming responsibility for one's own part in the food economy. Eaters should understand that eating takes place inescapably in the world, that eating is inescapably an agricultural act and that how we eat determines, to a considerable extent, how the world is used. Far from reducing this to the responsibility of the individual eater, it is part of a relationship to history and the market, the region and empire that makes this so potent in the context of Australia. As Christopher Mayes argues, "Food has been vital to the settler-colonial project, as a necessary means of survival, but also as an avenue through which the land was possessed an a culture cultivated" (2018: 2).

Conclusion

Distinguishing between the attitudes of colonial settlers and contemporary gourmets on the enjoyment of native foods is clearly misleading. The emphasis placed on the introduction of species established for world trade transformed the environment into a 'productive' colony, but the current interest in native foods has also been driven by commercial concerns, even as ethical and sustainable practices factor in consumer choice. The contemporary interest in native foods has been presented as a reflection of change in how indigenous flora and fauna are evaluated and in recognition of histories and relationships with Indigenous people. However, colonial consumption and enjoyment of native foods undermines this argument and complicates any suggestion that eating practices, without broader change, are a satisfactory shift from colonialism. In contrast to John Newton's suggestion for "culinary reconciliation" (2016), Bruce Pascoe has argued that "you can't eat our food if you can't swallow our history" (in Fairhall, 2019). If we have been eating native food since the beginning of settlement, merely enjoying it now offers little in terms of change. Understanding how legacies of colonialism inform food culture, historically and in contemporary practices, rather than presenting the two as distinct, shows a continuum and challenges the separation of past and present. While the monotonous plantations of macadamia have certainly changed the local landscape, the biggest single income earner in the region is still beef cattle: such a potent symbol of English identity in the nineteenth century. Some Indigenous chefs and initiatives have raised the profile of native foods and built opportunities for communities and knowledge sharing, but the industry as a whole is dominated by non-Indigenous people. Engaging Indigenous communities, knowledge and histories and connecting the foods to place requires a decolonising of culinary knowledge that acknowledges rather than marginalises Traditional Owners. Skye Krichauff has also concluded that unsettling settler descendants' consciousness of the colonial past and connecting Aboriginal people with people and places known to settlers in their everyday life can enable a connection between Aboriginal histories and experiences (2017). However, the historical elements that contribute to the identity of the Northern Rivers have largely been divided between Indigenous, colonial and new settler experiences, and disconnecting past and present. The gastronomic landscape of the North Coast is a *transnational* one, with the effects of history resonating into the contemporary period.

Historical factors are critical to food preferences, and these can change over time according to the way existing conditions converge with tradition to shape how foods are used. Even if the same plants are being grown, however, this does not signal a return to a precolonial landscape any more than it suggests a postcolonial agricultural movement. Increasing their exchange value, rather than just their use, may contribute to a reassessment of local native foods outside the region, but unless Bundjalung people are involved and acknowledged, colonial sovereignty is exercised unimpeded and the relationships built upon the legacy of colonialism are ongoing. In the words of Bruce Pascoe, "If we are to make a nation rather than a mere economy we have to absorb the history".

References

Abbott, E. 1864. *The English and Australian Cookery Book. Cookery for the Many, as well as for the 'Upper Ten Thousand'*. London: Sampson Low, Son, and Marston.

Ager, W. 1919. "Decentralisation Will Kill Sydney Octopus." *The Voice of the North.* May 16, p. 8.

Ainsworth, J. 1987. *Reminiscences: Ballina in the Early Days: 1847–1922.* Ballina: Apex 40.

Banner, S. 2005. "Why Terra Nullius? Anthropology and Property Law in Early Australia." *Law and History Review* 23(1): 95–131.

Bannerman, C. 2006. "Indigenous Food and Cookery Books: Redefining Aboriginal Cuisine." Pp. 19–36 in *Culinary Distinction*, edited by Costantino, E., and Supski, S. Perth: API Network/Australia Research Institute.

Beeton, I. 1982. *Mrs Beeton's Cookery Book and Household Guide.* London: Ward, Lock and Co. Ltd.

Berry, W. 2009. "The Pleasures of Eating." *What are People For?* [1990] *Center for EcoLiteracy* (www.ecoliteracy.org/article/wendell-berry-pleasures-eating).

Black, S. 2010. "'Tried and Tested': Community Cookbooks in Australia, 1890–1980." PhD Thesis. University of Adelaide.

Borch, M. 2001. "Rethinking the Origins of Terra Nullius." *Australian Historical Studies* 32(117): 222–239.

Callicott, J. B. 2000. "Contemporary Criticisms of the Wilderness Idea." Pp. 24–31 in *USDA Forest Service Proceedings*. RMRS-P-15 Volume 1.

Connor, M. C. 2005. *The Invention of Terra Nullius: Historical and Legal Fictions on the Foundation of Australia.* Sydney: Macleay Press.

Connors, L. 2015. *Warrior: A Legendary Leader's Dramatic Life and Violent Death on the Colonial Frontier.* Sydney: Allen & Unwin.

Craw, C. 2012a. "Gastatory Redemption? Colonial Appetites, Historical Tales and the Contemporary Consumption of Australian Native Foods." *International Journal of Critical Indigenous Studies* 5(2): 13–24.

Craw, C. 2012b. "Tasting Territory: Imagining Place in Australian Native Food Packaging." *Locale: Pacific Journal of Regional Food Studies* 2: 1–25.

Fairhall, L. 2019. "Bruce Pascoe Rewrites History." *Dumbo Feather*, 28 February. Retrieved April 2019 (https://www.dumbofeather.com/conversations/bruce-pascoe-interview/).

Ferguson, H., Kijas, J., and Wessell, A. 2017. "Towards Reflexive Localism: Exploring the Diverse Co-creators of Alternative Food Across Time in the Northern Rivers of New South Wales, Australia." *Journal of Historical Geography* 56: 14–21.

Fittal, K. 2013. "Homegrown: New Italy, Richmond River District, NSW." *SBS Food* October 29. Retrieved November 2018 (www.sbs.com.au/food/article/2012/08/26/homegrown-new-italy-richmond-river-district-nsw).

Fredericks, B., and Stoter, R. 2013. "We've Always Cooked Kangaroo. We Still Cook Kangaroo. Although Sometimes We Use Cookbooks Now: Aboriginal Australians and Cookbooks." *Text* Special Issue October 24, 2013 (www.textjournal.com.au/speciss/issue24/Fredericks&Stoter.pdf).

Gammage, B. 2011. *The Biggest Estate on Earth: How Aborigines Made Australia.* Crows Nest: Allen & Unwin.

Harper, D., and Bali, M. 2018. "Coutts Crossing Villagers Vote Against Name Change Despite Links to Brutal Past." *ABC News.* July 5. Retrieved October 2018 (www.abc.net.au/news/2018-06-29/coutts-crossing-residents-keep-town-name-despite-a-murky-past/9921206).

Harrison, R. 2004. *Shared Landscapes: Archaeologies of Attachment and the Pastoral Industry in New South Wales.* Sydney: University of New South Wales Press.

Hoff, J. 2006. *Bundjalung Jugun: Bundjalung Country* Lismore: Richmond River Historical Society.

Holt-Gimenez, E. 2017. *A Foodies Guide to Capitalism: Understanding the Political Economy of What We Eat.* New York: Monthly Review Press.

64   *Adele Wessel*

Honan, K., and McCarthy, M. 2018. "Native Bush Food Demand Outstripping Supply Says Industry as More Growers Encouraged." *ABC Rural*. August 30. Retrieved September (www.abc.net.au/news/rural/2017-08-30/native-bush-food-demand-outstripping-supply-says-industry/8855058).

Irvine, G. 2003. "Creating Communities At the End of the Rainbow." Pp. 63–82 in *Belonging in the Rainbow Region: Cultural Perspectives on the New South Wales North Coast*, edited by Wilson, H. Lismore: Southern Cross University Press.

Jackson, S. W. 1935. "Native Citrus Trees." *The World's News*. November 6, pp. 13, 30.

James, T. 2018. "School of Arts and Social Sciences Annual Lecture." Lismore Regional Gallery. October 25.

Janke, T., and Kearney, J. 2018. "Rights to Culture: Indigenous Cultural and Intellectual Property (ICIP), Copyright and Protocols." *Terri Janke and Company*. January 29. Retrieved September 2018 (www.terrijanke.com.au/single-post/2018/01/29/Rights-to-Culture-Indigenous-Cultural-and-Intellectual-Property-ICIP-Copyright-and-Protocols).

Johnstone, R. A. 1904. "Sketcher: Spinifex and Wattle." *The Queenslander*. February 20, p. 21.

Kerkhove, R. 2014. "Tribal Alliances with Broader Agendas? Aboriginal Resistance in Southern Queensland's 'Black War.'" *Cosmopolitan Civil Societies: An Interdisciplinary Journal* 6(3) (https://epress.lib.uts.edu.au/journals/index.php/mcs/article/view/4218/4491).

Kijas, J. 2003. "'From Obscurity Into the Fierce Light of Amazing Popularity': Internal Migration on the Far North Coast." Pp. 21–40 in *Belonging in the Rainbow Region: Cultural Perspectives on the New South Wales North Coast*, edited by Wilson, H. Lismore: Southern Cross University Press,.

Kneafsey, M., Cox, R., Holloway, L., Dowler, E., Venn, L., and Tuomainen, H. 2008. *Reconnecting Producers, Consumers and Food: Exploring Alternatives*. Oxford: Berg.

Krichauff, S. 2017. *Memory, Place and Aboriginal-Settler History: Understanding Australians' Consciousness of the Colonial Past*. London: Anthem Press.

Lang, J. D. 1847. *Cooksland in North-Eastern Australia: The Future Cotton-field of Great Britain: Its Characteristics and Capabilities for European Colonization, with a Disquisition of the Origin, Manners and Customs of the Aborigines*. London: Longmans, Brown, Green and Longmans.

Laurie, A. 1959. "The Black War in Queensland." *Journal of the Royal Historical Society of Queensland* 6(1): 155–173.

Lydon, J. 1996. "'No Moral Doubt . . .' Evidence and the Kangaroo Creek Poisoning, 1847–1849." *Aboriginal History* (20): 151–175.

Macpherson, E. 1860. *My Experiences in Australia: Being Recollections of a Visit to the Australian Colonies in 1856–1857*. London: J. G. Hope.

Massey, D. 1995. "Places and Their Pasts." *History Workshop Journal* (39): 182–192.

Mayes, C. 2018. *Unsettling Food Politics: Agriculture, Dispossession and Sovereignty in Australia*. London: Rowman & Littlefield.

McFarlane, J. 1980. *A History of the Clarence River District 1837–1915*. Maclean: Clarence Press.

McSwan, E. H. 1992. *Maclean – The First Fifty Years 1862–1912*. Maclean: Maclean District Historical Society.

Melchior, A. 2011. *Interview with Adele Wessell*. Lismore. Recording held by the author.

Newton, John. 2016. *The Oldest Foods on Earth: A history of Australian Native Foods with Recipes*. Sydney: New South.

Offord, B. 2003. "Mapping the Rainbow Region: Fields of Belonging and Sites of Confluence." Pp. 41–62 in *Belonging in the Rainbow Region: Cultural Perspectives on the New South Wales North Coast*, edited by Wilson, H. Lismore: Southern Cross University Press.

O'Neill, K. 2016. "The Noma Effect Is Natural." *Byron Shire News*. July 9. Retrieved October 2018 (https://www.byronnews.com.au/news/the-noma-effect-is-natural/3059292/).

Page, J. 2010. "Common Property and the Age of Aquarius." *Griffith Law Review* 19(2): 26.

Papas, C. 2018. "Lemon Myrtle in Every Cupboard: A Conversation with Mark Olive." *Field Guide Fortnightly*. May 2. Retrieved September 2018. https://fieldguide.org.au/journal/mark-olive/.

Pascoe, B. 2014. *Dark Emu Black Seeds: Agriculture or Accident?* Broome: Magabala Books.

Pascoe, B. 2018. "Australia: Temper and Bias." *Meanjin* 77(3), Spring 2018. Retrieved January 2019 (https://meanjin.com.au/essays/11312/).

Popular Guide to the Centennial Exhibition with Which is Incorporated the Stranger's Guide to Melbourne with Plans Compiled from Various Sources. 1888. W. H. Williams: Melbourne.

Potts, A. 2005. "F. S. Peppercorne on the Richmond River." *Richmond River Historical Society Inc. Bulletin* 16(194) September: 13–14.

Rawson, Mrs. L. 1992. Rawson, Mrs. Lance. [1895] *The Antipodean Cookery Book and Kitchen Companion*. Kenthurst: Kangaroo Press.

Rozin, E., and Rozin, P. 1981. "Culinary Themes and Variations." *Natural History* February: 6–14.

Ryan, L., Richards, J., Pascoe, W., Debenham, J., Anders, R. J., Brown, M., Smith, R., Price, D., and Newley, J. (2018). *Colonial Frontier Massacres in Eastern Australia 1788. 1930, v2.1*. Newcastle: University of Newcastle. Retrieved October 30, 2018 (http://hdl.handle.net/1959.13/1340762). This project has been funded by the Australian Research Council (ARC).

Ryan, M. 1999. *The Days and Ways of Old Time Nimbin*. Nimbin: Nimbin Chamber of Commerce.

Ryan, M., and Smith, R. 2001. *Time and Tide Again: A History of Byron Bay*. Lismore: Northern Rivers Press.

Ryan, M., and Smith, R. 2006. *Lismore: From Lios Mor to Tuckurimba*. Lismore: Northern Rivers Press.

Santich, B. 2011. "Nineteeth-Century Experimentation and the Role of Indigenous Foods in Australian Food Culture." *Australian Humanities Review* 51. November.

Singley, B. 2012. "'Hardly Anything Fit for a Man to Eat': Food and Colonialism in Australia." *History Australia* 9(3): 27–42.

Singley, B. 2017. 'Parrot Pie and Possum Curry: How Colonial Australians Embraced Native Food." *The Conversation*. January 26. Retrieved January 2017 (https://theconversation.com/parrot-pie-and-possum-curry-how-colonial-australians-embraced-native-food-59977).

Smith, A. N. 2011. 'Waterbirds and Their Habitat on the Clarence River Floodplain: A History." *Australian Zoologist* 35(3): 788–809.

Stubbs, B. J. 2001. "From 'Useless Brutes' to National Treasures: A Century of Evolving Attitudes Towards Native Fauna in New South Wales, 1860s–1960s." *Environmental History* 7(1): 23–56.

Stubbs, B. J. 2007. *Thematic History of Richmond Valley Local Government Area*. Casino: Richmond Valley Council.

Sunday Times. 1905. "A Valuable Australian Nut.' September 17, p. 1.

The Queenslander. 1867. "Bush, Farm & Garden." April 6, p. 11.

The Queenslander. 1889. "Useful Native Plants of Australia." March 9, p. 452.

Town and Country Journal. 1881. "A Trip to the Richmond District II." August 27, p. 26.

Tweed Shire Council. 2011. "Tweed Sustainability Agriculture Strategy Discussion Paper." September. Retrieved September 2018 (www.yoursaytweed.com.au/15829/documents/28524).

Waterhouse, R. 2004. "The Yeoman Ideal and Australian Experience, 1860–1960." Pp. 440–459 in *Exploring the British World: Identity, Cultural Production, Institutions*, edited by Darian-Smith, K., Grimshaw, P., Lindsey, K., and Mcintyre, S. Melbourne, Vic: RMIT Publishing (https://search.informit.com.au/documentSummary;dn=873090227183116;res=IELIND).

Waterhouse, R. 2006. "Agrarian Ideals and Pastoral Realities: The Use and Misuse of Land in Rural Australia." In *The Great Mistakes of Australian History*, edited by Crotty, M., and. Roberts, D. A. Sydney: University of NSW Press.

Wilkinson, J. 1999. *Dairy Industry in New South Wales: Past and Present*. Briefing Paper No. 23/99. NSW Parliamentary Library Research Service.

Wilson, H. 2003. *Belonging in the Rainbow Region: Cultural Perspectives on the New South Wales North Coast*. Lismore: Southern Cross University Press.

Wotherspoon, J. 1936. "Early Lismore." *The Northern Star*. June 27, p. 5.

3 Terraform and Terra Firma

Transnational economies of image, landscape and location in screen production in Queensland

Allison Craven

Introduction: nature, culture and the talented landscapes of Queensland

In outlining the Cultural Asset Mapping Project in Regional Australia (or CAMRA, which ran from 2008–2014), Ross Gibson (2015) poses the question of whether "nature" – in the form of weather, light, or landforms – is ever "apprehensible as culture" or "cultural capital" when it is "actively contextualised as part of the enriched and sustaining experience available in a region" (3). I say this is indeed the case when regional landscapes become locations for film production. In the process, natural phenomena are transformed into cultural assets. The cases in point are in the Australian state of Queensland, where for some years the iconic value of regional landscapes has been integral to participation in the transnational film industry and contributed to the steady rise of Queensland to prominence among the state-based film industries in Australia (see Craven 2016).

The watershed development was the establishment of Village Roadshow Studios on the Gold Coast in the late 1990s. The industry hub it stimulated is described by Ben Goldsmith, Susan Ward and Tom O'Regan (2010) as a "local Hollywood" or a hub of "film-friendliness", a quality defined by the combination and coordination of financial incentives and favourable conditions to attract film industry activity for which the Gold Coast was situated as a "Greenfield location" (61, 163). Village Roadshow now forms one of three major studios in Australia, with substantial production output that is predominantly networked with transnational interests. Its growth and prosperity has occurred amidst significant changes in conditions for film production in Australia and worldwide.

The first is the global sea change of digital technology innovation that has transformed twenty-first century filmmaking practices in all budget scales. Not only transformative of the medium of film, it has expanded the channels for industry participation through the range of digital effects that are now routinely part of high-end filmmaking. Second, and more directly relevant to Queensland's place in film economies, is the shift in funding structures for feature film production in Australia, namely the advent of taxation offsets offered by the federal government since 2007 through its agency, Screen Australia, and topped up by state governments seeking to attract international industry activity. A range of offsets are offered, including the Producer Offset and (the currently coupled) Location and PDV (Post, Digital and Visual Effects) Offsets (Screen Australia n.d.). These incentives have significantly enhanced the film-friendliness of Australian production locations (see Mark David Ryan [2017] for further comment on the offsets regimes). In combination with savvy entrepreneurship by screen agencies, these financial incentives have led to renewed identity for the Australian screen industries, with the Producer Offset now regarded as a "fundamental component of production business models" (Screen Australia 2017).

In Queensland, the combination of these changes has led to distinct regional images emerging as markers of the state's film industry that correlate with two particular hubs of filmmaking and signify production assets both natural and cultural that attract a range of the offsets. The first is the image of tropical Queensland, which descends from the longstanding folk myth of Queensland as 'paradise' in national cultural discourses (Molloy 1990; Moran 2001; Craven 2010, 2016) and vaunted since the early twentieth century in tourism and state marketing. The tropical aura is particularly renewed in the many marine-themed films made at Village Roadshow Studios (Craven 2018). A number of these films blend studio production with location filming (on the beaches and hinterland of the Gold Coast and a range of other locations around Queensland and interstate), and the film montage is typically engineered with digital effects. In recent work on *The Shallows* (Jaume Collet-Serra 2016) and *Kong: Skull Island* (Jordan Vogt-Roberts 2017), I characterise the images as 'terraform tropics', adapting the term 'terraforming' from science fiction (where it refers to the modification of a planetary surface) to suggest the imaginary geographies created through the convergent blend of studio and location production and digital engineering (Craven 2018). Terraforming results in images that are both generic of the 'tropics' and unique to the specific film copyrights.

The second hub, on a much smaller and fledgling scale, is centered around the tiny town of Winton in Western Queensland, around 1,200 kilometres inland, where a spate of filmmaking has occurred by interests drawn to the spectacular arid landscapes that surround Winton. More significantly for the discussion of regionality, the productions have been stimulated and encouraged by the residents and regional council in cultivating the film-friendliness of the town in their efforts to sustain the survival of Winton. In cultivating the remoteness and 'outback' attributes of inland Queensland, spinoff initiatives have established a festival program, including an annual film festival, expanding Winton's existing cultural infrastructure and place in national folklore, as discussed later in the chapter.

A range of films have been made near Winton since 2004, including *The Proposition* (John Hillcoat 2005), *Gone* (Ringan Ledwidge 2006), *Mystery Road* (Ivan Sen 2013) and *Goldstone* (Sen 2016). These and other productions have utilised images of the landscapes for the gothic resonances of *terra nullius*, or the generic resemblance of the landscapes to the settings of American genre 'Westerns', or, as in the case of Hillcoat's and Sen's films, for *both* effects. While it has been observed elsewhere that "there has been a long tradition of dis-associating the pastoral landscape from issues of ethnicity, race and racism" (Neal and Agyeman cited in Luckman 2012: 45), in the films made in the Winton region, the history of racial dispossession is expressly signified by both the particular and generic characteristics of the images of the land.

Coastal or remote outback, the production activities in the Gold Coast and Winton re-signify regions once identified with a range of other industries and that incurred the dispossession of Indigenous people and which now sustain a renewed identity for Queensland as a centre for screen production. Both case studies, in quite different ways, therefore reflect Susan Luckman's (2012) analysis of the role of nature and affect in aesthetic practices of regional creativity (her work is based on the British Lake District): "Ever since the Romantic era, nature *qua* source of inspiration has become an established discursive trope, and certainly it is well accepted that 'locality can be a source of aesthetic inspiration'" (31). More particularly, she refers to the role of "affect" in the "contemporary affordances of place" and how "[c]reative industries discourse can be said to have its own way of conceiving of this intangible . . . connection, namely, the enabling apparatus of a locale's 'soft infrastructure'" (31–32). Following Landry, she identifies elements such as "atmosphere" and the "emotional realm of experiences" in alluding to "the kinds of feelings, moods and inspirations people receive from nature" as something other than "clichéd Romantic holdover" and more directly about "emplaced nature as an enabling soft infrastructure" (32–33).

Luckman's framework is pertinent in several ways to the discussion that follows and in responding to Gibson's question about the cultural aspects of natural phenomena. The uses of regional landscapes in film production are definitive examples of "emplaced nature" as "enabling soft infrastructure" that are commodified in several ways: as offset incentives, as cinematic spectacles and as the 'affective affordances of place' that are harnessed in the practices of film friendliness. Whereas film-friendliness is an industrial-scaled practice on the Gold Coast that capitalises the tropical mythos of coastal Queensland, in remote Winton, in comparison, it is currently largely sustained through municipal and community endeavour. In both cases, the affective affordances of the "feelings, moods and inspirations" of the imaged landscapes emanate in complex ways in the films, from the terraformed images of the tropics to the deliberate resonances of *terra nullius* in images of Winton's arid region.

In exploring this further in the discussion that follows, I develop a view that 'region' is a concept, in the film industry at least, that is formed in the relationship between nature and culture. Region only indirectly correlates with the notion of 'place' which signifies something relatively concrete and takes identity from the way "it is performed . . . the way spaces, and the people and artefacts wrapped up in them become shared concerns, get discussed, become chronicled in census and names" (Bingham–Hall 2017: 67). Region, I suggest, is

70 *Allison Craven*

more abstract, even phantasmatic, and gains identity with geographic or climatic markers in combination with the cultural practices that span the geography – like regional foods, wares or films – of which the territorial extent is indistinct and essentially borderless. The identity of a region is often sustained by mytho-poetic discourses or the stories that are told about it (Carter 2015: 15). This is no less than the role of feature film in framing regions as images that signify narrative fictions for transnational consumption.

Terraforming the tropics

The advent of Village Roadshow Studios on the Queensland Gold Coast has led to a growing number of films that, elsewhere, I term 'marine adventure dramas' that utilise the studio facilities supplemented with location footage from around the state and elsewhere (Craven 2018). These films construct what I call the terraform tropics, a digitised image that circulates amidst the transnational flows of cinema, although it stems from the longer history of film, tourism and commercialisation of lifestyle in Queensland throughout the twentieth century.

Queensland as 'paradise' or the holiday tropics in Australian cinema has variously centred on portrayals of the Gold Coast in Southeast Queensland and the Great Barrier Reef and Far North Queensland. The coastal and underwater reaches of the northern marine environment figured in silent films as early as the 1920s in the cinematography of Frank Hurley (Landman 2006) and Zane Grey (Speed 2017). The growing cinematic spectacle of the Great Barrier Reef emerged more in the institutional media of the Commonwealth Film Unit from the 1940s (Moran 1989) and acquired a Hollywood-styled narrative in *Will the Great Barrier Reef Cure Claude Clough?* (Milson 1967/68), in which footage of the Reef is captured in a mockumentary about the said Claude, whose need for a getaway takes him first to a psychiatrist and then to an island off Queensland. The brilliantly colourful, moving imagery of the Reef represented the technical advances of colour and underwater cinematography that emerged more in the commercial cinema and television in the 1960s. Exemplary is the artist's escape to paradise in *Age of Consent* (Michael Powell 1969), a Columbia Pictures production on Dunk Island, North Queensland.

While the setting of *Age of Consent* retains historical identity with Queensland, it prefigures the flexibility of Hollywood production locations for tropical settings over subsequent decades. The flexibility arises, as Chua Beng Huat (2008) observes, because the tropics form a "geography of the mind", an ideological construction that is harboured in cultural discourses like cinema and urban design and is predominantly connected to nature in that heat and climate persist in the definitions, whether the films are made in Hollywood or elsewhere and regardless of how the mythos of the breezy tropics is dissonant with the seasonal realities. This historical tendency is renewed within what Grau and Veigl (2013) term the "image phenomena" of the twenty-first century and the culture of the "virtual, spatial image", with its promise of interactive "all-embracing audiovisual[ity]" where "temporal and spatial parameters can be altered at will" (3). Such is the effect of terraform production, or the layering of location footage with digital visual effects (sometimes called 'vfx') that leads to generic images without geographic referents at all. Whereas the fictions of the Queensland tropics attained a degree of identity in films from the twentieth century, the combination of transnational production practices and digital engineering results in a more ambiguous and generic image today.

Elsewhere I have examined blockbuster films produced at Village Roadshow Studios, namely Columbia Pictures' *The Shallows* and Warner Brothers' *Kong: Skull Island* (see Craven 2018). Both productions were incentivised by offsets, and the terraform effect is apparent in the way the (very limited quantity) of location footage is digitally modified to suggest the unique fictional places in the films. In *The Shallows*, the minimal location footage was captured interstate on Lord Howe Island (in New South Wales) and engineered to suggest the film's setting in Mexico and a theme of mystical feminine power (Craven 2018). Prima facie, this is not objectionable except that it implicitly contradicted the Queensland State Government's claims about the benefits of their (large) investment in the film for the reputation of the state. A comparable case was the state's investment in *Aquaman* (James Wan 2018), for which the location footage was controversially shot in New South Wales (see Riley and Harper 2017).

Interstate rivalries over locations are not at issue here. But it is the awarding of offsets that are touted as economic returns to the nation with little close scrutiny of the cultural or aesthetic values represented by the films that is more in question, as well as the impact on local or independent filmmakers. Indeed, a longstanding debate among scholars of Australian cinema concerns the risk of the so-called 'Hollywood backlot', or that such practices create a profile of Australia as a service industry to Hollywood. Even so, there is no avoiding the contemporary reality that high-budget film production is characteristically transnational in scope, and the biggest projects are typically sourced from the USA. Furthermore, films like *Guardians of the Tomb* (Kimball Rendall 2018), the latest (at the time of writing) of the Australia-Chinese co-productions (made under an agreement negotiated at federal government level some years ago) which was produced at Village Roadshow Studios, are examples of transnational collaborations that are not perceived as the 'backlot' stereotype but represent the promise of new cross-cultural industry directions and alliances.

These films typify the practices of the motion picture industry described by Andy Pike (2015), with its global capital "centered on Hollywood, California" that "utilizes the 'blockbuster' franchise model" that "deliberately avoids particular geographical referents in its films, except those with widespread and even global resonance to reap the scale economies of global distribution and marketing while minimizing potential mis-readings in specific geographical markets" (Pike 2015: 44). Accordingly, the terraformed images of *The Shallows, Kong: Skull Island* or *Guardians of the Tomb* are not conceived to identify Queensland as anything more than a 'location' and to merge its commodified image within global media flows.

72 *Allison Craven*

The culture industries are not unique for re-signifying tropical spaces in Queensland. Various landforms and landscapes have been subject to shifting frames of meaning in other contexts. The re-designation of 'the wet forest' as 'the Wet Tropics' (aka the rainforests of Far North Queensland) occurred, along with the repatriation of colonial artefact collections to the descendants of the Indigenous people who made them, as the result of shifts in criteria "based on evolutionary science and ethnographic classifications" to those "based on ecology, biodiversity" and cultural diversity (Erckenbrecht et al. 2010: 352–364). Another example, closer to that of the film industry, is the way the islands of the Great Barrier Reef have transmuted from "Australian bush to generic [tropical] ideal" through the influence of colour visual media in tourist literature through the twentieth century (Pocock 2002: 374–376). These histories of change speak directly to the historical and material impact of cultural practices in redefining natural environments and settler and Indigenous identities.

However, attracting the international screen industries to Queensland entails a further level of commodification through offsets and film copyrights, and this affects the way, to adapt Pike, a "place gets into goods" (Pike 23). Meaning and value are not only constituted of geographic elements, and these can be "uneven" and disparate (32). In modern transnational supply chains, where component parts of commodities are made and assembled in various places, the discursive effects of the places of making, materials or copyright ownership represent "hybrid configurations" (65–68), and this is so for cars, planes or terraformed films. Hybridity is variously detectable in the provenance of the films made at the Gold Coast and, to a lesser extent, in the second case study in outback Winton. The films produced in that region are largely unmodified digitally, in spite of the fact that the landscapes are sometimes sought by filmmakers due to the striking resemblance to the landscapes of genre Westerns. But as Australia offers a range of arid settings, the attraction of Winton has also depended on the film friendliness of the community and growing regional investment in co-attractions to encourage remote location production in the region.

A remote boom: Terra firma in Winton region

Winton is a tiny town with just one main street and a permanent population of about 900 people. Its commercial infrastructure consists of several pubs and service stations and a handful of shops as well as municipal buildings that house social programs and civic events. From the Queensland coast, Winton is hundreds of kilometres inland and emerges out of the dust of the vast landscape around 80 kilometres down the road from its nearest neighbour, the hamlet of Corfield, a former railway siding when the trains once ran to Winton. Apart from residents, the roads in and out are traversed by grey nomads and travellers and road trains, and the partakers of the annual bush race meetings held in Corfield and further inland and similar events throughout the year. Many of Winton's current residents are born and raised there; and its core population is distributed in a wide region and in families that dwell both within and far from Winton, either because of migration or through part-time residency in other places. Its cultural infrastructure is deeply embedded in its relationship to the land and the town's remote location.

To this extent, Winton is an ideal case study of "regions living in the aftermath of old-pastoral economies" and a community "dispersed widely across space and [generational] time" (Gibson 2015: 8 and 11, although Winton is not among their CAMRA case studies). Historically, Winton was the centre of a vast region of agriculture, predominantly grazing and wool growing. Key elements of its contemporary cultural infrastructure pertain to this heritage, including its proximity to the site where the bush poet, Banjo Patterson, is believed to have composed the iconic national song, 'Waltzing Matilda'. Winton's central hub is the Waltzing Matilda Centre, where the prized connection to Banjo Patterson is preserved and celebrated. However, Winton exists today largely in the shadow of its history, as the wool industry has transformed, and the army of sheep shearers who once mined the rich pickings of its seasonal produce are now ghosts and legends rather than an annual visitation.

Over time, the people of the district have grappled with the changed conditions. A key enterprise is the Australian Age of Dinosaurs, a pre-historic heritage trail that now extends throughout western Queensland and is centred in Winton (see Australian Age of Dinosaurs Limited 2018). It was developed by pastoral interests after a grazier, David Elliott (now OAM), came across what proved to be a dinosaur bone on his property in 1998 and subsequently founded a company to exhibit the findings of the archaeological research since and ongoing. It is now a mainstay of tourism in the region. When Winton's Waltzing Matilda Centre burned to the ground in 2015, it was rapidly rebuilt within three years and redesigned to expand its accommodation and exhibits and to aesthetically align with the design of the Australian Age of Dinosaurs visitor centre, around 25 kilometres away. Winton is therefore an answer to the question posed in the CAMRA project asking if *remote* "regional culture be seen as an *asset* compared with the seemingly endemic *debits* of isolation, under-population and stigma imposed from outside on these relatively 'off-road' places"; and, conversely, "from *inside* these regions, what are the riches, what are the edges and what counts as culture?" (Gibson 2015: 3). This question besets research in the regions insofar as a natural deficit of remote places is somewhat assumed to apply outside or beyond the normalised spaces of creativity. Accordingly, Gibson, Luckman and Willoughby-Smith (2012) declaim the tendency of remote dwellers to "disavow distance", and they frame their perspectives between the "curse of remoteness" and the "pleasures of isolation" (29–30). Remoteness, they argue, presents "particular challenges for creative workers" who are "a long way from key centres" and are challenged to "[stay] in touch with key gatekeepers" and "[maintain] visibility in these larger markets" (26). (However, it must be noted that I adapt their claims because the discussion by Gibson et al. concerns Darwin, Northern Territory, for its relative distance to east coast centres like Sydney and Melbourne.) Winton turns around this presumed deficit in the way its residents and visitors revel in its remoteness as a source of power, most recently in their efforts to attract the film industry to their region. The commitment of the Winton Shire Council and townspeople to generate economic viability for their town and outlying community has coalesced with the popularity of the space with filmmakers over the last 10 years or so. In participating in the pro-community activities that enhance film friendliness, the residents look upon their enterprise as attracting creatives into their town and for the benefits to the local economy and reputation that this will afford for its ongoing contribution to national values and folklore. The film friendliness that now thrives in Winton is essentially one of hospitality – the hosting of film industry personnel and interests. The landscape does the rest!

Filmmaking in the region goes back a long way, to the earliest Australian cinema in the first years of the twentieth century (see Gaunson 2010), but has not been sustained since that time. The breakthrough film in its current era was *The Proposition*, which was shot on private station properties and the Bladensburg National Park late in 2004. The locations around Winton were selected by the director John Hillcoat and his collaborators with the persuasion of the local tourism officer of the time, in preference to the district of Bourke in New South Wales (Craven 2010). Since then, a number of domestic and international films and an American television series have been (wholly or partly) shot in the region by filmmakers seeking locations that resemble the visual territories of the American Western and stimulated by industry word of mouth. A film studio is now under development with the support of the Queensland State Government. If it goes ahead, it will bring another dimension to the boon of filmmaking by facilitating studio and post-production onsite in Winton rather than, as is now the case, offsite either a flight or a long drive away at significant expense.

While filmmakers are attracted to the aesthetics of the landscapes, it is the people of Winton and its council who plough its appeal and gatekeep its interests in supporting the productions that go out there. In turn, this has stimulated a secondary industry of cultural festivals, initiated with the Vision Splendid Film Festival that commenced in 2013 (see www.visionsplendidfilmfest.com). Named in homage to Banjo Patterson ("the vision splendid" is a famous line from his poem, *Clancy of the Overflow*), the annual festival is staged in another unique feature of Winton's built environment: a 100-year old open-air cinema with a super-wide vintage screen, the last of its kind in Australia. Under the winter stars, during Winton's coolest months, festival audiences recline in canvas chairs and snuggle under rugs provided by Screen Queensland for the coldest of screenings. A state government grant brings a specialist projectionist to town who adapts the technology for digital projection amidst the cinematic memorabilia of reels and man-sized speakers and projectors.

Dr Greg Dolgopolov, a lecturer in film at the University of New South Wales, is the artistic director of the festival, a role that is integral with his academic practice. Dolgopolov's expert knowledge of Australian cinema and his commitment to Winton is combined in devising a program of around 35 films centred on the theme of Australian landscape. In addition, Dolgopolov and his collaborators bring students from their film programs to make films in the landscape and to engage in production training and industry networking with the celebrity personnel who travel to attend the festival (see, for example, the student-made documentary about the festival activities and townspeople, *Winton Splendid – a UNSW/GFS Documentary* [2016] available at: www.vision splendidfilmfest.com/about/winton-film-locations/) In a press interview, Dolgopolov comments: "'During the festival, we don't just screen films. We plan films, we talk about films, we . . . work together'" (MacIntyre 2017). In addition, the festival provides a forum for screening of new films, including "world" and "Queensland premiers [sic]" and he refers to the "special" audience that is "found in Australia's Outback Hollywood" (MacIntyre 2017).

Elsewhere, Dolgopolov (in publications with others) has noted the growth of festival culture in Australia. He sees the value not only for audiences but for the industry for whom conditions of distribution are constrained and challenging (Stevens, Dolgopolov and Harris 2016; see also Van Hemert and Ellison 2015). For audiences, festivals offer "experiential" modes of engagement and "participatory elements" that draw on the appeal of "the ephemeral live (and 'lived') experience and more established attractions of place, hospitality and the cinema itself" (Stevens, Harris and Dolgopolov 2015: 187). This is nowhere truer than in Winton, where the thematic program of landscape films screened in the Vision Splendid festival forms a cinematic fund of attention to the spectacle of the landscape that Winton inhabits and that its film friendliness supports. For instance, to suggest how this emerged in 2018, the festival theme of 'Wide Open Road' embraced a range of classic, art and contemporary 'landscape' films, some on Indigenous themes, including Ivan Sen's films *Mystery Road* (2013) and *Goldstone* (2016), both of which were made in the surrounding district. Another highlight was the documentary *Black Panther Woman* (Rachel Perkins 2014), about the Indigenous musician and activist Marlene Cummins, who grew up in Winton's district. Cummins participated as a guest speaker at the screening and also performed her music in another of the festival's events.

Furthermore, the film festival is not the sole event infrastructure. Winton's annual calendar now features a series of festivals surrounding the Vision Splendid event, all of which contribute to its attractiveness to visitors. There is the Way Out West Music Festival (www.facebook.com/WintonsWayOutWest Fest/) and the Outback Writers Festival (outbackwritersfestival.com.au/) that precedes the film festival each year. The staging of the festivals facilitates the steady streams of visitors to the town. Their patronage of festival events and local businesses supports the town's economy, in conjunction with dinosaur tourism, year round. For the film festival, the audience circulates within a small radius of events located in the cinema, the North Gregory Hotel and the alternative screening venue in the Waltzing Matilda Centre. The visitor population also includes the projection crew, industry guests and students who attend and the odd member of the research community. I attended in 2018 as a paying

76   Allison Craven

participant, combining research with a personal reunion with an old friend whose maternal family, the Everts, belong to Winton and own the cinema. Among the other visitors, I met a family on a road trip from Western Australia who had decided to stop in for a couple of days; a retired academic who travels every year from New South Wales; and couples from the land having an occasional day out in town.

While this floating population of festival patrons is debatable as a stimulant to commercial film production – aside from the prospects of the student films created during the festival – the economic benefits would seem a mainstay in the ongoing viability of Winton's capacity for film-friendliness. More sustaining are the local and municipal energies and the kinship networks and their affordances of social connections, which are not incidental in generating human infrastructure for the festival. These connections likely form part of what Robyn Mayes (2012, citing Kong) describes as the "inherent tensions in the economic and social roles of cultural activities" (21). The Evert family, for example, have a quest to preserve the cinema as both family and town heritage, which has gained impetus from the film festival. For instance, my reunion was accommodated at the newly minted Airbnb of the relatives of my old friend, a renovated Queenslander family home with a large verandah 'sleepout'. The family has invested in restoring the house on the promise of the festival activity and owing to the dearth of accommodation in town apart from the camping grounds.

While some locals speak of recovery of the grazing industry, the move to establish a film studio in Winton suggests that, while it may not entirely eclipse agriculture, the place of film production in the economy holds potential to grow. However, while Winton takes the credit(s), it is the land around Winton that attracts the filmmakers and forms the aesthetic spaces of the films made. In the images of the landscapes is resignification of the region stemming from the history of Australian cinema.

Outback unmodified

Outback landscapes are synonymous with Australian film and literature. The landscape trope has long gained critical attention for the connotation of European society in the Antipodes which construed land as empty space, overlooking foregoing inhabitants or culture, and unassimilated into the European symbolic order except, as Ross Gibson (1994) has described, as a motif of a "sublime, structuring void" (45) that came to be equated with the colonial notion of *terra nullius*. Since the 1990s, outback spaces in Australian films more register what Felicity Collins and Therese Davis (2004) memorably describe as the "aftershock" of the Mabo Native Title legislation of 1992 that overturned the legal fiction of *terra nullius*. Collins and Davis show how a range of film settings – urban, tropical and outback – carry the aftershock of Mabo and represent the same colonial histories as arid spaces, a history of violence that is increasingly documented. (A current project is the mapping of the colonial frontier by Professor Lyndall Ryan, Newcastle University. See: c21ch.newcastle.edu.au/colonialmassacres/map.php. See also Koori Mail 2018; and Parris 2018.) While arid film locations pre- and post-Mabo have emerged from around the country, particular sites in Central Australia and near Bourke in New South Wales have gained repeated use in a number of domestic and international productions like *Wake in Fright* (Kotcheff 1971) and *The Adventures of Priscilla, Queen of the Desert* (Elliott 1994) and more.

The appeal of Winton's landscapes in contrast is based on the dual potential to signify *terra nullius* and, with its distinctive butte-shaped landforms, to resemble the mid-western American landscapes of the Western, a genre that Peter Limbrick (2010) argues has been adapted in multiple national settings because it represents a colonial settler narrative in spaces that are disputed. It is precisely this narrative of disputed space that is adapted in *The Proposition* and in Ivan Sen's films *Mystery Road* and *Goldstone*, with Sen purposefully utilising genre (Western) conventions to confront the history of Australian racism by placing its conflict at the core of the aesthetic discourses of his films.

Mystery Road and *Goldstone* are both chapters in the life and times of Sen's creation, the cowboy detective Jay Swan played by Aaron Pederson. Both films utilise a distinct "production recipe" which "integrates genre, high-profile actors, focused artistic control and a tough Indigenous thematic" (Dolgopolov 2016: 11). Sen has spoken of how the landscapes around Winton inspired his decision to film there for the potential to signify histories of Aboriginal dispossession and discrimination and of his choice to adopt a genre template as a vehicle to broaden the market reach of his films (Luskri 2013). Sen skilfully works this potential in his films, emphasising the magnificence of the visual spectacle of the land as a decolonising effect of the narratives about the *ownership* of the land – in *Mystery Road*, through Jay's pursuit of the criminal farmer whose land holdings fill the frames, and, in *Goldstone*, in depicting the (fictional) conflict over the development rights of the mining company that traffics sex workers and negotiates deals with a corrupt Aboriginal land council.

His project mitigates assimilation into a generic class of outback images, and the landscape images, as I am aware, are not subject to technical modification comparable to the terraformed layering of the tropics (in the marine adventure films), notwithstanding the normality of digital-effects engineering in contemporary cinema. However, the much-acclaimed spin-off television mini-series of *Mystery Road* (Perkins 2018–) did not return to Winton for production but was filmed entirely in the Kimberley region of Western Australia (ABC 2018). (Sen did not direct this production but was involved as an executive producer.) Whatever the reasons for this decision, whether due to funding, production or aesthetic reasons, it suggests the competition that Winton faces and the potential for its filmmaking boom to migrate from it in the future. It is all the more reason why its festival culture and educational setting for young filmmakers and the film-friendliness of the town must continue to prosper if Winton is to remain competitive in the production sphere.

The aura of the region as image

In his ruminating discussion, Gibson (2015) asks: "Can regions sometimes be legitimately understood as 'country' in such a way that 'nature' and 'culture' suffuse each other to become something else yet again?" (3). This riddling question alludes to the Indigenous connotation of 'country' as ancestral land as much as to the settler meaning of rural 'countryside' that barely extends to the kinds of remote situations of the Australian outback. With passing reference to Walter Benjamin's (1969) notion of 'aura', which pertains to the cult value of an object that is displaced by its 'exhibition' value when it is subjected to the mechanical means of reproduction, I want to suggest that suffusion does not occur but is arguably simulated in the phenomenon of the image and the practice of filmmaking.

The case studies here do not speak of 'regional film industries' so much as an industry in which regions form component parts and how the commodity values are enhanced through a range of practices on industrial and community scales. At the outset, I emphasised the context of change in which these practices have rapidly developed, namely the changing structures of film financing and the advent of the Hollywood-style studios on the Gold Coast, which are the main anchor and magnet for these activities at present. At the Gold Coast, the film friendliness is built on the glamour and technical capacities of a 'local Hollywood', while in Winton, the townspeople work to generate industry attention to their region in the interest of economic sustainability of their town. But whereas, on the Gold Coast, the natural environs and its 'affective affordances' have become substitutable or expendable as assets of the production hub, in Winton, at present at least, the 'emplaced' landscape and heritage culture of the town form indispensable soft infrastructure that attracts production activity. This may change if the film studio goes ahead, and even as, in some instances in Winton, the layers of history of the land are implied in the films that remember *terra nullius* in the quest to overturn its long-lasting impact.

At both sites, surplus emerges in uses of land through its commodification as film-friendly locations and as the offset value of the costs of production as well as the exhibition value of the images created. These land uses, like earlier ones, change over time and suggest the renewability of the identity and aura of regions. Rather than suffusion, it is this quality of renewability that gives rise to the phantasmatic and gilded potential of (a) region to resonate as iconic and subject always to the dual and symbiotic forces of nature and culture.

Acknowledgements: I am grateful to Michael Watson, Maureen Kelleher, Janice Evert and Peter Evert for their generous recollections of the cinema and the history of Winton.

References

Australian Age of Dinosaurs Limited. 2018. "Australian Age of Dinosaurs Winton, Q." Retrieved November 5, 2018 (www.australianageofdinosaurs.com/).
Australian Broadcasting Corporation. 2018. "Mystery Road." *ABC TV*. Retrieved October 30, 2018 (www.abc.net.au/tv/programs/mystery-road/).

Benjamin, W. 1969. *Illuminations,* trans. by H. Zohn. New York: Schocken.

Bingham-Hall, J. 2017. "Imagined Community and Networked Hyperlocal Publics." Pp. 64–71 in *4d Hyper-local: A Cultural Tool Kit for the Open Source City,* edited by Bullivant, L. Oxford, UK: John Wiley & Sons (http://ebookcentral.proquest.com/lib/jcu/detail.action?docID=4833698).

Carter, P. 2015. "Common Patterns: Narratives of 'Mere Coincidence' and the Production of Regions." Pp. 13–29, in *Creative Communities: Regional Inclusion and the Arts,* edited by McDonald, J., and Mason, R. Bristol and Chicago: Intellect.

Chua, B. H. 2008. "Tropics, City and Cinema: Introduction to the Special Issue on Cinematic Representation of the Tropical Urban/City." *Singapore Journal of Tropical Geography* 29: 1–7.

Collet-Serra, J. dir. 2016. *The Shallows,* Motion Picture, Columbia/Weimarana Republic/Ombra Films, USA.

Collins, F., and Davis, T. 2004. *Australian Cinema After Mabo.* Cambridge, UK: Cambridge University Press.

Craven, A. 2010. "Paradise Post-National: Landscape, Location and Senses of Place in Films Set in Queensland." *Metro* 166: 108–113.

Craven, A. 2016. *Finding Queensland in Australian Cinema: Poetics and Screen Geographies.* London: Anthem.

Craven, A. 2018. "Escape to the Terraform Tropics: Geography and Gender in Marine Adventure Films in Queensland." *Screening the Past* 43 (www.screeningthepast.com/2017/12/escape-to-the-terraform-tropics-geography-and-gender-in-marine-adventure-films-from-queensland/).

Dolgopolov, G. 2016. "Balancing Acts: Ivan Sen's *Goldstone* and outback noir." *Metro* 190: 8–13.

Elliott, S. dir. 1994. *The Adventures of Priscilla Queen of the Desert,* Motion Picture, Polygram/Australian Film Finance Corporation/Latent Image Production, Australia.

Erckenbrecht, C., Fuary, M., Greer, S., Henry, R., McGregor, R., and Wood, M. 2010. "Artefacts and Collectors in the Tropics of North Queensland." *Australian Journal of Anthropology* 21(3): 350–366.

Gaunson, S. 2010. "Bushranger." Pp. 88–92 in *Directory of World Cinema: Australia and New Zealand,* edited by Goldsmith, B., and Lealand, G. Bristol, UK: Intellect.

Gibson, C., Luckman, S., and Willoughby-Smith, J. 2012. "Creativity Without Borders? Rethinking Remoteness and Proximity." Pp. 25–38 in *Creativity in Peripheral Places: Redefining the Creative Industries,* edited by Gibson, C. London and New York: Routledge.

Gibson, R. 1994. "Formative Landscapes." Pp. 45–60 in *Australian Cinema,* edited by Murray, S. St Leonards, NSW: Allen & Unwin.

Gibson, R. 2015. "Orientation: Remote, Intimate, Lovely." Pp. 7–15 in *By-roads and Hidden Treasures: Mapping Cultural Assets in Regional Australia,* edited by Ashton, P., Gibson, C., and Gibson, R. Crawley, Western Australia: University of Western Australia Publishing.

Goldsmith, B., Ward, S., and O'Regan, T. 2010. *Local Hollywood: Global Film Production and the Gold Coast.* St Lucia, Queensland: University of Queensland Press.

Grau, O., and Veigl, T. 2013. *Imagery in the 21st Century.* Cambridge, MA and London, UK: MIT Press.

Hillcoat, J. dir. 2005. *The Proposition.* Motion Picture, Surefire Films, London UK.

Koori Mail Pty Ltd. 2018. "New Online Map Shows Frontier Wars Massacres." Retrieved November 5, 2018 (http://koorimail.com/new-online-map-shows-massacres-from-frontier-wars/).

Kotcheff, T. dir. 1971. *Wake in Fright.* Motion picture, NLT Productions/Group W, Australia/USA/UK.

80   *Allison Craven*

Landman, J. 2006. *The Tread of a White Man's Foot: Australian Pacific Colonialism and the Cinema, 1925–1962*. Canberra, Australian Capital Territory: Pandanus Books.

Ledwidge, R. dir. 2006. *Gone*, Motion picture, Universal Pictures/Working Title Films/Australian Film Finance Corporation.

Limbrick, P. 2010. *Making Settler Cinema: Film and Colonial Encounters in the United States, Australia and New Zealand*. New York: Palgrave Macmillan.

Luckman, S. 2012. *Locating Cultural Work: The Politics and Poetics of Rural, Regional and Remote Creativity*. Basingstoke, UK: Palgrave Macmillan.

Luskri, C. 2013. "In conversation with Ivan Sen." Melbourne International Film Festival, in *Mystery Road*, dir. Sen.

MacIntyre, E. 2017. "Vision Splendid Outback Film Festival Arrives in Winton." June 19. Retrieved August 30, 2018 (www.northweststar.com.au/story/4738022/splendid-visions-for-film-lovers/).

Mayes, R. 2012. "Postcards from Somewhere: 'Marginal' Cultural Production, Creativity and Community." Pp. 11–23, in *Creativity in Peripheral Places: Redefining the Creative Industries*, edited by Gibson, C. Abingdon, UK and New York: Routledge.

Milson, J. dir. 1967/8, *Will the Great Barrier Reef Save Claude Clough?* Short Film, Australian Commonwealth Film Unit, Australia.

Molloy, B. 1990. "Screensland: The Construction of Queensland in Feature Films." Pp. 66–77 in *Queensland Images in Film and Television*, edited by Dawson, J., and Molloy, B. St Lucia, Queensland: University of Queensland Press.

Moran, A. 1989. "Constructing the Nation: Institutional Documentary Since 1945." Pp. 148–171 in *The Australian Screen*, edited by Moran, A., and O'Regan, T. Ringwood, Victoria: Penguin.

Moran, A. 2001. *Queensland Screen: An Introduction*. Brisbane: Queensland Griffith University.

Parris, M. 2018. "Newcastle Professor Lyndall Ryan's Massacre Map Plots More of Australia's Untold History." July 27. Retrieved November 5, 2018 (www.theherald.com.au/story/5548387/newcastle-professors-massacre-map-plots-more-of-australias-untold-history/).

Perkins, R. dir. 2014. *Black Panther Woman*. Documentary Film, Blackfella Films, Australia.

Perkins, R. dir. 2018. *Mystery Road*. Television Mini-series, Bunya Productions, Australia.

Pike, A. 2015. *Origination: The Geographies of Brands and Branding*. London, UK: Wiley.

Pocock, C. 2002. 'Sense Matters: Aesthetic Values of the Great Barrier Reef." *International Journal of Heritage Studies* 8(4): 365–381.

Powell, M. dir. 1969. *Age of Consent*. Motion picture, Nautilus Productions/Columbia Pictures.

Rendall, K. dir. 2018. *Guardians of the Tomb*. Motion picture, Nest Holdings/Sleeping Otters Productions, China/Australia/Russia/Thailand.

Riley, S., and Harper, D. 2017. "Aquaman Movie Given Permission to Film at Hastings Point, Despite Locals' Anger." *ABC News*. June 30. Retrieved December 10, 2017 (www.abc.net.au/news2017-06-30/aquaman-gets-green-light-but-mayor-in-tears/8668176).

Ryan, M. D. 2017. "Australian Blockbuster Movies." Pp. 51–76 in *Australian Screen in the 2000s*, edited by Ryan, M., and Goldsmith, B. Cham, Switzerland: Palgrave Macmillan.

Screen Australia. n.d. "Location and PDV Offsets; Other Australian Government Incentives for Screen Production." *Screen Australia*. Retrieved November 5, 2018 (www.screenaustralia.gov.au/funding-and-support/producer-offset/location-and-pdv-offsets).

Screen Australia. 2017. "Report Released–A Decade of the Producer Offset." *Media Release*. Retrieved November 5, 2018 (www.screenaustralia.gov.au/sa/media-centre/news/2017/11-15-a-decade-of-the-producer-offset-report).

Sen, I. dir. 2013. *Mystery Road*. Motion picture, Bunya Productions/Screen Australia/Mystery Road Films, Australia.

Sen, I. dir. 2016. *Goldstone*. Motion picture, Bunya Productions/Dark Matter, Australia.

Speed, L. 2017. "Fishing the Waters of Life: Zane Grey's White Death, Exploitation Film and the Great Barrier Reef." *Studies in Australasian Cinema* 11(1): 5–17 (doi 10.1080/17503175.2017.1308906).

Stevens, K., Dolgopolov, G., and Harris, L. C. 2016. "Distribution and Film Festivals: Editorial Introduction." *Studies in Australasian Cinema* 10(1): 97–99 (doi:10.1080/17503175.2016.1141921).

Stevens, K., Harris, L. C., and Dolgopolov, G. 2015. "Special Section: Inside Looking Out – Film Festival Reports." *Studies in Australasian Cinema* 9(2): 187–189 (doi:10.1080/17503175.2015.1058645).

Van Hemert, T., and Ellison, E. 2015. "Queensland's Film Culture: The Challenges of Local Film Distribution and Festival Exhibition." *Studies in Australasian Cinema* 9(1): 39–51 (doi:10.1080/17503175.2014.1002269).

Vogt-Roberts, J. dir. 2017. *Kong: Skull Island*. Motion Picture, Warner Bros/Legendary Entertainment/Tencent Pictures, USA/China.

Wan, J. dir. 2018. *Aquaman*. Motion Picture, DC Comics/DC Entertainment/Panoramic Pictures, Australia.

4 Landscape as tension

The Blue Mountains and cultural economies of place

Eduardo de la Fuente

Introduction

In this essay, I suggest that what John Wylie (2007: 1) terms *landscape-as-tension* – a tension "between proximity and distance, body and mind, sensuous immersion and detached observation" – occurs at the both the *practical* and *theoretical* levels, and that cultural and economic practices surrounding landscape also mirror the distinction recent theorists have made between the "representational" and the "nonrepresentational" (Waterton 2013). I develop my argument through a case study in landscape and place-based cultural economies. I consider the Blue Mountains, a region where the landscape looms large in constructions of regional identity, cultural value and community aspirations. My contention will be that the representational and nonrepresentational shape not only the kinds of practices and systems of valuation that are generated with respect to landscape but also the kinds of limitations and contradictions that human–nature relations entail. Novelist and local resident Delia Falconer (2016: np) has written of the most visited tourist attraction in the Blue Mountains, a site which epitomises the landscape in the representational register, that the lookout at Echo Point, Katoomba, revolves around a central "tension between the beautiful and the *kitsch*". The lookout, gazing out over the majestic scenery and pristine wilderness, sits oddly with the tourist coaches dropping tourists off at the location and the various "trinkets" for sale at the nearby Visitor Information Centre. But, if the representational economy is based on viewing platforms, "picture-postcard" images of landscape and a tension between the beautiful and the aesthetics of "mass tourism", then, in the case of the nonrepresentational, the tension is between the kinds of unique experiences promised and the types of capital (economic, cultural, spiritual and even physical) required to access such cultural and experiential goods. The presence of such tensions – indeed, for Wylie (2007: 7), the "tensions which animate landscapes have proved enduringly creative and productive" – makes the Blue Mountains region not only a rich case study; arguably, it also leaves the door ajar for the development of new and innovative responses to landscape and place. The chapter ends by examining community and grassroots innovations that are responding to the dualities of nature and culture (Macnaghten and Urry 1998), "exotic" and "native" (Jones and Cloke 2002), landscape and place (Williams 1960; Cresswell 2015), in novel ways and which are helping to redefine the *ecologies of belonging* available to both residents of and visitors to the Blue Mountains.

Case study: the Blue Mountains as valued/valuable landscape

The value of the Blue Mountains landscape has not always been about economic imperatives. The Blue Mountains are considered by some as the birthplace of nature conservation in Australia (Mosley 1999), and much of the Greater Blue Mountains Area is protected from economic exploitation in that it consists of "eight national parks or reserves which combine to form more than one million contiguous hectares of protected land" (Thomas 2004: 27). Interestingly, the landscape was initially considered to hold very little "value". As noted by a book about the geology, poetics and cultural history of the "sandstone country" surrounding the Sydney basin, entitled *Wasteland, Wilderness, Wonderland*, Gregory Blaxland, William Lawson and William Charles Wentworth may be famous for showing the "seemingly impassable Blue Mountains" could be crossed, but their initial reaction was to see the Blue Mountains "as a barren no-man's land" or wasteland due to the "texture of rugged and labyrinth sandstone landscapes" (Jones 2013: 11). Interestingly, the response of early explorers to the Blue Mountains echoed the same visceral reactions by North American explorers to the Grand Canyon. One participant, during an expedition to the Grand Canyon in 1858, wrote: "The plateau is cut into shreds by these gigantic chasms and resembles a vast ruin. . . . The region . . . is of course, altogether valueless" (cited in Nye 2003: 75).

Another of the aesthetic–cum–geological obstacles to Europeans valuing the Blue Mountains landscape came in the shape of terminology. "Geologically, the escarpment is a series of sandstone plateaus", and, when one is standing at the cliff edge, one can see that "[t]hese valleys, gorges, are the opposite to mountains. . . . Instead of gazing or climbing skyward, the path goes down" (Thomas 2004: 32, 37). Adam Ford (2017: 47) makes the point that, for the "European hiker", the Blue Mountains provide the "odd experience . . . of starting at the top and walking down into the valleys then back up to the top at the end of day". He adds in parentheses that such an experience seems to confirm "the childhood prejudice" of northern hemisphere inhabitants, that in the Antipodes, "everything . . . is upside down" (Ford 2017: 47). Landscape expectations are deeply embedded, and, of all landscape forms, mountains are one of the most mythologised and archetyped. The mountain landscape is often judged "for its grandeur, beauty and conformity to the idealized Alpine horn" (Urry 1990: 45). I remember my own high school geography teacher repeatedly asserting that Australia didn't really have mountains and that the Blue Mountains were a case in point. Technically, of course, the naysayers are correct. Thomas Griffith Taylor, a pioneer of Australian geography, referred to the range as the "Blue Plateau" and the "Blue Mountains Plateau" (Tredinnick 2009: 269). Plateau not

84 *Eduardo de la Fuente*

only has different "value" connotations to mountains; it arguably also shifts the emphasis from visuality to the implied "affordances" of landscape.

The shift from "wasteland" to "wilderness", and the fact the Blue Mountains were able to cement their place in the popular imagination as "mountains", occurred during the middle decades of the nineteenth century. Thus began the "long history of [the Blue Mountains] been promoted . . . based on sightseeing and other landscape qualities" (Porter 2016: 20). In *The Pursuit of Wonder*, Julia Horne (2005: 110) notes that the Blue Mountains were "one of the first places for extensive commercial tourist development" within the Australian colonies, including hotels, resorts and other types of guest accommodation; by the 1880s, Blue Mountains tourism was no longer "only for the upper classes in search of something novel and interesting, but a leisure activity for anyone who wanted to and could afford to retreat from the everyday" (ibid).

The value of the landscape became synonymous with either the aesthetic-spiritual uplift it could provide or the types of pleasures/sensory recalibrations it was able to afford. Burke (1988: 99) recounts how each generation of tourists has "brought their specific social beliefs, aspirations and self-images to the Blue Mountains". She continues:

> To a refined gentleman of the 1870s the Blue Mountains spoke of a majestic landscape wherein contemplation of nature uplifted the soul. Staying at the house of his dear friend, the Chief Justice, out gentleman would discourse on the botany and geology of the area after the servants had cleared the dinner away. . . . In the 1930s the Mountains were smart and upbeat. It was unnecessary for motorists to exert themselves with walking at all: great views could be seen from projecting lookouts and the sights were floodlit at night for those whose days were taken up playing golf.
>
> (Burke 1988: 99)

Horne (2005: 4) suggests the period which saw the development of the Blue Mountains as a recreational and leisure landscape entailed a "complex relationship between people, culture and nature". The relationship was complex because it involved the simultaneous deployment of discourses and practices from fields as diverse as botany and aesthetics, hospitality and sanitoriums. While "initially restricted to middle- and upper-class explorers and tourists", in the long run the fascination and engagement with the natural landscape had "far-reaching social and cultural effects" for "mass tourism", the local "tourist industry" and people's "enduring interest in the natural environment" (Horne 2005: 110). She documents how places such as the Blue Mountains, the Dandenongs, Mount Macedon and the Mount Lofty Ranges came to be valued not just for their spectacular vistas but also for the atmospheric and transformative qualities provided by ferns and gullies, waterfalls and creeks, altitude and cooler climates. These characteristics of mountainous or higher landscapes came to be seen as "intrinsically valuable for a society's emotional health" and as providing important "non-human forces" that could "spur fruitful contemplation and the pursuit of knowledge" (Horne 2005: 4). Arguably, the emphasis on "higher landscapes" and "non-human forces" is still with us and continues to shape both the practices and types of value bestowed upon the Blue Mountains landscape.

While, in the case of the Blue Mountains, the sources of landscape value have been varied, one process cemented its "universal" cultural and aesthetic standing. In keeping with other significant landscapes around the globe, such as Tuscany (Gaggio 2011) and the Lake District (Scott 2010), the Greater Blue Mountains area acquired UNESCO World Heritage listing in 2000. The nomination was initiated by New South Wales National Parks and Wildlife Service. together with Environment Australia and local Blue Mountains stakeholders, based on the "outstanding universal significance of eucalypt-dominated vegetation, of which it represents the best single example" (cited in Thomas 2004: 27). Human and cultural dimensions also played their part. The nomination emphasised the thousands of years that Aboriginal groups had both occupied and managed the landscape, as well as the "symbiotic" relationship that had developed between the Greater Blue Mountains and the (now) global "City of Sydney" since the early nineteenth century. With respect to the latter, the nomination asserted that the "Greater Blue Mountains exemplify the links between wild places and human aspirations" (cited in Thomas 2004: 27). As Kowalski (2011: 87) proposes, attaining such a UNESCO World Heritage listing bestows upon a landscape a "cultural wealth" or "objective capital" that, because it is in "accordance with the convention's procedures" and marshalling of expertise, ensures a landscape's "cultural capitalisation" as well as long-term "economic value" (i.e. tourism, experiential and cultural goods connected with the landscape). In short, the listing, and its notion of "universal value", add the imprimatur of supra-national governance to other measures of landscape value, thereby ensuring that landscape is less subject to variations in taste and other deflators of economic and cultural capital. In addition, the UNESCO listing of the Greater Blue Mountains Area has also been invoked in political campaigns regarding controversial planning developments that might directly impact the landscape in question (for example, the current campaign to stop the raising of the Warragamba Dam wall).

Any consideration of the value of the Blue Mountains landscape also needs to take on board the highly mediated and explicitly cultural nature of that landscape. In his award-winning book about how European-Australians have "imagined" the Blue Mountains, *The Artificial Horizon*, Martin Thomas (2004: 14) claims the "mountains have a double presence: semiotic and topographical"; in today's mediated consumer culture, "the possibility exists that the [Blue Mountains] can be felt, anywhere at any time, across the globe". Indeed, some have suggested that, due to its presence in everything from feature films to souvenirs, the "Blue Mountains epitomizes the mediated character of landscape" (Porter 2016: 1). And, the types of mediation that have shaped perceptions of the landscape have been varied:

> The Blue Mountains have been conceptualized and represented in many ways, from the Dreaming of the six Aboriginal language groups and their connections to country that are relived during walkabouts, the early

86 *Eduardo de la Fuente*

travel writings of colonial explorers, the media releases of today's brand strategists, the landscape photographs of professionals and the snapshots of day-trippers, the website advertisements of public authorities and private businesses, and the physical modifications of the land in the form of numerous lookouts, roads and gardens.

(Porter 2016: 1–2)

Attempts at controlling "messaging" about the Blue Mountains landscape have a long history. They predate what is now referred to as "place" or "destination" branding. But recent image-management has become more professionalised and systematic than its (sometimes "informal") predecessors. Today, consultants are regularly hired by local councils and tourism authorities to maximise "place marketing" strategies. As such, "[i]n 2004 the Blue Mountains became one of a growing list of places to be officially branded ... to capture and communicate the identity of the place, and, it was hoped, ensure its market appeal and economic prosperity" (Porter 2016: 76). The brand identity that resulted from the project in question (and which is still operational) placed landscape at the core of the Blue Mountains branding and produced the aforementioned tag line: "Elevate your senses" (cited in Porter 2016: 77). The elevation theme is also

Figure 4.1 BMCC front entrance and slogan.
Source: Author

present in Blue Mountains Cultural Centre (BMCC) branding, which features the following at the entrance to the building and in print advertising: "Just below the clouds is a place for artists and art lovers". In other words, branding by Blue Mountains organisations freely draws upon an "assemblage" (on brands as assemblages see Lury 2009) of people and things that includes landscape and emotion, art and place, architecture and clouds or human infrastructure and the "atmospheres" provided by mountainous altitude (see Figure 4.1).

The omnipresent tourist gaze: the Blue Mountains as visual landscape

The ubiquitous nature of landscape within the region in question, one that highlights Falconer's aforementioned tension between the beautiful and the *kitsch*, was brought home for me recently by an experience at a Blue Mountains petrol station lavatory. After acclimatising to my surroundings, I noticed that two of the walls had striking glossy photos of Blue Mountains panoramas: one of the Three Sisters from the Echo Point lookout and the other of the Scenic World Skyway cable car suspended over the Jamison Valley with the Three Sisters in the background (see Figure 4.2). While at first shocked that such an iconic and World Heritage–listed landscape might be encountered in this "profane" context, there was also a sense in which this odd juxtaposition of landscape "postcard" views and tourist "toilet" amenities spoke loudly about the iconography and "aura" surrounding the Blue Mountains landscape and also how locals were prepared to sell the place to others (i.e. to the kind of passerby who would be using the facility). The landscape as image, or as famous landmarks seen from popular vantagepoints, is what the Blue Mountains has become for many visitors to the region. And, in the petrol station lavatory, I had some of the essential Blue Mountains vistas that any tourist might aim or want to see. But, as a consequence, the "real" Blue Mountains are partially, if not largely, erased.

Ross Brownscombe (1997: 8) comments on the irony that, in turning the Blue Mountains into an object of visual pleasure, tourist and other authorities have "relentlessly promoted a narrow strip" of land that follows the Great Western Highway, "convincing generations of people that once at the cliff edge at Govett's Leap or Echo Point, they are looking *from* the Blue Mountains into some other place". In other words, the visual gaze also involves a kind of shrinkage of what constitutes the Blue Mountains as landscape and unified object. For many visitors to the region, the Blue Mountains is now synonymous with the vistas afforded from the famous network of lookouts:

> [E]very lookout leads out on to another. The fenced vantagepoints within the mountains have names like Echo Point, Sublime Point, Inspiration Point, Princes Rock. You do look outwards – but also downwards. The sandstone cliffs cut a crooked amphitheater; below a sea of trees.
>
> (Thomas 2004: 37)

Figure 4.2 Landscape image on wall of men's toilet at service station on the Great Western Highway in the Blue Mountains.

Source: Author

The reduction of the Blue Mountains to a set of visual panoramas to be enjoyed from a network of lookouts that emphasise visuality, has been a long time in the making and parallels developments in other parts of the world. As Sue Luckman (2012: 18; 18–19) states with respect to the emergence of the Lake District as a site of tourism, "human intervention was required in eighteenth-century Britain to 'educate' people about the specifics of how to properly 'appreciate' the qualities of 'nature'"; and it was artists, poets and others associated with the Romantic movement who "undertook the work of teaching others how to 'appreciate', that is look at nature as, the picturesque". The same occurred with respect to the Blue Mountains. As mentioned earlier, even after the first successful crossing of the Great Diving Range by European explorers, the sandstone escarpments and thick forests of eucalypts were considered something of

Landscape as tension 89

a wasteland. But, as Burke (1988: 102) suggests, the next fifty years after the famous crossing coincided with the dominance of the "cult of the Sublime and the Beautiful" – which together with the aforementioned "Picturesque" – led to a reassessment of nature's aesthetic and psychological powers. What had been seen as "too rugged" and "inhospitable" became "revered as a vast panorama of awesome cliffs and chasmic valleys" (Burke 1988: 102). And, as had been the case in the northern hemisphere, visual artists and other creative professionals played an important agential and discursive role. Paintings such as Eugene von Guerard's *Weatherboard Creek Falls* (the original name for "Wentworth Falls") of 1862, which depicts the grand panorama observable from the cliff edge where the water descends into the Jamison Valley, a scene also described in naturalist Charles Darwin's travel diaries, was the kind of colonial-era landscape painting that helped to shift attitudes and perceptions towards the Blue Mountains and the Australian landscape more generally. But it wasn't only so-called "highbrow" or "fine" artists who helped to shift the landscape visual gaze. Burke (1988: 100) explores the history of the Blue Mountains visual gaze via "historical records, publications and photographs" from such organisations as the railways, tourist bureaus and municipal councils, as well as entrepreneurs who operated "photographic studios, souvenir vendors and hotel interests".

The presence of such visual culture artefacts attests to the fact the Blue Mountains could be said to be the first place in Australia where what John Urry (1990) terms the "tourist gaze" was imposed upon the local landscape. The concept of the tourist gaze is explicitly visual, and its author sees such a gaze as operating in conjunction with broader cultural and creative goods and services. Urry (1990: 3) writes that the tourist gaze is "directed at features of landscape . . . [that] are taken to be in some sense out of the ordinary". He adds that the "viewing of such tourist sights often involves a much greater sensitivity to visual elements" and that, through media such as "photographs, postcards, films, models and so on", the tourist visual gaze can be "endlessly reproduced and recaptured".

Urry offers an ideal-typical distinction of relevance to discussions of Blue Mountains landscapes and the kinds of cultural infrastructures, goods and services that developed (or fail to develop) in connection with tourism. He suggests that consumption of landscape and its visual elements tends towards either what we might call the "Solitary-Romantic and the Collective-Mass" tourist gazes (Urry 1990: 45). Much of Urry's discussion of this typological distinction is framed around mountainscapes and the modalities of engagement they mobilise. Thus, mountains provide the best example of the Solitary-Romantic modality of the tourist gaze whenever the "emphasis is on solitude, privacy and a personal, semi-spiritual relationship with the object of that gaze" (Urry 1990: 45). This echoes a point made by Roland Barthes (1972: 74) in *Mythologies* when he claims that, in Western culture, "mountains, gorges, defiles and torrents" are the landforms that are seen as best "encourage[ing] morality of effort and solitude". The "alternative" is the "collective tourist gaze", which revolves around things like observation platforms and lookouts which "would

90 *Eduardo de la Fuente*

look strange if they were empty. It is other people that make such places" (Urry 1990: 45).

There is an uncanny parallel between Urry's typological distinction between the Solitary-Romantic and Collective-Mass forms of the tourist gaze and the history of Blue Mountains tourism and which aspects of landscape have been privileged or most valued. We might suggest that, in the era when the Solitary-Romantic tourist gaze dominated, landscape sites such as Govett's Leap and Wentworth Falls were dominant. The vistas from such vantage points complied with the dominant landscape ideology "that Nature taught Mankind and that the greatness of mountains served to impress with the sense of man's own little-ness" (Burke 1988: 102). In addition to been depicted by prominent landscape artists, in the nineteenth century these "Mountain sights" also "received the most consistent representation in published works, such as the *Railway Guides*" (Burke 1988: 102). There were also attempts, for example, to promote certain parts of the Blue Mountains landscape, such as Grose Valley panoramas, as "Australia's Yosemite", a project conceived by a wealthy art patron who funded artistic expeditions to the Blue Mountains and then displayed the results at some of the International Exhibitions of the era (Snowden 1988: 133).

The swing to the Collective-Mass mode of Blue Mountains landscape con-sumption began in the late nineteenth century with the building of viewing platforms but then greatly accelerated with the arrival of the motor car, flood lighting of mountain features at night time and the arrival of mass photogra-phy with "smaller, lighter cameras and then roll film" (Snowden 1988: 146). It is with the shift to congregated viewing of the landscape at lookouts that the Three Sisters and Echo Point start to dominate the visual and cultural iconog-raphy of the Blue Mountains. To cite again from Falconer:

> Echo Point, high above the Jamison Valley . . . on the southern edge of Katoomba . . . is the most popular scenic lookout in the Blue Moun-tains. . . . Viewed from a height of almost a kilometer above sea level, the undulant blue-green contours of the valley floor resemble a sea or gentle labyrinth; the huge valley often filling with spectacular formations of mist and cloud. . . . Echo Point is most famous for the iconic Three Sisters . . . rock formation, to the immediate east of the viewing platforms.
>
> (Falconer 2016: np)

The author adds of the Echo Point viewing platform, which can now accom-modate several hundred people across various tiers: "It is an uncanny site which for almost a century has combined a 'holiday playground' atmosphere with the sublime" (Falconer 2016: np). But "sublime" and "holiday playground" atmos-pheres are complex and, at times, opposed material and affective constructs. In the case of Echo Point's competing cultural logics, they proved difficult to bal-ance in the long term and also vulnerable to the dictates of fashion (e.g. Blue Mountains tourism declined and the region's cultural identity suffered as beach culture became more popular). Indeed, as we shall see, the cultural economy of landscape-as-representation eventually gave way to economic and aesthetic decline – especially, in the case of Katoomba.

From "Jewel in the Crown" to "Tawdry Theme Park" and beyond: landscape as backdrop to Katoomba's changing fortunes

From the late nineteenth century through to the mid-twentieth century, Falconer's aforementioned formula of landscape "sublime" plus "holiday playground atmosphere" made the Blue Mountains a prime destination for Sydneysiders "in search of something novel and interesting" (Horne 2005: 110). The success wrought by the imposition of the tourist gaze to the region generated hospitality infrastructures and the provision of mass-transport services to "the mountains". As Urry (1990: 3) notes, the tourist gaze thrives by working in conjunction with the material, technological and logistical "relationships [that] arise from a movement of people to, and their stay in, various destinations". These infrastructures and logistical frameworks, in turn, develop their own cultural and affective rationales (for example, they become associated with certain individual or collective rituals). Thus, by the 1930s, Katoomba and its network of guesthouses and hotels had become the major honeymoon destination in New South Wales (Burke 1988: 115), and Katoomba became a "tourist town" as famous for its grand resorts, cafes and bars, picture theatres, dance halls and golf course as for its access to pristine wilderness and its panoramic scenery. Indeed, it might be difficult to fathom, given the international coverage now given to Sydney's annual New Year's celebration, that during the 1920s and 1930s, Katoomba was the place to "see in" the arrival of the new calendar year. A 2019 article in the local newspaper, *The Blue Mountains Gazette*, entreats contemporary readers to the festive atmospheres associated with the "Golden Years" of Blue Mountains tourism and urban celebrations:

> In the 1920s, guesthouses spearheaded Katoomba's New Year's Eve celebrations. Their merriment overflowed [o]nto the streets where thousands of day visitors partied. Katoomba Street closed at 8pm . . . allowing those 'dressed in fancy costume, Sheiks, cowboys, princesses, Turks and others to mingle in kaleidoscopic array' . . . Throughout the Depression, Katoomba still celebrated the arrival of the new year with 'merry madness'. . . . Special trains from Sydney carried thousands of revellers. Celebrations focused on the procession. Guesthouses and business and community organisations created floats. Individuals dressed up. In 1935, a . . . description of the parade and the countdown to midnight were relayed to 2CH in Sydney by 2KA, Katoomba, the first occasion a country station relayed a program to city listeners.
>
> (Ridge 2019: np)

But the long post-war boom was not kind to the cultural and leisure economies that had developed around the Blue Mountains landscape. By the time of

92   *Eduardo de la Fuente*

mass car ownership and the adoption of suburban living, the Blue Mountains became a site of "recreation" and short visits. As Peter Spearritt (2000: 228) puts it in *Sydney's Century*, the type of economic and spatial modernity that had set in by the 1950s meant that, for suburban Sydneysiders: "Work life was usually associated with the city and inner suburbs, while recreation . . . was linked with the harbour, the ocean beaches, Botany Bay and the Blue Mountains". The latter became connected with leisure rituals such as the "day trip" either by private motor vehicle or in one of the many large coaches that one regularly sees parked near lookouts such as Echo Point. These developments were problematic for the local economy and for the symbolic landscape of Katoomba or its cultural-cum-leisure "status". By the 1960s and 1970s, "day trippers . . . had replaced long stay tourists", and the "arrival of supermarkets forced many old-style shop keepers out of business, to be replaced by coffee shops, galleries and souvenir shops" (Merriman 2008: np). What particularly impacted perceptions of Katoomba's decline is that many "old hotels and guest houses gradually lost patronage and many fell into disrepair" (Merriman 2008: np). Arguably, the impact of such decline was less palpable in villages such as Wentworth Falls, Leura and Mount Wilson, which managed, in the transition from a long-term to a day-trip tourist economy, to maintain some of the ambience of stately homes and impressive "cool climate gardens" (i.e. an aesthetic harking back to the Solitary-Romantic mode of landscape consumption).

However, despite the vestiges of architectural and landscaping heritage, it must be said that much of the Blue Mountains region has been impacted by "suburbanization" – a process involving brick veneer houses and streetscapes that would not look out of place in Sydney "middle class" areas such as the Hills District, and which, at times, replicates the urban aesthetics of Western and South Western Sydney due to the size of houses constructed and blocks. The loss of Blue Mountains "character" was remarked upon by a "landscape consultant" in a chapter for a 1976 publication commissioned by UNESCO about human-landscape relations in Australia. The author comments that "Katoomba-Leura in the Blue Mountains" was acquiring the "visual quality" of Australia's "sprawling dormitory . . . suburbs" (Mackenzie 1976: 306). The commentator in question suggests Australia's "ability to replace the highly distinctive with the barely distinguishable" was, in the case of Katoomba-Leura, all the more remarkable given that the suburban aesthetic was being imposed upon "a rugged plateau about 900 metres high overlooking deep canyons of great grandeur" (Mackenzie 1976: 306).

The juxtaposition of magnificent landscape and "low-brow" plus suburban aesthetic values becomes more pronounced towards the end of the twentieth century and the start of the twenty-first century. In the evocative landscape memoir, *The Blue Plateau*, one of Mark Tredinnick's (2009: 258) "real" historical characters, Les – whose biography spans much of the changes the Blue Mountains experienced throughout the twentieth century – is reported as having said "in his old age that Katoomba had become nothing but a tourist attraction . . . a tawdry theme park, perched in astonishing terrain". Towards the close of the last century, Katoomba, the jewel in the Blue Mountains tourism economy during the 1920s and 1930s, started to give the region a decidedly "liminal" feel. Writing in the 1990s, geographers Peter Murphy and Sophie Watson (1997) note the presence in "mountain towns, particularly Katoomba, [of] a growing number of poor single parents". They suggest a major type of demographic shift due to the Blue Mountains becoming the site of "the welfare migration of those who cannot afford to live in the city and find rentals or cheap houses to buy in the mountain towns" (Murphy and Watson 1997: 132).

However, Katoomba's image of "liminality" also created new opportunities. While, it undoubtedly involved a period of stagnation and associated "stigma" (North Katoomba, in particular, came to be seen as "Bogan central"), there were advantages to the area's relative economic backwardness. For one, it meant that the streetscape of Katoomba remained more untouched by developers than might otherwise been the case. For another, the cheap rents and inexpensive property prices also attracted creatives and knowledge workers – whom now live in the Blue Mountains in greater numbers than the state median (Stevenson et al. 2017). In recent times, there have also been important urban reactivation projects that have drawn on the tarnished "visual gaze" and emphasised Katoomba's "grungy" urban credentials, such as the award-winning "street art walk" (www.streetartmurals.com.au/street_art_walk/).

Another indicator that Katoomba may be experiencing early signs of a creativity-led recovery is the emergence of the twice-yearly crowdfunded publication *Blume Illustrated*. An illustrated magazine designed to open "a window into [the] region's unique and very contemporary creative culture", and to benefit "not only our local community and businesses, but also benefit our many colleagues, readers and visitors from all over the world" (Wilson 2019: 5), *Blume Illustrated* combines art and commerce, heritage with contemporaneity. As the magazine's title suggests, landscape and the region's flora play an important, if metaphoric, role. The magazine's editor, Faye Wilson (2019: 5), writes in one of her editorial columns, "Blume translates from the German as . . . flower. In English you can bloom to your potential". Within this creative project, locality and landscape are intimately connected: "Blume is nurtured by the rich cultural soil that is Katoomba" (Wilson 2019: 5). However, despite its celebration of contemporary creative and commercial local culture, what is interesting is that *Blume Illustrated* doesn't ignore or sidestep Katoomba's past. The visual iconography of *Blume Illustrated* and the creatives who contribute to it freely draw from the social and cultural history of the Blue Mountains (including its commercial and promotional visual and material culture). Men wearing Victorian or Edwardian suits that would not look out of place in advertising material circa 1900 are depicted shopping – hardly a "masculine" pursuit – above the tagline: "Keep Katoomba Odd". A similar self-conscious appropriation of past visual culture is also present in the design of goods for sale in the BMCC shop. Here, tea towels and posters depict escarpments and valleys, waterfalls and Blue Mountains flora and fauna, not as unmediated landscape, but rather as icons or symbols depicted in the tourism and marketing of yesteryear. Landscape and its objects re-appear as potent symbols of how much nature and culture/collective memory are entwined to remind us that landscape is as much a part of commodity culture as the more obvious objects of consumption (see Figure 4.3). The vintage quality of the image (as with the visual style of many of the images in *Blume Illustrated*) suggests a complex set of temporalities in which past and present, heritage and modernity, combine.

The point I am trying to make is that while the landscape-driven cultural economy of visuality resulted, in many cases, in *kitschification* and subsequent decline, the representational infrastructure of tourist images and patinated streetscape have, in the case of Katoomba, served to (a) foster new types of cultural production and experiences and (b) allow for the flourishing of an aesthetic that serves to unify and anchor local creative lifestyles, goods and experiences. As with other cases of urban renewal through the creative industries, this has (quite literally) come at a price: namely, gentrification and increases in property prices in places like Katoomba, which on occasion has outpaced house price increases in Sydney (Williams 2018). With its microbrewery, multiple galleries, cute workers cottages, "slow fashion" retail outlets and increasingly sophisticated café scene, "liminal" Katoomba is said to be morphing (according to the real estate discourse, at least) into the Blue Mountains equivalent of Sydney's "Inner West" (or, perhaps, the Inner West as it was 25 years ago).

Figure 4.3 Tea towels for sale in BMCC shop.
Source: Author

The "Nonrepresentational": the Blue Mountains as landscape to walk and immerse oneself

Wylie (2005: 242) notes that terms such as beautiful, picturesque and the sublime – which, as we earlier noted, underpinned the emergence of the visual tourist gaze and "taught" modern subjects how to see "nature" in a new light – are predicated on "a cleaving apart of subject and world". Walking, by contrast, involves being "[i]n the thick of it. . . . Limbs and lungs working hard in a haptic, step-by-step engagement with nature-matter. Landscape becoming foothold" (Wylie 2005: 239). To be in the "thick of it" seems like an apt description of walking in "the Mountains". It also involves a shift in cultural rhetoric and the performative repertoires surrounding nature-induced forms of subjectivity. Thus, Burke (1988: 108) makes the point that the building of "fences and stairways", and paths along valley floors, such as that between Leura and Katoomba known as the "Federal Pass", led to a new type of Blue Mountains imagery: namely, one involving "tiny figures . . . against a backdrop of sheer cliffs". For her, this new staging of the individual in nature signalled that the "sublime was losing its exclusive stronghold as the Mountains became a landscape for walking in" (Burke 1988: 48). Rather than the assertion of control implied by the detached visual gaze, descending from the sandstone cliffs down into the rainforests below is often described as being overwhelmed. This is how one contemporary walking enthusiast and author on its spiritual benefits, who emanates from the United Kingdom, describes his first walk in the Blue Mountains:

> [H]aving descended a steep staircase, I ventured only a short way out into the forest along a clearly marked track. A waterfall cascaded so far down the cliffs behind me that it turned into spray . . . ferns flourished. The forest wrapped itself around me, enveloping me. . . . When you walk in the forest you feel so overwhelmed that your head turns in everyday direction all the time . . . a complete, mixed panoramic view, of a rich organic world.
>
> (Ford 2017: 48–49)

The author's experience of a multi-perspectival and multi-sensorial world, where one experiences sound and vision, rocks, trees, sky, ground, up and down, more or less simultaneously, reminded him of paintings he had recently seen: Australian landscape painter William Robinson's *Creation* series from the early 1990s. He suggests "Robinson's cleverness" in the *Creation* works is that he "had painted the holistic *experience of walking* in the forest and not just the scene" (Ford 2017: 49).

Through an interesting piece of intellectual and cultural serendipity, William Robinson's art has played a role in the "place branding" of the Blue Mountains. The Brand Blue Mountains Manual, produced in 2004, explicitly references Robinson's "distinctive 'multi viewpoint' style", which attempts to draw the viewer in as "an active participant". The Manual also waxes lyrical about the benefits of adopting a "dynamic perspective" and of imagery that depicts "people actively engaging with the environment . . . in extreme

96 *Eduardo de la Fuente*

perspective, characterized by acute angles, subjects viewed from above, below or contrapuntally" (Porter 2013: 243). In echoing Robinson's aesthetic, the Brand Blue Mountains Manual could be said to be engaging in a practical – as against purely theoretical – demonstration of the benefits of an immersive approach to landscape in branding and logo design. Porter (2013: 243) writes of the aesthetic that informed the Brand Blue Mountains logo design: "Unlike panoramic detached views, [Robinson's] work evokes the sensory qualities of immersive landscape experience . . . the relative certainty of the picturesque is abandoned for the distortions of the less familiar and disorientating point of view." In this respect, the Brand Blue Mountains visual aesthetics could be said to be replicating an important dimension of non-representational geography/landscape theory's aims with respect to dwelling in landscape: namely, that rather than "fusion" of self and world, landscape practices and processes can produce instances of defamiliarization and force one to experience "with", rather than gaze "at", the world (Wylie 2009).

Brewing the landscape: walking in the forest and making beer

Early on in the research for this chapter, I came across a story in the local paper, *The Blue Mountains Gazette*, about a young couple, Harriet and DJ McCready, who had plans to set up a "craft brew pub" in Katoomba. Given the exponential growth rate of microbreweries in Australia and elsewhere, and also the "hipster" connotations of this kind of creative entrepreneurship, the fact that the Blue Mountains would acquire another craft brewery was interesting without necessarily being earth-shattering. But what caught my eye was the following: "DJ McCready wants to give the true flavour of the Blue Mountains to some of his brews so he plans to collect yeast from canyon floors, from wild flora and from pristine wilderness areas" (Curtin 2018: 6). McCready "reassured the *Gazette* that collecting yeast is not invasive" and that his "wild or 'sour' beers . . . will really allow the consumer to 'taste' the Mountains" (Curtin 2018: 6).

The main economic development body for the region, Blue Mountains Economic Enterprise (BMEE), has also identified "specialist beverage businesses" as an emergent strength and is attempting to organise "[b]eer brewers, kombucha fermenters, cider makers, coffee roasters, wine makers and specialist syrup makers" with respect to opportunities for growth and tapping into the visitor economy (Fehon 2019: 25). BMEE's CEO writes in an opinion piece on the subject that a "well-crafted, uniquely local beverage will make a visit" to the Blue Mountains "even more memorable". But what makes a drink "uniquely local"? The fact it is made by people who reside in the Mountains? The use of ingredients either grown or foraged there? Or do products evince a greater degree of Blue Mountain-ness if they are consumed in Blue Mountains settings (i.e. while gazing out at a Jamison Valley vista)? Or perhaps what links gastronomic or beverage production to place is some unspoken "Blue Mountains" style or sensibility amongst microbrewers, coffee roasters, gastronomes or creatives in general? In the case of Harriet and DJ McCready and the "wild beers" they hope to brew in Katoomba, the newspaper article in question mentions the following connections between product and place: "the couple marry and begin to spend a lot of time in the Mountains, visiting Harriet's mum in Leura"; they "kept coming back and kept falling in love with the area more and more"; during their visits they engage in "bushwalking and rockclimbing . . . [as] well as looking for somewhere to set up their brewpub"; and they successfully apply for "$100,000 from the state government 'heritage near me' grants" to restore a building on Parkes St that once housed the newspaper, *The Blue Mountains Echo*, and more recently Civic Video (Curtin 2018: 6). But, as mentioned earlier, the key ingredient will be the yeast, which the brewer says "is responsible for 80% of flavour" in wild or sour beers and which he plans to collect from the canyon floors (Curtin 2018: 6).

Will the harvesting technique have the desired effect on drinkers and potential consumers? Will they also experience the "authentic" taste of "the Mountains"? The range of economic goods that lay some claim to possessing place qualities are long and intriguing. They include, for example, a local Katoomba butcher named "Mountain Fresh Meats" whose reference to mountain beef is only likely to be "linguistic" at best, although wild cattle can be found in various part of the Blue Mountains National Park and an artisan grazier/beef producer operates from the Megalong Valley. The latter, however, are unlikely to be experienced unless one undertakes a "food tourism" tour or dines at the right restaurant. There is a lot that needs to happen culturally, technologically and even geologically (as in the concept of *terroir*) for food or drink products to embody what Amy Trubek (2008) has termed the "taste of place". Thus, there is no guarantee that the McCreadys will achieve their desired sense of "localness" for their craft beers. We will not know until the beer has been brewed, drunk, paired or not paired with other activities (such as socialising, eating, being the subject-object of beer tastings, being featured in tourism marketing campaigns etc.). What we do know, however, is that one craft beer entrepreneur will be walking into the forest and immersing himself within the sensorium that the landscape offers in order to harvest "wild yeasts" – what this particular artisan thinks will be the key ingredient in the alchemical process of brewing beer. That a substance created on the canyon floor will play a crucial role in the product speaks volume about the role of landscape as "material" and "imaginary" fact in the context of the Blue Mountains.

Foraging and *ecologies of belonging*: beyond the "Economics of Singularity"?

A useful way to think about taste and place is in terms of what Callon, Meadel and Rabeharisoa (2005) label the "economics of qualities" and Karpik (2010) terms the "economics of singularities" – that is, goods that are valued for their purported unique qualities, where uniqueness often involves acts of translating or smoothing out otherwise "incommensurable" qualities. Karpik's (2010)

98   *Eduardo de la Fuente*

study of "singularities" identifies seven different types of value-regimes prevalent in the judgment/legitimation of seemingly singular goods: the authenticity regime, the mega regime, the expert opinion regime, the common opinion regime, the reticular regime, the professional regime and the inter-firm regime. While various of these regimes might be at play in the case of craft or microbrewing (for example, increasingly craft beer approximates wine in that expert opinion is starting to play a bigger role in shaping judgment), I would contend that the "authenticity regime" is predominant. And, in the case of the McCreadys, and their wild beer project, the emphasis is on the socio-technical and performative rituals which will produce said authenticity: namely, the act of foraging in Blue Mountains forests.

Foraging is currently going through something of a renaissance as a way of sourcing food and ingredients. What is interesting about the politics and ethos of foraging is that it tends to put the emphasis on re-valuing the under-valued or what is currently deemed unproductive: as in harvesting what are otherwise considered "weeds" or, in the case of the forests of the Greater Blue Mountains Area, harvesting a bio-organic material such as yeast in a non-evasive way. Melissa Poe et al. (2014: 901) speak of the synergistic relationship that foraging establishes between dwelling and place as an act that highlights "relational ecologies of belonging". They define the latter as:

> [The] interactive and networked aspects of the ways that relationships between people, place, and more-than-human nature are formed, legitimated, and mobilized in discursive and material ways. Tending to the flows of material life, not as fixed or finished products, but as processes of becoming.
>
> (Poe et al. 2014: 905)

Foraging, then, can be conceived as a way of constructing home and giving shape to various types of ecologies of belonging (e.g. how one sustains a living, lives a good life etc.). Interestingly, Tredinnick (2009: 259) – who draws direct homologies between the Blue Mountains landscape and creativity and sees a certain porousness between people and place – also emphasises belonging as an ensemble of practical activities when he writes: "Home is a word – sometimes it is a whole sentence – for the ecology of belonging".

However, ecologies of belonging can be either exclusionary or inclusionary if we don't watch out. Thus, the "economics of singularity" and the types of value it relies on (e.g. hipster "craft brewers", foraging for yeast in World Heritage-listed forests) can be either a powerful tool for promoting local identity (Schnell and Reese 2003; Flack 1997) or it can contribute to the kind of post-industrial gentrification that we earlier noted places like Katoomba have started to experience and which some analysts of both the creative industries and the craft beer industry have identified as unintended consequences of the rapid growth of such industries (Peck 2005; Matthews and Picton 2014).

Yet this qualification needs another qualification: namely, the Blue Mountains have also spawned creative, experiential and cultural ecologies that seem to fly in the face of the regularly reported post-industrial dysfunctions. Alongside the economics of singularity have arisen more communal and collectivist solutions. Thus, for example, it is interesting that the Blue Mountains Economic Enterprise MTNS MADE Creative Industry Cluster includes within its purview organisations such as The Blue Mountains Food Co-Op. Listed under the category of "Artisan Food" on the MTNS MADE website, the latter has existed since 1981 as a "member-based organisation committed to providing the local community with fresh food that doesn't cost the earth" (see: https://mtns made.com.au/listing-category/blue-mountains-artisan-foods/). There have been other attempts to move even further beyond a creative economy defined by existing measures of economic and/or exchange value. The Blue Mountains City Council now co-sponsors with Scenic World and Bendigo Bank an annual Blue Mountains Edible Garden Trail, which, although it does feature small-scale producers who supply local farmers markets and/or restaurants, is on the whole dominated by "backyard growers" who grow food either for themselves or for their immediate community and by community and school gardens which are based on a collective ethos.

The Edible Garden Trail has a pedagogic function to the extent the featured "[h]ome gardeners . . . share their secrets on how they are composting, mulching, companion planting, worm farming and enjoying their own fresh food" (Tabone 2019: np). It also involves the redefinition of local landscape aesthetics by recognising that the Blue Mountains landscape is not only a hybrid of natives and exotics but also a combination of the "productive" and the "ornamental", as well as everything in between. The nonrepresentational landscape can engender its own types of creativity, and, as evidenced in the contrast between craft brewing and something like the "collective intelligence" of the Edible Garden Trail, creativities can be more or less inclusive, more or less communal (on Australian leisure preferences, including bushwalking and gardening, in relationship to class, gender and age see Bennett, Frow and Emmison 1999).

Conclusion

My analysis has suggested the Blue Mountains landscape is undoubtedly a construct, one that has evolved over time and through various material and cultural frameworks. However, echoing the representational-nonrepresentational theoretical debate in fields such as geography and landscape studies, we might suggest that these constructs have varied greatly in how they mobilise the practical or embodied dimensions of landscape experience. Looking upon deep gorges or extended valleys from cliff-edge platforms up high is very different to immersing oneself on the forest floor while walking or canyoning. Furthermore, my argument has been that there are cultural or creative economy equivalents to the representational and nonrepresentational. Just as there are

100 *Eduardo de la Fuente*

those creatives who depict and evoke the landscape through media such as photography, painting and the moving image, there are those who seek to tap into the Blue Mountain-ness of taste through foraging, and others who are attempting to build a new landscape by curating community events such as the annual Edible Garden Trail. Underlying these different activities are not just competing landscape frameworks but also competing notions of the "good work" to which landscape can be put (on creative work as "good work" see Luckman 2012).

References

Barthes, R. 1972. *Mythologies*. London: Jonathan Cape.

Bennett, T., Frow, J., and Emmison, M. 1999. *Accounting for Tastes*. Cambridge: Cambridge University Press.

Brownscombe, R. 1997. *Blue Rivers*. Kingsdene, NSW: Forever Wild Press.

Burke, A. 1988. "Awesome Cliffs, Fairy Dells and Lovers Silhouetted in the Sunset: A Recreational History of the Blue Mountains." Pp. 99–117 in *The Blue Mountains*, edited by Stanbury, P. Leura: Second Back Row Press and Macleay Museum, Sydney University.

Callon, M., Meadel, C., and Rabeharisoa, V. 2005. "The Economy of Qualities." Pp. 58–79 in *The Cultural Economy Reader*, edited by Amin, A., and Thrift, N. Oxford: Blackwell.

Cresswell, T. 2015. *Place* (2nd ed.). Oxford: Wiley Blackwell.

Curtin, J. 2018. "Beer Plan for Old Newspaper Office." *Blue Mountains Gazette,* Wednesday August 22, p. 6.

Falconer, D. 2016. "Echo Point." *The Dictionary of Sydney*. Retrieved April 23, 2019 (https://dictionaryofsydney.org/entry/echo_point).

Fehon, B. 2019. "Craft Beverage Cluster Here." *Blue Mountains Gazette* Wednesday April 17, p. 25.

Flack, W. 1997. "American Microbreweries and Neolocalism: 'Ale-ing' for a Sense of Place." *Journal of Cultural Geography* 16(2): 37–53.

Ford, A. 2017. *The Art of Mindful Walking*. London: Leaping Hare Press.

Gaggio, D. 2011. "Selling Beauty: Tuscany's Rural Landscape Since 1945." Pp. 43–58 in *The Cultural Wealth of Nations*, edited by Bandelj, N., and Wherry, F. Stanford: Stanford University Press.

Horne, J. 2005. *The Pursuit of Wonder*. Melbourne: Miegunyah Press.

Jones, G. 2013. *Wasteland, Wilderness, Wonderland*. Lawson: Blue Mountains Education and Research Trust.

Jones, O., and Cloke, P. 2002. *Tree Cultures*. Oxford: Berg.

Karpik, L. 2010. *Valuing the Unique*. Princeton, NJ: Princeton University Press.

Kowalski, A. 2011. "When Cultural Capitalization Became Global Practice: The 1972 World Heritage Convention." Pp. 73–89 in *The Cultural Wealth of Nations*, edited by Bandelj, N., and Wherry, F. Stanford: Stanford University Press.

Luckman, S. 2012. *Locating Cultural Work: The Politics and Poetics of Rural, Remote and Regional Creativity*. London: Palgrave Macmillan.

Lury, C. 2009. "Brand as Assemblage." *Journal of Cultural Economy* 2(1–2): 67–82.

Mackenzie, B. 1976. "Design with People." Pp. 305–313 in *Man and Landscape in Australia*, edited by Seddon, G., and Davis, M. Canberra: Australian Government Publishing Service.

MacNaghten, P., and Urry, J. 1998. *Contested Natures*. London: Sage.

Mathews, V., and Picton, R. M. 2014. "Intoxifying Gentrification: Brew Pubs and the Geography of Post-Industrial Heritage." *Urban Geography* 35(3): 337–356.

Merriman, J. 2008. "Katoomba." *The Dictionary of Sydney*. Retrieved April 23, 2019 (https://dictionaryofsydney.org/entry/katoomba).

Mosley, J. G. 1999. *Battle for the Bush*. Sydney: Envirobook.

Murphy, P., and Watson, S. 1997. *Surface City – Sydney At the Millennium*. Sydney: Pluto Press of Australia.

Nye, D. E. 2003. "Visualizing Eternity: Photographic Constructions of the Grand Canyon." Pp. 74–95 in *Picturing Place*, edited by Schwartz, J. M., and Ryan, J. R. London: I. B. Tauris.

Peck, J. 2005. "Struggling with the Creative Class." *International Journal of Urban and Regional Research* 29(4): 740–770.

Poe, M. R., Le Compte, J., McLain, R., and Hurley, P. 2014. "Urban Foraging and the Relational Ecologies of Belonging." *Social and Cultural Geographies* 15(8): 901–919.

Porter, N. 2013. "'Single-Minded, Compelling and Unique': Visual Communications, Landscape and the Calculated Aesthetic of Place Branding." *Environmental Communication* 7(2): 231–254.

Porter, N. 2016. *Landscape and Branding*. London and New York: Routledge.

Ridge, R. 2019. "New Year's Eve Fun in Katoomba." *Blue Mountains Gazette*. January 11, 2019. Retrieved August 2, 2019 (www.bluemountainsgazette.com.au/story/5845354/new-years-eve-fun-in-katoomba/).

Schnell, S. M., and Reese, J. F. 2003. "Microbreweries as Tools of Local Identity." *Journal of Cultural Geography* 21(1): 45–69.

Scott, A. J. 2010. "The Cultural Economy of Landscape and Prospects of Peripheral Development in the Twenty-First Century: The Case of the English Lake District." *European Planning Studies* 18(10): 1568–1589.

Snowden, C. 1988. "The Take-Away Image: Photographing the Blue Mountains in the Nineteenth Century." Pp. 133–156 in *The Blue Mountains*, edited by Stanbury, P. Leura: Second Back Row Press and Macleay Museum, Sydney University.

Spearritt, P. 2000. *Sydney's Century*. Sydney: UNSW Press.

Stevenson, D., Rowe, D., Caust, J., and Cmielewski, C. 2017. *Recalibrating Culture: Production, Consumption, Policy*. Parramatta: WSU.

Tabone, J. 2019. "The Second Year of the Blue Mountains Edible Garden Trail." *Blue Mountains Gazette*. February 28, 2019. Retrieved May 25, 2019 (www.bluemountainsgazette.com.au/story/5916876/edible-garden-trail-grows/).

Thomas, M. 2004. *The Artificial Horizon*. Melbourne: University of Melbourne Press.

Tredinnick, M. 2009. *The Blue Plateau: A Landscape Memoir*. St Lucia, Queensland: University of Queensland Press.

Trubek, A. B. 2008. *Taste of Place*. Berkeley and Los Angeles: University of California Press.

Urry, J. 1990. *The Tourist Gaze*. London: Sage.

Waterton, E. 2013. "Landscape and Nonrepresentational Theories." Pp. 66–75 in *The Routledge Companion to Landscape Studies*, edited by Thompson, I., Howard, P., and Waterton, E. London and New York: Routledge.

Williams, R. 1960. *Border Country*. London: Chatto and Windus.

Williams, S. 2018. "Sydneysiders Flee to the Blue Mountains." *Domain*. April 13, 2018. Retrieved May 25, 2019 (www.domain.com.au/news/sydneysiders-flee-to-the-blue-mountains-the-region-with-a-median-price-of-680250–20180413-h0y9rb/).

Wilson, F. 2019. "About Blume/From the Editor." *Blume Illustrated* 3: 5.

Wylie, J. 2005. "A Single Day's Walking: Narrating Self and Landscape on the South West Coast Path." *Transactions of the Institute of British Geographers* 23: 435–454.

Wylie, J. 2007. *Landscape*. London and New York: Routledge.

Wylie, J. 2009. "Landscape, Absence and Geographies of Love." *Transactions of the Institute of British Geographers* 34(3): 275–289.

5 Deck-chair innovation

Innovation within arm's reach for regional Australian architecture: A little of what we found when we rode the Grand Section across Australia's girth in 2017

Bobbie Bayley and Owen Kelly
Inspired by and co-authored with John Roberts

Introduction

Useful innovation in design and construction of buildings for regional and remote Australia may only be possible if we move counter to the culture of *efficiency* (Williams and Tsien 1999). Deck-chair innovation offers an alternative: it involves slowing down to self-immerse in a place. For this chapter *place* is a wonderfully loose term we use to encapsulate the broadest understanding of *somewhere*. It is inclusive of climate, topography, ecologies and social and cultural backgrounds (Clare and Clare 2007). It is flexible in what it describes, from a particular campsite (Fig 5.3) to locations frequented by particular locals that influence their understanding and the embedded memories associated with those locations. Deck-chair innovation involves being stationary, reclining on a verandah observing with a critical eye, taking inspiration and understanding from what's within view, watching where dogs go in the heat of the day, looking at what happens to the ground during heavy rain or seeing where people gather. Deck-chair innovation is architectural foraging, using observation and conversation to understand place and people through the buildings used. Through this process, we may be able to design buildings that are a resource for a place, not just use the place as a resource.

Regional (and remote) Australia (GISCA et al. 2006) is at the heart of Australia's identity; it is our spiritual centre (Tawa 2002). It is this neglected unurbanised part of our country that offers opportunities that urban Australia does not. It is precisely this regionalism that allows architecture to embody local particularities of climate and culture (Rybczynski 1992). It is in regional Australia where buildings are less likely to be subject to maintenance, development and forgiving climates. It is these tough conditions that play a part for us to observe the role of design more clearly, its successes and failures. The architecture of regional Australia responds directly to the effects of place. It is this awareness of buildings over time that should inform architectural design (Rybczynski 1992).

This chapter discusses how the work of the Grand Section offers a direction for place-specific deck-chair innovation based on an awareness of regional Australian architecture. This *regional Australia* is specifically the route taken by the Grand Section, a meander along latitude 25 (Fig. 5.2). The Grand Section was a 2017 bicycle trip and architectural study across the girth of Australia, which we – Bobbie Bayley and Owen Kelly – made as students as a reaction to a lack of educated knowledge about our own country. In architecture, we are preoccupied with European design, and yet architecture is "predominantly a product of place" (Beck 1996: Inside Front Cover). The Grand Section was inspired by architectural trips of the 1970s to seek out an education founded on the reality of the country, notably the 1975 "Australian Communications Capsule" (Harris 2016) and the 1977 Troppo kombi trip around the exterior of the country where four architecture students (in shorts) studied Australian contemporary architecture as it is used by everyday people in the context of the country. On their website they quote Max Freeland's 1968 words as inspiration:

> A country's architecture is a near perfect record of its history. Every building captures in physical form the climate and resources of a country's geography, and the conditions of its society. . . . Every building explains the time and place in which it was built.
>
> (Welke et al. 1978)

In deference to these epic voyages we aimed to go beyond the "girt" of the coastal Australia to better understand its *girth*.

As part of the Grand Section we stayed for one week in each of 19 towns, embedding ourselves in communities, conversing with locals, documenting local buildings, and, at the end of each week, holding a public exhibition of our analysis. This is the process of deck-chair innovation, careful observation of the *specifics of place* (Clare and Clare 2007) to inform place-responsive design. This is tangential to innovation in architecture, which focuses on new computational modelling or digitalised production in the work of architects like Frank Gehry (Abel 2004; Boland et al. 2008). This is not an attack on Gehry, who has an amazing and creative body of work, but is proposed as a counterpoint to the *innovation* that often uses his work as precedent. We propose that deck-chair innovation provides an alternate way for architecture to be an on-going resource for a place and its people in that it particularises, enriches, embellishes, complements and heightens understanding of place, including celebrating the unmade places. It is architecture that leads to better climatic suitability and community engagement and can meet appropriate needs of social and cultural backgrounds (Pholeros 1999; Clare and Clare 2007).

Before delving into the built form of regional Australia, it is important to understand why we need to look at Australia's architecture rather than elsewhere. Australia is the driest inhabited continent in the world (Argent 1996), as Figure 5.1 indicates. Seventy percent of its landmass is arid or semi-arid (Australian Bureau of Statistics 2018); however, Australian inhabitation of "Australia" is largely limited to the edges of the continent, with only 27% living in

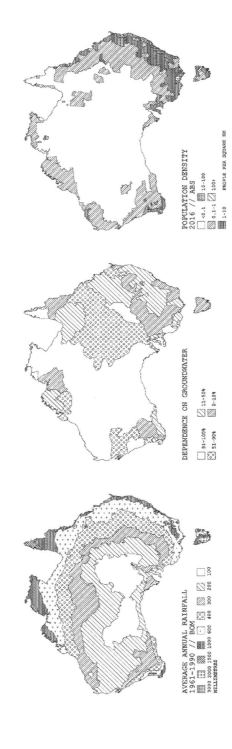

Figure 5.1 Maps of annual rainfall, groundwater and population density in Australia.

Source: Authors, based on the Bureau of Meteorology and the National Centre for Groundwater Research and Training 2013

regional areas (Coleman 2016). To design for the large parts of regional Australia, perhaps we need to reconsider our coastal understanding of the rest of the sunburnt country.

Our approach to this was architectural: we began mapping the "layers" of Australia in the same way we would begin to design a building. Analogously, we studied the "site plan" of the country (Fig 5.2). After experiencing some of the "girth", we realised the current map of Australia, with its orthogonal state borders, tells us very little about the realities of the continent and is about as useful as "tits on a three-legged goanna" (an expression of a local from Mt Perry, Queensland, whose colourful vernacular was a constant source of delight. This expression means "useless"). It became clear to us that this vast place was actually foreign to us, and its architecture equally so.

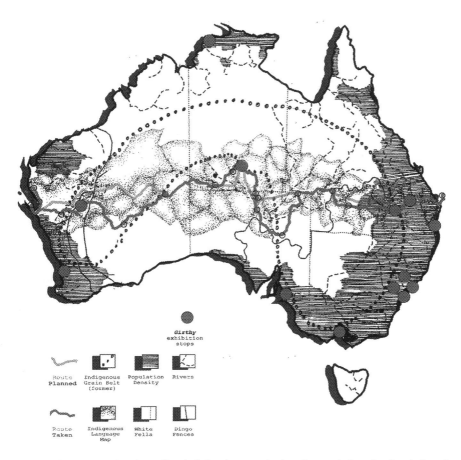

Figure 5.2 Re-mapping Australia: dark hatch around edges is population density, dark red line is Grand Section route.

Source: Authors

An off-hand comment, from Australian place-centric architect Paul Pholeros, that the best first year of architecture would be to walk from Uluru to Sydney (Pholeros 2014) was the impetus for slowly seeing our own country. We rode push bikes (or as we affectionately called them, *Experience Amplifiers*), as they provide complete sensory place-immersion. This was our best tool for understanding place and for starting conversations (especially when riding a push bike into a town of 80 people that is 400 km from its closest neighbour). It is precisely this bodily movement through an environment, rather than a "mind in a body", that reveals the place (Ingold 2011); it reminds us that "we are only one of the animals, we should not forget that" (Leplastrier 2013).

This kinaesthetic and dialectical process (Tawa 2002) has deep roots in Australia, from Indigenous songlines (Page, Smith and Yovich 2017) to contemporary Australian thinkers and slow travellers like Andrew Harper and Robyn Davidson, who say the country reveals itself through their interconnectedness with the environment and the animals they travel with (Davidson 1995; Harper 2014). We would add that this interconnectedness extends beyond just the natural environment and into social and cultural understanding in the form of varied conversations, experiences and observations. Slow travel then becomes a tool to gain better community and cultural insights.

Push bikes may be the (time-) poor man's walking. With their help we began to learn to read particular places. We were able to choose a campsite that didn't flood when we weathered the tail end of cyclone Debbie in March 2017 (Fig 5.3). We arrived in towns with the place embedded in us, afforded through participating in the place (Ingold 2000). For architecture, this awareness of natural systems embodies sustainable practice (Tawa 2002) and allows us to better know what climatic conditions buildings and materials have to be designed for.

In the same way that the natural environment reveals itself, so does community and culture. Slowing down, stopping easily and more often, provides opportunity to hear local anecdotes: "anecdotes start conversations, conversations form relationships, and relationships make architecture" (Banney 2017). By accumulating these anecdotes, a cultural and social understanding of a place is jig-sawed together; it is a fluid process, alive and vibrant with contradictions (Banney 2017).

Nature and culture are inseparably intertwined. Giving cultural meaning to natural objects is an ancient and on-going practice (Ingold 2000). Shot dingoes (Fig 5.4) provide a political-physical fence, a boundary signifying particular "pest" management strategies and avoiding reliance on physical fences, a contentious issue in pastoralism (Emmott 2017). Apart from giving something to talk about at the next stop, slow movement through country provides a prelude to environmental and cultural ways of thinking. We now know a *dingo museum* wouldn't be popular with *all* locals.

Perhaps Australia's best example of nature and culture being inseparable is Uluru, but as a symbol of Australian culture, it seems to embody a paradox of understanding. Architectural commentators often claim "harsh climate" as intrinsic to Australian architecture (Butler 2018), even though we

Figure 5.3 Understanding place from immersion and camping dry, near Roma, QLD.
Source: Authors

predominantly build in coastal urban areas with very liveable climates. The view of Uluru from the Indigenous Mutitjulu community is of the short east elevation (Fig 5.5) rather than the touristic long north elevation. Perhaps our understanding of the country is more *postcard* than informed: for architecture, this can mean buildings that don't understand the climatic or cultural conditions in which they are built.

If we were to reduce local conditions to climate alone, and architecture as something that responds to its immediate climate, would we really know how to design for regional Australia? Before the Grand Section journey we wouldn't have. The passive design principles that suit urban coastal Australia (Hollo 2011; McGee 2013) are not always appropriate for the arid and semi-arid climates of regional and remote Australia. With these climates comprising 70% of the continent, deck-chair innovation offers place-immersion to understand what good design entails in an unfamiliar climate; riding a bike through 47-degree Celsius days really drives home the difference between temperate and semi-arid climates.

The experts of regional architecture, Indigenous Australians, provide examples of appropriate design (Figure 5.6). Many of these would change multiple

108 Bobbie Bayley and Owen Kelly

Figure 5.4 Shot dingoes, hung in tree for all to see, political pastoralism, a different experience of a place . . . on show, near Quilpie, QLD.

Source: Authors

times a year to adapt to climate, food sources, social or cultural events (Memmott 2007). How radical! Australia's contemporary architecture is heavily influenced by European design (Apperly, Irving and Reynolds 1989; Beck 1996), which has rarely had to design for principally arid and semi-arid landscapes.

Figure 5.5 Uluru from Indigenous community Mutijulu exit, an Australian icon that looks very different from a different point of view, Northern Territory.

Source: Authors

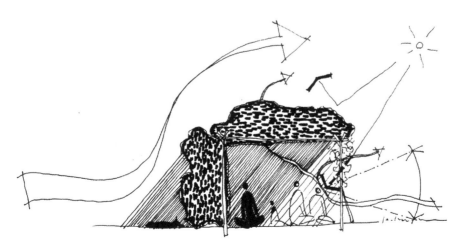

Figure 5.6 Arid Australian architecture with ventilated shade and its back to the wind, Mimili camp, Everard Ranges, SA.

Source: Bobbie Bayley from (Memmott 2007)

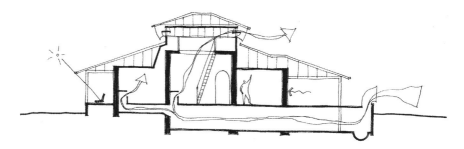

Figure 5.7 Arid design in a more western style, Adelaide house in Alice Springs, Northern Territory; air is cooled by bringing it under the house, through wet hessian and up through the building.

Source: Bobbie Bayley

Learning how to design for regional Australian climates is where deck-chair innovation can be useful. By taking the time to observe what is required of a building through place-immersion and anecdotal jig-saw puzzles, we can then *design forage* architectural techniques to create buildings that are place-responsive (Fig 5.7). In the same way that foraging requires a knowledge of the specifics of place, so does place-responsive architecture.

Design foraging is in contrast to the use of modern homogeneous construction, recently infiltrating the inland in the form of lightweight Dongas: transportable, prefabricated buildings used extensively for temporary mining camps and fly-in-fly-out workers (Fig 5.8). Dongas are generic and ubiquitous, with mechanical cooling working overtime, and when the life of the Donga is up, it is sold to local communities where it decays on the outskirts of towns. This is in contrast to some pre-Donga mining architecture such as Big Bell, WA, which boasted the longest bar in the southern hemisphere and had at its height a population of 850 people. All caused by the opening of a new gold mine. When the mine closed down, many of the buildings were re-used in surrounding areas (Bayley and Kelly 2017d). However if we look at existing design principles, we can *design forage* solutions that provide more longevity to regional architecture.

Often these design principles can cross time and contexts. One principle used for some Dongas is a double skin roof. A double-fly canvas tent was a common sight in early white settlements in regional and remote Australia. The twin fly greatly reduces radiant heat by creating a ventilated gap between two pieces of canvas fabric (Fig 5.9). This setup also became a staple to reduce heat loading on the Grand Section. To be able to reduce heat loading year-round is crucial to reduced carbon emissions, cheaper running costs, better health (Healthabitat 2007; Winter 2017) and the ability to have longer lasting buildings.

Adaptations to buildings and structures can be good indicators of place-responsiveness. In Birdsville, Queensland, clotheslines have a shade-cloth

Figure 5.8 The common regional architecture of Australia. Mechanical heating and cooling is a must for Dongas, Laverton, Western Australia.

Source: Authors

covering to protect plastics (including pegs) and clothes from intense heat and UV. The old Betoota hotel, Queensland (QLD), (Figure 5.10) has adapted its western awning, dipping low to provide shade year-round and reducing unwanted radiant heat effects. Extensive shading provides shelter from heat

112 Bobbie Bayley and Owen Kelly

Figure 5.9 Heat is a major design problem for regional Australia. The Grand Section adopted the double fly tent as tried and tested method to reduce heat loading, north of Leonora, Western Australia.

Source: Authors

and weather, extending over the high thermal mass earth walls surrounding the building. These design techniques to maintain thermal comfort are part of rapidly disappearing pre-air-conditioning architecture. With buildings accounting for nearly 50% of the world's carbon emissions, cutting out air-conditioning can reduce this by up to 70% (Winter 2017). There are lessons in regional architecture that we, as urban Australians, may have to re-learn.

The importance of learning from the low awning of the Betoota Hotel (Fig 5.10) becomes clear when looking at other high thermal mass construction in a similar climate. A contemporary rammed earth house in Birdsville, Queensland, (Fig 5.11) was commissioned to be liveable without air conditioning. The house follows passive design principles for a temperate climate (McGee 2013), although, anecdotally, the building stays hot throughout summer, as the thermal mass of the rammed earth walls absorb and hold heat from the high daytime temperatures and direct sunlight. The lack of large eaves and shading has also led to some weathering from UV, heat and weather (Bayley and Kelly 2017a).

Deck-chair innovation prompts us to look at what is already working rather than thinking that new is necessarily better. A new office building in Leonora,

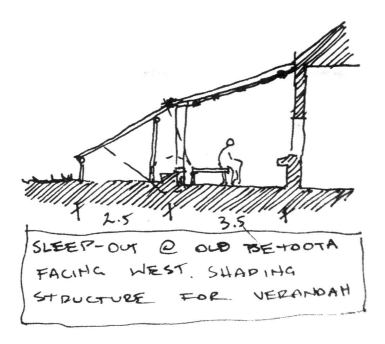

Figure 5.10 Adaptations to buildings often indicate good design considerations. Low sloping western sleep-out, Betoota Hotel, Betoota, Queensland is one example.

Source: Authors

Figure 5.11 Contemporary rammed earth house for a temperate climate, Birdsville, Queensland.

Source: Authors

114 *Bobbie Bayley and Owen Kelly*

Figure 5.12 Lenora government services building, Western Australia, the shiniest building on the street.

Source: Authors

Western Australia, seems to exemplify innovation for its own sake. Shiny, gold and black, it sticks out like a bowtie on a singlet (Figure 5.12). This government services building provides office space that even the government services can't afford. Anecdotally, the paid car parking out back is also unused as there is ample free street parking out front (Bayley and Kelly 2017c).

In contrast to the Laverton bow-tie, the church at Warburton, Western Australia, painted a striking lime green (Figure 5.13), looks almost unused, even vandalised – yet while we were there it was one of the most used buildings in the town. The main outdoor space, used by locals, has shade, fire drums, moveable seats and a plug-and-play PA system that blares eclectic 1990s hits late into the night (Bayley and Kelly 2017b). This building appears to be preferred (by local badasses) over architecturally designed spaces, government buildings and other designated communal areas. Studying the existing built environment gives us clues for appropriate design. Deck-chair innovation suggests that sometimes the best design is to build less, offer autonomy and play more music.

This deck-chair innovation approach can be applied across the continent. The process employed by the Grand Section offers a slow method to *design*

Deck-chair innovation 115

Figure 5.13 Warburton Church, Western Australia, one of the most used buildings in the community. Lime green glory. PA system on 44-gallon drums under bell tower.
Source: Authors

forage for place-specific architecture that provides one way for architecture to be an on-going resource for a place and its people. Through sensory immersion and immersion in community, an understanding arises that particularises, enriches, embellishes, complements and heightens our understanding of place, including celebrating the unmade places, through architecture.

References

Abel, C. 2004. *Architecture, Technology and Process*. Oxford: Architectural Press.

Apperly, R., Irving, R., and Reynolds, P. 1989. *Identifying Australian Architecture Styles and Terms from 1788 to the Present*. Sydney: Angus and Robertson.

Argent, D. R. M. 1996. "Chapter 7: Inland Waters." *Australia: State of the Environment 1996*. Australian Government Department of the Environment and Energy: Canberra.

Australian Bureau of Statistics. 2018. "Population Density." Retrieved November 9, 2018 (www.abs.gov.au/ausstats/abs@.nsf/Previousproducts/3218.0Main%20Features752016?opendocument&tabname=Summary&prodno=3218.0&issue=2016&num=&view=).

Banney, M. 2017. *Anecdotal Evidence*. Doctor of Philosophy PhD Thesis, RMIT University.

Bayley, B., and Kelly, O. 2017a. "The Grand Section Guardian #09 – Stop 07 Birdsville." *The Guardian*. January 7, 2017. Retrieved November 10, 2018 (www.thegrandsection.com/blog/2017/7/1/the-grand-section-guardian-009-stop-07-birdsville).

Bayley, B., and Kelly, O. 2017b. "The Grand Section Guardian #015 – Stop 015 Warburton." *The Guardian*. February 10, 2017. Retrieved November 10, 2018 (www.thegrandsection.com/blog/2017/10/2/the-grand-section-guardian).

Bayley, B., and Kelly, O. 2017c. "The Grand Section Guardian #016 – Stop 16 Laverton." *The Guardian*. October 16, 2016. Retrieved November 17, 2018 (www.thegrandsection.com/blog/2017/10/16/the-grand-section-guardian-016-stop-16-laverton).

Bayley, B., and Kelly, O. 2017d. "The Grand Section Guardian #017 – Stop 17 Meekatharra." *The Guardian*. November 8, 2017. Retrieved November 17, 2018 (www.thegrandsection.com/blog/2017/11/8/the-grand-section-guardian-017-stop-17-meekatharra).

Beck, H. 1996. "Editorial." *UME*. Melbourne, Victoria: Haig Beck.

Boland, R., Jr, J., Collopy, F., Lyytinen, K., and Yoo, Y. 2008. "Managing as Designing: Lessons for Organization Leaders from the Design Practice of Frank O. Gehry." *Design Issues* 24(1): 16–20.

Butler, K. 2018. "How is Australian Architecture Unique?" Retrieved November 9, 2018 (www.modernhouse.co/how-is-australian-architecture-unique/).

Clare, L., and Clare, K. 2007. "Cultural Connection – The Queensland Gallery of Modern Art (GoMA)." *Material Thinking of Display* 12(6): 3–4.

Coleman, S. 2016. "Australia State of the Environment 2016: Built Environment." P. 2 *Australian Government Department of the Environment and Energy*: Canberra.

Davidson, R. 1995. *Tracks: A Woman's Solo Trek Across 1700 Miles of Australian Outback*. New York: Vintage.

Emmott, A. 2017. "Why Do Some Graziers Want to Retain, Not Kill, Dingoes?" *The Conversation*. Retrieved November 23, 2018 (https://theconversation.com/why-do-some-graziers-want-to-retain-not-kill-dingoes-77457).

GISCA, T. U. o. Adelaide, A. G. G. Australia and A. B. o. Statistics. 2006. "Map of Australia Showing Areas of Varying Geographic Remoteness." Retrieved January 6, 2019 (https://aifs.gov.au/publications/families-regional-rural-and-remote-australia/figure1).

Harper, A. 2014. "Bio." Retrieved January 9, 2018 (www.andrewharper.com.au/).

Harris, J. 2016. "On the Buses: Mobile Architecture in Australia and the UK, 1973–1975." *Architectural Histories* 4(1): 6–12.

Healthabitat. 2007. "Temperate Control Insider the House – Cool Houses in Hot Climates." Retrieved November 11, 2018 (www.healthabitat.com/products/temperature-control-inside-the-house-cool-houses-in-hot-climates).

Hollo, N. 2011. *Warm House, Cool House: Inspirational Designs for Low-Energy Housing*. Sydney: NewSouth.

Ingold, T. 2000. *The Perception of the Environment: Essays in Livelihood, Dwelling and Skill.* London: Routledge.

Ingold, T. 2011. *Being Alive: Essays on Movement, Knowledge and Description.* Milton Park, UK: Routledge.

Leplastrier, R. 2013. "The Cave Interview. C. Hunter." *Oris Magazine* 85: 13.

McGee, C. 2013. "Passive Design – Your Home, Australia's Guide to Environmentally Sustainable Homes." Retrieved January 6, 2019 (www.yourhome.gov.au/passive-design).

Memmott, P. 2007. *Gunyah, Goondie + Wurley: The Aboriginal Architecture of Australia.* Brisbane: University of Queensland Press.

Page, A., Smith, D., and Yovich, U. 2017. "Songline Audio Journey." (www.nma.gov.au/explore/blog/songlines-audio-journey).

Pholeros, P. 1999. "Organic Architecture." P. 86 in *Avalon, Landscape & Harmony*, edited by Burley Griffin, W., Stewart Jolly, A., and Ruskin Rowe, H. J. Roberts. Avalon Beach: Ruskin Rowe Press.

Pholeros, P. 2014. "PP: Looker, Listener, Teacher, Learner, Leader, Artist, Australian. J. Roberts." *Architecture Bulletin.* Retrieved January 8, 2019 (http://architecturebulletin.com.au/spring-summer-2016/reflections-on-paul-pholeros-and-the-thingness-of-things/).

Rybczynski, W. 1992. *Looking Around: A Journey Through Architecture.* New York: Penguin Books.

Tawa, M. 2002. "Place, Country, Chorography: Towards a Kinesthetic and Narrative Practice of Place." *Architectural Theory Review* 7(2): 45–58.

Welke, A. C., Hill, J. J., Hayter, J. N., and Harris, P. N. 1978. *Influences in Regional Architecture.* Adelaide: Troppo.

Williams, T., and Tsien, B. 1999. "On Slowness." Retrieved November 9, 2018 (www.twbta.com/3031).

Winter, T. 2017. "Moving from Air-Con to A 'Cool Living' Future." Retrieved November 11, 2018 (www.humanities.org.au/issue-item/moving-air-con-cool-living-future/).

Section 2

Placing knowledge and innovation economies

Regional universities, ecosystems and Fab Labs

6 The troubling third tier

Small cities, small universities and an ambivalent knowledge economy

Tara Brabazon

Introduction

Gerry Rafferty composed songs of travel, mobility, excitement, change, disappointment and loss. Best known for 'Baker Street' (1978), the literary-saturated fictional home of Sherlock Holmes, Rafferty transformed the base for the super-sleuth into a mournful lament to the loss of love, life and expectations. Yet beyond his greatest hit, and included on the same album, was 'City to City', conveying the passage from love to work, Glasgow to London. The ambivalence of both journeys, carried by Caledonian sleeper trains, captured the strain of managing professional and personal success, noting the cost of both.

Gerry Rafferty was a situated musician and geographically anchored his lyrics. Yet he did not locate his music in his home. His focus on first-tier cities like London and the powerfully competing second-tier cities Glasgow and Edinburgh masked the place of his birth: Paisley. Most famously known as the location of Glasgow Airport, positioned – significantly – outside of Glasgow, this small city of 76,000 people is part of the commuter belt but also has another significant feature. It encloses a university. The University of the West of Scotland (UWS) maintains campuses in Paisley, Hamilton, Dumfries and Ayr, alongside the oddly global city location that regional universities seem to doggedly maintain. For UWS, they maintain a campus in London. For Charles Sturt University in regional New South Wales, Australia, the institution maintains a building in Sydney. Third-tier cities, it appears, are rarely branded sufficiently to gain leverage in the international student market.

While Paisley was invisible in Gerry Rafferty's musical career, the city has not forgotten him, but his tribute is ambivalent at best. Gerry Rafferty Drive has been named after him. It is a suburban street, with conventional housing and nothing to mark it as distinctive except its signage. Rafferty had to leave Paisley – physically and imaginatively – to sing his songs of loss, regret, work and love. Popular culture is rarely drawn to – or draws from – these small cities and large towns. However universities do have a presence. But like Gerry Rafferty Drive, that existence is ambivalent, oddly unsatisfying, unstable and under-theorised.

122 *Tara Brabazon*

The challenges confronting small cities – with or without a university – are vast: underemployment, decline in health and educational services, and depopulation. Development remains uneven (Harvey 2006). My chapter investigates the opportunities and problems when third-tier cities like Paisley become education cities. These small cities and large towns are a trifling slice in the corporate cake of higher education as either the outlier campus of a metropolitan institution or part of a cluster of locations for a 'regional' university. Yet these campuses – in an environment of quality-assurance monitoring and research assessment – confront multiple threats. This chapter explores the struggles confronted by 'regional universities' and their pivotal role in the movement from an industrial to a knowledge economy. The chapter works through economic, social and cultural variables for the formation and success of a third-tier university city, then concludes with how these institutions can – while enabling some higher education – also cap the expectations of their students. This capping emerges through restricting the course and subject offerings, restricting the availability of doctoral supervision or relying on casual staff for teaching undergraduates.

Urbanity on the third tier

Third-tier cities are small urban environments that do not sustain the profile or touristic branding of global cities, like New York, London, Tokyo or Cairo, or second-tier cities, like San Francisco, Manchester, Osaka or Alexandria. As the Paisley example that commenced this chapter shows, third-tier cities are not well known or internationally recognised but are facing structural economic challenges that worsened after the Global Financial Crisis and are therefore requiring the invention of new reasons for their existence.

To configure such a model for urbanity requires the construction of a relational model.

This relational definition is important, as policy designations are not easily shared between nations. Number of residents is not a reliable indicator. In Australia, the determination of a 'city' is statistically constituted, being granted to a place with a minimal range of 10,000 to 30,000 people. The state of Tasmania is at the lower end of this population designation. Western Australia is at the top of the scale. Therefore, even within one nation, the definition of a 'city' is variable.

Figure 6.1 Global, second-tier and third-tier cities.
Source: Tara Brabazon

Cities have signified excitement, movement, chaos, political intrigue and opportunity since – at least – the industrial revolution. Karl Marx and Friedrich Engels developed the theories for political change while watching the twisting Manchester landscape bending and buckling under the speed of economic and social change triggered by the automated weaving loom in the textile industry.

The relationship between industrialisation and the growth of an urban workforce is clear. As industrialisation transformed, so did employment, underemployment and unemployment. Post-manufacturing economies required new agents and opportunities to build a labour force. Phrases – clichés – such as the gig economy and portfolio careers capture some of the new realities of this new model of contract, casualised work. Since the first set of creative industries policies were instigated by the Tony Blair government in 1997, economic development and city development – rather than cities and revolutions – have been tethered. Through the 2000s, researchers such as Richard Florida, Charles Landry and Charles Leadbeater aligned economic progress with urbanity. Through the history of the creative industries, the challenges and specificities of small, third-tier cities were invisible. There was little money to be made. Little low-hanging fruit to pick. These small places were not the engines for economic growth in difficult times. But this absence has meant that assumptions have dominated the creative industries literature. The most damaging and seductive is the theory of city modelling, with researchers such as Florida and Landry suggesting that the practices that operate(d) well in San Francisco in the United States or Manchester in England hold relevance and resonance in Wagga Wagga or Invercargill. Such assumptions summon flawed analyses and policymaking. Regeneration has become a bland word that defaults to an automatic positive connotation.

Regeneration has meant in the last twenty years – simply – a rise in building construction. Phil Jones and James Evans presented this process ruthlessly – but with productive bite (2008).

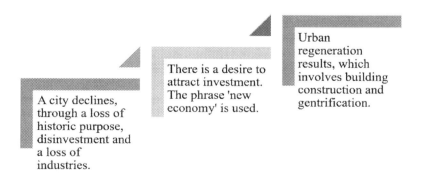

Figure 6.2 Diagram constructed by Tara Brabazon, based on Phil Jones and James Evans, *Urban Regeneration in the UK*, (Los Angeles: SAGE, 2008).

Source: Tara Brabazon

After the global financial crisis – which revealed the lie in this form of urban regeneration as a proxy for sustained economic and social development – the issue remains how stability and perhaps even growth can be created beyond global cities (Dekker and Tabbers 2012). How do those of us living in small urban environments manage deindustrialisation, depopulation, environmental damage and decrepit infrastructure? Are sustainability and resilience unproductive, empty words? Global cities continue to do well, attracting the money, businesses and well-educated population. Third-tier cities are left with the poor, the less educated, the less mobile and the less skilled. They are places of residuals, waste and deficits: the Edgelands (Farley and Roberts 2011). Howell confirmed that, "large populations bring their own amenities and agglomeration effects ... making consolidated cities more attractive" (2014: 900). However, the presence of universities can intervene in this narrative of decline and decay.

While the spaces and population size of large cities create productive internal markets, the problems confronting small cities are not only a question of geography, but of time, through the speed of change and accelerated culture. The changes in our economic systems – globalisation, digitisation, hyper consumption and increasing interests in intellectual property rights and copyright – are radical reconfigurations in cultural life. In conservative and unstable times, an unusual historical combination, it is easy to perpetuate the narrative of small cities as insular (inward), safe (dull) and dependable (lacking imagination and dynamism). These "place-based social norms" (Myrdahl 2013) hold a debilitating effect on the people that do not fit within the narrow definitions of love, sex and families. But this place branding for liveability has to be carefully managed for education cities in the third tier. These everyday geographies do matter, and liveability can slide into conformity and unproductive stability. The ideologies can be detrimental to higher education.

Besides slicing cities into tiers, urban development can also be categorised as fast, slow and still. Time can be added to the modelling of space.

Global cities are associated with speed, movement and change. Second-tier cities are more embedded in their histories, but can mobilise opportunities if and when they are presented. For example, the Beatles emerged from Liverpool. Beatles tourism grew from the 1980s. The slower, third-tier cities often rely on agricultural rather than industrial time – using seasons – rather than the vagaries of a stock market opening and closing. There is potential to brand and utilise the slow and the still to attract residents in accelerated times.

Spaces and times, geographies and histories, the land and the clock, create a momentum for change or a blockage to innovation. Yet another binary opposition is also significant: mind and the body. Physical cultural studies, and research into movement cultures more generally, requires different techniques in the third tier (Brabazon, McRae and Redhead 2017). Assumptions about 'public health' and the capacity to exercise require bespoke strategies in these small places, as infrastructure is lacking. But to complete the Cartesian dualism, the mind – education – remains important, particularly in these neglected areas and regions.

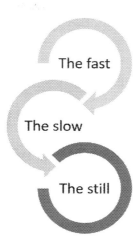

Figure 6.3 A model of city time, derived from a phrase by Gilles Duranton (2007) in "Urban Evolutions: The Fast, The Slow, and the Still".

Source: Tara Brabazon

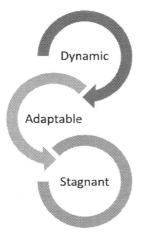

Figure 6.4 How cities and their citizens manage change.

Source: Tara Brabazon

A provocative maxim to consider, which bubbles through this chapter, is: the smaller the city, the more important the university. While second-tier cities encase multiple institutions, and global cities like London, New York and Sydney feature a matrix of further and higher education options, the small cities often feature only one university or the outlier campus of a larger university. Even with these restrictions of choice, this is still a valuable contribution

126   *Tara Brabazon*

to a region. John Hogan, the registrar at Newcastle University in the United Kingdom, verified the accuracy of this assumption about universities and small cities:

> Imperial [College London] is a fantastic institution, but if it closed, would London notice? Probably not. But if Newcastle closed, or Northumbria, Durham, Teesside or Sunderland [universities] closed, it would be a catastrophe for the local and the bigger region, because there's not a lot else going on in the North East. . . . The relative importance of these universities is so much more important than some of the outstanding institutions you might find in London.
>
> (cited in Cunnane 2012: 8)

This role is aggregating in its importance because regional inequality increases when public spending declines. Health and education funding is valuable far beyond those sectors. Therefore, in a declining economy, regional injustices heighten, and at such a time, the economic role and significance of a university is amplified. Considering many post-industrial third-tier cities were also founded on a single industry, this means that the university becomes crucial to creating generational options and alternatives. Education tourism and event management – from convocations to graduation – means that thousands of people come to a city, using hotels, restaurants and visiting local sites. However many of these 'new industries' are also casualised with short-term, contract appointments. Guy Standing, in crafting his 'precariat' (2013), used the university workforce as a key example of new, transitory, difficult employment conditions.

After the Global Financial Crisis and rise of the precariat, the assumptions, theories and models of branding and urban regeneration not only appear brittle but corrosive. Joel Kotkin confirmed, with brutality and accuracy:

> Among the most pervasive, and arguably pernicious, notions of the past decade has been that the "creative class" of the skilled, educated and hip would remake and revive American cities. The idea, packaged and peddled by consultant Richard Florida, had been that unlike spending public money to court Wall Street fat cats, corporate executives or other traditional elites, paying to appeal to the creative would truly trickle down, generating a widespread urban revival. . . . Indeed in many ways the Floridian focus on industries like entertainment, software, and social media creates a distorted set of economic priorities. The creatives, after all, generally don't work in factories or warehouses. So why assist these industries? Instead the trend is to declare good-paying blue collar professions a product of the past.
>
> (Kotkin 2013)

'Cool cities', such as San Francisco, did not provide methods, strategies, trajectories or scenarios for assisting deindustrialised cities. It took a Global Financial

Crisis to provide the stark, brutalising mirror that made the followers of Richard Florida recognise the flaws in their theories and research through the 2000s. By January 2013, Richard Florida admitted this reality in public, stating that, "the past couple of decades have seen America sort itself into two distinct nations, as the more highly skilled and affluent have migrated to a relatively small number of cities and metro areas" (Florida cited in Kotkin 2013). Cities with diverse economies and skilled workers increased their viability and skill base. The others suffered decline as the educated, the skilled, the young and the taxpayers left one location and moved to another. Florida's intoxicatingly simple ideas for economic growth meant that manufacturing and agricultural industries were neglected. Urban planners and local and regional governments were sold bohemia, startups and coffee shops, all of which proved cardboard cut-out solutions unable to withstand the hurricane of financial capital. Regeneration failed. The creative class did not arrive. Indeed, as Gibson, Carr and Warren have suggested, the binary of manufacturing and creativity, however it was and is defined, is false (2015).

Third-tier cities are the canary in the mine of capitalism, functioning at the mono-industrial edge. It is difficult for these areas to gain an identity and image beyond the manufacturing past. Because of their diversity, it is very difficult to create uniform and proven policy solutions for these small cities and large towns. In a remarkable study, Erickcek and McKinney mapped and categorised eight types of small cities:

1 Dominated by an older industry in decline
2 Private-sector dependent, with little public sector employment
3 Dispersed geography and function
4 Company towns attempting to survive when a company leaves
5 University and college cities where graduates leave after graduation
6 Company towns surviving after the company leaves, but with a remaining social purpose
7 Cities growing through the engine of the new economy and creative industries
8 Cities growing through university/government/business clusters (2004: 14–22).

By this list, third-tier university cities occupied two of the eight categories. The graduates remaining or vacating the urban environment is the differentiating factor between the two. This difference can also be captured by an emerging phrase in this field: Entrepreneurial Learning City Regions (James, Preece and Valdes-Cotera 2018). This phrase recognises that lifelong learning – continuing to return to education – is the enabler of sustainable development. A workforce can grow, transform and change through the trans-local economic reconfigurations.

With or without a university, problems cluster in third-tier cities. Transportation and telecommunication are lacking. Because of the lack of a diverse employment base, the population is declining, and health and educational facilities are reducing. Abandoned and derelict buildings proliferate. Environmental problems, hazards and pollution result from the aftereffects of de-industrialisation. With a narrow range of jobs available, young people move away. It is difficult to attract new residents, the population declines, schools close, hospitals close and the tax base reduces.

To arch beyond these problems and challenges, to ensure that tourism links up industries, population, events and education, a four-stage city modelling is required. Firstly, it is necessary to understand the specificity of the city's history, noting the period of its greatest economic and social success, along with its causes, consequences and legacy. A second stage is to recognise the present environment and reality of living in this city, including the social and institutional gaps and challenges. The city or regional council's structure matters. Is it fit for current purpose, or are the departmental structures blocking innovation? Thirdly, explore the similarities and differences with other third-tier cities around the world, noting effective and inefficient strategies for change. What worked in Morecombe in England? What did not succeed in Oshawa in Canada? How did Albany in Western Australia promote cycling tourism (Brabazon, McRae and Redhead 2015)? The final stage in city modelling is to take an example, strategy or policy that works well in one location and test it in another. If the goal is food and wine tourism linked with the music industry, look at the Shiraz and seafood weekenders in the Swan Valley in Perth, Western Australia. If the focus is as a university city, then the mistakes made by the University of Ontario or the challenges confronting the University of Bolton are incredibly relevant (Brabazon 2012).

The key challenge is managing the lack of diversity in economic and working options and opportunities. Flint in Michigan and Oshawa in Canada manufactured motor vehicles. Napa (still) makes wine and has flourishing wine-tourism enterprises. Blackpool was a destination for working-class tourism. Rockhampton in Australia was a service hub for the cattle industry with a huge meat works. A university cannot solve these problems, but it can provide the salve for movement and change.

Digitisation is one such salve, enabled through university infrastructure. Third-tier cities do not require a determinant – analogue – relationship with the second-tier and global cities. Different networks and relationships can be configured. E-commerce enables more direct relationships (Melin 2018) beyond a nation. But there is no checklist for recovery that is widely applicable. Transferability of strategies is difficult to predict. As David Bell and Mark Jayne realised:

> Small cities have been ignored by urban theorists who, in seeking to conceptualize broad urban agendas and depict generalizable models (for example relating to epochal urbanism, the structure and nature of the urban hierarchy, global cities and global city-regions), have tended to obscure as much as they illuminate. Given that study of 'the city' has been vital to

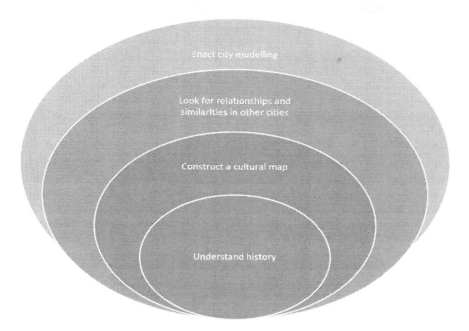

Figure 6.5 Stages to intervene in third-tier city outward development.
Source: Concept and diagram by Tara Brabazon

broader advances in the social sciences, this neglect of smaller urban centres has profound consequences for urban studies.

(2009: 683)

Since these words were published, the literature on third-tier cities is growing, but unevenly. The place of universities in these urban environments is a very small part of the scholarship. There is innovation and interest burgeoning in this specialist field – of which Greg Richards and Lian Duif's *Small Cities with Big Dreams* (2019) is a fine example – but the role of education in this 'placemaking' is un(der) specified. All cities encase myriad urban experiences, for leisure, work, tourism, the night-time economy and education. But it is the education city that remains disconnected from other specialisations. There is a reason for that disengagement. Third-tier cities are diverse, as are the educational institutions within them. Cambridge has little connection to Ballarat. Both are third-tier cities with universities. Yet that is the end of the similarity.

Terminology is part of the challenge. I am using the phrase third-tier university cities with intent. These locations are distinct in ideology and branding from the 'college town', a phrase frequently used in the United States and

130   *Tara Brabazon*

Canada, and 'university town' in Europe. Indeed, the university town was a characteristic of the ancient institutions encircling the Cambridge and Oxford colleges. These towns were built because of, around and in support of the university. The population was highly educated and mobile. Third-tier cities, while including these college and university towns, have a different story that emerges from the expansion of the higher education sector and post-industrialisation. As the number of universities expanded alongside the student population, these institutions moved into regional and remote areas that already existed yet were discarded in the 'new economy'. Some lost their primary manufacturing industry – such as Oshawa in Canada after General Motors moved out and the University of Ontario moved in. Others simply occupied a region that had been un-serviced by higher education. Central Queensland is an example of this latter configuration. So instead of a town organically emerging from and intertwining with an elite university, these new universities were positioned in already existing small cities and large towns. The studentification of these cities (Smith 2005) created specific challenges in this context, with housing, transportation and the excesses of student culture jarring with divergent and distinctive industrial or regional histories (Gumprecht 2003). The town and gown separation in these cases can be damaging to the already delicate urban cultures in these locations. However, there are benefits to residents. Housing downturns are mitigated in university cities as students require places to live during their studies (Gopal 2008). This remains a volatile real estate economy, reliant on the fortunes of the institution but also the cycles of terms and semester. Similarly, the cultural life of the university provides touring and institutional events that would not be available to residents if the campus did not exist. Therefore, the remaining sections of this chapter take these economic and cultural variables and apply them to this unique location.

Economic stability or stagnation?

Universities are employers of staff. Significantly, the diversity of that staff group is often underplayed. Because universities are so poorly represented in popular culture – with the *Good Will Hunting* and *Wonder Boys* model of salacious, narcissistic male professors a dominant narrative palette – the employees beyond academics are frequently invisible. Universities UK, in their 2014 report *The Impact of Universities on the UK economy*, dedicated an entire chapter to the Employment Profile of UK Universities. An advocacy document confirming the economic value of institutions, the argument in this report is that a remarkable range of employment opportunities exist in institutions. While academics dominate, an array of retail and customer service, caretakers, sports and leisure workers, childcare specialists, gardeners, chefs, librarians, marketing professionals and technicians gain their living through a university (Kelly, McNicoll and White 2014). While the report does not differentiate between tiers of cities or geographical location – unsurprisingly, as the Universities UK commissioned the research – it is not difficult to apply the argument to demonstrate that the employment generated for Bolton, Stoke and Falmouth from their universities is more valuable than that created for Manchester, Sheffield and Edinburgh because of the lack of alternative jobs in the region. In post-manufacturing industrial cities where the work has disappeared, the university remains a key, pivotal and central employer.

The third-tier university cities are also key employers for early career academics. My current role as Dean of Graduate Research at Flinders University in Adelaide, Australia, a research and teaching university in a second-tier city, requires that I manage the research master's and PhD programmes. Professional development and employability of graduates is a key imperative. In one of my weekly vlogs, and accompanied by Professor Steve Redhead, we discussed the strengths and weakness of each type of city and university for early career researchers (Brabazon and Redhead 2016). The importance of regional universities as a gateway post for graduate researchers was stressed while also noting the instability and vulnerability of these economies through a lack of alternative employment.

While the function of the university as a diverse employer is clear, the relationship between economic development and university development is neither linear nor causal. A study funded by the South African Department of Higher Education and Training and completed by Kruss et al. (2015: 22–31) confirmed that, while higher education does increase skills for workers, other variables must contextualise those workers and skills to ensure a higher income for well-educated individuals and wider economic development. There must be attention to the network of companies available to offer employment, the geography of the regions and the already available skilled workforce. As Simon McGrath argued, "Development is actually deeply contextualized . . . not just thinking it's a simple case of investing in education and leaving it to the markets. That will only do so much" (McGrath in Goodchild van Hilten 2015). It is clear that the revenue created by students in a city and the employment of staff remain the key economic drivers of universities (Swinney 2011).

It is much harder to study and quantify the research transfer and community engagement. The research that has been done on the harder edge of research transfer – patents, licensing agreements and startup creation – found that downtown universities (noting the North American inflections to the language and study) have a much higher rate of research transfer than rural and suburban universities (Andes 2017). These downtown studies, though, are just as likely to be placed in global and second-tier environments as the third tier. Andes' study focuses on Pittsburgh, Chicago, Atlanta, Austin, New York and Houston. Flint's downtown is not of interest because it – seemingly – is not so easily available for regeneration. Significantly, most post-industrial cities have a downtown. Once more, the global and second-tier downtowns are successful and visible in proxies for research engagement. But what makes this study interesting – and perhaps useful for third-tier cities – is that 'research impact' emerges because of the geographic proximity between the university and local businesses. Andes did not make that connection himself. Instead, he recommended in his report that

132   *Tara Brabazon*

the universities located in small cities needed to be more urban (Andes 2017: 22). Therefore the distinctiveness and specificity is lost, rendering regional and rural locations as 'urban' – as if it has a singular definition and that a freedom of choice is available. Also, he did not recognise the contradiction in his own argument. If the downtown universities are successful because of their proximity, then the types of businesses in rural and regional towns and cities are different from Atlanta or Chicago. They gain success from their proximity, servicing different needs, students and consumers. The music industries are different, as are health and education industries, tourism and sport. If proximity is the key for value adding to research, then it must be geographically and economically appropriate to the region from which it emerges. Andes' research is also counter to the urban planning literature from the Environmental Protection Agency in the United States, which argues strongly for the use of local assets to rebuild economic, social and cultural success (Johnson, Kackar and Kramer 2015).

A cultural turn to education

Urbanisation has been (too easily) aligned with economic, cultural and social development (Henderson 2010). Through the industrial revolutions in the 19th century, urbanity and development were locked into a productive embrace, if brutalising to the agrarian social structures. In post-industrial locations, it is more ambivalently placed. The challenge with such easy correlations is that urbanisation – like development – is not a singular, agreed entity or concept. As the argument progresses, the infrastructure of global cities creates agglomeration and economies of scale. The ease of such an argument is disrupted by third-tier cities. What happens to development when agglomeration is ambivalent, at best? Depopulation is a key challenge for third-tier cities. Accompanying depopulation is the loss of doctors, hospital services, childcare facilities and schools. University students and staff make a difference to this population stability. The recent Economic Contribution of the Finnish Universities report (BiGGAR Economics 2017) confirmed that the Finnish towns and cities with universities had a population growth rate twice that of the national average.

Small cities and large towns have advantages. In North America, there is even a marketing methodology to 'rank' the best college towns. The resultant article on this survey begins with the supposed cliché that "everyone knows that small college towns are desirable places to live, often well after graduation" (CVO Staff 2015). Their ranking assesses cost of living, unemployment rate, crime rate and a 'Wow Factor', a unique feature of value. As has been shown throughout the third-tier literature, the characteristics and networks of third-tier cities are far more nationally distinctive than the theorisations of global and second-tier cities. That is not a surprise. Global cities are globalised and built on networks of commerce and finance capitalism. Money, ideas and people move between them, creating homogeneity. While second-tier cities are more diverse, particularly with regard to immigration history, they are known internationally for something significant, such as Liverpool and the Beatles, Seattle and grunge,

Manchester and acid house, to use music as one clustering trope. But to assume that the 'small college town' is a generalisable, globally agreed, attractive location is not internationally transferable. What is required, and Bonifacio and Drolet's research is forging a new path in this field (2017), is an understanding of how immigration impacts on third-tier cities. These scholars demonstrate the incredible diversity of immigration experiences when considering the pathways and trajectories of students and migrants beyond Toronto and Vancouver, beyond global and second-tier cities.

'Gown and town', like Morecambe and Wise, is too glib a combination and requires careful scholarship into the terms to create meaning. Much of the research literature on university cities focuses on the students, either their economic benefit or complaints about student behaviour. Yet Noah Smith (2018) has confirmed that the cultural benefit to the 'town' from the 'gown' arches far beyond the student presence. Students may leave at the completion of their degree. Therefore what remains through these cycles of admissions and graduation?

The answer to that question is that the 'value' is located in the academic staff, the professional staff and the support staff. The retention rate for students after graduation oscillates widely. In the United States, graduates stay in Texas, California and Illinois because of the large cities and potential employers. The converse is also true. Small cities are lacking the employment base, so students leave (Smith 2018). Therefore, is the benefit of a university in a small city wasted? With the focus on the research generated by the academic staff, the benefit seems wide but also difficult to measure and monitor. Academics consult for local businesses and provide spaces and opportunities for business owners and employees to meet with and exchange ideas with academics.

Beyond teaching and learning, university research – carefully disseminated and translated – can create a space for the exchange of ideas, knowledge engagement and impactful scholarship. One personal example can demonstrate this worth. While working as the Head of School of Teacher Education and Professor of Education at Charles Sturt University in Bathurst and Dubbo, managing students gaining accreditation from early childhood education through to vocational education, I continued my research as an academic, including my focus on small cities, sports tourism and GLAMs (galleries, libraries, archives and museums). During my tenure as the Head of School, *Unique Urbanity* was published (Brabazon 2015). This book solidified the relationship with Bathurst Council and then Mayor Gary Rush. That productive relationship resulted in many consultancy opportunities. I was the only member of Charles Sturt University to be invited to present and consult with delegates at the 2015 Local Government NSW Tourism Conference, where I presented a keynote on "Small Cities, Big Ideas" and conveyed the current research on economic, social and cultural development within small urban environments (Local Government NSW 2015). From this point, I was able to advise an array of even smaller local councils in New South Wales on the horizontal integration of their event tourism with wider economic opportunities. While my formal role at CSU

134   *Tara Brabazon*

was in academic management of teacher education, the 'value add' of research demonstrated the capacity for impact and engagement through the exchange of ideas between regional tourism professionals and a regional university.

My narrative from Bathurst, Australia, is anecdotal and individualised. The research tells a different story and demonstrates that my experience is not generalisable. The capacity of an educated population from a university, beyond the students, to influence and transform a small city or town has been discredited by Sean Grady's research (2017). While his focus is on the raising of human capital in students, via the proxy of post-graduate income, the role of the town around the gown is more ambivalently configured:

> There are no real visible results, at least in the research conducted in this paper, [that] people gain anything from living in a college town by itself. A certain College town may be becoming more sustainable, it may even be a prettier place to live, but if you have a college degree you can do just as well anywhere else.
>
> (2017: 61)

Sustainability, potential, capacity and the logging of specific impact stories between cities and universities will be required to move the research beyond a teaching and learning – and student – focus. Assuming that a relationship will be created simply through the presence of a university is naive. However, what Rebecca Warden described as "engaged universities" (2014) are not only employers and consumers of goods and services in the city or town. Making social decisions can transform the employment base, such as hiring women, creating family-friendly workplaces or employing ethnic minorities or men and women with impairments. Research and its targeted benefits to the local community remain integral to Warden's argument, with attention to the two-way transfer of information. This requires work, intellectual generosity and goodwill from academics and denizens. With dialogue and collaboration emerges choices and options. This is not about individual academics or administrators. Instead, it is about an institution offering different policies to attract the best staff who will stay in the town or small city.

The language used by Birch, Perry and Taylor is important here. They refer to universities as "anchor institutions" (2013). Students and staff may be mobile, but the institution is stable and remains through the vagaries of national governments, national education policies and international financial upheavals. For local governments, this enables planning and stable collaborations if a strong outreach culture is in place. Yet this role and value is stymied in some national systems, of which the Canadian network of third-tier cities is a clear example. Jennifer Massey, Sean Field and Yolande Chan studied the consequence of 'young, creative' graduates leaving the small cities (2014). They argued that a positive relationship between university and city officials was crucial to the creation of local employment opportunities and the building of relationships between students and the communities in which they study. The examples of these overt relationships include the Town and Gown Committee of the City of Windsor, the Town and Gown Advisory Committee of the City of Brantford and the 2010 Town and Gown Strategic Plan developed between the City of Kingston, the Kingston Economic Development Corporation (KEDCO) and Queen's University. This is not simply a university 'problem'. Town and city councils can make an incredible difference. Mark Funkhouser offered one model: a HERO (Higher Education Relations Officer). The function of this role would be to strategically deploy the colleges and universities, with regard to goods and services, research funding, the arts and the development of a cultural life (2015). This process ensures that tenders and engagement opportunities are well utilised.

These small cities will never be able to compete with the second-tier and global cities for corporate investment. With a considered understanding of the creative industries suite, not only including entertainment industries, but strong affiliations to sport and tourism, a relatively sustainable economic, social and cultural matrix where the university is the anchor can be achieved. The imperative is to track, following on from the research Shumin Qiu, Xielin Liu and Taishan Gao, that there is a "spillover effect" between universities and local businesses that is difficult to map and track (2017). Criteria and strategies for its evaluation will enhance our research in international city imaging scholarship.

The problem of third-tier cities and towns is invisibility. When the British Council wrote its report *Mutual Influence? Universities, Cities and the Future of Internationalisation* (2017), their case studies were Amsterdam, Dublin, Glasgow and Hannover. Second-tier cities hold a profile and distinctiveness while being small enough to render students visible and reveal the impact of the education industries. The internationalisation of Paisley, Windsor or Renmark requires research from scratch. Much more attention is required on the third-tier cities, particularly as international economic retraction, borders and barriers renders these vulnerable places even more vulnerable. The final section therefore shows how third-tier city universities limit their own capacity and the trajectory of their students.

The capping of expectations

As argued throughout this chapter, third-tier cities are incredibly diverse in terms of geography, industries present, workforce, leisure, health and educational facilities, and transportation options. There are many ways to categorise and codify them, but the labels of 'regional,' 'rural' and 'remote' usefully align, agitate and organise third-tier cities. The deployment of these terms is volatile and dynamic. In the Australian context, 'regional' refers to the towns and small cities that exist beyond the capital cities: Sydney, Melbourne, Brisbane, Perth, Adelaide and Canberra. Through this definition, 8.8 million people are in regional areas, contributing one-third of the national output and employment for one in three Australians (Regional Australia Institute 2018). Rural is determined in opposition to urban based on agricultural industries. Rurality is an ideology as much as a designation of a place. Remote locations are configured through not only distance from a metropolis but a lack of infrastructure.

136 *Tara Brabazon*

There is a wider international theory to frame and encircle the Australian experience. Jason Cervone's remarkable monograph, *Corporatizing Rural Education: Neoliberal Globalisation and Reaction in the United States* (2018), is so important because these third-tier rural cities have been buffeted by the waves of neoliberal globalisation. The white working class in regional and rural areas voted for Donald Trump. These "angry, white men and women" (Cervone 2018: 1) were not validated or addressed by any of the major political parties. Yet the point about these locations – and how neoliberalism has framed their city imaging – is far more complex and damaging than any simple labelling of Donald Trump voters may suggest. Cervone argues that

> the corporatization of rural schools is based in the same ideology that has affected rural communities throughout US history, the ideology that shapes rural communities as backward and in need of modernization.
>
> (2018: 16)

This is a powerful and important analysis. Configuring the rural and regional as backward – summoning the cascading identities of redneck, yahoo, gronk or bogan (depending on the nation) – opens these environments to market-driven and profit-motivated 'programmes' for modernisation. The rural and regional are configured through a deficit model, and the citizens that live in these locations are deficient, requiring the market economy – rather than public services – to rectify the weaknesses and deficits. Instead of public providers for health, education and correctional services – to name three key examples – neoliberal corporations move into these rural and regional locations to extract profit. Therefore, 'modernisation' is mashed with exploitation: of people, animals and the land. Education is cheapened and public schooling undermined. With a poor schooling system and few choices for alternative providers, the rural and regional citizens continue to have fewer choices and options than those from larger cities.

The labelling of 'rednecks' therefore has nothing to do with the reality or lived experience of rural, regional or remote environments and instead is a product of configuring these spaces and the people within them as lacking, underdeveloped and anti-modern. Such an ideology poses particular challenges for universities in these environments. Regional schools confront instability, including the churn of teaching staff, which impacts the quality of education for students.

The options available to students in regional and rural areas are constricted economically, intellectually and socially, and even further restricted in remote areas. There is a variance in opportunity determined by the mode of university present in third-tier cities:

1   A single institution: a self-standing university in a large town or small city.
2   A regional university with campuses spread through third-tier cities.
3   An outlier campus of a major university, located in a third-tier city.

The second and third modes dominate the international numbers of third-tier cities. The challenge and problem with these models is that expectations are capped. Even in the first model, if the institution is a community college, with the great advantage of partnerships between further education and higher education to widen the participation in education, there is a cap on the capabilities and qualifications of students. The point is, "Small-Town Harvards" (Semuels 2017) do not exist outside of Harvard. The type of university that exists in these struggling third-tier cities is – so often – a struggling university. Everything is more difficult. The Vice Chancellor and senior staff that are hired are often inexperienced, and it is their first post at that level. The deans appointed to faculties, similarly, are in that role for the first time. Fields of candidates for appointments are smaller. Attracting staff to live in these small cities, away from the facilities in larger urban environments, is challenging. If they are hired, then some of the staff become part of the FIFO (Fly In Fly Out) academic workforce, not living permanently in the location of their employment. Therefore, gown and town relations are truncated.

Such a problem manifests acutely in rural and remote education, where these locations are framed as appropriate for professional placements or clinical practices, but not nested, organic, situated education (Kaden, Patterson and Healy 2014). In other words, students are sent out to regional locations. Their supervisors visit them. But the notion of students, supervisors and locations authentically contextualising regional experiences is rare in the literature. Currently, these are places to visit for a short placement and then leave. Change is required. Intervention is necessary. They are locations to live and develop situated teaching learning and research. This reality is absent for many industries and professions, with just over one-quarter of nurses in Australia working in regions with populations between 5,000 and 100,000 people (Mills, Francis and Bonner 2005). This workforce sees a churn, a rapid turnover of staff, is older than the urban nursing population, and has fewer opportunities to engage in professional development and upskilling. This problem is made worse through the lack of comprehensive education institutions in many of these towns and cities.

Robert Chambers' landmark study of rural development (2013) is appropriate to understanding how universities operate in third-tier cities. Insider knowledge – insider research and insider teaching – is rare. When considering "cores and peripheries of knowledge" (2013: 4), outsiders bring their – mistakenly configured – "superior knowledge and superior status" (2013: 6) to study communities that are, by definition, ignorant or backward. Also, the curriculum in the outlier campuses of major universities is capped. To use the Augustana campus, in Camrose, from the University of Alberta as an example, only undergraduate and some master's courses are offered. The doctoral programme is only available on the 'main' campus in Edmonton. So while higher education is delivered in Camrose, the expectations are capped. This is distinct from Otago and Massey Universities in Dunedin and Palmerston North in New Zealand. Both are comprehensive research and teaching universities in third-tier cities.

138 *Tara Brabazon*

Education is the central employer in both cities (Penny 2015). A full doctoral programme is provided in both these universities.

The more elite the qualification, the less research appears in the cross-hairs of theories of teaching and learning, doctoral studies and third-tier cities scholarship. When sourcing material on doctoral education and supervision in these small environments, the absence and silence is chilling. The focus remains on supervising placements in rural and regional areas, rather than teaching and learning in situ. Importantly, the lack of refereed material – or even blogs – on how to supervise research master's and doctorates in regional, rural and remote environments is telling. My Digital Doctorate project (Brabazon 2018) demonstrates how the 3 Ds (Digitisation, Disintermediation and Deterritorialisation) can shape a high-quality learning experience for students outside of capital cities. But the capacity for a highly qualified and experienced supervisor to be living and working in Camrose, Renmark or Skye is not high. Yet with a labour surplus of academics, the ability to choose to live and work in Vancouver, Melbourne or Edinburgh may no longer exist. Currently these outlier campuses are teaching factories, pumping out undergraduate degrees in health and education in particular. Policies and procedures (and leadership) are FIFO-ed into these locations. Authentic learning from these small places for the staff and students that live and work there is rare.

Aligning critical geography, urban studies and cultural studies provides a theoretical platform for university cities to be understood. Their diversity is both troubling and remarkable. There can never be a singular model for a university city. But in each case study and context, the university offers an anchor, an employer, a font of expertise, a drawcard for (even temporary) residents and an enhanced cultural life of public lectures and events, the performing arts and book launches to offer incidental, inspirational and conversational events that are rarely measured or presented in the research. At their best, universities in third-tier cities enable not only "smart diversification" (Suwala and Micek 2018) but also stability and perhaps growth through the corrugated iron development after the Global Financial crisis.

Learning and teaching matters. Thinking matters more. As economic development and social opportunities become more fractured and frayed, small cities hold advantages. A tough place requires Theoretical Times (Redhead 2017). One solution to the claustropolitanism framed by environmental damage, inequality, homelessness and underemployment is to see education and urbanity as complex, intricate and diverse. While Gerry Rafferty sung of London, he was born in Paisley. Like third-tier city universities, these ambivalent places are worthy of research, even though the sources, evidence and methods to investigate their specific stories remain hidden, ignored or marginalised.

References

Andes, S. 2017. *Hidden in Plain Sight: The Oversized Impact of Downtown Universities*. Washington, DC: Brookings Institution.

Bell, D., and Jayne, M. 2009. "Small Cities? Towards a Research Agenda." *International Journal of Urban and Regional Research* 33(3): 683–699.

BiGGAR Economics. 2017. "Economic Contribution of the Finnish Universities." *Penicuik*. Retrieved January 12, 2018 (www.unifi.fi/wp-content/uploads/2017/06/UNIFI_Economic_Impact_Final_Report.pdf).

Birch, E., Perry, D., and Taylor, H. 2013. "Universities as Anchor Institutions." *Journal of Higher Education Outreach and Engagement* 17(3): 7–16.

Bonifacio, G., and Drolet, J. 2017. *Canadian Perspective on Immigration in Small Cities*. Gewerbestrasse: Springer.

Brabazon, T. 2012. "Wasted? Managing Decline and Marketing Difference in Third-tier Cities." *JURA (Journal of Urban and Regional Analysis)* 4(1): 5–33 (www.jurareview.ro/2012_4_1/p_5_33_2012.pdf).

Brabazon, T. 2015. *Unique Urbanity*. Gewerbestrasse: Springer.

Brabazon, T. 2018. "Vlog 102: The Digital Doctorate." *Office of Graduate Research YouTube Channel*. Retrieved May 23, 2019 (www.youtube.com/watch?v=GV7pH-Vtv0s).

Brabazon, T., McRae, L., and Redhead, S. 2015. "The Pushbike Song: Rolling Physical Cultural Studies Through the Landscape." *Cultural Geographies* 9(2) (http://humangeographies.org.ro/articles/92/a_92_5_tara.pdf).

Brabazon, T., McRae, L., and Redhead, S. 2017. "Recession, Recovery, Regeneration and Resilience: Newport and the Creation of Movement Cultures." *Human Geographies* 11(2) (http://humangeographies.org.ro/articles/112/a_112_1_brabazon.pdf).

Brabazon, T., and Redhead, S. 2016. "Vlog 15: Where Will You Work? Education Cities." *Office of Graduate Research YouTube Channel*. May 23, 2019 (www.youtube.com/watch?v=_DoRbuKgKeE).

British Council. 2017. *Mutual Influence? Universities, Cities and the Future of Internationalisation*. London. British Council.

Cervone, J. 2018. *Corporatizing Rural Education: Neoliberal Globalisation and Reaction in the United States*. New York: Palgrave Macmillan.

Chambers, R. 2013. *Rural Development: Putting the Last First*. Abingdon: Routledge.

Cunnane, S. 2012. "Univer-cities Told to Learn Some Home Truths." *Times Higher Education*. May 3, pp. 8–10.

CVO Staff. 2015. "50 Best Small College Towns in America." *College Values Online*. July. Retrieved May 23, 2019 (www.collegevaluesonline.com/features/best-small-college-towns-in-america/).

Dekker, T., and Tabbers, M. 2012. "From Creative Crowds to Creative Tourism: A Search for Creative Tourism in Small and Medium sized Cities. *Journal of Tourism Consumption and Practice* 4(2): 129–132.

Duranton, G. 2007. "Urban Evolutions: The Fast, the Slow, and the Still." *American Economic Review* 97(1): 197–221.

Erickcek, G., and McKinney, H. 2004. "Small Cities Blues: Looking for Growth Factors in Small and Medium-Sized Cities." *Upjohn Institute for Employment Research*. Working Paper 04–100. Retrieved May 23, 2019 (http://research.upjohn.org/cgi/viewcontent.cgi?article=1117&context=up_workingpapers).

Farley, P., and Roberts, M. 2011. *Edgelands: Journeys into England's True Wilderness*. London: Jonathan Cape.

Funkhouser, M. 2015. "The Benefits of a Better Town-and-Gown Relationship." *Governing*. Retrieved May 23, 2019 (www.governing.com/gov-institute/funkhouser/gov-college-town-relationships.html).

140 *Tara Brabazon*

Gibson, C., Carr, C., and Warren, A. 2015. "Making Things: Beyond the Binary of Manufacturing and Creativity." Pp. 86–96 in *The Routledge Companion to the Cultural Industries*, edited by Oakley, K., and O'Connor, J. Abingdon, UK: Routledge.

Goodchild van Hilten, L. 2015. "We Need to Look at Geography, Skills and Local Companies to Accelerate Development." *Atlas: Research for a Better World*. July. Retrieved May 23, 2019 (www.elsevier.com/atlas/story/people/higher-education-is-key-to-economic-development).

Gopal. P. 2008. "College Towns: Still a Smart Investment." *Business Week*. March. Retrieved May 23, 2019 (www.primepropertyinvestors.com/businessweek.pdf).

Grady, S. 2017. "The Economics of a College Town." *The Park Place Economist* 25(1): 52–62.

Gumprecht, B. 2003. "The American College Town." *The Geographical Review* 93(1): 51–80.

Harvey, D. 2006. *Spaces of Global Capitalism: Towards a Theory of Uneven Geographical Development*. London: Verso.

Henderson, J. 2010. "Cities and Development." *Journal of Regional Science* 50(1): 515–540.

Howell, M. 2014. "The Logic of Urban Fragmentation: Organizational Ecology and the Proliferation of American Cities." *Urban Studies* 51(5): 899–916.

James, J., Preece, J., and Valdes-Cotera, R. 2018. *Entrepreneurial Learning City Regions*. Gewerbestrasse: Springer.

Johnson, N., Kackar, A., and Kramer, M. 2015. *How Small Towns and Cities Can Use Local Assets to Rebuild Their Economies: Lessons from Successful Places*. Washington, DC: U.S. Environmental Protection Agency.

Jones, P., and Evans, J. 2008. *Urban Regeneration in the UK*. Los Angeles: SAGE.

Kaden, U., Patterson, P., and Healy, J. 2014. "Updating the Role of Rural Supervision: Perspectives from Alaska." *Journal of Education and Training Studies* 2(3): 33–43.

Kelly, U., McNicoll, I., and White, J. 2014. *The Impact of Universities on the UK Economy*. London: Universities UK.

Kotkin, J. 2013. "Richard Florida Concedes the Limits of the Creative Class." *Joelkotkin.com*. Retrieved May 23, 2019 (www.joelkotkin.com/content/00717-richard-florida-concedes-limits-creative-class).

Kruss, G., McGrath, S., Petersen, I., and Gastrow, M. 2015. "Higher Education and Economic Development: The Importance of Building Technological Capabilities." *International Journal of Educational Development* 43, Issue C: 22–31.

Local Government NSW. 2015. "Local Government NSW Tourism Conference 2015." Retrieved May 23, 2019 (www.lgnsw.org.au/files/imce-uploads/166/final_Tourism%20Conference%20Program_CON5.pdf).

Massey, J., Field, S., and Chan, Y. 2014. "Partnering for Economic Development: How Town-gown Relations Impact Local Economic Development in Small and Medium Cities." *Canadian Journal of Higher Education* 44(2): 152–169.

Melin, H. 2018. "Online Commerce Allows Regional Economies to Depend Less on Capital Cities." *LSE Business Review*. February 28. Retrieved May 23, 2019 (http://blogs.lse.ac.uk/businessreview/2018/02/28/online-commerce-allows-regional-economies-to-depend-less-on-capital-cities/).

Mills, J., Francis, K., and Bonner, A. 2005. "Mentoring, Clinical Supervision and Preceptoring: Clarifying the Conceptual Definitions for Australian Rural Nurses." *Rural and Remote Health* 5 (www.rrh.org.au/journal/article/410).

Myrdahl, T. 2013. "Ordinary (Small) Cities and LGBQ Lives." *ACME* 12(2): 279–304.

Penny, J. C. 2015. "University Towns in New Zealand – Their Impacts on the Community and Economy." *ID Blog*. June 19. Retrieved May 23, 2019 (https://blog.id.com.au/2015/population/new-zealand-population-census/how-do-universities-affect-our-population-housing-and-industries/).

Qiu, S., Liu, X., and Gao, T. 2017. "Do Emerging Countries Prefer Local Knowledge or Distant Knowledge? Spillover Effect of University Collaborations on Local Firms." *Research Policy* 46: 1299–1311.

Rafferty, G. 1978. *Baker Street*. London: United Artists.

Redhead, S. 2017. *Theoretical Times*. Bingley: Emerald.

Regional Australia Institute. 2018. "What is Regional Australia?" Retrieved May 23, 2019 (www.regionalaustralia.org.au/home/what-is-regional-australia/).

Richards, G., and Duif, L. 2019. *Small Cities with Big Dreams: Creative Peacemaking and Branding Strategies*. New York: Routledge.

Semuels, A. 2017. "Could Small-town Harvards Revive Rural Economics?" *The Atlantic*. May 2017. Retrieved May 23, 2019 (www.theatlantic.com/business/archive/2017/05/rural-economies-colleges-development/525114/).

Smith, D. 2005. *"Studentification": A Guide to Opportunities, Challenges and Practice*. London: Woburn House.

Smith, N. 2018. "How Universities Make Cities Great: It's Not Just About Education." *Bloomberg.com*. March 6. Retrieved May 23, 2019 (www.bloomberg.com/view/articles/2018-03-06/how-universities-make-cities-great).

Suwala, L., and Micek, G. 2018. "Beyond Clusters? Field Configuration and Regional Platforming: The Aviation Valley Initiative in the Polish Podkarpackie Region." *Cambridge Journal of Regions, Economy and Society* 11: 353–372.

Swinney, P. 2011. "What Impact do Universities Have on City Economies?" *Centre for Cities*. May 5. Retrieved June, 2019 (http://centreforcities.typepad.com/centre_for_cities/2011/05/what-impact-do-universities-have-on-city-economies.html).

Warden, R. 2014. "Engaged Universities Contribute to Economic Development." *University World News* 344. Retrieved May 23, 2019 (www.universityworldnews.com/article.php?story=20141119095107901).

7 Locating knowledge in Australian cities

The Knowledge City Index

Lawrence Pratchett, Michael James Walsh, Richard Hu and Sajeda Tuli

Introduction

In the digital era, there is a tendency to consider knowledge and its creation to be increasingly freed from place. No longer limited by linguistic, cultural and geographic barriers, knowledge can be created, acquired and shared with ease on a global scale. In part enabled by the "'lifting out' of social relations from local contexts of interaction and their restructuring across indefinite spans of time-space" (Giddens 1992: 21), work, knowledge and social life have gradually become untethered from time and space. Richard Florida (2005: 28) suggests this supposed untethering has led to one of the greatest myths about the nature of cities: geography is dead, due in part to advances in our information communication technology and transportation systems. The implied logic in this argument suggests that work is no longer physically confined to specific localities and, as a result, workers need not congregate to undertake economic activities.

While the proliferation of communication technologies has led to an even greater uncoupling of the "relationship between physical settings and social situations" (Meyrowitz1985: 7), place has not become completely outmoded. We argue that the untethering of knowledge from place has been greatly exaggerated and that such arguments overlook the ongoing, and often renewed, importance of locality in creating and sustaining knowledge. In this context, it is worth considering the relationship between traditional and online social interactions and the extent to which they place a greater emphasis on place. Indeed, in contemporary social life, face-to-face interaction no longer has the structural importance it once did; consider the various social and economic endeavours that continue to migrate online (Cetina 2009: 63). Information technologies underpin almost every aspect of economic and social life and continue to transform the ways in which we interact with one another (Frey and Osborne 2017). While work and social life become increasingly conducted through mediated technologies, a good deal of our experiences remains in the realm of physical reality. In this respect, work and social life are increasingly mediated between online interactions and geographical realities; components of work remain anchored to physical environments. The ubiquity of information technologies creates greater emphasis on place, allowing the intrinsic value of a locality for an individual or family to be privileged over the traditional constraints of communication. Such intrinsic values might include the physical, social and cultural attractions of a place, values that once might have been over-ridden by the need to have access to specific communication channels. We see this in particular with respect to regional economies and cities where people not only remain highly concentrated in geographical centres but also are reflected in the distribution and concentration of economies that are anchored in specific localities (Florida 2005: 28).

Place also matters in terms of a locality's capacity to transition into a knowledge economy. Our interest in this topic stems from a broader curiosity regarding debates around the future of work and the predicted impact of artificial intelligence, machine learning and other technologies on various industries (Frey and Osborne 2017). In summary, this debate contends that the most in-demand workers in the future will be those based within knowledge industries or professions, able to drive and benefit from the knowledge economy that is emerging from the so-called fourth industrial revolution (Schwab 2016).

In this chapter, we argue that location matters in terms of the generation of knowledge; the knowledge economy along with its various digital technologies provide cities and regions with new opportunities to develop knowledge capabilities that are locally contingent and also globally connected. Our central concern is the ability of cities and regions to nurture knowledge capacity and to function as knowledge economy sites that represent anchorage points in the generation and diffusion of knowledge. To develop our argument, we construct a Knowledge City Index (KCI) for 25 Australian cities which showcases the connections and tensions between the knowledge capacity and the knowledge economy within these localities. Our analysis finds an interesting and important variation in the potential for Australian cities to engage with the emergent knowledge economy. Some cities appear to be well positioned to prosper in the knowledge economy, with workers whose skills and creativity will become increasingly valued and harnessed by knowledge-intensive activities. At the same time, however, our index suggests that other cities, where workers and their skills are connected to less knowledge-based occupational practices, are at risk of becoming increasingly outmoded. We argue that these transitions and tensions are importantly played out within different Australian cities and are contingent on their regional locality. Understanding and exploring this context of knowledge, its creation and implications that stem from its geography is crucial. The findings will provide insight into the changing nature of work practices and, from this, the cities and regions that are likely to be most and least susceptible to the uneven social and economic transitions currently underway as a result of the rise of the knowledge economy.

Contextualising the measurement of knowledge across Australia

In many sectors of the economy, automation, artificial intelligence, big data, machine learning and other innovations are claimed to have the potential to make many current jobs in traditional industries redundant or at least change them in significant ways (Frey and Osborne 2013, 2017). In Australia, we have seen considerable changes to the economy as it has transitioned from agriculture and manufacturing towards a greater emphasis on services sector, which might be considered forerunners to knowledge-intensive industries. This restructuring is clearly demonstrated in the proportions of gross domestic product (GDP) that various sectors now contribute. While the agricultural and manufacturing sectors have played significant roles in Australia's economy over the previous century, their proportional contributions to GDP have continued to decline from the second half of the twentieth century (see Figure 7.1). While these sectors made significant contributions to the economic base and collective identity of the nation, the greater rise of the service sectors and its associated industries have not merely taken a foothold but have come to dominate the Australian economy.

While agriculture and mining have played an important role in long-term Australian economic history, we note that other sectors not known for their contributions to Australia's economy have been principal sectors of the economy since federation. Indeed, as the Australian Treasury notes, it is the service sector that has represented the largest portion of the Australian economy since the middle of last century (Australian Treasury 2001). While we do not mean to imply by this that knowledge work (in our contemporary understanding) has existed prior to post-industrial society, it is significant that, in an Australian context, knowledge work emerges from this historical context that has emphasised service provision in terms of the share of the national economy.

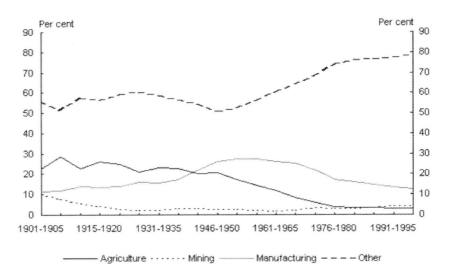

Figure 7.1 Industry shares of GDP, 1901–2000.

Source: ABS yearbooks (various editions) for the period 1975–2000; Treasury for the period 1940–74; Butlin, N. G. (1962) for the period 1901–39; Australian Treasury (2001)

Locating knowledge in Australian cities 145

It is for these reasons that our focus in this chapter is on the knowledge-intensive elements of our economy that render increasingly relevant the service sectors as broadly defined and as a key contributor to Australia's social and economic outlook. When considering the role of the service sector in light of potential challenges that arise in terms of the longevity of these industries, it is not simply unskilled or semi-skilled workers who face exposure to increasingly precarious labour thanks in part to new technologies and the changing nature of work within the economy. Increasingly, many skilled and professional occupations are being affected by these same technologies and their associated economic and social transformations, leading some to question the very future of many professions as they are currently structured (Susskind and Susskind 2015). Moreover, there are also predictions that roughly half of the jobs that currently exist in developed economies could be automated or otherwise made redundant by 2030 (Frey and Osborne 2015). It is not sufficient, therefore, to think only of the sectors that are prospering in our economy but also the types of work, and their attendant skills and knowledge that will underpin those sectors in the future. As will be seen below, our analysis seeks to take account of such changes by drawing on Frey and Osborne's (2013) distinction between occupations most exposed to automation or technological redundancy and those which appear to have the least exposure.

Critically, as some occupations are replaced by technologies and ways of undertaking routine tasks, other occupations are likely to emerge as new economic activity ramps up, signifying the changing nature of the Australian economy and the future of work. As Figure 7.1 indicates, when we look at the long-term trend, we can see that economic activity is constantly changing; rather than attempting to fix or stabilise economic activity, understanding and responding to longer term changes is critical. In this respect, the development of new occupational categories will require different sets of skills and attributes that contrast from activities in the past. Greater focus will be directed towards new forms of industries and sectors across Australia's cities and regions.

In an Australian context, some national predictions suggest that the service sectors will continue to dominate and expand their role in the economy. Healthcare, professional, scientific and technical services, construction and education and training are all predicted to grow and are forecast to provide 61.5 per cent of total employment growth over the five years to 2022 (see Figure 7.2). However, these projections in the employment structure of the economy will be offset with declines forecast in sectors such as manufacturing; electricity, gas, water and waste services; and agriculture, forestry and fishing, which are to be balanced by long-term shifts towards service sectors (Department of Jobs and Small Business 2017). Of course, such economic restructuring will not be evenly spread across the country; developments in the service sector, and especially those aspects of it that constitute or support the knowledge economy, are likely to benefit disproportionately urban and metropolitan areas.

These projections indicate that occupations that will prosper will be in the information, knowledge and service sectors, especially those occupations that

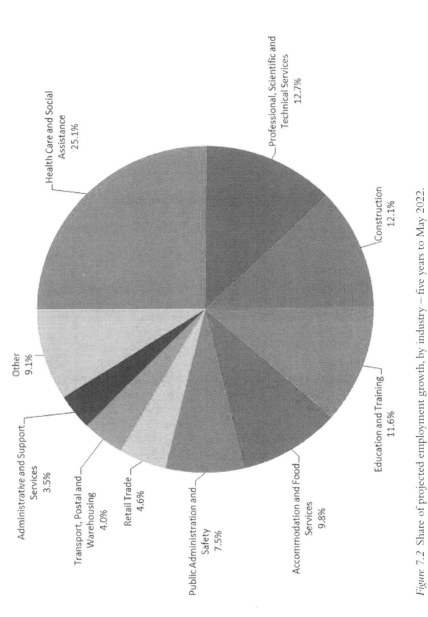

Figure 7.2 Share of projected employment growth, by industry – five years to May 2022.

Source: Department of Jobs and Small Business (2017), Industry Employment Projections, ABS Labour Force Survey

privilege advanced perception and manipulation, social intelligence or creative intelligence (Frey and Osborne 2017) in non-routine tasks or applications. Occupations that require human creativity, interpretation and perception skills rather than the repeated application of rules and procedures presumably will flourish. Augmented interpersonal and communication skills increasingly will be critical in that, while autonomous technologies may attempt to replicate these qualities, they arguably will be unlikely to master these attributes.

The likelihood of these new and emerging jobs being geographically dispersed is limited. As Richard Florida (2005) notes, not only do people in these industries remain in the same locations, but the economy itself tends to remain geographically anchored. Therefore,

> the high-tech, knowledge-based, and creative content industries which drive so much of economic growth – continues to concentrate in specific places from Austin and Silicon Valley, to New York City and Hollywood, just as the automobile industry once concentrated in Detroit.
>
> (Florida 2005: 28)

In an Australian context, we take this argument to mean that in order to be successful, city and regional authorities must develop the capacity to attract talent and workers to their localities through providing the quality of life that appeals to talented workers. By developing the quality-of-life experiences for occupants of a region, this strategy is critical for producing suitable conditions to attract high-tech as well as knowledge industries (Florida 2005: 50). One strategy therefore suggested is that different localities could develop distinct knowledge focuses that connect with the amenities of a given place rather than building or reengineering cities or regions to suit their desired knowledge focus of a given locality. Van Winden and Carvalho's (2016) typology of knowledge-work locations indicates how distinct forms of knowledge work (e.g. symbolic, synthetic, and analytical) become configured in distinct spatial localities and therefore suggests that distinct forms of knowledge work might be predisposed to a given location's existing infrastructure. The first type of knowledge location they identify is *symbolic* knowledge work that typifies the creation of cultural or aesthetic artefacts and symbols that attract particular workers who, more often than not, reside in, and congregate around, distinctive, 'buzzing' and vibrant urban environments. These forms of knowledge work tend to be situated in inner city environs that mix up time and space and that are predisposed to more contingent or temporary projects (van Winden and Carvalho 2016: 57–58). The second form of knowledge work identified is *synthetic* knowledge work: pertaining to the application of existing knowledge practices related to customisation and problem solving, which shows preference for frequent face-to-face contact and interactions with clients in a functional urban region that engenders a 'business climate' that typically is said to be associated with advanced IT activity and machinery-related industries (van Winden and Carvalho 2016: 58). And finally, in a similar vein to synthetic work,

148   *L. Pratchett et al.*

van Winden and Carvalho identify *analytical* or science-based knowledge work that refers to medical or biotechnical activity that tend to be located in close proximity to other scientists in large urban regions that do not rely on the same vibrant urban surrounds (van Winden & Carvalho 2016: 58). In this respect, we suggest that if different knowledge work shows a predilection for distinct amenities and infrastructure, then cities and regions would best focus on forms of knowledge work most closely situated to their current characteristics.

The transformation enabled by new technologies and the emerging service sectors of the economy create significant demand and opportunities for certain dimensions of the knowledge economy in an Australian context. The work and job roles that are most likely to decline in the near future are those associated with the older segments of the economy that are reducing in their share of contribution to the national economy. We also have some sense that other jobs and sectors, like the service and knowledge sectors of the economy, are likely to be most resilient and grow into the future. But most significantly, this dichotomy of decline and growth is not equally distributed neatly across the geography of Australian cities and regions. Some regions of Australia are well positioned to grow and advance in the emerging service and technology-driven dimensions of the knowledge-based economy, but others lack the infrastructure and capacity to adapt to, and survive, the impacts that are associated with the structural transformations occurring. Just like for individual workers, for some Australian cities and regions, it will become increasingly precarious. To provide some understanding about the nature of these changes associated with work that arise from the shifts in the national economy, we have developed a Knowledge City Index that provides insights into the knowledge performance of 25 Australian cities and their regions. In the index, we highlight some of the geographical areas of Australia that will require further support as they transition from older economic structures and also indicate regions of the nation that will be placed at the centre of change ushered in by the continuous transitions occurring in Australia's economy.

Constructing the Knowledge City Index

To better understand these impacts on our cities and regions, this chapter builds a Knowledge City Index (KCI) for Australian cities. We examine the 25 largest urban areas in the country and analyse each of them according to knowledge capital (the underlying knowledge infrastructure of a city that includes human and non-human assets) and knowledge economy (the knowledge activation and performance within a city).

In presenting the KCI, we note that statistical information can operate in ways that affect the phenomena under consideration. In this respect we are mindful of the bind that researchers can find themselves in, as MacKenzie (2006: 12) suggests with respect to the use of statistics, in that they can shift the ontological basis of our understanding of the economy and function like an engine that feeds into the phenomena under consideration rather than merely providing a representation, like a camera. In presenting our index, we are mindful of this tendency for statistics to be used to "make up people" as objects of scientific inquiry (Hacking 2006). We also note that the production of indices has come under criticism in that they tend to privilege and isolate dimensions of the economy without considering the interconnections. In constructing our index, we are mindful of these critiques and provide our index with the important qualification that we use proxy measures that only approximates, rather than directly signals, the knowledge-intensiveness of Australian cities.

We combine six different measures through a data-standardisation process to provide a comparative overview of all 25 cities. In doing so, we employ an approach that attempts to compare regions and cities across Australia for the purpose of providing details into the changing nature of work and how it is impacting on geographical areas in distinct ways. The framework can also be extended to comparisons of other cities around the world and will be repeatable over time in order to understand the changing nature of Australian cities and regions. The Knowledge City Index presented in this chapter has been developed to allow for comparisons of 25 significant urban areas (SUAs): that is, geographic boundaries that are delimited with a methodology provided by the Australian Bureau of Statistics to represent cities and towns with populations over 10,000 people. Unlike adopting conventional administrative boundaries to define cities and regions, our use of SUAs aims to focus on labour markets that evolve and seep across administrative boundaries. By focusing on these geographical areas, we then explore qualities associated with knowledge that are situated across two core domains:

- Knowledge capital, which measures the existing knowledge infrastructure of a locality and the resources, both human and technological, which the local knowledge economy can draw upon.
- Knowledge economy, which examines the knowledge activity located in a particular city's region and that is related to its prosperity.

We suggest that these two domains are essential to create and sustain successful knowledge cities. Knowledge capital provides the capacity to generate the knowledge artefacts that are the economic products of the city. At the same time, the value of the artefacts needs to be understood and measured in the context of the knowledge economy. Our model brings these two domains together with the aim of measuring both the capacity of generating knowledge and also the economic value of such knowledge generation (see Table 7.1): in other words, two different sides of the same coin. While conceptually these domains work in tandem, it is also necessary to operationalise them in order to give them empirical value. The operationalisation of the domains enables the index to compare different localities by drawing upon six indicators; three in each conceptual domain.

150   L. Pratchett et al.

Table 7.1 Indicators and measures of the KCI

	Indicators	Measures	Explanation
Knowledge Capital (KC)	KCI: Knowledge Capacity	Residents with tertiary qualifications	This measures a city's locally based human capital.
	KCII: Knowledge Mobility	Migrant residents working in knowledge intensive industries	This measures a city's attraction to knowledge workers from elsewhere in Australia and overseas who newly moved into the city.
	KCIII: Digital Access	Dwellings with Internet connection	This measures the accessibility to digital infrastructure.
Knowledge Economy (KE)	KEI: Knowledge Industries	Workers for knowledge intensive industries	This measures the knowledge base in the local economy.
	KEII: Income	Workers earning the highest bracket of income	This measures the high-value-added part in the local knowledge base.
	KEIII: Smart Work	Non-commuting workers	This measures the practice of non-commuting work facilitated by digital technology and the knowledge economy.

For the *knowledge capital* domain we draw upon the following measures:

- Knowledge capacity, which is a measure of human capital that focuses on the educational qualifications of residents; namely, the proportion of residents in the SUA who have a tertiary level qualification (bachelor's degree or higher). This is because tertiary education is a widely recognised measure of strong human capital (Raghuram 2013).
- Knowledge mobility, which is another measure of human capital that examines the number of migrant workers in knowledge-intensive industries. Migrants are defined as people from outside of the SUA who have moved to it within the last five years and can include both Australians from other areas as well as workers from overseas. This measure is important because it emphasises the extent to which a city and region attracts talent from outside of its own locality to pool resources. The measure demonstrates the capacity of a city to attract workers that are diverse in nature to a locality, and this is key in developing and retaining high-technology and knowledge industries (Florida 2005: 137).
- Digital access, which is a proxy measure of the physical infrastructure that underpins the knowledge economy. We use the number of households with an Internet connection, but we also recognise that more nuanced measures (such as speed of connection etc.) may become more appropriate as census data is enhanced.

Locating knowledge in Australian cities 151

For the *knowledge economy* domain we draw upon the following measures:

*   Knowledge industries, which is a measure of the importance of the knowledge base to the local economy. The measure we use here is the number of people employed in knowledge-intensive industries within the area. These knowledge-intensive industries were defined on the basis that their major output is knowledge or that they are instruments for the reception, processing or transmission of knowledge. Their selection was informed by a wide range of literature on knowledge production, knowledge employment and knowledge workers (Brint 2001; Florida 2002, 2003; Frey and Osborne 2015; Hu 2016; Machlup 2014; Mellander 2009). Knowledge-intensive industries were selected from 126 sub-industries from the following eight broad industry groups in the Australian and New Zealand Standard Industrial Classification (ANZSIC) (Commonwealth of Australia 2006): Information Media and Telecommunications; Financial and Insurance; Professional, Scientific and Technical; Manufacturing; Public Administration and Safety; Education and Training; Health Care and Social Assistance; and Arts and Recreation. This selection of industries includes the creative class defined by Richard Florida (2005) as well as the emerging technology-enabled sectors.
*   Income, which is an indication of a proxy for the value-add that knowledge work contributes to the local economy. The specific statistical measure we used here was the number of workers earning an annual income within the top income bracket as identified on the Census of Population and Housing (i.e. more the $104,000 pa). We recognise that this measure may miss parts of the knowledge and innovation ecology such as startups and low-income aspects of the creative fields. However, this distinction is important because we are interested in the measurable economic value of the knowledge artefacts that are produced in a locality rather than solely the artefacts themselves.
*   Smart Work, which is an indicator that measures the number of workers who do not commute but work from home. This final statistical measure provides an important understanding of the knowledge economy, as it reflects the increasing trend of changing work practices that allow for and indeed encourage work to be displaced from central office localities within a city (Wilmot et al. 2014). As companies continue to encourage the reduction of their physical footprints through reductions in office space, knowledge work is increasingly undertaken outside of the office, and this is one particular feature of the emerging knowledge economy (Pratchett et al. 2015; Hu 2016).

In constructing this index, we have been deeply aware of the importance of data quality, especially for local and regional areas that typically struggle to obtain direct and accurate statistical information about their locales. In order to ensure greater accuracy as a basis of measures for our index, the data source we draw on is the Census of Population and Housing. One of the greatest strengths of the census as a data source is that it provides a more detailed picture of the local geographical level than is possible with survey instruments; none are more sensitive to geographic differences than the census. In exploring locational variation in knowledge across different cities, this source is ideal in that it provides consistent and robust data while also allowing for a greater level of fidelity at the small geographical scale. Because every household ideally completes the census, it is much more comprehensive than surveys that sample only a proportion of the population. As a consequence, we are able to drill down into, and compare, geographic regions across Australia: a feature that is not possible with similar levels of fidelity with the use of national surveys. While we recognise that the 2011 data that we are currently applying to the KCI has matured, we balance with the clear advantages it offers our current analysis. Moreover, as the analysis will show, even using 2011 data reveals significant divergences between Australian cities.

We note that for the knowledge capital measure, the *place of usual residence* data was used to reflect the people who 'live' in the specific city, while for the knowledge economy measures, the *place of work* data was used to reflect the people who 'work' in the given city. These two census categories have important differences in that people may reside in one area but work in another. Our decision to use *place of usual residence* for knowledge capital measures reflects our desire to measure the potential knowledge base of the city. Equally, our decision to use *place of work* data for knowledge economy measures reflects our desire to focus on the ways in which cities are exploiting knowledge capital, regardless of whether the human capital resides within the area or commutes. Ultimately, this methodology has been constructed for measuring and comparing cities and their regions. For more precise information about how the calculation for the Knowledge City Index has been undertaken, please see Pratchett et al. (2017).

Cities and regions of contrast: the Knowledge City Index

According to our KCI, some cities show that it is the best of times, and for other cities, it has the potential to be troubling, especially in light of the changes and growth in service and knowledge sectors of the economy, with corresponding declines in the manufacturing and agriculture sectors. The KCI suggests that some cities and their regions perform exceptionally well given their size and the components of their economic bases, whereas other cities show signs of limited development and capacity to transform themselves in light of the increase in the knowledge intensive nature and burgeoning service orientation of the Australian economy. While, to some extent, it is the biggest metropolitan areas that top the index, the distinction is much more nuanced than simply a metropolitan/non-metropolitan divide; some significant metropolitan areas perform poorly.

The index provides an understanding of the knowledge strengths and weaknesses of different Australian cities and their regions. Here we provide some insights into the broader economics of these regions through statistics, showcasing the knowledge intensiveness of different cities and, as a result, those

Locating knowledge in Australian cities 153

cities that are likely to be more resilient to the transitions occurring as Australia pivots towards a fully-fledged knowledge-based service economy. In 2016, Australia's third-biggest export sector was not a physical commodity, but was education in the form of international students who came to study in an educational institution. After iron ore and coal, Australia's key export industry is knowledge-based, contributing $32 billion to the national economy in 2018 (Universities Australia 2018). This trend is therefore understandable given the transition towards a knowledge economy.

The following presents the KCI in three ways: first the index is presented by proportion; then by raw size; and then finally as a measure of proportion and overall size (a combination of the first and second representations). We present these three versions of the index because they illustrate different aspects concerning the nature of knowledge cities. After all, comparing cities of differing sizes without attempting to control for scale and proportion may hide or diminish the knowledge capacity of different cities included in our analysis. These different versions of the index also paint slightly different pictures about the knowledge intensiveness of Australian cities in that the knowledge bases that constitute these cities can be located in different components of the index. The final version of the index balances the proportion with the size of the knowledge indicators and demonstrates that five Australian cities appear strongly placed to withstand the changes afoot in terms of the transformation occurring with the emergent knowledge economy. With this picture, we learn that the size of a city is not the only thing that matters; the extent to which cities focus and concentrate around service and knowledge roles as well as attract workers to regions while providing a relatively high income are also critical. While these measures provide only a concentrated overall picture of Australian cities and their regions, they nonetheless illuminate comparative differences that are critical in cities of different sizes across the nation.

The KCI presented here represents the picture of Australian cities by proportion of those living and working in the locality. In this version of the index, we see that Canberra-Queanbeyan has the highest percentage according to five

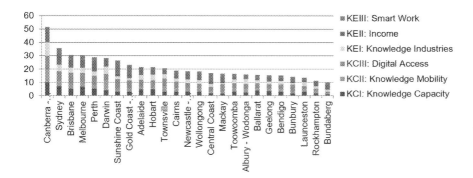

Figure 7.3 Knowledge City Index – by proportion.

of the measures that are used to construct the KCI. Canberra-Queanbeyan's only limitation is its measure of smart work. Canberra's concentration of public sector organisations and concentration of educational institutions contributes not only to affluence but to the number of workers that find themselves working in the knowledge and service sectors. By proportion, Sydney is positioned second, then Brisbane and then Melbourne. However, it should be noted that this version of the index only covers the intensity of knowledge within a city and overlooks how this might be impacted by scaling up the size of the city. In this measure we treat all cities and their regions as if they were all made up of an equal number of people. In this sense, within this version of the index we can conduct a thought experiment that compares cities on the basis of what constitutes their components without taking into consideration their size.

As cities are understood as the collection of dwellings in close proximity to one another (Weber, Martindale and Neuwirth 1958), it would be overly simplistic to disregard this principle when considering the scale of different cities. Therefore in this version of the KCI, we account for the size of the city by its population of residents and workers. When we examine the measures by focusing on absolute size, it is unsurprising that cities such as Sydney and Melbourne stand out as significantly out-performing all other cities given the scale of these cities. Sydney is positioned in first place in terms of knowledge capability in Australia because it measures the highest score across all six measures that constitute the index. Melbourne stands in second position, considerably ahead of Brisbane in third place. Canberra-Queanbeyan has expectably fallen to a lower position on the index given its relatively small size, followed by Perth and Adelaide.

To develop an effective measure of the knowledge-intensive nature of cities, this final version of the index incorporates the proportion of knowledge-intensive activity within a city and the overall size of the locality. Integrating both the proportion of knowledge measures and the size of the city in question is important for considering the extent to which these components contribute to its position on the index. In this sense, the approach is different from conventional measures of absolute numbers because here we factor both components to standardise each city without completely reducing each locality on the index

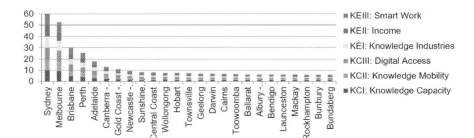

Figure 7.4 Knowledge City Index – by size.

Locating knowledge in Australian cities 155

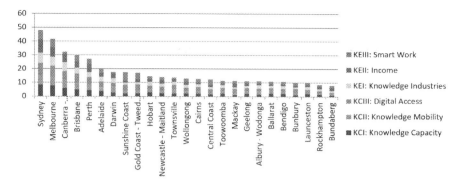

Figure 7.5 Knowledge City Index – by proportion and size.

to the exact same number (given the cities in question range from approximately 65,000 people to four million people).

For this final version of the index, we adopted a data standardisation process that ensures the index accounts for these different elements of scale and proportion. The integrated version of the KCI means that we are no longer overlooking the considerably different variation of population across these cities. This final version of the index provides the most revealing story about the knowledge capacity of Australian cities. It shows that Sydney still out performs all other cities as it has the highest scores across all six indicators, followed by Melbourne in second position and then followed by Canberra-Queanbeyan, Brisbane and Perth. The index also shows that smaller to medium-sized cities also have considerable opportunity to develop in particular areas.

Overwhelming, the index informs us that the top five cities are well prepared for the knowledge transition that is currently taking place. These cities we identify as 'knowledge' cities in that they possess a concentration of knowledge capital that is reflected in the share of service and knowledge jobs that are mooted as key areas of growth in short to medium term. The remaining 20 cities that we have included in the index have knowledge limitations to varying degrees that place them in more acute positions in terms of the transition occurring in the economy more broadly as we pivot away from manufacturing and agricultural industries. We would also note that Canberra-Queanbeyan in particular represents one of Australia's leading knowledge cities despite its comparatively smaller population and employment bases. It has higher proportions of its population situated within the knowledge economy, and this shows up as the number of workers that labour in the knowledge-intensive parts of the local economy as compared with other cities on the index. Canberra-Queanbeyan's regional context is also significant in that it not only serves as the nation's capital and formal seat of the federal government but also services the large regional locality of southwestern New South Wales.

The index suggests that other regional centres might go some way in responding to and mitigating themselves from the changing nature of Australia's economy by positioning themselves to capitalise on the transitions from the traditional economy to the new service and knowledge sectors that result in the changing nature of work practices. Were regional economies to position themselves in growth industries and sectors that are projected to increase in scale and size, this could be one means of redressing some of the limitations in the structural make-up of cities located at the lower end of the index. While cities that traditionally possessed a concentration of manufacturing and mining industries for employment tend to be less efficient in generating knowledge capital and therefore have not developed the knowledge-intensive parts of their economy, they also potentially have some capacity to draw upon talent and people who are displaced. As Richard Florida notes, it is no coincidence that companies tend to concentrate in locations associated with previous economic activity because of the ability to mobilise labour from these pre-existing concentrations and that it is a "tremendous source of competitive advantage for companies in our time-driven and horizontal economy" (Florida 2005: 29). The challenge for areas wanting to address aspects of decline in the knowledge economy is to focus not only on the workers that they wish to attract but also the broader conditions that might create the physical, social and cultural infrastructure that is attractive to those workers.

Conclusion

The rise of the knowledge economy, along with improvements in digital technology, has endowed cities and regions with greater geographic importance. Technological developments assist business and government to overcome some of the geographical limitations that arise from living in a nation that is simultaneously a continent, reducing costs while increasing productivity, reliability, scalability and security. The movement of people around the globe has increased steadily, which has been coupled with an increase in the mobility of global talent. People, companies and countries are less restricted by borders and great distances, and consequently, the world is a more connected place. In this respect, we might suggest that the world is developing into one large global market, including its labour components, rather than a series of distinct national markets – providing access to previously unreachable opportunities in business and employment (Hajkowicz et al. 2016: 36). We suggest that to prosper in this globalised world, cities and regions need to focus on knowledge-based urban development to attract and retain globally mobile talent. With technological advancements and infrastructure development, human capital is increasingly becoming more mobile and less confined to specific locations that enable for the increasing movement of people. In this context, while mobility abounds for workers, the cities and regions that house knowledge work are required to compete more actively in creating conditions that will attract and retain these workers.

Locating knowledge in Australian cities 157

Cities and regions therefore will not become displaced as centres of economic and cultural anchorage. Indeed, cities are becoming increasingly important, as we have suggested, as locations of knowledge-based activities that pervade society and economy more generally. It is evident from our study that knowledge-intensive industries are concentrated and are situated in locations that appear linked with drivers of economic growth for cities and regions. As such, the future of cities depends on the ability to make them attractive places that lure knowledge workers to live, work and enjoy city life (Glaeser, Kolko and Saiz 2001). As Florida remarks, global competition is no longer seen between the trading of services, goods or capital flows, but the ability to "harness the creative energy of a country's domestic population" and "attract creative people from around the globe" (Florida 2005: 173). It is investments and focused action that cultivates knowledge production that will prepare and equip cities and regions for the changing nature of work in times of increasing volatility and uncertainty.

References

Australian Bureau of Statistics. 2001. *Year Book Australia 2001* (Catalogue Number 1301. 0.30.001).

Australian Treasury. 2001. "Economic Roundup Centenary Edition: Australia's Century Since Federation at a Glance." *Canberra.* Retrieved November 8, 2018 (https://treasury.gov.au/publication/economic-roundup-centenary-edition-2001/article-2-australias-century-since-federation-at-a-glance).

Brint, S. 2001. "Professionals and the 'Knowledge Economy': Rethinking the Theory of Postindustrial Society." *Current Sociology* 49(4): 101–132.

Butlin, N. G. 1962. *Australian Domestic Product, Investment and Foreign Borrowing 1861–1938/1939.* Cambridge: Cambridge University Press.

Cetina, K. 2009. "The Synthetic Situation: Interactionism for a Global World." *Symbolic Interaction* 32(1): 61–87.

Commonwealth of Australia. 2006. *Australian and New Zealand Standard Industrial Classification* (ANZSIC). Australian Bureau of Statistics. (https://www-abs-gov-au.ezproxy.canberra.edu.au/AUSSTATS/abs@.nsf/DetailsPage/1220.02006?OpenDocument).

Department of Jobs and Small Business. 2017. "Industry Employment Projections." Retrieved November 8, 2018 (http://lmip.gov.au/default.aspx?LMIP/GainInsights/Employment Projections).

Florida, R. 2002. *The Rise of the Creative Class: And How It's Transforming Work, Leisure, Community and Everyday Life.* New York: Basic Books.

Florida, R. 2003. "Cities and the Creative Class." *City & Community* 2(1): 3–19.

Florida, R. 2005. *Cities and the Creative Class.* New York and London: Routledge.

Frey, C. B., and Osborne, M. 2013. *The Future of Employment. How Susceptible are Jobs to Computerisation.* Oxford: University of Oxford.

Frey, C. B., and Osborne, M. 2015. "Technology at Work: The Future of Innovation and Employment." Oxford: Oxford Martin School and Citi GPS. Retrieved November 8, 2018 (www.oxfordmartin.ox.ac.uk/downloads/reports/Citi_GPS_Technology_Work.pdf).

Frey, C. B., and Osborne, M. A. 2017. "The Future of Employment: How Susceptible are Jobs to Computerisation?" *Technological Forecasting and Social Change* 114: 254–280.

158   *L. Pratchett et al.*

Giddens, A. 1992. *The Consequences of Modernity*. Cambridge: Polity Press.

Glaeser, E. L., Kolko, J., and Saiz, A. 2001. "Consumer City." *Journal of Economic Geography* 1(1): 27–50.

Hacking, I. 2006. "Making Up People." *London Review of Books* 28(16): 23–26.

Hajkowicz, S. A., Reeson. A., Rudd, L., Bratanova, A., Hodgers, L. M. C., and Boughen, N. 2016. "Tomorrow's Digitally Enabled Workforce: Megatrends and Scenarios for Jobs and Employment in Australia Over the Coming Twenty Years. CSIRO, Brisbane." Retrieved November 8, 2018 (www.acs.org.au/content/dam/acs/acs-documents/16-0026_DATA 61_REPORT_TomorrowsDigiallyEnabledWorkforce_WEB_160128.pdf).

Hu, R. 2016. "Concentration and Mobility of Knowledge Workers: An Intercity Analysis of Sydney, Melbourne, and Brisbane." *Journal of Urban Technology* 23(1): 1–18.

Machlup, F. 2014. "Knowledge Industries and Knowledge Occupations." Pp. 14–21 in *Economics of Education: Research and Studies*, edited by Psacharopoulos, G. Oxford: Pergamon Press.

MacKenzie, D. 2006. *An Engine, Not a Camera: How Financial Models Shape Markets*. Cambridge, MA: MIT Press.

Mellander, C. 2009. "Creative and Knowledge Industries: An Occupational Distribution Approach." *Economic Development Quarterly* 23(4): 294–305 (doi:10.1177/08912424093 43808).

Meyrowitz, Joshua. 1985. *No Sense of Place: The Impact of Electronic Media on Social Behavior*. New York: Oxford University Press.

Pratchett, L. Hu, R., Buick, F., and Carmody, L. 2015. *Smart Work in the ACT and Region*. Canberra: University of Canberra.

Pratchett, L., Hu, R., Walsh, M., and Tuli, S. 2017. "The Knowledge City Index: A Tale of 25 Cities in Australia – 2017." Retrieved November 8, 2018 (www.canberra.edu.au/ research/faculty-research-centres/nexus-centre-for-research/research-progeammes/ research-programs/research-areas/the-knowledge-city-index-a-tale-of-25-cities-in-australia).

Raghuram, P. 2013. "Theorising the Spaces of Student Migration." *Population, Space and Place* 19(2): 138–154.

Schwab, K. 2016. *The Fourth Industrial Revolution*. New York: World Economic Forum.

Susskind, R., and Susskind, D. 2015. *The Future of the Professions: How Technology Will Transform the Work of Human Experts*. Oxford: Oxford University Press.

Universities Australia. 2018. "International Students Inject $32 Billion a Year into Australia's Economy – Boosting Aussie Jobs and Wages [Press release]." Retrieved November 8, 2018 (www.universitiesaustralia.edu.au/Media-and-Events/media-releases/International-students-inject–32-billion-a-year-into-Australia-s-economy–boosting-Aussie-jobs-and-wages#.W-T-nPkzY2w)./

van Winden, W., and Carvalho, L. 2016. "Urbanize or Perish? Assessing the Urbanization of Knowledge Locations in Europe." *Journal of Urban Technology*, 23(1): 53–70 (doi:10.1080/ 10630732.2015.1090194).

Weber, M., Martindale, D., and Neuwirth, G. 1958. *The City*. New York Free Press.

Wilmot, K., Boyle, T., Rickwood, P., and Sharpe, S. 2014. *The Potential for Smart Work Centres in Blacktown, Liverpool and Penrith*. Sydney: University of Technology Sydney.

8 Universities and regional creative economies

Donna Hancox, Terry Flew, Sasha Mackay and Yi Wang

Introduction

The relationship of universities to regional creative economies is a topic requiring further exploration given its overall significance. The prominent role played by universities in the promotion of knowledge clusters and innovation is well documented, and there has been much debate about the importance of creativity and the creative industries to cities and regions worldwide. The role specifically played by universities in the regional creative economies of non-metropolitan centres requires further attention for three reasons.

First, there is the distributional question that rises for the arts and creative industries and how this relates to university campuses. The distribution of university campuses is often quite decentralised. In Australia, there were 89 cities and towns that hosted a university campus in 2016, and 21 cities which hosted the main campus of an Australian university. The higher education sector is therefore relatively dispersed compared to many other industries, with cities and regions such as Townsville, the Gold and Sunshine Coast, Toowoomba, Newcastle, Lismore, Armidale, Bathurst, Wollongong, Ballarat and Geelong all being major centres alongside the eight state and territory capitals (Universities Australia 2016). This is comparable to other parts of the world, notably the United States, where the tradition of "college towns" has a history going back to the nineteenth century, and Europe, where it has been common for a city to develop around a long-established university.

Second, the relationship of universities to the arts and creative industries, and the scope for local institutions to reverse tendencies towards the concentration of jobs and businesses in the arts and creative industries, is an important concept to be explored. In the United Kingdom (UK), the Nesta studies of the geography of creative industries find that these sectors are, on average, 50% more concentrated in London and the South-East of England than jobs and business in the UK economy as a whole, with over 50% of creative industries employment in this prosperous and globally connected region (Bakhshi and Mateos-Garcia 2016: 13). At the same time, a number of highly significant creative clusters can be identified elsewhere, measured in terms of their importance to the local economy. These include major cities such as Edinburgh, Glasgow, Manchester, Leeds, Bristol, Sheffield, Newcastle and Cardiff. They also include particular regions, such as the regions around Bath-Bristol, Brighton-Eastbourne-Hastings, Manchester-Wigan-Chester-Crewe and Cambridge-Chelmsford-Colchester (Bakhshi and Mateos-Garcia 2016: 17). In these regions, universities have often played a key role as incubators of creative talent. Bakhsis and Mateos-Garcia describe the role played by universities in the generation of local creative clusters in these terms:

> If there is one feature that all creative clusters share, it is their reliance on creative talent, often highly skilled and supplied by universities. Research at universities also creates a knowledge base that R&D-intensive creative businesses in particular draw on. Universities also undertake knowledge exchange activities which transform this knowledge into impact, through entrepreneurship, training and dissemination activities. For all of these reasons, universities are widely acknowledged as central players in the local ecosystems that drive the success of creative clusters.
>
> (Bakhshi and Mateos-Garcia 2016: 24)

Third, many regional universities have established themselves as global leaders in particular fields, even when there are not significant clusters of relevant industries in their immediate vicinity. In Australia, James Cook University in Far North Queensland is a global leader in marine science research, drawing upon its geographical proximity to the Great Barrier Reef. The University of Southern Queensland in Toowoomba has been known as an international leader in the international delivery of online higher education, drawing upon its history in open and distance education going back to the 1920s. The relationship between the location of universities and their fields of research specialisation is not random: in Australia, it remains advantageous to be located in Sydney if the aim is to build linkages with the screen industries, as jobs and capital remain highly concentrated in that city. But it is also not pre-ordained by locational destiny. The University of Newcastle in New South Wales has sought to position itself as playing a key role in the development of creative industries in the Hunter region as the city adopts a "post-industrial" strategy to respond to the closure of its iconic steel mills.

This chapter expands on these ideas through three case studies which examine the relationships between universities and regional Australia around arts and culture, and in particular looking at three key aspects of regional arts: knowledge exchange, program delivery and evaluation. These case studies help to tease out the opportunities and challenges in the partnership between universities, regional communities, government and arts organisations to grow creative economies in often marginalised communities. The case studies also illuminate innovative models being explored in Queensland, which is the most decentralised state in Australia.

Cross-sector innovation and collaboration

The innovation evolution we are witnessing in the university-industry-government (UIG) sector can be understood in part through the Triple Helix framework (Etzkowitz 2003; Ranga and Etzkowitz 2013). Advocates of this framework argue that the UIG interplay is important for innovation. However, few studies of the creative industries have applied the Triple Helix framework to the creative sector.

The increased flux of knowledge intensity across sectors and regions tend to resonate with interaction and collaborative relationships. Collaboration and interaction can be expected to engage with boundary-spanning mechanisms such as networks of entrepreneurial universities, digital innovation and multi-institutional knowledge exchange. In the Triple Helix framework, knowledge creation, exchange and communication are regarded as the main interactions that shift the dynamics in modern science, technology and innovation. For example, well-known cases such as Silicon Valley (Colapinto 2007) and the Waterloon region displayed that entrepreneurship among universities was a key dynamic in fostering and motivating economic development. With the development of Silicon Valley, Stanford University can be regarded as an innovation force with a long history in technology and entrepreneurship. The Stanford Innovation Survey (Eesley and Miller 2018) gathered data from staff and alumni in Stanford University from 2011 to show that the institution has contributed to the growth of local and global economies, and nurtured an entrepreneurship ecosystem in terms of its regional impact. As Flew and Cunningham (2010) point out, the evolving policy of creative industries within urban regeneration has promoted economic growth and creative capital in a way that fosters emerging export markets and broader international cooperation. Numerous studies of the role of innovation, arts and culture emphasise creative industries and the knowledge exchange process in the context of digital media's contribution, which is to foster creativity and innovation in creative societies. Furthermore, it can be argued that a new character of academic institutions as stakeholders in interconnections of socio-cultural shifts in creative economics has led to wider engagement with communities and cities (Comunian, Taylor and Smith 2014).

Knowledge exchange has become the central interaction in UIG networks for regional development. The concept of knowledge exchange was proposed from the Arts and Humanities Research Council to "increase the flow, value and impact of world-class arts and humanities research from academia to the UK's wider private, cultural and public sectors" (Arts & Humanities Research Council 2018). Given the discussions among academics researching the collaboration process between different sectors around the UK, few studies use empirical research to explore the practice of knowledge exchange.

Moreton (2016) explores the ways in which higher education institutions and creative sectors can best collaborate in arts and humanities disciplines. Four

162   *D. Hancox et al.*

AHRC-funded knowledge exchange hubs in his case study reflect the uncertain relationship between academics and creative industries in the knowledge exchange process. However, as Morton points out, there is a tendency towards the commercialisation of cultural and artistic development between academic and creative sectors. In this sense, the existing knowledge exchange patterns in creative spaces are presented as innovation processes that require new institutional functions and creative practices. Morton argues that the approaches with more coherence and impact should be the focus of future research about the possibilities of interaction and practices that could foster and operate networks through spaces in different sectors in the arts and humanities. Morton's argument suggests a need to explore new models of knowledge exchange engagement in creative industries between the spaces and networks of this field.

Creative economies and regional arts

The term "regional arts" is used as a catch-all for vastly different activities and areas, from large prosperous regional centres to isolated remote townships. The access to arts activities and participation in cultural events between these areas varies dramatically. Just over 30% of Australians – around eight million people – live outside major cities, according to ABS data in Regional Population Growth Australia (2018). The capacity of regional communities to contribute significantly to the Australian economy and Australian culture is offset by unequal rates of poverty and disadvantage. Research from the National Rural Alliance and the Australian Council of Social Service (ACOSS) titled *A Snapshot of Poverty in Rural and Regional Australia* (2013) indicates that despite the fact that the rate of poverty in rural and regional areas is slightly higher than in capital cities, it is rarely the focus of national policy attention. Regional Australians live in a variety of social and economic conditions, with personal social and economic wellbeing often tied to the overall outcomes of their local area. To further develop and support regional Australia, strong sustainable communities are needed, and there is a great deal of evidence and research (see Holden 2004; Dunphy 2009) to suggest that arts and culture can make an important contribution to community wellbeing and success. The positive impact and benefit of arts and culture is well documented in the areas of health, civic pride, crime reduction, economic opportunities and development; however, arts policy and funding remains outside the government approach to regional policy.

In the past five years, the understanding of the role of the regions in arts and culture nationally has developed considerably; however, for much of the 2000s, the global focus around arts and culture has been on cities. The twenty-first century has been described as a "new metropolitan age" (Isar, Hoelscher and Anheier 2012: 1), where global, national, regional and local forces coalesce within and around densely populated metropolitan centres and where cities – and associated city-regions – are the "motors of the global economy" (Scott et al. 2008: 15). An extensive academic literature developed around global cities (Taylor 2004; Sassen 2006; Timberlake and Ma 2007) and creative cities (Hall

2000; Landry 2000; Currid 2007; Florida 2014). The rise of cities also promised newer and more cosmopolitan forms of urban citizenship (Holston 2008) capable of transcending the nation-state, as the shift from manufacturing industries to knowledge, service and creative industries aligned with globalisation to make major cities nodes in increasingly complex global networks (Castells 1996; Howard 2011).

Richard Florida's "creative class" thesis, upon which creative city strategies around the world were based, clearly overstated the geographical mobility of creative workers (see Flew and Gibson 2012). The perceptions of creatives and arts workers in regional Australia demonstrates the ways in which location significantly affects the trajectory of their careers. Data from Australia Council for the Arts in the recently released *Connecting Australians: Results of the National Arts Participation Survey* (2017) shows that regionally based artists have increasingly negative perceptions about the impact of their location on their practice. Artists living in the regions earn almost a third less than their city counterparts for creative work, diminishing sustainability and career pathways, which in turn impacts on the sector as a whole. Yet, regional artists are critical to a vibrant arts sector that reflects Australia's depth and diversity. Since the previous Australia Council for the Arts survey, negative perceptions about the impact of being a regional artist have increased: 42% of artists in regional locations say their location has a more negative than positive impact on their practice, up from 25% in 2009. There are a range of factors influencing these perceptions, and a number of recent articles and reports, such as *Restless Giant* by Lindy Hume (2017), have sought to understand the degree to which artists can maintain and grow a creative practice and career in regional Australia.

The focus thus far has been on "push" factors that would lead to creative industries workers moving out of cities. But there are very strong "pull" factors that promote the location of creative people in regional areas. One factor is the value attached to space and particular landscapes and environments that provide cognitive and mental stimulation and minimise the factors that inhibit creativity, such as long journeys to and from work. In her study of the movement of artists to post-industrial towns in the north-east of the United States, Breitbart (2013: 14) found that "artists want to live in places that look like places, and are affordable". There is also a life-cycle element to such movements: people often seek greater personal space when establishing families and are prepared to trade off access to inner-urban centres for a more spacious and less-constricted living environment (Flew 2012). Quality-of-life considerations have therefore figured strongly in the new regionalism that prioritises diversity, community and sustainability as much as it does access to global markets or urban cultural amenity.

The contribution arts and cultural activity make to regional and remote communities has been documented sporadically over the past 20 years; however, governments at all levels tend to underestimate their importance. The social outcomes of regional towns are tied to the prevalence and sustainability of arts and culture programs that are developed and delivered from within the community.

164   *D. Hancox et al.*

Towns and the people in those towns thrive when creativity and innovation are fostered, shared and sustained. Further data from Australia Council for the Arts' *Connecting Australians: Results of the National Arts Participation Survey* (2017: 18) shows that "living in a regional area does not substantially affect arts attendance, with around seven in ten people attending the arts in regional Australia (69%)". However, this percentage does not reflect the range of arts experiences detailed in the report which are available to regional communities. What the figure does indicate is that Australians living in regional centres want access to arts products, while federal and state governments in Australia have long struggled to develop and deliver arts programs to regional areas that foster a sense of agency and cohesion for those areas. Through a series of case studies, this chapter explores recent models of collaboration between universities and regional communities to create innovation avenues to harness the expertise and experience of all stakeholders. These case studies point to the role universities may play in supporting regional arts and raise considerations around what the future of regional arts and regional creative economies could look like.

Case studies

Knowledge exchange: writing the digital futures

Increasingly, universities throughout the world are being encouraged – quite robustly – to engage meaningfully with industry as part of their mission. These collaborations take many forms and have differing levels of success, often depending on the strength of the relationship and the shared vision. In the UK, the Knowledge Transfer Partnership scheme has created a framework and set of KPIs for collaboration between universities and industry. In the UK, one way the government encourages university engagement with industry is through Knowledge Transfer Partnerships (KTPs) in which an industry partner and a higher education institution work with a KTP associate, who is an appropriately experienced graduate who is mentored through the process in a three-way partnership on a project with the specific intent to increase the competitiveness of the industry partner (Technology Strategy Board 2010). For industry partners, the objectives vary depending on need, but might for example be the development of new products or processes or new approaches to delivering services (Ferguson 2014: 178).

In a climate, both in the UK and Australia, of funding austerity in the creative arts and regional arts, these partnerships are emerging as important pipelines for innovation and sustainability. One such partnership was the *Writing the Digital Futures* project, a three-year (2014 to 2017) project funded by Arts Queensland to create a network of programs and information exchange between creative practitioners and researchers from Queensland University of Technology and a range of regional and remote communities. The particular focus was around digital technology and writing and publishing, which had been identified as a creative field that was popular throughout regional areas and also a creative

Universities and creative economies 165

practice that could be deployed as something of a Trojan horse, ostensibly designed to deliver creative workshops while also increasing digital literacy in novel ways in areas that lacked some of the access to developing digital knowledge and confidence available in urban areas. The overall aim of *Writing the Digital Futures* was to bring together international knowledge and expertise in digital writing to cement Queensland as a centre of innovation in writing and publishing within Australia and to shift community and professional perceptions of storytelling and publishing in a digital age, with particular emphasis on transmedia/multi-platform storytelling, self-publishing and digital storytelling.

The research team conducted workshops throughout Queensland in Townsville, Cairns, Rockhampton, Bundaberg, Roma, Emerald and Longreach. Each workshop was tailored to the particular needs of the town and was developed in collaboration with the Queensland Writers' Centre, local arts organisations and Arts Queensland. The research team brought on board high-profile creative practitioners from around Australia, including Matt Blackwood and Dr Christy Dena, in an effort to deliver expert-quality creative workshops alongside digital literacy skills. In Townsville, award-winning writer and interactive designer Dr Christy Dena conducted two day-long workshops at the Townsville library about interactive narratives, particularly focusing on designing narratives to facilitate maximum audience engagement. The participants in the workshop quickly understood the ways these skills may benefit their employment prospects or their ability to promote their business through creative branding and storytelling. Unlike other workshops in regional towns, this became an intensive workshop dealing with professional applications for the creative practice. What could seem like a novel or fun way to spend a day was transformed – by the participants and the facilitators – into a significant sharing of specialist knowledge.

For the Roma workshops, the team engaged Matt Blackwood, a writer from Melbourne who works with locative media to create place-based stories. Both the Queensland Writers' Centre and Arts Queensland had indicated that Roma was a town known to be interested and active in oral histories and local history. The workshops focused on teaching traditional digital stories that involved participants bringing personal photographs and video to create a two-minute audio/visual story about a specific moment or memory. Around half the participants worked on this, while the other half explored ways to use locations around the town as story sites using analogue and digital methods. Six months after the Roma workshop in 2016, an event held as part of Brisbane Writers' Festival – Story Plus – was live-streamed to the Roma Library for participants and interested community members, and participants were able to ask questions and make comments via Facebook. Story Plus was an event focused on digital innovations in storytelling, and in 2016 it hosted Google Creative Lab's Director Tea Uglow and award-winning digital writer Professor Kate Pullinger. This provided a unique opportunity for writers and storytellers in a remote location to be part of a conversation with international experts and to contribute rather than simply receive. Both of these events (along with the other workshops)

166   D. Hancox et al.

were extremely successful, with 100% of participants in the post-workshop survey stating they enjoyed the workshops "very much" and that the workshops extended their understanding of digital writing.

Writing the Digital Futures represents a possible mode of collaboration and partnership for universities and regional communities around arts-based projects. In a sense, the delivery of key skills development, some consultation and knowledge exchange was outsourced by state government to a team of researchers who could design and develop a series of face-to-face workshops and panel events for regional and remote Queensland to deliver on some of the government's election promises to regional Queensland. The opportunity for a team of experts in a field to engage appropriately skilled people to deliver specialised knowledge in specific workshops in an accessible forum was one of the great strengths of this project. However, this was an ad hoc project and, as such, lacked strategic development and sustained follow-up with communities: a key to successful relationships with community partners. The next case study, of the recent RASN framework, will explore a more considered partnership between state government and a university for regional arts delivery.

Delivery: the Regional Arts Services Network and Central Queensland University

The Regional Arts Services Network (RASN) is a new model of arts service delivery in Queensland and offers an example of a long-term, strategic partnership between state government, a university and regional communities. Announced in 2017, RASN was developed by state government arts body Arts Queensland in response to consultations with stakeholders that highlighted the need for a coordinated approach to the delivery of arts programs in regional and rural Queensland that was also attuned to the nuances and needs of individual communities. Arts Queensland sought expressions of interest from "suitably qualified and experienced companies to support, strengthen and promote vibrant and sustainable regional arts delivery" (Arts Queensland 2018a) and in early 2018 announced the eight regional arts service providers from across Queensland selected to form RASN. As described by Arts Queensland, the eight service providers work with their local arts sectors, their communities and key stakeholders to determine specific arts and cultural priorities for their region and coordinate to deliver arts services for, and from within, their communities (Arts Queensland 2018b). The arts services provided include securing arts funding across all levels of government and the private sector; facilitating and delivering community arts and cultural development programs; facilitating new employment and training opportunities in regional and remote Queensland; and increasing opportunities for Aboriginal and Torres Strait Islander communities, amongst other key deliverables (Arts Queensland 2017). A State Coordination Office provides a secretariat function, connects and supports the network of service providers from across the state and leads the development of a state-wide strategy (Queensland Music Festival 2018). RASN is a decentralised approach to the delivery of arts services in Queensland which intends to support regional communities to have meaningful input into the arts and cultural investment made in their communities while fostering partnerships, collaborations and a sense of cohesion.

Central Queensland University (CQUniversity) was selected to be the service provider for the central Queensland region, which comprises 14 regional government areas. Dr Liz Ellison from CQUniversity states that having a number of campuses spread throughout Central Queensland meant the university was well positioned to become the service provider for the central Queensland region, although the initial call was not for universities per se (personal communication 25 September 2018). The CQUniversity model of administering RASN is as a series of clusters that correlate with three of its campuses – Mackay, Rockhampton and Bundaberg – and buffer the logistical challenge of working across such a large geographic area. Each cluster takes their own approach to programming discrete arts events and activities while a central steering group coordinates cross-regional projects, learning programs to support the professional practice of artists and groups, and develops a research and evaluation arm to measure the impact of arts in the regions (CQUniversity 2018).

Universities can bring together diverse expertise, stakeholders and networks, as well as infrastructure, and have the capacity to leverage those elements in unique ways to enhance the sustainability of arts in the regions. As a university with campuses throughout the state, CQUniversity has for many years partnered with regional governments on creative and community building projects and is a research and evaluation partner for various regional activities, one example of which is outlined in the next section. Its networks, breadth and capacity mean it is potentially well placed to manage the partnerships with governments, arts organisations and stakeholders in its role as arts service provider for Central Queensland. However, one of the challenges for the university in this role may be engaging with communities and with organisations and groups outside of government who are often more difficult to build and maintain relationships with.

The development of an evaluation framework for regional arts is one of CQUniversity's primary aims in their role as part of RASN and is a key benefit of the role for all stakeholders. Working collaboratively with local governments, arts organisations and practitioners across Central Queensland, CQUniversity's evaluation model will measure the impact of arts in their region. A strong evaluation framework that measures outcomes on a micro and macro level, and then guides the development of new programs throughout the region, will strengthen the regional arts sector in Central Queensland. The next case study further explores the value of university-led evaluations for the regional arts sector by outlining an evaluation partnership between CQUniversity and a regional arts organisation.

Evaluation: creative regions and CQUniversity

Quantifying and articulating cultural value and impact is a requirement for arts funding. In recent years particularly, existing systems of cultural measurement have become increasingly contested, and developing efficient and appropriate processes for evaluating creative activities remains a challenge for creative practitioners and arts companies. This section describes an evaluation partnership between CQUniversity and regionally based arts production company Creative Regions as a means of addressing such challenges and as an example of a mutually beneficial regional arts organisation and university collaboration. For Creative Regions, partnering with a regional university provided a means of developing processes for capturing data, measuring the value of their work for audiences and participants, identifying key learning experiences for the organisation and articulating these to their partners and sponsors.

Creative Regions is a not-for-profit organisation situated in the regional Queensland coastal city of Bundaberg. Founded in 2008, the company's core business is socially engaged art, creative place-making, and the design and delivery of the Bundaberg region's annual arts festival. The mission of the company is "to produce arts and cultural experiences that are relevant to regional people and that add value to regional communities" (Creative Regions 2018a), and it secures philanthropic funding and state and local government investment to support the delivery of their core programs. Between 2012 and 2014, Creative Regions developed a partnership with CQUniversity for evaluation of *Afloat*, a creative recovery and participatory arts program the company delivered in the aftermath of the 2010 and 2011 Queensland floods in collaboration with local governments, other Queensland-based arts organisations and community service providers Red Cross and UnitingCare Community (Creative Regions 2018b). CQUniversity health and social services researchers evaluated *Afloat* to assess the project's contribution to building community resilience (Madsen, Chesham and Pisani 2015). Following *Afloat*, Creative Regions maintained its partnership with CQUniversity for the evaluation of projects which were either wholly or partly supported by government, including the domestic violence awareness theatre production *It All Begins With Love* (2015). From the company's perspective, such a partnership was essential for demonstrating to funding bodies and stakeholders the social and economic value of their work. External evaluation led by a university enabled Creative Regions to achieve a level of rigour and objectivity in its data collection and reporting that it would not have been able to achieve alone.

While evaluation reports are important for reporting back to funding bodies on the outcomes and impacts of projects, rigorous evaluations of arts programs can contribute to an ongoing cycle of improvement for organisations such as Creative Regions (Gattenhof 2017: 3). Despite attempts by governments to measure arts impact through standardised cultural measurement tools such as CultureCounts, these tools and the data they collect can be inadequate for capturing the ways in which a project was or was not successful and highlighting the learning opportunities for the practitioners involved. Creative Regions trialled the digital application CultureCounts in 2016 to capture data on the annual arts festival delivered as part of the company's contract with the local council. Accessed on an iPad at each event, CultureCounts was convenient for capturing some of the data required for grant acquittals and annual reports such as event attendance and audience members' age, gender and postcode; however, the tool seemed inadequate for capturing "data about intrinsic value centred on how experiencing arts and culture affects individuals or communities in an emotional sense or evidence rooted in subjectivity and judgement" (Gattenhof 2017: 31). Further, it is not designed to provide arts practitioners with insights into how they might improve their work. Rigorous evaluations may help companies such as Creative Regions and the practitioners they employ to develop programming that continues to meet the needs of communities.

In 2017, Creative Regions integrated evaluation centrally into its business plan by directing a portion of their state government funding into the establishment of an evaluation partnership with CQUniversity. For Creative Regions, a partnership with CQUniversity could enable it to develop an evaluation framework that was appropriate for the company, their stakeholders and their mission by designing means of assessing project outcomes against the needs and interests of the community it was designed for rather than generalised concepts of artistic quality or cultural value. A CQUniversity health and social sciences researcher worked with the company's Artistic Director and project producers to design and lead evaluations for discrete projects, for core programs and for the company as a whole. Evaluation reports were provided to the company and often published in academic journals in the field of arts and health, which helped Creative Regions make its work more widely known.

The context-specific nature of CQUniversity's evaluations enabled the company to assess a project's value for particular members of a community and identify long-term and sometimes unexpected outcomes. For example, during 2014 and 2015, the company partnered with community service provider UnitingCare Community to develop creative works and community arts activities that would raise the Bundaberg community's awareness of domestic and family violence. A series of creative workshops that guided children to express their physical and emotional feelings when confronted with violent or dangerous situations was delivered during this partnership, and a story book entitled *My Big Bear Story* (2015) was produced based on the children's creative responses, illustrations and descriptions. Two years after the project's conclusion, the CQUniversity researcher designed an evaluation to determine how this picture book could be a useful resource for counsellors working with children who had been exposed to domestic and family violence (Madsen and O'Mullan 2017). The researcher led semi-structured interviews with the counsellors from various community agencies, the writer and the illustrator who had collaborated with Creative Regions to produce a story "that not only provided an avenue for children's voices to be heard but that could support the counselling of children who had also experienced DFV" (Madsen and O'Mullan 2017: 4). The evaluation not only investigated the ways involvement in the project had been professionally worthwhile for the writer and illustrator but also focused on how the counsellors involved in the project had continued to use the book as a tool in their practice. The evaluation concluded that *My Big Bear Story* has been

170   D. Hancox et al.

identified as a useful therapeutic tool for counsellors working with children between the ages of 4 and 12 and recommended the book be "promoted to child counsellors as a useful bibliotherapy tool for children who have experienced domestic and family violence, provided it is used as part of normal therapeutic processes" (Madsen and O'Mullan 2017: 9). Such an evaluation usefully measured the project against its core aims and gave Creative Regions a thorough and objective summary of the project's continued successes to share with partners and sponsors. CQUniversity's evaluations of *It All Begins With Love* and *My Big Bear Story*, particularly, have been vital to the company establishing itself as a leading producer of socially engaged art in regional Queensland.

Conclusion

The three case studies in this chapter demonstrate the opportunity for universities to assert themselves in the arts sector, contribute to capacity building for arts practitioners in regional communities and have significant input into regional arts policy. Accessible skills development workshops such as *Writing the Digital Futures*, tailored to the identified needs and interests of specific regional communities, represent important means through which universities can engage with, and contribute to, the development of the regional arts sector. For communities, such workshops bring specialist knowledge to their doorstep and help defuse some of the geographic and financial challenges of accessing skills development opportunities. The types of collaboration and engagement between government, industry and universities that were illustrated through *Writing the Digital Futures* and other projects in these case studies also signal a potential shift in the ways that communities can have a direct voice in professional skills development needed for the regional arts sector and also in the ways they are delivered. A more nuanced and responsive approach to creative and entrepreneurial skills in regional communities could have a significant impact on the economic and creative sustainability of regional and remote towns.

While state and federal governments and policies have historically struggled to position arts and creativity within the whole of government regional policy, initiatives such as RASN may facilitate this from the inside out by supporting regional communities to define and express the types of art and cultural experiences that are meaningful to their communities. This particular model allows for more projects and activities to be developed from within the community and for more sophisticated evaluation that takes into account local indicators of success and impact. As the case of Creative Regions suggests, external researcher-led evaluations are increasingly important for arts companies in a climate of funding austerity. Another potential development that might result from the case studies discussed is a more holistic and integrated consideration of the role of the arts in regional communities and a possible move away from concepts of the creative economy and its attendant assumptions about urbanism and its relative cultural superiority and instead to this idea of new regionalism

Universities and creative economies 171

and with it the possibility that solutions, innovations and creative futures already exist within regional communities.

References

Arts & Humanities Research Council. 2018. "Knowledge Exchange and Partnerships." Retrieved Month May 20, 2019 (https://ahrc.ukri.org/innovation/knowledgeexchange/).

Arts Queensland. 2017a. "Regional Arts Services Network Expressions of Interest: Information for Providers." Retrieved May 20, 2019 (www.arts.qld.gov.au/images/documents/artsqld/Guidelines/Regional-Arts-Services-Network-EOI-Information-For-Providers-finalv3.pdf).

Arts Queensland. 2017b. "Title." Retrieved May 20, 2019 (http://www.arts.qld.gov.au/projects-and-initiatives/regional-arts-services-network-outcomes).

Arts Queensland. 2018a. "Regional Arts Services Network Expressions of Interest." Retrieved May 20, 2019 (www.arts.qld.au/projects-and-initives/regional-arts-services-network-eoi).

Arts Queensland. 2018b. "Regional Arts Services Network." Retrieved May 20, 2019 (www.arts qld.gov.au/projects-and-initiatives/regional-arts-services-network.eoi).

Australia Council for the Arts. 2017. *Connecting Australians: Results of the National Arts Participation Survey*. Sydney: Australia Council.

Australian Bureau of Statistics. 2018. "Regional Population Growth, Australia, 2011." Retrieved May 20, 2019 (www.abs.gov.au/ausstats/abs@.nsf/mf/3218.0).

Bakhshi, H., and Mateos-Garcia, J. 2016. *The Geography of Creativity in the UK: Creative Clusters, Creative People and Creative Networks*. London: Nesta.

Breitbart, M. 2013. "Examining the Creative Economy in Post-industrial Cities: Alternatives to Blueprinting Soho." Pp. 1–29 in *Creative Economies in Post-industrial Cities: Manufacturing a (Different) Scene*, edited by Breitbart, M. Burlington, VT: Ashgate.

Castells, M. 1996. *The Rise of the Network Society*. Malden, MA: Blackwell.

Central Queensland University. 2018. "CQUni Chosen as a Service Provider for State's New Regional Arts Services Network [Media Statement]." Retrieved May 20, 2019 (www.cqu.edu.au/cquninews/stories/general-category/2018/cquni-to-host-a-regional-arts-services-network-for-wider-cq-region).

Colapinto, C. 2007. "A Way to Foster Innovation: A Venture Capital District from Silicon Valley and Route 128 to Waterloo Region." *International Review of Economics* 54(3): 319–343.

Comunian, R., Taylor, C., and Smith, D. N. 2014. "The Role of Universities in the Regional Creative Economies of the UK: Hidden Protagonists and the Challenge of Knowledge Transfer." *European Planning Studies* 22(12): 2456–2476 (doi:10.1080/09654313.2012.790589).

CQU 2018. "CQUNI Chosen as a Service Provider for State's New Reginal Arts Service Network." Retrieved August 13, 2018 (https://www.cqu.edu.au/cquninews/stories/general-category/2018/cquni-to-host-a-regional-arts-services-network-for-wider-cq-region).

Creative Regions. 2018a. "About Creative Regions." Retrieved May 20, 2019 (www.creativeregions.com.au/about/).

Creative Regions. 2018b. "Afloat Creative Recovery." Retrieved May 20, 2019 (www.creativeregions.com.au/portfolio-item/afloat-creative-recovery/).

Currid, E. 2007. *The Warhol Economy: How Fashion, Art and Music Drive New York City*. Princeton, NJ: Princeton University Press.

172   *D. Hancox et al.*

Dunphy, K. 2009. *Developing and Revitalising Rural Communities through Arts and Creativity*. Melbourne: Cultural Development Network Victoria.

Eesley, C. E., and Miller, W. F. 2018. "Impact: Stanford University's Economic Impact via Innovation and Entrepreneurship." *Foundations and Trends in Entrepreneurship* 14(2): 130–278 (https://doi.org/10.1561/0300000074).

Etzkowitz, H. 2003. "Innovation in Innovation: The Triple Helix of University-Industry-Government Relations." *Social Science Information* 42(3): 293–337 (https://doi.org/10.1177/05390184030423002).

Ferguson, M. 2014. "Knowledge Exchange between Universities and Creative Industries in the UK: A Case Study of Current Practice." *Industry and Higher Education* 28(3): 177–183 (https://journals.sagepub.com/doi/pdf/10.5367/ihe.2014.0207).

Flew, T. 2012. "Creative Suburbia: Rethinking Urban Cultural Policy: The Australian Case." *International Journal of Cultural Studies* 15(3): 231–246.

Flew, T., and Cunningham, S. 2010. "Creative Industries After the First Decade of Debate." *The Information Society* 26(2): 113–123.

Flew, T., and Gibson, M. 2012. "Melbourne and Brisbane: The Claims of Suburbs." Pp. 235–242 in *Cities, Cultural Policy and Governance,* edited by Anheier, H., and Isar, Y. Los Angeles, CA: Sage.

Florida, R. 2014. *The Rise of the Creative Class* (2nd ed.). New York: Basic Books.

Gattenhof, S. 2017. *Measuring Impact: Models for Evaluation in the Australian Arts and Cultural Landscape*. London: Palgrave Macmillan.

Hall, P. 2000. "Creative Cities and Economic Development." *Urban Studies* 37(4): 639–649.

Holden, J. 2004. *Capturing Cultural Value: How Culture Became a Tool of Government Policy*. London: Demos.

Holston, J. 2008. "Urban Citizenship and Globalization." Pp. 325–348 in *Global City-Regions: Trends, Theory, Policy* (2nd ed.), edited by Scott, A. Oxford: Oxford University Press.

Howard, P. 2011. *Castells and the Media*. Cambridge: Polity.

Hume, L. 2017. *Restless Giant: Changing Cultural Values in Regional Australia*. Strawberry Hills, NSW: Currency House Inc.

Isar, Y., Hoelscher, M., and Anheier, H. 2012. "Introduction." Pp. 1–12 in *Cities, Cultural Policy and Governance*, edited by Anheier, H., and Isar, Y. Los Angeles, CA: Sage.

Landry, C. 2000. *The Creative City*. London: Earthscan.

Madsen, W., Chesham, M., and Pisani, S. 2015. "Keeping Afloat After the Floods: Evaluation of a School-Based Arts Project to Promote Resilience." Pp. 44–54 in *Community Resilience, Universities and Engaged Research for Today's World*, edited by Madsen, W., Costigan, L., and McNicol, S. London: Palgrave Pivot.

Madsen, W., and O'Mullan, C. 2017. "Breaking the Cycle of Violence: How a Children's Story Book Can Contribute to Early Intervention." Retrieved Month XX, Year (www.creativeregions.com.au/wp-content/uploads/2017/10/MBBS-final-report.pdf).

Moreton, S. 2016. "Rethinking Knowledge Exchange: New Approaches to Collaborative Work in the Arts and Humanities." *International Journal of Cultural Policy* 22(1): 100–115.

National Rural Health Alliance Inc., & Australian Council of Social Service. 2013. "A Snapshot of Poverty in Rural and Regional Australia." Retrieved June 12, 2018 from Rural Health Organisation database.

Queensland Music Festival. 2018. "State Coordination Office." Retrieved May 20, 2019 (https://qmf.org.au/abousus.sco/).

Ranga, M., and Etzkowitz, H. 2013. "Triple Helix Systems: An Analytical Framework for Innovation Policy and Practice in the Knowledge Society." Pp. 107–148 in *Entrepreneurship and Knowledge Exchange*, edited by Mitra, J., and Edmondson, J. New York: Routledge.

Sassen, S. 2006. *Cities in a World Economy* (3rd ed.). Thousand Oaks, CA: Sage.

Scott, A., Agnew, J., Soja, E.; and Storper, M. 2008. "Global City-Regions." Pp. 11–32 in *Global City-Regions: Trends, Theory, Policy*. edited by Scott, A. Oxford: Oxford University Press.

Taylor, P. 2004. *World City Networks: A Global Urban Analysis*. London: Routledge.

Technology Strategy Board. 2010. "Knowledge Transfer Partnerships Strategic Review." Retrieved October 12, 2018 from The National Achieves database.

Timberlake, M., and Ma, X. 2007. "Cities and Globalization." Pp. 254–271 in *The Blackwell Companion to Globalization*, edited by Ritzer, G. Malden, MA: Blackwell.

Universities Australia. 2016. "University Profiles." Retrieved December 11, 2018 (www.universitiesaustralia.edu.au/australias-universities/university-profiles#.XAL62hMzbuQ).

9 The role of Fab Labs and Living Labs for economic development of regional Australia

Ana Bilandzic, Marcus Foth and Greg Hearn

Introduction

Innovation is the key driver of economic growth (Schumpeter 1934). While its definition varies (Hauschildt and Salomo 2011), it mostly refers to a novel creation that is commercialised (Kline and Rosenberg 1986; Porter 1990; Arteaga and Hyland 2014). Broader definitions recognise innovation as widely spread inventions or discoveries that significantly differ to a (former) state of comparison (Schumpeter 1934; Hauschildt and Salomo 2011; Usher 1954; Couger, Higgins and McIntyre 1990; Howard 2012). Moreover, innovation brings social and environmental benefits (Pavitt 2001), e.g. increase in living standards, and improvement in safety, health, and our relationship with the natural environment. Rickards (1985: 119) describes innovation as a process "whereby individuals discover and implement the means for meeting environmental needs," and Holly (as cited in Saul 2010: 51) as a mix of products and processes that translate "new ideas into tangible societal impact." Aiming for a holistic definition with societal meaning, we define innovation as creating a novelty that is widely adopted or creates added value for an individual, business, (governmental or non-profit) organisation, or community. Although its impact can be measured by how much money it generates, it is not restricted only to this commercial sense; rather, the value can also be created through environmental or social effects (social innovation). Then the value lies in the responsibility of the innovation, which van Lente, Swierstra and Joly (2017: 255) explain: "As long as they [innovations] can be marked as 'responsible' their uptake in firms, economic sectors and society at large can be expected to be success[ful]." In this case, the scale of penetration is no longer a priority if the innovation improves an individual's life, circumstance, attitude, work process, or anything else as long as it is 'responsible.'

Theories of regional economic development and innovation are often contested (e.g. Storper 2011; Pugalis and Gray 2016). However, recent practice has recognised the importance of place-based mobilisation of public and private, and tangible and intangible, resources, as well as the importance of local creativity, innovation, and knowledge. This is particularly so when regions face the challenge of diversifying or reinventing their economy or the need to respond to a shifting demography with associated employment challenges and opportunities. Developing immersive hubs facilitating collaboration and networking within regional cities cannot be achieved solely by local governments; rather, it requires many parties to be involved, e.g. the community, private sector, and not-for-profit organisations (Voyce 2016). Novel approaches to producing and measuring value are also needed – and not only economic value. Rather, strategies need to consider social innovations, upon which public and private sector innovation can grow. The basic building blocks of social innovations are ideas, values, and proclivities consistent with innovation, skills, and trusted relationships between individuals and organisations. A key economic and social outcome of multiple forms of value is work – including self-employment and voluntary work. Local jobs are key to sustainable regional economies. Seeing an occupation as "a set of knowledge practices, or more expansively, knowledge, skills, identity formations, social relationships and practices" (Hearn 2014: 90) reminds us that jobs have a social context as part of their spatial location (Gordon and de Souza e Silva 2011). Thus, social innovation and economic development are tightly tied together.

It is well accepted in studies of economic development that urban agglomeration provides the kind of diversity, experimentation, and creativity that lead to social and economic renewal (Scott and Storper 2015; Desrochers and Leppälä 2011). To the extent that non-urban regions may lack such characteristics and competencies, the role of what we call Casual Creative Environments (CCE) (e.g. Fab Labs and Living Labs) in regional areas as experimental spaces is an interesting possibility. In practical terms, the intention of Fab Labs and Living Labs is to allow exploration, experimentation, and creative solutions to be followed by evaluation through action research or market testing (Tacchi, Foth and Hearn 2009). This then feeds subsequent iterations of innovation or scaling up of the solution through markets or open innovation networks. From scholarship on urban agglomeration (Adkins et al. 2007; Desrochers and Leppälä 2011; Scott and Storper 2015), we know that the precise dynamics of urban cluster "generativity" are complex, although a number of reasonably well-established principles are at play, which we posit may be relevant to the role of Fab Labs and Living Labs in regional innovation. These include:

- *Creative ideation.* Innovation in regions requires creativity, and the presence of well-educated creative individuals creates productivity both through creation of new technologies as well as the recognition and application of technology from elsewhere (Lobo et al. 2014).
- *A learning-oriented environment; knowledge exchange.* Learning, and especially learning by doing, allows rapid take up of ideas into useful innovations. Knowledge spillovers are important to allow innovation to move across sectors (Desrochers and Leppälä 2011; Lankester, Hughes and Foth 2018).
- *Digital platform technologies* which spread across different industries and sectors can be a major driver of innovation including social innovation (Dezuanni et al. 2018).

CCEs are spaces, offices, or labs that people, e.g. digital nomads, choose to work from. They do so because they have the freedom to decide from where, when, and how they want to work and pursue their innovative and entrepreneurial endeavours. Such spaces are often tagged with words such as coworking, innovation, maker, hacker, fabrication, creativity space, or hub and are proliferating in numbers (Kojo and Nenonen 2014; Bouncken and Reuschl 2016; Bilandzic and Foth 2017). Their open and playful setting (Blythe and Wright 2005; van Meel and Vos 2001) allows for informal learning (Bilandzic and Foth 2013) and idea exchange (Bouncken and Reuschl 2016) and might be a reason for their success in challenging conventional innovation environments where people are creative and innovative (DeGuzman and Tang 2011), e.g. wet and dry laboratories in universities or research and development departments in industry. Continuous knowledge and information flow, mutual connected and informal learning, and group formation evolving from social interactions are some of the benefits that involved actors reap. This is often referred to as 'buzz' (Bathelt, Malmberg and Maskell 2004; Storper and Venables 2004). Although buzz can result in innovation (Pancholi, Yigitcanlar and Guaralda 2015), Shearmur (2012: S16) criticises the notion of "buzzing cities," which take other parts of the innovation system out, e.g. non-metropolitan regions, the diversity advantage of the creative fringe and other precursors to innovation that are not immediately obvious (Bilandzic et al. 2018). Creative industries and their innovations that are based on symbolic knowledge rely on buzz and face-to-face communication (Asheim, Coenen and Vang 2007). In terms of CCEs, Capdevila (2015: 24) found that "temporary clusters" in coworking spaces provide individuals who are part of the "local buzz" with opportunities of knowledge exchange with external actors, such as event attendees or foreign workers hosted by a CCE temporarily.

In Australia, demographer Bernard Salt (2016) coined the term "e-change" to describe a new social movement of people moving from metropolitan to regional cities seeking better lifestyles, more happiness closer to nature, and decreased living costs. This suggests that the new urban crisis in metropolitan areas may in turn cause a revival of regional areas that comes with new economic and socio-cultural opportunities. CCEs might be entities that set a playground for innovation in regions where new businesses emerge and provide employment to local people, hence contributing to the socio-economic development in the area. Further, CCEs are often associated with a lifestyle shaped by travel (Isaacson 2011), fun (Blythe and Wright 2005), and coworking (Bilandzic and Foth 2013). A CCE affords people space for experiences, social interaction, and connected, informal learning. These activities teach them skills such as critical thinking, problem solving, creativity, communication, and collaboration (Bilandzic and Foth 2013). People equipped with these skills may recognise approaches to innovation that are not just narrowly focussed on economic benefits but also take social and ecological values into account. That is contrary to how governments often measure innovation. For example, 3.11% of Australia's gross domestic product was spent on research and development

(R&D) in 2015 (Department of Industry, Innovation and Science n.d.-a). The government uses R&D expenditure, patent and trademark applications, and new business creations as indicators of Australia's innovation activities (Department of Industry, Innovation and Science n.d.-b). The impact of innovation is often reported only on businesses, industry, and national performance (Commonwealth of Australia 2018) and neglects social innovation and its role in producing social and environmental benefits.

Nevertheless, there is a lack of understanding of precursors, processes and outcomes with regards to entrepreneurship and business model innovation (Bouncken and Reuschl 2016). Further, Bouncken and Reuschl (2016) suggest further research to explore processes, collaboration, and communication techniques that shape learning, community, entrepreneurship, and innovation. With this in mind, analysing CCEs and their activities for social innovation in regional Australia can inform new support strategies and policies tailored to the regional context.

The following sections present in order: the study's methodology; three case studies; a discussion of our findings across the triad of people, place, and technology; and our conclusions.

Methodology

Eversole (2017: 306) points out that regions are "geographic areas with shared characteristics ... defined differently depending on what characteristics are of interest." Foci could be economic, demographic, environmental, or social, for example. Further, in Australia, unlike other countries, the term regional mostly refers to areas excluding state and national capital cities. Common statistical classifications include:

- Australian Bureau of Statistics' Statistical Geography Standard SA1 (200–800 populations) to SA4 (100,000 to 300,000),
- Postal Code Areas,
- Local Government Areas, and
- Electorates.

Since the aim of this study is to understand the functioning of CCE within a local regional economy, we utilise Local Government Areas (LGA). With regional areas getting less attention from policy makers and investors for development than urban agglomerations, they might pursue different approaches to innovation. In the city of Brisbane, several innovation hubs are state or local government owned and focus on tech startups, e.g. The Capital committed by Brisbane City Council (www.choosebrisbane.com.au/digital-brisbane/the-capital) or The Precinct (https://advance.qld.gov.au/precinct) funded by the Advance Queensland initiative, which makes them more likely to exclude other approaches or outcomes of innovation (Bilandzic et al. 2018; Casadevall, Foth and Bilandzic 2018). The State of Queensland (2017) recently introduced its

Advancing Regional Innovation Program to harness innovation in its regions by supporting innovative communities that represent "the diversity of Queensland's regions" and encourage grassroots entrepreneurial activities. Yet, in order to generate appropriate levels of support, advice, and advocacy, we first need to learn and understand the strengths, weaknesses, and needs of approaches to innovation that are regionally specific, rather than risking forcefully importing solutions from metropolitan cases that may not fit the regional context.

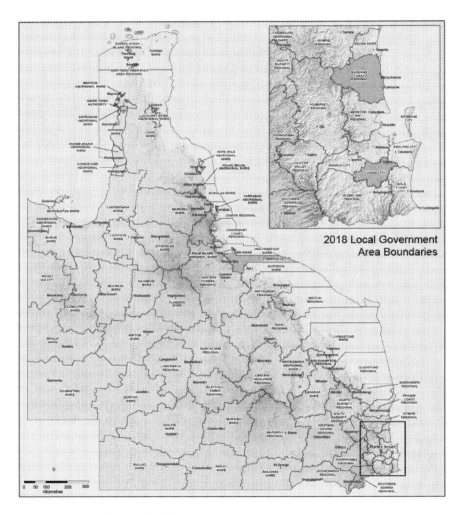

Figure 9.1 LGAs of Queensland.

Source: Map was retrieved from Queensland Government (2018) and modified to highlight regions that are the focus in this study

In this study we looked at three CCEs in three LGAs in Queensland: the City of Townsville in North Queensland; Nambour in the Regional Council of Sunshine Coast; and the City of Logan (see Fig. 9.1). The three CCEs are Innovate NQ (iNQ) in Townsville; The Old Ambulance Station in Nambour, and Substation33 in Logan. The three CCEs have each their own unique story and focus, but they share passion and purpose to attract and keep talent in the region and make their region thrive. Each has been reported in the media as having actively contributed to the development of an innovation culture in their respective region: the local magazine DUO and 7 News Townsville acknowledge iNQ contributing to Townville's startup and innovation ecology (Millios-Hullick 2016; 7 News Townsville 2016); ABC News reported on the role of The Old Ambulance Station in reviving Nambour by turning towards creative industries (Coghill 2015a, 2015b); and ABC News also reported on Logan's Substation33's contribution to reducing e-waste going to landfill by recycling technology and teaching long-term unemployed people to upcycle and repurpose technology while gaining new skills and finding employment (ABC News 2018; Hamilton-Smith 2018). Due to their relatively recent occurrence, ours was one of the first academic studies that sought to shed light on these CCEs' role in fostering economic development of regional Australia.

We conducted desktop research to gain data about each site from their websites, their social media presence, and media coverage in news and magazines. We applied a threefold lens of people, place, and technology to analyse our data (Foth et al. 2011). This approach borrows from the research practice of urban informatics, which conceptualises "the city as an ecology that consists of technological, social, and architectural layers" (Foth et al. 2011). Foth et al. (2011: 4) define urban informatics as:

> the study, design, and practice of urban experiences across different urban contexts that are created by new opportunities of real-time, ubiquitous technology and the augmentation that mediates the physical and digital layers of people networks and urban infrastructures.

Urban informatics can be a powerful tool that guides research and development in real-world applications and contexts, not just in metropolitan cities but also for regional centres and areas (Foth et al. 2011). Figure 9.2 illustrates disciplinary influences for each layer of the triad but also at the intersections between the layers. We chose this approach for our analysis of the three regional CCEs to understand the meaning and impact on innovation of each layer, i.e. people, place, and technology, for each CCE. The urban informatics paradigm allows us to holistically capture and analyse the CCEs from a hybrid view that takes both physical and digital aspects into account. Resembling aspects of communicative ecology research (Foth and Hearn 2007; Hearn and Foth 2007), this data analysis approach fits our study's purpose due to both its spatial and transdisciplinary qualities, which other, more traditional data-gathering methods often lack.

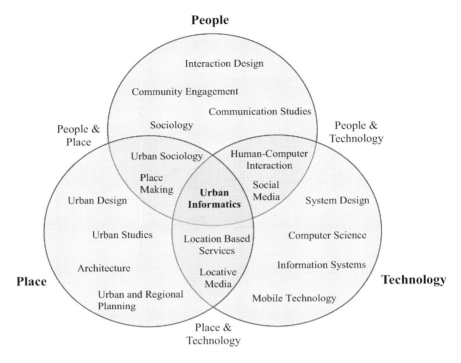

Figure 9.2 The Urban Informatics Transdisciplinary Paradigm – People, Place, and Technology.
Source: Author reconstruction of illustrations by Foth et al. (2015) and Johnstone, Choi and Leong (2016)

Case studies

We chose three case studies of CCEs in regional Queensland for presentation and in-depth discussion because of their success in developing an innovation culture that is unique to each region. Although some started as bottom-up initiatives, e.g. The Old Ambulance Station (Johnstone, Choi and Leong 2016), it appears more appropriate to recognise them as middle-out interventions that "draw on the collective knowledge from stakeholders at the top and everyday people at the bottom" (Fredericks, Caldwell and Tomitsch 2016). For instance, The Old Ambulance Station was awarded a grant from the Advance Queensland Regional Innovation fund, and iNQ works closely with the Queensland State Government and is involved with the Advancing Regional Innovation Program. Table 9.1 summarises data on our three case study regions from 2016 as published by the Australian Bureau of Statistics (2018). We simplified the LGAs City of Townsville, Sunshine Coast Regional Council, and the City of Logan to the town names Townsville, Nambour, and Logan, respectively. Data in the table refers to each region's population, unemployment rate, percentage

The role of Fab Labs and Living Labs 181

Table 9.1 An overview of population data by regional data. Data refers to year 2016.

Category	Townsville	Nambour	Logan
Population (number)	192,058	303,389	313,785
Unemployment rate (%)	8.9	7.2	8.9
Aboriginal and Torres Strait Islander People (%)	**7**	1.9	3.2
Citizenship (%)	86	86	79.5
• Australian	5.7	7.7	**13.6**
• not Australian	8.3	6.3	6.9
• not stated			
Speaking Language other than English at home (%)	7.6	5	**15.9**
Median age (years)	33.8	42.4	33.8

Source: Australian Bureau of Statistics (2018)

of Aboriginal and Torres Strait Islanders, citizenships, and percentage of households that speak a language other than English. The table allows for comparison between the regions; however, we will refer to this data in the following sections where we introduce our case studies. A few numbers are highlighted because their value (almost) doubles the values of the other two regions in the same category. The following sections will introduce our case studies, i.e. iNQ in Townsville, The Old Ambulance Station in Nambour, and Substation33 in Logan.

iNQ in Townsville

iNQ is a community-driven not-for-profit incubator in Townsville that opened its doors in August 2016 (Powell 2016b). It aims for "becoming the driving force behind the growth and success of North Queensland's startup ecosystem," and being the home for creatives, makers, entrepreneurs, and innovators in the region (iNQ n.d.). Besides supporting tech-oriented innovations and startups, iNQ welcomes and hosts entrepreneurs and innovators whose passion and growth lies in the creative, educational, sustainable development, or other industries. It is located in the entertainment precinct in Townsville and offers various facilities to its members and the public depending on their needs and preferences, e.g. hot desks, permanent offices, and meeting rooms. Further, it organises regular events for its members, the public, and even children to provide them with opportunities for exploring creativity, networking, collaboration, and skill development. iNQ has its own website (i-nq.com.au) and social media channels on Facebook, Twitter, and Instagram. iNQ uses its online presence to inform members and the public about the space, membership opportunities, and plans, news, and past and future events. It is a hub for people who are at the early or scaling stages of their innovative and entrepreneurial endeavours. However, rather than focusing only on developing and scaling businesses, it also takes children into account and provides programs to educate and support future generations for innovation (see Fig. 9.3).

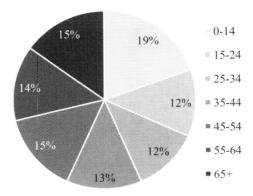

Figure 9.3 Nambour's population by age. Data refers to year 2016.
Source: Australian Bureau of Statistics (2018)

In 2016, the population of Townsville was 192,058, of which 50.13% were men and 49.87% were women (Australian Bureau of Statistics 2018). Children and young adults aged between 0–14 and 15–24 years old were 20% and 16% of Townsville's population, respectively (Australian Bureau of Statistics 2018). This shows the meaning of iNQ's efforts in integrating young people – who are the region's future – into the city's innovation ecosystem. Townsville has the highest percentage of Aboriginal and Torres Strait Islanders, i.e. 7% of its population, compared to Nambour's 1.9% and Logan's 3.2%. Further, 5.7% of its population hold a different citizenship than Australian, and more than 7% speak a language other than English at home. This quantitative data indicates the diversity of people in Townsville.

The Old Ambulance Station in Nambour

The Old Ambulance Station is also known as "The Ambo" among its community members (Johnstone, Choi and Leong 2016; Coghill 2015a). It is "A Creative Space for Creative Businesses" in Nambour (The Old Ambulance Station n.d.). Nambour is a town in the Regional Council of the Sunshine Coast bordering in the south with Moreton Bay. The Ambo is owned by the Sunshine Coast Council and managed by eight board members of the Sunshine Coast Arts Industry Precinct Inc. Its space is divided and offers configurations as diverse as a theatre, gallery, meeting room, cinema, offices, and retail space. It provides creative people with a space to thrive, develop ideas, and establish their businesses. The Ambo facilitates regular events for the local community to exchange ideas and conversation and irregular events depending on the needs of its short- and long-term tenants and businesses from the creative sector.

The role of Fab Labs and Living Labs 183

Its website (theoldambulancestation.com) and Facebook profile share general information and news about The Ambo, provide an overview of past events accompanied with photographs, advertise upcoming events, and provide information regarding involvement and occupation opportunities for the community and potential tenants. The Ambo is an established hub for creative people in and around Nambour that genuinely takes care of its visitors and tenants and, hence, has succeeded in building up a thriving community in the region (Coghill 2015a). This success is meaningful and brings new hope to keep and attract talent (back) to the region of the Sunshine Coast. Previously, Nambour was a socio-culturally and economically strained town (Johnstone, Choi and Leong 2016; Coghill 2015a) when its sugar mill closed down in 2003 (Queensland Government 2015). Nambour counted 303, 389 citizens, of which 48.39% were men and 51.61% were women in 2016 (Australian Bureau of Statistics 2018). Its unemployment rate was 7.2% and the lowest in our three regions, with both Townsville and Logan at 8.9%. In comparison to Townsville and Logan, whose populations' median age was 33.8 years, Nambour's population had a median age of 42.4 years. Figure 9.3 shows its population by age that is evenly spread between the age groups. Further, if we look at 5% of residents speaking a language other than English at home, 1.9% Aboriginal and Torres Strait Islanders, and 7.7% holding a citizenship other than Australian and use those indicators for socio-cultural diversity, Nambour is the least diverse of our three regions. However, The Ambo manages diversity in a different way, including how it engages with people across different age groups. Nambour's population is almost evenly split when looking at age groups (see Figure 9.3).

Substation33 in Logan

Substation33 is a social enterprise focussing on electronic waste (e-waste) recycling by not-for-profit organisation Youth and Family Service funded by the Australian and Queensland Governments. It is located in a warehouse in the City of Logan south of Brisbane. The warehouse is mainly an open area divided into bigger and smaller sections for different steps in the recycling and upcycling processes (see Fig. 9.4).

Furthermore, Substation33 has two separate rooms. One room is the reception for visitors and the check-in and check-out counter for its workers and volunteers. The other room accommodates the IT team that keeps control of the tracking software for the warning signs for flooded roads, which is a product by Substation33 in partnership with Logan City Council (Substation33 2017a). Substation33 found its unique way to innovate services and products for both commercial and educational purposes. The social enterprise provides people with the opportunity to learn new skills and find employment through recycling and upcycling e-waste. Its manager, Tony Sharp, recognised the opportunity to keep e-waste away from landfill and give batteries, computers, monitors, and other electronic equipment a second life by exploiting the technologies to their fullest capacity in innovative services and products. Substation33 provides

Figure 9.4 Recycling e-waste at *Substation33*.

Source: https://substation33.com.au/tony-sharp/?doing_wp_cron=1538105194.9974870681762695312500

online information about its operations, services and products, involvement opportunities, and news on its website (substation33.com.au), but also via social media. Tony Sharp's approach to recycle and upcycle e-waste is part of an emerging group of thought leaders who are pioneering a circular economy for electronics. In the time of consumerism and an ever-rising divide between rich and poor, Substation33 could be said to be 'killing two birds with one stone' by upcycling e-waste and providing (unemployed) people with opportunities to learn new skills and transition into employment.

Logan's population was 313,785 in 2016 and was represented by 49.67% male people and 50.33% female people (Australian Bureau of Statistics 2018). Its socio-cultural diversity can be understood when looking at statistics that show 15.9% of its population speak a language other than English at home, 3.2% are Aboriginal and Torres Strait Islanders, and 13.6% hold a non-Australian citizenship. Furthermore, Figure 9.5 shows overseas-born population by origin for our three regions, with Townsville in blue, Nambour in orange, and Logan in green. Logan leads in almost all categories of overseas-born people.

Discussion

This section discusses three case studies that represent a CCE particular to their region. The discussion is thematically grouped into people, place, and technology. Although the urban informatics approach considers them jointly, for our purpose here we discuss each layer in turn. While we acknowledge

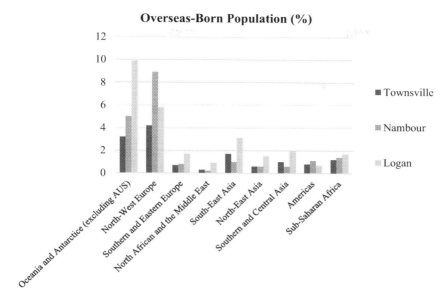

Figure 9.5 Overseas-born population for Townsville, Nambour, and Logan. Data refers to year 2016.

Source: Australian Bureau of Statistics (2018)

thematic overlaps between two or more layers, we chose to structure our discussion in this way for reasons of clarity and scope. Our data analysis revealed that each CCE has – implicitly or explicitly – a focus on one of the three areas with respective implications for the other two areas. For example, Susbstation33 appears to have a clear technology focus with its goal of upcycling e-waste; however, as a result, our data confirms interesting implications for social and spatial relationships within the City of Logan, too. Similarly, The Ambo appears to have a primary focus within the people lens, and iNQ within the place lens.

People

Foth et al. (2011: 3) argue that the city "only meaningfully exists when it is occupied by a sustained stream of people. In this sense, people are the core of the stream of the city." Similarly, innovation only exists because people invent and discover innovation (Gladwell 2000). Although the potential to innovate might depend on people's exposure to political and cultural forces surrounding them, the meaning and role of people as active creators of innovation is apparent, because they are the innovators.

Since the closure of its sugar mill, Nambour has been socio-culturally and economically strained (Johnstone, Choi and Leong 2016). Michael Doneman, who is the president of The Ambo, was the initiator who found purpose in a defunct ambulance station with a vision to turn it into a creative hub for Nambour's creative community. The Sunshine Coast Arts Industry Precinct Inc board members volunteer their services to The Ambo. Currently, The Ambo is occupied by six tenants from different industries; for example, Spiral aims to provide an environment for people with disabilities to link them to the community and build capacity, ElevenPM Studios provides a recording facility for online publishing, and Jewellery Collective is a jewellery school that offers co-working space and workshops. The variety of business tenants gives an idea of the diversity of people at The Ambo. At the same time, it might also be surprising in the sense that these businesses and their industries are barely associated with each other, and yet they share facilities at The Ambo. The types of businesses convey the idea of what The Ambo calls "grunge entrepreneurship" (Doneman 2017), or what is more commonly known under the name of 'innovation agenda.' The businesses show social responsibility and care for environmental sustainability and are value-creating enterprises that bring benefits to the local community. Although, at present, (digital) technologies as well as the notion of fast growth seem to be less of a focus for the business tenants at The Ambo. Moreover, The Ambo facilitates a variety of events that are inclusive of, or organised by, young people, people with disabilities, students, people from abroad, and seniors. This suggests that The Ambo is a hub where everyone is welcome to come and engage with the creative community. The tenants' rents are a source of income; hence, *The Ambo* is less dependent on external funding (Johnstone, Choi and Leong 2016). The role of people, their dedication to volunteering for the community, and their welcoming of old and new members to The Ambo demonstrates The Ambo's focus on a socio-cultural diversity of *people*.

iNQ appears to focus less on diversity, as their approach is distinctly themed around the STEM (science, technology, engineering, maths) sector and technology startups inspired by Silicon Valley success stories such as Google and Tesla. However, they do aim to foster collaboration amongst its community members who are passionate about building up, growing, and making the region's startup ecosystem successful. Members pay a yearly membership fee that ranges between AUD\$99 for individuals and AUD\$2,500 for corporate organisations. These fees seem to be more affordable in comparison to other innovation hubs. For example, River City Labs in Brisbane charges AUD\$550 per month membership just for a dedicated desk (River City Labs 2018). iNQ also takes future generations into account and provides free membership for children. Children get free access to iNQ's network and mentors, one hour for consultancy with a team member, and 50% discounts on the hub's events and workshops, e.g. coderdojo (coderdojo.com) programming classes for children between 7 and 17 years of age. While the attention devoted to caring for the next generation of innovators is commendable, it remains unanswered whether those young people who want to explore a career path outside the tech/STEM sector, e.g. in the arts or design, find any support or resources provided by iNQ. If we want to be serious about encouraging innovation that will bring prosperity

The role of Fab Labs and Living Labs   187

to regional Australia and sustain a future for younger generations, we need not just STEM to come to the rescue, but we need to nurture all forms of innovation (Foth 2015a, 2015b).

Substation33 is a volunteer-based social enterprise that employs a few technical specialists and people who started at Substation33 as volunteers. It welcomes people from all backgrounds to volunteer in its re- and upcycling process to learn new skills, gain confidence, and potentially transition to employment. Technical specialists who bring the know-how help with the development and commercialisation of innovative products and services. In this regard, Substation33 found the right way to facilitate collaboration between specialists and volunteers who are mostly long-term unemployed people. The social enterprise gives volunteers the opportunity to re-start and gain confidence through meaningful work. It sometimes hires volunteers. However, its turnover rate of employees and volunteers is two years, meaning that employees and volunteers leave Substation33 on average after two years because they found employment with another company. Besides benefiting the individuals who find themselves in employment, as a consequence, it also positively impacts on society's welfare system when the unemployment rate goes down.

Although iNQ and Substation33 make efforts in helping people to *stand-up before start-up* by teaching them new skills and providing them with equipment and facilities to be entrepreneurial and innovative, we found that The Ambo has the biggest focus on *people* out of our three case studies. The Ambo helped to revitalise Nambour, which suffered when its sugar mill closed down. Its volunteer-based and bottom-up approach is inclusive of 'fringe' innovators, 'grunge' entrepreneurs, and older generations. The Ambo successfully created an authentic community profile with 'street credibility,' and provides a place for local creatives to be entrepreneurial.

Place

Urban informatics examines the city as a "hybrid space" (de Souza e Silva 2006: 262) that comes with a complexityand hence requires "*real-time* examination with both tangible and intangible constituents . . . between the physical and digital" (Foth et al. 2011: 2). Although people have been striving for innovation in 'conventional' places, such as universities using wet and dry laboratories (Harman 2010) or research and development departments in companies (Ulku 2007), CCEs provide new places for people to work, create, be entrepreneurial, and innovate. For instance, coworking spaces are more open, transparent, and playful (van Meel and Vos 2001) and host "a diverse group of people" (DeGuzman and Tang 2011: 23). People who pursue their work and entrepreneurial and innovative endeavours independent of specialist equipment and machinery can become nomads who traverse the urban environment and make the city their office (Foth et al. 2016).

iNQ Central is iNQ's space in Townville, with almost 300 square metres of co-working area (Powell 2016a). Its space is flexible in use and can accommodate small offices, permanent desks, hot desks, and meeting rooms to facilitate work for individuals, startups, and larger groups of up to 120 people (Powell 2016a). Honeycombes Property Group donated the facility to iNQ to support it in building an ecosystem for local creative thinkers, entrepreneurs, and innovators (Powell 2016a). iNQ uses its facilities to host events such as startup community meetups, coderdojo programming classes for children, and its "pizza and brews" monthly night for members to catch up (iNQ n.d.). At the iNQ Central launch on 8 August 2016, founding member Warwick Powell said in an interview with 7 News Townsville (2016): "The businesses that have been associated with iNQ in terms of the start-up community have already created around 40 jobs in Townsville." This shows that iNQ started its mission to develop an innovation and entrepreneurial ecosystem in Townsville even before it had a dedicated space. The launch was accompanied by four special guests who are leaders in innovation activities in Queensland and Australia. After the industry breakfast launch, the special guests spread across Townsville for discussing opportunities and challenges for iNQ's mission (Powell 2016b). Rather than focusing only on its new facility for hosting seminars and discussion events, iNQ uses the whole city of Townsville to create and encourage innovation and entrepreneurship (Lankester, Hughes and Foth 2018). iNQ follows a decentralised approach and spreads its activities across the city. This approach, which rightly recognises that regional areas operate differently to larger, metropolitan cities with a designated CBD, seems to pay off. Following its aim, it supports and collaborates with other organisations in the region's startup community. For instance, it is involved in innovation activities at James Cook University (Powell 2016a) and Mixhaus (Foth et al. 2018). Further, it also reaches out to entrepreneurs in the UK, the US, Hong Kong, Taiwan, and Singapore to build new networks and opportunities in new markets (Powell 2016a). These examples suggest that iNQ has a more dispersed and decentralised focus on *place*, i.e. not just on iNQ Central itself but on Townsville as a region, to inspire, support, and build a creative entrepreneurial and innovative ecosystem in the region rather than centralising innovation activities within its own facilities. However, this approach has been met with some opposition when the Australian Government picked Townsville as one of four regions to enter into a City Deal with (Chan 2016). These federal-local government partnerships trigger investment and subsidies but come with conditions. In the case of Townsville, the City Deal borrows metropolitan growth strategies in an attempt to bolster the Townsville CBD, which goes contrary to iNQ's regionally dispersed focus.

The Ambo has its focus on *people* to bring creatives together and build a community. Its facility, which used to be an ambulance station in Nambour, can facilitate events with different purposes such as theatre plays, exhibitions, workshops, or individual work stations. The Ambo hosts events where community members come together to build creative capacity (Johnstone, Choi and Leong 2016). For instance, the Long Table Dinner takes place on the 16th of every month and is a free event to which people bring and share their homemade food and have conversations. The Ambo's 'street credibility' is also mirrored in its spatial facilities. Rather than providing a modern minimalistic and clean space that may remind someone of an airport architecture and vibe, its spatial design looks unfinished and yet to be designed. This seems to align with the hub's creative community spirit and communicates an ongoing movement, process and creation in the space. The Ambo uses *place* as a central destination to gather the creative community of the region.

Substation33 makes use of its space similar to The Ambo. Its main business process, i.e. re- and upcycling of e-waste, happens on site of the warehouse. In some cases, it might arrange for e-waste pick-up service or send volunteers or employees off-site as part of its service for maintaining its innovative products, e.g. warning signs that are deployed on flooded roads nearby. Besides its usual business including recycling e-waste, monitoring and evaluating its products in-use, and innovating product and services, Substation33 hosts Engineers Without Borders Makerthons that encourage teams to produce prototypes providing solutions to real-world problems (Substation33 2018).

As opposed to iNQ, The Ambo and Substation33 have a much more centralised focus on their facilities. They use their facilities to host events, gather their community members, volunteers, or employees, and provide a space for them to work. iNQ uses its space similarly, but spreads its activities and services across the wider Townsville region, putting the focus on a regional understanding of activating *place*.

Technology

The web (Leadbeater 2009) and digital technology (Castells 2010) have affected the structure of information flow between people in ways that "are still difficult to foresee entirely" (Barthelemy 2016: 246). They also enabled workers to become digital nomads (Foth et al. 2016). Through the *technology* lens, urban informatics acknowledges that people in the creative industries can take advantage of technology, harnessing its innovative opportunities either as new creativity outlets and tools or as means for sharing, discussing, and publishing findings and results (Foth et al. 2011). Our three case studies use digital and physical technologies in different ways.

Substation33 uses digital technology such as its website and social media platform for publicity and to inform the public about its projects, services, involvement opportunities, and news. However, Substation33 has a focus on physical computing and ubiquitous technology. It uses e-waste, e.g. old computers, laptops, phones, and other electronics with a battery or plug, for re- or upcycling purposes (Substation33 2017b). Through the process of collecting, processing, and recycling e-waste, it aims to reduce the amount of electronics that goes into landfill. Here then, social innovation involves a way of decreasing the amount of e-waste. At the same time Substation33 uses the process of recycling to educate its volunteers by teaching them new skills and helping them gain confidence to find employment. Dismantling e-waste helps participants to understand how the technology was put together and how it works. In a way, volunteers and employees are learning while doing at Substation33. Substation33 uses valuable parts and re-assembles them to create novel products and services that are conceived in its innovation lab. *Technology* builds the core of Substation33's business. It is not only used as a one-way communication tool to inform the public about its operations, but technology is the subject of its business operation, as Substation33 recycles it.

The Ambo predominantly relies on word-of-mouth marketing (Johnstone, Choi and Leong 2016), complemented by technology-assisted digital communication. Its website, social media profiles and email newsletters inform community members and public audience about past and upcoming events, activities, and news. The Ambo faces challenges to introduce new technologies to the space due to limited financial resources (Johnstone, Choi and Leong 2016).

iNQ focuses on technology not just for its web presence and social media platforms in order to communicate upcoming events and information that is of interest to its creative and entrepreneurial community. It also has a notable focus on primarily supporting startups that use technology and STEM. Warwick Powell occasionally takes the opportunity to write about iNQ in DUO Magazine, e.g. in the August 2016 issue (Powell 2016a: 16–17). Further, iNQ provides its community members with the opportunity to take part in workshops on online branding and software development. While it advocates for an inclusive approach to build its innovation ecosystem, the community is not as diverse as The Ambo's. A combination of social and technology-assisted interventions and initiatives may assist in attracting other disciplinary profiles to iNQ. An example of a social initiative is Hack the Evening at the State Library of Queensland's coworking space and digital culture centre The Edge, which provides library "visitors with opportunities for connected learning in relation to hacking, making and do-it-yourself technology" (Bilandzic 2016). Examples of technology-assisted interventions are Gelatine, a digital 'check in' system at The Edge that facilitates encounters between coworkers (Bilandzic et al. 2013), and Skunkworks Finder, a website providing its users with the opportunity to find innovation spaces and marginalised networks on the creative fringe (Bilandzic et al. 2018; Casadevall, Foth and Bilandzic 2018). Due to its operational profile, we find that Substation33 focuses most on technology when compared to The Ambo and iNQ. All case studies maintain an online presence to be visible to the public and their community. However, their efforts in using technology as a tool to innovate and pursue entrepreneurial endeavours differs.

Conclusion

In this study we aimed to better understand the role of CCEs in regional Australia. This allowed us to examine some of the specifics governing their approaches to innovation that help to make them unique and distinct from the common genre of innovation spaces found in larger cities that often focus on technology startups. We analysed three case studies of CCEs in regional Australia through the lenses of people, place, and technology.

For our study, we conducted desktop research and collected data about each case study through their websites, social media platforms, and media releases, e.g. news and magazines. Our findings show that the three case studies have different approaches to innovation, hence, their foci vary: iNQ has a focus on space, The Ambo cares primarily about people, and Substation33 prioritises technology. Nevertheless, they have a "middle-out" approach (Fredericks, Caldwell and Tomitsch 2016) to innovation in common. They are community-based and volunteer-based. They welcome new members independent of their socio-cultural or socio-economic background, indicating an all-inclusive approach and recognition of value in all individuals. Further, they believe in, and support, informal learning (Bilandzic 2016) and knowledge exchange (Bouncken and Reuschl 2016) for developing new skills, hence, increasing the capacity for innovation within the local community. Their approach and activities are reminiscent of Narendra Modi, the prime minister of India who gave a speech on "Start-up India; Stand-Up India," calling for incentives and support to encourage women, youth, and those historically seen at the bottom of the caste hierarchy for entrepreneurial training to mobilise them towards innovation (PTI 2015). In this sense, our case studies provide tools and give opportunities to their community members for learning, tinkering, and creative development before innovation occurs. In a way, these spaces provide their community members with a "skunkworks" (Foth 2015a) where they can gather, learn, train, experiment, and innovate in preparation for entrepreneurial activities.

Based on our findings, we believe policies and development strategies should recognise the uniqueness of regional CCEs and support them with 'responsible' solutions. CCEs in larger cities might benefit from learning and adapting a similar all-inclusive approach rather than almost exclusively focusing on tech start-ups and commercial innovations as the only economic development approach. Our case studies provide examples of different approaches to innovation. Their spaces as CCEs give possibilities for experimentation, testing, learning, and creation and show their potential as a different approach to economic development in regional areas. Society as a whole would benefit of a broader, more holistic understanding of innovation, such as considering and valuing more less-obvious parts of the innovation process in particular its precursors. For instance, CCEs in metropolitan areas could support and provide more tools helping people first to stand up before startup. Our future research will investigate these issues. Although each of our case studies has its own focus, they all provide a novel approach to foster diversity in their respective region where various stakeholders come together, share encounters, and build a community. Other regions could learn from our case studies, because innovation can thrive on serendipitous encounters and diversity, e.g. through providing individuals with access to more than one social network (Granovetter 1973); gathering people with different characteristics, knowledge, skills, know-how (Callon 1990; O'Connor 2006; O'Connor and McDermott 2004; Roberts and Fusfeld 1982) or motivations (Battistella and Nonino 2013); and providing a variety of channels that

192 *Ana Bilandzic, Marcus Foth and Greg Hearn*

allow people to express their ideas in different ways (He 2013). However, our case studies suggest that diversity requires curation, e.g. from volunteering board members who are committed to the community, to afford opportunities for creative and innovative ideas to emerge from shared encounters and serendipity. Furthermore, research could focus on getting a deeper understanding of the precursors that enable people to be innovative and entrepreneurial in regional CCEs, hence, leading to thriving regions in Australia. Leveraging the knowledge of locally involved community members could enhance the understanding of how the CCEs operate and provide a nurturing ground for innovation in regional Australia. Foth (as cited in Parliament of Commonwealth of Australia 2018) argues for the value in seeing "regionality as an asset." In his expert witness account, Foth recommended to the Australian Parliament to reject the cookie-cutter mentality that often sees regional LGAs merely adopting undifferentiated urban growth and urban sprawl strategies of their metropolitan counterparts and, by doing so, inheriting the same problems that capital cities face: pollution, congestion, and housing unaffordability. Foth argues that an investigation of "the qualitative aspect that actually allows us to differentiate what to grow and what not to grow [referring to businesses], what to increase and what to decrease" will help to identify a region's uniqueness rather than looking for the next Elon Musk or forcefully injecting a Silicon Valley innovation culture (Foth as cited in Parliament of Commonwealth of Australia 2018).

References

7 News Townsville. 2016. "7 News Townsville – New Jobs Hub." *Innovation Hub: Full Story*. Retrieved September 20, 2018 (www.facebook.com/7NewsTownsville/videos/new-jobs-hub/1130246877021397/).

ABC News. 2018. "Substation33 on ABC News February 17, 2018." *Australia: YouTube*. Retrieved October 31, 2018 (www.youtube.com/watch?v=GemmBw5putY).

Adkins, B. A. et al. 2007. "Ecologies of Innovation: Symbolic Aspects of Cross-Organizational Linkages in the Design Sector in an Australian Inner-City Area." *American Behavioral Scientist* 50(7): 922–934.

Arteaga, R., and Hyland, J. 2014. *Pivot – How Top Entrepreneurs Adapt and Change Course to Find Ultimate Success*, New Jersey: John Wiley & Sons.

Asheim, B., Coenen, L., and Vang, J. 2007. "Face-to-Face, Buzz, and Knowledge Bases: Sociospatial Implications for Learning, Innovation, and Innovation Policy. Environment and Planning." *Government & Policy* 25(5): 655–670.

Australian Bureau of Statistics. 2018. "Data by Region." Retrieved September 19, 2018 (http://stat.abs.gov.au/itt/r.jsp?databyregion#/).

Barthelemy, M. 2016. *The Structure and Dynamics of Cities: Urban Data Analysis and Theoretical Modelling*. Cambridge: Cambridge University Press.

Bathelt, H., Malmberg, A., and Maskell, P. 2004. "Clusters and Knowledge: Local Buzz, Global Pipelines and the Process of Knowledge Creation." *Progress in Human Geography* 28(1): 31–56.

Battistella, C., and Nonino, F. 2013. "Exploring the Impact of Motivations on the Attraction of Innovation Roles in Open Innovation Web-Based Platforms." *Production Planning & Control* 24(2–3): 226–245.

The role of Fab Labs and Living Labs   193

Bilandzic, A. et al. 2018. "Social and Spatial Precursors to Innovation: The Diversity Advantage of the Creative Fringe." *The Journal of Community Informatics* 14(1): 160–182.

Bilandzic, M. 2016. "Connected Learning in the Library as a Product of Hacking, Making, Social Diversity and Messiness." *Interactive Learning Environments* 24(1): 158–177.

Bilandzic, M., and Foth, M. 2013. "Libraries as Coworking Spaces: Understanding User Motivations and Perceived Barriers to Social Learning." *Library Hi Tech* 31(2): 254–273.

Bilandzic, M., and Foth, M. 2017. "Designing Hubs for Connected Learning: Social, Spatial and Technological Insights from Coworking, Hackerspaces and Meetup Groups." Pp. 191–206 in *Place-Based Spaces for Networked Learning*, edited by Carvalho, L., Goodyear, P., and de Laat, M. Abingdon: Routledge.

Bilandzic, M., Schroeter, R., and Foth, M. 2013. "Gelatine: Making Coworking Places Gel for Better Collaboration and Social Learning." Pp. 427–436 in *Proceedings of the 25th Australian Computer-Human Interaction Conference (OzCHI 2013)*. New York: ACM.

Blythe, M. A., and Wright, P. C. 2005. "Funology." Pp. XIII–XIX in *From Usability to Enjoyment*, edited by Blythe, M. A. et al. New York: Kluwer Academic Publishers; Springer Science + Business Media.

Bouncken, R. B., and Reuschl, A. J. 2016. "Coworking-spaces: How a Phenomenon of the Sharing Economy Builds a Novel Trend for the Workplace and for Entrepreneurship." *Review of Managerial Science* 1–18.

Callon, M. 1990. "Techno-economic Networks and Irreversibility." *The Sociological Review* 38(1): 132–161.

Capdevila, I. 2015. "Co-working Spaces and the Localised Dynamics of Innovation in Barcelona." *International Journal of Innovation and Technology Management* 19(3): 25.

Casadevall, D., Foth, M., and Bilandzic, A. 2018. "Skunkworks Finder: Unlocking the Diversity Advantage of Urban Innovation Ecosystems." In *Australian Conference on Computer-Human Interaction* (OZCHI 2018). ACM.

Castells, M. 2010. *The Rise of the Network Society*. West Sussex: Wiley Blackwell.

Chan, G. 2016. "Heart of Modern Politics is on the City Fringes, says Turnbull's Urban Thinker." *The Guardian*. Retrieved December 12, 2018 (www.theguardian.com/australia-news/2016/jul/30/heart-modern-politics-city-fringes-turnbulls-urban-thinker).

Coghill, J. 2015b. "Sunshine Coast Town Turns to Creative Industries after Economic Struggle." *ABC News*. Retrieved October 31, 2018 (www.abc.net.au/local/photos/2015/09/18/4315396.htm).

Coghill, J. 2015a. "Nambour Old Boy Teaches Business to Fringe Dwellers." *ABC News*. Retrieved September 27, 2018 (www.abc.net.au/news/2015-11-19/old-boy-michael-doneman-leads-nambour-revival/6954324).

Commonwealth of Australia. 2018. "Startups and Entrepreneurs." Retrieved March 20, 2018 (www.innovation.gov.au/audience/startups-and-entrepreneurs).

Couger, J. D., Higgins, L. F., and McIntyre, S. C. 1990. "Differentiating Creativity, Innovation, Entrepreneurship, Intrapreneurship, Copyright and Patenting for I.S. Products Processes." Pp. 370–379 in *Twenty-Third Annual Hawaii International Conference on System Sciences*. IEEE.

de Souza e Silva, A. 2006. "From Cyber to Hybrid: Mobile Technologies as Interfaces of Hybrid Spaces." *Space and Culture* 9(3): 261–278.

DeGuzman, G. V., and Tang, A. I. 2011. *Working in the Unoffice: A Guide to Coworking for Indie Workers, Small Businesses, and Nonprofits*. San Francisco: Night Owls Press LLC.

Department of Industry, Innovation and Science. n.d.-a. "Industry Monitor – Innovation." Retrieved March 20, 2018 (https://industry.gov.au/Office-of-the-Chief-Economist/Publications/IndustryMonitor2018/innovation/index.html).

Department of Industry, Innovation and Science. n.d.-b. "Innovation Map." Retrieved March 20, 2018 (https://industry.gov.au/Office-of-the-Chief-Economist/Publications/AustralianIndustryReport/innovation-map.html).

Desrochers, P., and Leppälä, S. 2011. "Creative Local Environments: The Case for Local Economic Diversity." *Creativity & Innovation Management* 20(1): 59–69.

Dezuanni, M. et al. 2018. *Digital Participation Through Social Living Labs: Valuing Local Knowledge, Enhancing Engagement.* Cambridge: Elsevier Limited.

Doneman, M. 2017. "The Old Ambo and The Regional Innovation Program. The Old Ambulance Station." Retrieved December 13, 2018 (http://theoldambulancestation.com/our-news/).

Eversole, R. 2017. "Economies with People in Them: Regional Futures Through the Lens of Contemporary Regional Development Theory." *Australasian Journal of Regional Studies* 23(3): 305–318.

Foth, M. 2015a. Australia Needs an Innovation "Skunkworks." *The Conversation.* Retrieved December 5, 2017 (https://theconversation.com/australia-needs-an-innovation-skunkworks-51326).

Foth, M. 2015b. "We Need to Fund More Than Just Science Priorities for Australia's Future. *The Conversation.* Retrieved September 28, 2018 (http://theconversation.com/we-need-to-fund-more-than-just-science-priorities-for-australias-future-50243).

Foth, M. et al. 2015. "From Users to Citizens: Some Thoughts on Designing for Polity and Civics." Pp. 623–633 in *OzCHI '15 Proceedings of the Annual Meeting of the Australian Special Interest Group for Computer Human Interaction.* OZCHI 2015. Melbourne: ACM.

Foth, M., Choi, J. H.-J., and Satchell, C. 2011. "Urban Informatics." Pp. 1–9 in *Proceedings of the ACM 2011 Conference on Computer Supported Cooperative Work,* edited by ACM. CSCW. Hangzhou, China.

Foth, M., Forlano, L., and Bilandzic, M. 2016. "Mapping New Work Practices in the Smart City." Pp. 1–13 in *Handbuch Soziale Praktiken und Digitale Alltagswelten,* edited by Friese, H., Rebane, G., Nolden, M., and Schreiter, M. Wiesbaden: Springer.

Foth, M., and Hearn, G. 2007. "Networked Individualism of Urban Residents: Discovering the Communicative Ecology in Inner-city Apartment Buildings." *Information, Communication and Society* 10(5): 749–772.

Foth, M., Lankester, A., and Hughes, H. E. 2018. "Mixhaus: Dissolving Boundaries with a Community Maker Space." Pp. 97–116 in *Digital Participation through Social Living Labs: Valuing Local Knowledge, Enhancing Engagement,* edited by Dezuanni, M. L. et al. Cambridge, UK: Chandos Publishing (Elsevier).

Fredericks, J., Caldwell, G. A., and Tomitsch, M. 2016. "Middle-out Design: Collaborative Community Engagement in Urban HCI." Pp. 200–204 in *Proceedings of the 28th Australian Conference on Computer-Human Interaction.* OzCHI 2016. New York: ACM.

Gladwell, M. 2000. *The Tipping Point.* Boston: Little, Brown.

Gordon, E., and de Souza e Silva, A. 2011. *Net Locality: Why Location Matters in a Networked World.* Chichester, UK: Wiley-Blackwell.

Granovetter, M. S. 1973. "The Strength of Weak Ties." *The American Journal of Sociology* 78(6): 1360–1380.

Hamilton-Smith, L. 2018. "One Person's Trash is Another's DIY 3D Printer." *ABC News.* Retrieved October 31, 2018 (www.abc.net.au/news/2018-02-17/using-ewaste-to-build-3d-printers-and-electric-bikes-brisbane/9449604).

Harman, G. 2010. "Australian University Research Commercialisation: Perceptions of Technology Transfer Specialists and Science and Technology Academics." *Journal of Higher Education Policy and Management* 32(1): 69–83.

Hauschildt, J., and Salomo, S. 2011. *Innovationsmanagement*. München: Vahlen.

He, L. 2013. "Google's Secrets of Innovation: Empowering its Employees." *Forbes*. M. L. Retrieved January 24, 2018 (www.forbes.com/sites/laurahe/2013/03/29/googles-secrets-of-innovation-empowering-its-employees/#d06671a57e7b).

Hearn, G. 2014. "Creative Occupations as Knowledge Practices: Innovation and Precarity in the Creative Economy." *Cultural Science Journal* 7(1): 83.

Hearn, G., and Foth, M. 2007. "Communicative Ecologies." *Electronic Journal of Communication* 17(1–2).

Howard, J. H. 2012. *Innovation, Ingenuity and Initiative: The Adoption and Application of New Ideas in Australian Local Government*, ANSZOG Institute for Governance.

iNQ. n.d. "Home – Innovate NQ." *Innovate NQ*. Retrieved September 17, 2018 (https://i-nq.com.au/).

Isaacson, W. 2011. *Steve Jobs*. New York: Simon & Schuster.

Johnstone, S., Choi, J. H.-J., and Leong, J. 2016. "Designing for Diversity: Connecting People, Places, and Technologies in Creative Community Hubs." Pp. 135–139 in *OzCHI '16 Proceedings of the 28th Australian Conference on Computer-Human Interaction*. OzCHI 2016: 28th Australian Conference on Human-Computer Interaction (HCI).

Kline, S. J., and Rosenberg, N. 1986. "An Overview of Innovation." Pp. 275–306 in *The Positive Sum Strategy*, edited by Landau, R., and Rosenberg, N. Washington, DC: National Academy Press.

Kojo, I., and Nenonen, S. 2014. "Evolution of Co-working Places: Drivers and Possibilities. *Intelligent Buildings International*, 1–12.

Lankester, A., Hughes, H. E., and Foth, M. 2018. "Mapping a Connected Learning Ecology to Foster Digital Participation in Regional Communities." Pp. 141–171 in *Digital Participation Through Social Living Labs: Valuing Local Knowledge, Enhancing Engagement*, edited by Dezuanni, M. L. et al. Cambridge, UK: Chandos Publishing (Elsevier).

Leadbeater, C. 2009. *We-think: Mass Innovation, Not Mass Production*, London: Profile Books Ltd.

Lobo, J. et al. 2014. "The Inventive, the Educated, and the Creative: How Do They Affect Metropolitan Productivity?" *Industry and Innovation* 21(2): 155–177.

Millios-Hullick, E. 2016. "Leading a Sustainable Future." *DUO Magazine* (118): 112–113.

O'Connor, G. C. 2006. "Open, Radical Innovation: Toward an Integrated Model in Large Established Firms." Pp. 62–81 in *Open Innovation*, edited by Chesbrough, H. W., Vanhaverbekem, W., and West, J. New York: Oxford University Press.

O'Connor, G. C., and McDermott, C. M. 2004. "The Human Side of Radical Innovation." *Journal of Engineering and Technology Management* 21(1–2): 11–30.

Pancholi, S., Yigitcanlar, T., and Guaralda, M. 2015. "Place Making Facilitators of Knowledge and Innovation Spaces: Insights from European Best Practices." *International Journal of Knowledge-Based Development* 6(3): 215–240.

Parliament of the Commonwealth of Australia. 2018. *Building Up & Moving Out*, Commonwealth of Australia.

Pavitt, K. 2001. "Public Policies to Support Basic Research: What Can the Rest of the World Learn from US Theory and Practice? (And What They Should Not Learn)." *Industrial and Corporate Change* 10(3): 761–779.

Porter, M. E. 1990. *The Competitive Advantage of Nations*. New York: Free Press.

Powell, W. 2016a. "Innovator's New Home." *DUO Magazine Duo Magazine* (123): 16–17.

Powell, W. 2016b. "iNQ Reflections – We're Away!" *LinkedIn*. Retrieved September 17, 2018 (www.linkedin.com/pulse/inq-reflections-were-away-warwick-powell-%E9%B2%8D%E9%9F%B6%E5%B1%B1).

PTI. 2015. "PM Narendra Modi Announces 'Start up; Stand up India" Initiative to Create More Jobs." *The Indian Express*. Retrieved January 31, 2018 (http://indianexpress.com/article/india/india-others/pm-narendra-modi-announces-start-up-stand-up-india-initiative-to-create-more-jobs/).

Pugalis, L., and Gray, N. 2016. "New Regional Development Paradigms: An Exposition of Place-based Modalities." *Australasian Journal of Regional Studies* 22(1): 181–203.

Queensland Government. 2015. "Nambour Section of the Moreton Central Sugar Mill Cane Tramway." *Queensland Government*. Retrieved September 19, 2018 (https://environment.ehp.qld.gov.au/heritage-register/detail/?id=602522).

Queensland Government. 2018. "Local Government Areas of Queensland." *Department of Local Government, Racing and Multicultural Affairs*. Retrieved September 27, 2018 (www.dlgrma.qld.gov.au/resources-ilgp/maps/local-government-maps.html).

Rickards, T. 1985. "Making New Things Happen: An Interpretation of Observed Innovation Strategies." *Technovation* 3(2): 119–131.

River City Labs. 2018. "Desk Membership – River City Labs." *River City Labs*. Retrieved September 20, 2018 (www.rivercitylabs.net/join/become-a-member/desk-membership/).

Roberts, E. B., and Fusfeld, A. R. 1982. "Critical Functions: Needed Roles in the Innovation Process." Pp. 182–207 in *Career Issues in Human Resource Management*, edited by Katz, R. Englewood Cliffs: Prentice Hall.

Salt, B. 2016. "Super Connected Lifestyle Locations." *Nbn*. Retrieved September 21, 2018 (www.nbnco.com.au/content/dam/nbnco2/documents/Super%20connected%20lifestyle%20locations_nbn%20report_FINAL.PDF).

Saul, J. 2010. *Social Innovation, Inc.* San Francisco: John Wiley & Sons.

Schumpeter, J. A. 1934. *The Theory of Economic Development. An Inquiry into Profits, Capital, Credit, Interest, and the Business Cycle*. Cambridge: Harvard University Press.

Scott, A. J., and Storper, M. 2015. "The Nature of Cities: The Scope and Limits of Urban Theory." *International Journal of Urban and Regional Research* 39(1): 1–15.

Shearmur, R. 2012. "Are Cities the Font of Innovation? A Critical Review of the Literature on Cities and Innovation." *Cities* 29(2): S9–S18.

Storper, M. 2011. "Why Do Regions Develop and Change? The Challenge for Geography and Economics." *Journal of Economic Geography* 11(2): 333–346.

Storper, M., and Venables, A. J. 2004. "Buzz: Face-to-Face Contact and the Urban Economy." *Journal of Economic Geography* 4: 351–370.

Substation33. 2017a. "Flooded Road Warning Signs." *Substation33*. Retrieved September 21, 2018 (https://substation33.com.au/projects/flooded-road-smart-warning-signs/).

Substation33. 2017b. "Our Services." *Substation33*. Retrieved September 21, 2018 (https://substation33.com.au/services/).

Substation33. 2018. "Engineers Without Borders Makerthon." *Substation33*. Retrieved September 21, 2018 (https://substation33.com.au/engineers-without-borders-makerthon/?doing_wp_cron=1537507716.8115549087524414062500).

Tacchi, J., Foth, M., and Hearn, G. 2009. "Action Research Practices and Media for Development." *International Journal of Education and Development Using Information and Communication Technology* 5(2): 32–48.

The Old Ambulance Station. n.d. "What's on at the Old Ambo." *The Old Ambulance Station*. Retrieved September 18, 2018 (http://theoldambulancestation.com/).

The State of Queensland. 2017. "Advancing Regional Innovation Program Guidelines." *Advance Queensland*. Retrieved March 13, 2018 (https://advanceqld.initiatives.qld.gov.au/entrepreneurs-startups/advancing-regional-innovation/guidelines.aspx).

Ulku, H. 2007. "R&D, Innovation, and Growth: Evidence from Four Manufacturing Sectors in OECD." *Oxford Economic Papers, New Series* 59(3): 513–535.

Usher, A. 1954. *A History of Mechanical Inventions*. Cambridge: Harvard University Press.

van Lente, H., Swierstra, T., and Joly, P. B. 2017. "Responsible Innovation as a Critique of Technology Assessment." *Journal of Responsible Innovation* 4(2): 254–261.

van Meel, J., and Vos, P. 2001. "Funky Offices: Reflections on Office Design in the 'New Economy.'" *Journal of Corporate Real Estate* 3(4): 322–334.

Voyce, B. 2016. "Social Innovation for Liveable Regional Cities – Regional Australia Institute." *Regional Australia Institute*. Retrieved September 27, 2018 (www.regionalaustralia.org.au/home/2016/05/social-innovation-liveable-regional-cities/).

Section 3

Regional creative industries and their potentials

Case studies and comparative perspectives

10 The Hunter Region

A creative system at work

Phillip McIntyre, Susan Kerrigan, Evelyn King and Claire Williams

Introduction

The Hunter Region in New South Wales (NSW), Australia, is a place where we can see a complex creative system at work (McIntyre 2013; Kerrigan 2013; McIntyre, Fulton and Paton 2016). This creative system can be seen in the actions of the creative industries, a set of related sectors comprised of a rich admixture of design, the arts, the media and information technology (Flew 2012: 84). In order to understand how these creative industries operate as a system of production, it is worthwhile to outline what is characteristic about systems themselves before detailing a set of specific examples from the Hunter Region which illustrate the ideas themselves.

Background to the study

Like innovation ecosystems (Andersen 2011; McIntyre 2011), creative systems "are a subset of all complex systems" (Frenkel and Maital 2014: 229). Frenkel and Maital point out that the manifestation of novel products, processes and practices of complex systems "cannot easily be predicted from underlying components" (West quoted in Frenkel and Maital 2014: 229) since these products, processes and practices emerge from the interactions and interrelationships of the system at work. First mooted by Lewes in 1859, the notion of emergence describes a process whereby "novel and coherent structure, patterns and properties [arise] during the process of self-organization in complex systems" (Goldstein 1999: 49). Self-organisation in complex systems is thus a process whereby a form of order arises from the ongoing interactions of the system at work. Frenkel and Maital go on to assert that "the 'whole' of the innovation system in a nation or region is . . . significantly different from the sum of its parts" (2014: 229).

The creative systems approach used here, which adheres to the above characteristics of all systems, was initially developed by psychologist Mihaly Csikszentmihalyi (1988, 1997, 1999, 2014). It "incorporates not just individual creators but also the social and cultural context in which they work. In many ways it satisfies Csikszentmihalyi's call for an amalgam of the psychological and the

202   *Phillip McIntyre et al.*

sociological" (McIntyre, Fulton and Paton 2016: 1–2). From a sociological perspective, Pierre Bourdieu (1977, 1990, 1993, 1996) suggests that:

> It is the interplay between a *field of works* which presents possibilities of action to an individual who possesses the necessary *habitus*, partially composed of personal levels of *social, cultural, symbolic and economic capital* that then inclines them to act and react within particular structured and dynamic spaces called *fields*. These fields are arenas of production and circulation of goods, ideas and knowledges. They are populated by other *agents* who compete using various levels of the forms of capital pertinent to that field. Bourdieu suggests that it is the interplay between these various spheres of cultural production that makes practice possible.
>
> (McIntyre 2009: 7)

Csikszentmihalyi also proposed something remarkably similar in developing his systems model of creative action. He argues that:

> Three major factors, that is, a structure of knowledge manifest in a particular symbol system (*domain*), a structured social organisation that understands that body of knowledge (*field*), and an individual agent (*person*) who makes changes to the stored information that pre-exists them, are necessary for creativity to occur. These factors operate through 'dynamic links of circular causality' (1988: 329) with the starting point in the process being 'purely arbitrary' (ibid) indicating the systems essential nonlinearity.
>
> (McIntyre 2009: 7)

Each component part of the system – field, domain and agent – is necessary but not sufficient, in and of itself, to produce creative action. In an analogous way, fire emerges from the interaction of tinder, oxygen and a spark. Take one component out and fire simply will not occur. Creative systems are similar, but the difference is they are active and dynamic, and they exhibit, like all systems – including innovation ecosystems – emergence, complexity, nonlinearity, complementarity, interconnectedness and scalability as features that identify them. Scalability, for example, describes the idea that a whole system is composed of a variety of sub-systems, each of which is complete in and of itself, but is at the same time a constituent of the larger system of which it is a part. These systems are scaled vertically both above and below the one being focused on. To demonstrate this idea of scalability, as a creative system in action the creative industries in the Hunter Region are local, regional and global all at the same time. The global is constituted in some sense by a variety of regions, and these, of course, are dependent for their constitution on the localities that constitute them. And, of course, neighbourhoods operate within global spaces. It is through their interactions that these spaces become local places (Tuan 1997: 73). As Paul Knox and Sallie Marston argue in their book *Human Geography: Places and Regions in Global Context*:

The Hunter region 203

It is in specific locales that important events happen, and it is from them that significant changes spread. Nevertheless, the influence of places is by no means limited to the occasional innovative change. Because of their distinctive characteristics, places always modify and sometimes resist the imprint of even the broadest economic, cultural, and political trends.

(Knox and Marston 2014: 14)

We can demonstrate the idea of a creative system at work, as described briefly above, through an elucidation of an Australian Research Council Linkage Project entitled *Creativity and Cultural Production in the Hunter: An Applied Ethnographic Study of New Entrepreneurial Systems in the Creative Industries*. The project consisted of a three-year ethnographic study drawing on statistical analysis, 115 in-depth interviews with key informants, artefact examination and participant observation of the creative industries across the Hunter Valley in regional NSW, Australia, from 2014–2017.

The Hunter Region

When many in Australia think of the Hunter they tend to think of the city of Newcastle – but cities, as systems of production and consumption, do not exist in isolation. They are both historically and geographically located, system within system within system. As Fernand Braudel (1990) pointed out, the geography of a locality or region effects its patterns of settlement and has some effect on the systems of trade, culture and politics that develop there. The way linked villages, towns and cities come to define themselves, and are defined further afield in national and global arenas, is dependent in many senses on their interactions, which are both constrained and enabled (McIntyre 2012) by the geographical factors on offer and the histories that have been enacted there. Hinterlands feed cities, and cities depend on their hinterlands for survival. Smaller towns draw trade, wealth, knowledge and ideas from their larger urban cousins, and the urban areas are sustained by migrations of people and goods to and from them. As Braudel explains:

Every urban settlement is bound to live by maintaining a balance between what it receives (or takes) and what it gives (or returns). The balance has perpetually to be adjusted, the point of equilibrium is never fixed. And the particular way a town draws on the outside world while modifying itself internally, the better to attach itself to its surroundings and dominate them is never simple.

(1990: 189)

In "explaining the system" (1990: 161–262), Braudel points out cities and towns exist in "circles of influence" (1990: 185). Similarly, cities operate within "zones of urban attraction" (Braudel 1990: 259). The multi-faceted influence of a regional capital, "political and cultural in the broadest sense of both terms"

204 *Phillip McIntyre et al.*

(ibid), tends to exceed its designated city limits. This system is scalable, inter-connected and interdependent. As an example, the Hunter Region in NSW is a contested space operating as a system of many interactions and identities (McIntyre 2015). It is not "just there to be described" (McManus, O'Neill and Loughran 2000: 3). This can be seen in the "emergence of the Hunter Region as a cultural bounding of physical space that has, itself, changed over billions of years" (ibid). Apart from the ongoing Indigenous presence in the valley:

> There is the water catchment regional boundary, the political regional boundary, the regional economy and the Hunter Region of every individual's geographical imagination. For some people, the Hunter Region is centred on Newcastle, for others it is focused on the vineyards or the coalfields, while for other people the Hunter Region is an area somewhere north of the Central Coast. For other people it is not Sydney!
> (McManus, O'Neill and Loughran 2000: 3)

In an area as geographically, socially and industrially diverse as the Hunter Valley in NSW, with its urban concentrations of more than 350,000 people and with rural and tourism centres and waterfront villages, there has been a fairly wide bandwidth of skills and market experiences on offer. Mining, defence, shipping, health, manufacturing, power generation, viticulture, education, agriculture and professional services are all evident in the region's profile, but steel and aluminium production, shipbuilding, manufacturing and even coal production have all decreased their contribution in recent years. Alongside these recent industry dislocations, a devastating earthquake and an increasing animosity between mining and agriculture, a number of innovative approaches to cultural and economic adaptation have become necessary as this region interacts with a neoliberal, globalised and digitised world (Davies and Sigthorsson 2013; McIntyre 2017; Kerrigan and Hutchinson 2016). As Schulz indicates, "the technological advances made in the last decade have been breathtaking. . . . It is the kind of sea change that can only be compared with nineteenth century industrialization, but it is happening much faster this time" (2015). With a fluid economic situation developing for what were traditionally significant and mature generators of jobs, and a shift in the related businesses that depended on them, there is an increasing recognition of, among other industries, the creative industries as an identifiable and potentially strong economic sector to help take the region forward.

As one example, Marcus Westbury's book *Creating Cities* (2015) is a useful one in that it partially sees the world in systemic terms. Westbury identifies the connectivity those in Newcastle, rather than the broader region, now experience, where every action taken in individual projects that are part of the Renew campaign for urban renewal:

> is a microcosm of a wider network. Each is distinctive. Most of them are very much from and of Newcastle; they literally could not have happened

anywhere else. Yet virtually all of them are connected. They are part of global movements, networks, dialogues and markets.

(Westbury 2015: 155)

Kerrigan and Hutchinson's (2016) work, also specifically on the region's capital, Newcastle, looks at the transformation of this city in systemic terms. It examines Westbury's development of the Renew project, as well as interviews four business owners from film, fashion, design and accounting. The paper argues for a connection between the shifts in the city's cultural identity and how this complements business confidence in working in the creative industries. They conclude that communities are just as important as individuals in achieving success in the creative industries.

As a further example of the importance placed on creative industries, it was indicated in the recent Newcastle City Council (NCC) *Newcastle's Economic Development Strategy 2016–2019* (NCC 2016), alongside the recognition of the importance of innovation and creativity (ibid: 5) the creative industries were specifically named as a strategic growth sector (ibid: 34). The NCC observed a strong set of links with the knowledge economy and the potential for future growth from the creative industries in the city. This situation may also be reflected in the region more broadly.

As a composite, the region is composed of eleven local government areas (LGAs): Lake Macquarie, Newcastle, Maitland, Port Stephens, Cessnock, Great Lakes, Upper Hunter, Singleton, Dungog, Gloucester and Muswellbrook. The region is also

> divided into the urban areas, based around Newcastle and Lake Macquarie, and the remaining semi-rural and rural areas. Together, Newcastle and the Lake Macquarie LGA's have 54.17% of the region's total population. Lake Macquarie has the larger of the two urban populations.
>
> (Wilkinson 2017: online)

As per ABS Data by Region statistics, as set out in McIntyre et al. (2019), the total population of the Hunter Region in 2017 was 675,199. As an example of scalability at work, the Hunter Region's Gross Regional Product (GRP), that is, the region's net measure of wealth generated, sat at $44.435 billion in 2017 (Remplan 2017: online). This figure constituted 2.86% of New South Wales' gross state product (GSP) of $538.513 billion and 0.93% of Australia's gross domestic product (GDP) of $1.655 trillion (ibid). The contribution of the region's urban centres, constituted by Lake Macquarie and Newcastle LGAs, is estimated at $15.386 billion, "representing 34.63 % of the entire region's GRP" (ibid). Since the creative industries on one measure constitute 2.91% of the employed population (CIIC 2013) in the region, they are estimated in simple terms to contribute $1.29 billion to the GRP of the Hunter Region.

Analysis of the collected quantitative data

The sectors used in this analysis were initially based on a similar list generated from a report into the creative industries to the NSW Department of State and Regional Development (NSWSRD 2009: 7). These creative industries sectors include advertising and design, fashion, architecture, visual arts, performing arts, music, publishing, film, television, radio and electronic games and interactive content sectors. While there have been a number of lists and models generated, no matter which one is used, they consistently include design, the arts, information technology and media industries (Flew 2012: 84). Therefore, based on six-digit ANZSCO '06 Occupation codes, a tranche of ABS data was collected from the 2011 census in the early phase of the research based on these groupings. The collected data shows that the advertising and design sector in the Hunter Region constitutes 43.9% of all people engaged in the creative industries. This surprisingly large sector is clustered around not only traditionally recognised graphic design but also fashion, advertising and marketing and public relations, although many of the occupations found in agencies, for example filmmakers and web designers, also occur across other sectors. This amalgamation of what were previously thought to be separate sectors accounts for its size.

The ABS occupation data also indicated that 18.1% of the creative industries cohort in 2011 in the Hunter was engaged in the electronic games and interactive content sector. Once again, this includes a wide variety of cross-sectoral occupations. The next largest sector was architecture at 13.4%. In total, these three sectors represented at least 75% of the total creative industries occupations occurring in the Hunter Region in 2011.

The urban centre of this region, as defined by the NSW Parliament (Wilkinson 2017: online), had, as would be expected, the greater number of people from the creative industries living in these areas. Of this urban centre, Newcastle has the greater share with 2,539 people, while Lake Macquarie has 2,074. Of the rural and semi-rural areas, Maitland houses 584, closely followed by Port Stephens with 481 people engaged in the creative industries living there. The Dungog LGA has the lowest number of creative industries residents, with the Upper Hunter understandably contributing just 65 to the overall total of 6,535.

A second round of statistical data was also collected. This data was drawn from *both* the 2011 and 2016 censuses, resulting in an initial table from the ABS statistics which contained the number of persons employed, the total who stated income as well as mean income for 35 selected industries (four-digit IND06P) and all other industries by all occupations (six-digit ANZSCO). Unlike the prior data, this latter tranche was not drawn from LGAs but was based instead on SA4 geographical areas. Significantly, the Trident Methodology, as developed at QUT, was used as the basis for these statistics as it

> focusses on the activities that define creative production capacity in both occupations and industries. It includes three categories: (1) creative occupations within the core creative industries (what we term 'specialists');

(2) creative occupations employed in other (non-creative) industries (termed 'embedded' creatives); and (3) non-creative occupations ('support staff') employed in the creative industries.

(Higgs and Lennon 2014: 1)

The resultant data analysed for the project by Peter Higgs shows that the number of people employed in the creative industries in the Hunter Region has risen from 2011 to 2016, with 7,895 people employed in these industries in 2016. The share of the total workforce also increased between 2011 and 2016, with a cumulative annual growth rate of 4.3% compared to an annual growth in the general workforce of 3.2%. While the percentage of specialist and support workers appears to have dropped marginally, there was certainly growth in the employment of embedded creatives, that is, those operating within sectors of other industries. In addition, overall earnings in all sectors of the creative industries in the region increased between 2011 and 2016, but the share of earnings fell in the specialist and support segments with commensurate growth in share of earnings for the embedded sector. What is significant is that cumulative annual growth rate of earnings for the total creative industries (specialist, support and embedded combined) at 7.8% has outpaced that of the total workforce where earnings grew at 6.3%.

An ethnographic approach to the creative system

The initial statistical summary briefly outlined above reveals a valuable descriptive understanding indicative of the creative industries in the Hunter Region. We argue that what the Trident Methodology is pointing toward – bounded in this case by its methodological and ontological assumptions, as all research is – is the "field". The field is a term used specifically by both Mihaly Csikszentmihalyi (1988) and Pierre Bourdieu (1993) to describe all those who form part of the social structure of creative activity in a certain domain of creative action and can contribute to and influence that domain. In this case, we should note here that the domain and field are inextricably linked. If we assume we are thus looking at fields of activity built on specific domains of knowledge, what this systemic situation then requires is one further step for analysis. We need to get some in-depth sense of those agents who have been immersed in certain domain knowledge and who actually constitute the field of each sector of the creative industries, rather than what occupational list might or might not indicate what occurs there, since it is the interaction of the field, the domain and various active agents that, in its entirety as a system, forms a crucial contribution to the emergence of creative processes, products and ideas within these entrepreneurial systems. The system, comprised of arenas of social contestation that are built on varying degrees of domain knowledge, can be seen, in part, as a collections of agents who contribute to the emergence of objects, services and experiences typical of design, architecture, film, theatre and so on. This system is not the same thing as an industry occupation list. Although they do

208   *Phillip McIntyre et al.*

share commonalities, systems are broader and more inclusive than the notion of an industry. This additional perspective might reveal – in a slightly different way – who is involved and what they contribute to the emergence of creative activity in these industries.

In this case, alongside the statistical descriptions provided by the quantifiable data, we also want to draw out a little of what was revealed via the in-depth ethnographic interviews and participant observations. These qualitative methods revealed that there are concentrations of successful creative practitioners engaging in collaborative activities who are increasingly making not only regional but national and global linkages. We present a very limited set of these stories here as indication of the wealth of activity that is actually occurring on the ground in the region but stress, again, as the full report of the study (McIntyre et al. 2019) indicates, there are many other stories to be told across a number of creative industries sectors right across the region.

Creating an innovative niche in the radio sector of the creative system

In the radio sector, Sean Ison, as an active choice-making agent working within the creative industries sub-system of radio, was intent on being part of this mainstream media form, but he found permanent entrée into it a little difficult, so he built his own radio station. His DIY punk musician background, the domain knowledge he had gained from this other field, stood him in good stead. Ison began his career 25 years ago, developing his initial cultural capital in the field of radio as a 'cart boy' working at various stations in the production side of commercial radio. In short, he was immersing himself in the domain knowledge of radio. He moved into on-air positions on community radio and from there moved to narrowcast broadcasting, in the process developing the habitus – the set of naturalised predispositions to action that are informed by a long-term way of being in the world – typical of a radio operative. He had also been immersed formally in the domain or knowledge system of radio, as he has a BA (Com. Stud.) from the University of Newcastle completed in 2004. He can demonstrate his symbolic capital by pointing to the title he now holds as the president of The Independent Australian Radio Broadcasters Association and has built a small media business that concentrates on successfully syndicating programming internationally, delivering content in narrowcast formats. He has also been developing streaming services. As an active decision-making agent within the business, he is nominally the product manager for Australian Broadcasting Media, originally Ison Live Radio (ILR). Along with Israeli investors, members of the field in Csikszentmihalyi's terms, he owns half of that company. For ILR, he oversees the music coming in from all online sources and the music going out. These songs also constitute a significant portion of the domain of radio, and the musicians who send them to him from across the globe also constitute a part of the field Ison deals with.

In terms of the products and programs his company creates, both of which are part of the field of works, Ison asserts that "every product that's created . . .

The Hunter region 209

has to be something we can either fly with advertising or something we can sell as a package to other radio stations or TV stations" (Ison May 2015). It is worthwhile noting here that when Ison refers to "we", he is indicating the partners he is working with, rather than a set of employees, as this business is not structured in the traditional way. It has no employees. In outlining ILR's operational methods, Ison claims that:

> [ILR] produces weekly radio programs for radio stations all around the world. In a range of formats our shows are heard by over a million free-to-air radio listeners each week. We also produce direct-to-radio programming from our studios 24 hours a day, 7 days a week. This is non-stop music programming in nine different formats, delivered via the Internet or via satellite straight through the mixing desks of Australian radio stations hooked up to our own ILR Media Server.
>
> (ILR 2016: online)

Ison indicates that "although web casting is a somewhat minor concern with us, we also have a substantial share in online radio in Australia with our daily webcasts reporting listeners from one end of the country to the other" (Ison May 2015). Ison has thus used the affordances the Internet provides to his own advantage. This was not always the case. He admits that, initially, "I had no real use for the Internet, no experience of it until I went back to university, and it opened up a whole world for me. And I was able to contact a lot of people and to make friends" (Ison May 2015). In developing this social capital, so important in being placed within the field, Ison admits these networks were heavily leveraged. As Ison explains,

> our products, the actual specific shows, carried word of mouth with other stations. We also were working with a lot of musicians for the music to come in from the musicians, and a lot of them actually put us on to stations, believe it or not, which was pretty good.
>
> (Ison May 2015)

Then in an able demonstration of the gift economy at work, Ison:

> set up an industry website called ausradiosearch.com and offered all kinds of free services and content as a package [subscribers] could sign up to for free. This attracted a lot of Australian and overseas traffic from radio stations (about 800 visitors a day at its peak). We then hitched onto this and offered them shows.
>
> (Ison May 2015)

It was this service, a gift to the community as it were, that demonstrated the value of reciprocity and which enabled the initial international contacts to be made. ILR was eventually delivering programs via the Internet to stations across

210   *Phillip McIntyre et al.*

Asia, Oceania, Europe and North and South America. Most of these have been concentrated in Europe and North America.

Popular music and the interplay of the local and the global

Morgan Evans' story also demonstrates a Newcastle-North American-Global connection. While the Hunter Region has produced its share of creative contributors to international popular music, including of course Silverchair and the Screaming Jets, Evans provides a more current example of the local and global interplay. He grew up in Newcastle, NSW. He undertook work experience in his final year doing his Bachelor of Communication at UON working for Foxtel as a production assistant. This led to full-time work at Foxtel, and then in 2013, after releasing two hit country EPs, Evans was named New Oz Artist of the Year at the CMC Music Awards. This was followed by four more trophies over the next two years, including Male Oz Artist of the Year a number of times. Evans then went to Nashville to record his debut album with an all-star group of A-list musicians and Nashville-based Aussie expat producer Jedd Hughes. The album, released in March 2014, quickly went to No. 1 on the iTunes and ARIA Country Album Charts and debuted at No. 20 on the ARIA Mainstream Album Chart. The album garnered three No. 1 singles and his first APRA nominations. He was invited to return to perform at Nashville's CMA Music Festival again as well as at the legendary Grand Ole Opry.

This exposure prompted William Morris Endeavor – the globe's largest talent agency – to sign Evans up for international representation. He was also signed as the face of Foxtel's Country Music Channel, which had nominated him for an ASTRA Award and a TV Week Logie Award – a first for an Australian country music star. He hosted television coverage of the CMC Rocks music festival, artist interviews and the CMC Music Awards and then was awarded the prestigious 2015 CMA Global Artist Award. Previous winners including Tommy Emmanuel, Kasey Chambers and Lee Kernaghan. Evans has since relocated to Music City (Nashville) in the USA, where country music operates to its own rhythms. As Evans indicated, "you can tour all year around here playing country music if you want to" (Morgan Evans April 2016). As a self-employed touring and recording artist Evans is also supported by a team of music professionals and is contracted to Warner Bros Records. In 2018, he had a No. 1 charting success in the USA and globally:

> Connecting with listeners stateside and across the world, the album [*Things That We Drink To*] has surpassed more than 72,000 album equivalents in America, while accumulating an impressive 110,000 album equivalents globally. The exciting release has also garnered 80 million combined streams.
>
> (Evans 2018: online)

For Evans, the skills he developed playing and writing in Newcastle, especially the live gigs he continues to play there, have been critical to his success around the world:

> I think the biggest skill that you can take from those, apart from obviously like being able to play a guitar and sing, is the ability to deal with the unknown and I think that's probably the only one that translates. . . . I see that a lot here in Nashville . . . it's so obvious, especially in the first year or two of people's career which way they came up and how they deal with live situations. You need to connect with 50,000 people instead of five, or 50 you know. . . . I'm totally comfortable in kind of situations like that because, you know, I've done it a million times at [Newcastle collaborator Mark] Wells's gigs and Wells's done it a million times with me. We've played weddings when the PA broke down and had to jump into the crowd and sing to people, you know, it's like what's the worst that can happen, it's already happened you know.
>
> (Morgan Evans April 2016)

Publishing as an interactive system

Jaye Ford, a *nom de plume* used by former Prime TV news journalist Janette Hankinson, is a quietly significant part of the publishing sector in the valley. She is an active agent in the publishing sector. This sector consists of multiple local newspapers; magazine publishing, both hard copy and online; and an increasing proliferation of blogs and zines. A lively book publishing scene is also represented by Catchfire Press and Mark MacLean and Christine Bruderlin's Hunter Press. Ford, who is a typical example of a creative industries professional who has actively moved across occupations, took her writing further afield. She is now contracted to a globally active publisher, Random House, and is promoted as a "bestselling author of five thrillers and two women's fiction novels" (Ford 2017: online).

Ford originally came from the northern beaches of Sydney and moved to Bathurst where she obtained a Communication Degree from the Mitchell College of Advanced Education – now Charles Sturt University. She started her career as a cadet journalist in radio before moving to both print and television journalism. She was "the first woman to host a live national sport show on Australian TV, fronting Sport Report on SBS. Later, she fronted Prime TV news in Newcastle" (Ford 2017: online). With years of broadcast journalism experience in the region, she left the news media and, like many creative industries professionals, transferred her skill set to a related occupation and began her own public relations consultancy. She also wrote unpublished fiction between jobs and 10 years later, after raising a family, "her first book, *Beyond Fear*, was published by Random House Australia. It was the highest selling debut crime novel in Australia in 2011, won two Davitt Awards for Australian women crime writers (Best Debut, Readers' Choice) and was shortlisted for Best Adult Crime" (ibid). Since

212   *Phillip McIntyre et al.*

then she has been writing fiction full time. Apart from her thrillers, Ford also writes women's fiction under the further *nom de plume* of Janette Paul. "Her first novel under that name, *Just Breathe*, was released in 2013 after her second thriller (*Scared Yet?*) and became a bestselling digital title" (ibid). Her next book, written as Janette Paul, is a romance entitled *Amber and Alice*. She is cognisant of the need to be an active member of the field, operating at various scales within the system, including at the global, national and local level. She is therefore, at one and the same time, part of all of these systems as each sits nested one inside the other:

> Jaye is a regular guest at libraries and author events to discuss her books and career. Jaye also hosts library events, interviewing other authors and chairing panel discussions. Other appearances have included participation in author panels and teaching workshops at writers' festivals and writers' conferences, including the Sydney Writers Festival, Byron Bay Writers Festival, Newcastle Writers Festival, the Romance Writers of Australia annual conference and Sisters in Crime events.
>
> (Ford 2017: online)

Ford has been interviewed for *Better Reading, intouch Magazine*, the *Newcastle Herald* and *Australian Women Writers*. She has been involved in the Australian Writers Centre podcasts, had stories about her discussed on pop.edit.lit, has engaged in Q&A sessions on Blog Talk Radio, is active on social media and does guest blogs for various online bloggers, as well as maintains her own author's website. Ford was also instrumental in setting up and running the ongoing writer's support network, Partners in Words, which meets regularly in the Hunter at venues such as the Prince of Wales Hotel in Merewether, where regional writers regularly host guests from the publishing industry to speak with them over dinner, linking the local to the national and hopefully from there to the global.

Fashion as a point of convergence in the creative system

Façon Australia magazine is the brainchild of Lara Lupish. It is an ambitious and high-quality luxury fashion magazine published out of Greenaway St, Wickham, an inner-city suburb of Newcastle. It features "Hunter-based models wearing the brands of local designers and established national designers, as well as global fashion juggernauts including Versace, Ferragamo, Armani, Burberry and Escada" (Green 2015: online). Lupish is the magazine's editor-in-chief and its creative director. She took extensive international experience as a stylist and applied it to magazine publishing.

Soon after graduating from the University of Newcastle, she moved overseas to Vancouver, where she says she "got thrown into the creative industries there, just by chance. That's where it started" (Lupish Oct 2016). Lupish moved on to successfully forge "an international career as a celebrity stylist, dressing some of the most beautiful and noteworthy people in the world" (Facon 2017a: online).

The Hunter region 213

When she finished her degree she, as many Hunter residents have, decided to go travelling the world:

> I stumbled into styling, [in Vancouver] starting with a photoshoot with one of the top rock photographers in the country. Then I moved on to London (as most Aussies do), expanding my styling resume there & making a conscious decision that this was what I wanted to do. . . . Having first worked as a wardrobe stylist in the film industry, styling music videos & TV commercials, I then progressed to feature film costume design [working] with cast members such as Naomi Watts, Sir Ian McKellen, Laura Dern & Mark Ruffalo. It was great to work with such high calibre actors so early in my career. My TVC work in North America was moulded by prominent & notorious Director Marcus Nispel. Working with US ad agencies was also an amazing experience and had an exponential learning curve attached to it. Returning to Australia I saw my career as a stylist move towards fashion & celebrity styling. I further added the title of 'style director' to my CV, working closely with and directing shows for various Australian designers. Currently my focus is on celebrity styling, advertising and editorial. The time I worked overseas was indispensable in building my skills.
>
> (Lupish 2011: online)

As an in-demand celebrity stylist she moved back to Sydney in 2009 and eventually returned to Newcastle in 2013, as many creative industries professionals have, but remained connected to her clients in Sydney:

> At first I didn't know where I would land so I wanted to keep my relationships with those brands in Sydney, bring them here – although I did keep it quiet that I had moved to Newcastle for probably a whole year. I rented a studio in Sydney because I was still involved in the Sydney market as far as styling went and I needed that as back-up. When I did those runways, I invited the Newcastle City Council people and the Museum people and the Art Gallery people, footballers' wives and the socialites of the city because I thought I'd do personal styling or I might dress them for events. I think I still wanted to be at that point what I was in Sydney to an extent. But the cards just laid down differently to what I thought and it pushed me in a different direction and what I got out of that was all the brands that I'd built a really strong relationship with in Sydney were still quite prepared to work with me and when Giorgio Armani would call me – not him personally but the brand – and say 'Look Lara, the new collection is here, do you want to shoot something?' And they would courier it to my door in Wickham I was quite astonished and that's how *Façon* started, actually. We started an Instagram page, we started shooting material for the Instagram page and I guess from there we spruiked the magazine because I thought that we should turn it into a hard copy.
>
> (Lupish Oct 2016)

214 *Phillip McIntyre et al.*

The genesis for *Façon* and the 2016 New Fashion Festival Newcastle came after Lupish and three other businesses – Matt Briggs Photography, Models & Actors Talent Management and Chic Artistry – moved into a refurbished factory space in Wickham in May. Lupish and Briggs were helping Models & Actors Talent Management style and photograph model cards for the agency's clients to take to auditions and castings when she saw more potential. *Façon* has now been on sale "in all major capitals and regional hubs; New Zealand; Singapore; Hong Kong, UAE, Thailand, Taiwan and Indonesia" (Facon 2019: online), but all issues are available online. Hunter fashion designers, such as Jean Bas, High Tea with Mrs Woo and Abicus, have been highlighted in the magazine alongside national and global brands. The magazine also features local models with shoots staged by local photographers. Lupish's task was made easier through an economic development grant from Newcastle City Council:

> Editor-in-chief Lara Lupish unveiled Façon Book Two, the Influencers Issue, in September 2016 to a well-dressed crowd of more than 100 people at Custom Eyecare on Darby Street in Newcastle. With all the elements needed to kick-start a party, the night was a huge success and the perfect way to reveal the cover and to release the book ahead of its national roll out the following day. In attendance included the Lord Mayor of Newcastle, Nuatali Nelmes, *Façon* cover girl – Gemma Sanderson, NXFM radio presenter Sophie Tiller, NBN news anchor, Natasha Beyersdorf, high profile business owners, creatives and supporters/friends of *Façon*. Music was provided by indie rock band, Dave the band, canapés by Sprout and wine by Yellowglen Peacock Lane.
>
> (Façon 2017b, online)

The magazine emerged from the popularity of the company's posts on Instagram and was then produced as a hard copy. "The reason I made the first one so glossy and drippy was I wanted it to sit on the stands next to Vogue which it did" (Lupish Oct 2016). It is also distributed in Hong Kong, Dubai, Malaysia and Singapore. "I'm very lucky that I've got a really good distributor. He was the Circulation Manager for ACP for 30 years and he just happened to take my call. I'm sure he rues the day! He's connected, and he knows" (ibid). Lupish also recognises that while Sydney has status, Newcastle is more liveable:

> There are a lot of Sydneysiders I work with who are struggling with the cost of Sydney and what it is to live there. I like to boast now that I have a nice home in Newcastle and we go to the beach after school and it's affordable, all that kind of stuff. Now I'm proud of it.
>
> (Lupish Oct 2016)

However, her skills and experience demand a certain standard. "I'm trying to train people to be what I used to be but I oversee the whole thing and make sure it is hopefully of an international standard – that's what we are trying to achieve"

The Hunter region 215

(Lupish Oct 2016). Lupish's intention is to demonstrate excellence. She wants to create an image and have "people feel like they could be in Sydney or London or New York or wherever" (ibid). She more seriously hopes that "it's not just about the look of the place but also the way we work, the way we behave and the image we project to the industry as well" (ibid). Bringing these international standards, experiences and skills back to the region they hailed from has paid dividends for creative industries professional like Lupish. Others have found the region after similar international experiences. David Fitzgerald is one.

Musical theatre: glocally oriented agents and the gift economy

David Fitzgerald moves continually between local productions and global touring commitments. He is a CONDA (City of Newcastle Drama Awards) winner for his work in musical theatre in Newcastle and lives with his family near Lake Macquarie. A Musical Director and Head of Audio, he works nationally and internationally, where he recruits musicians for the international shows he directs as well as supplying tech specs for the audio parameters of those shows. "I switch between both, being an MD onstage or an MD at the audio, front of house audio position" (Fitzgerald April 2017). He was trained as a classical concert pianist but also studied business through an MBA and now operates under his own trading name of Full Fat Jazz. This is an extension of his theatre work, as he has "some production values in terms of funding, organising, managing, directing, producing, and that again comes under that Full Fat trading name" (ibid). He now "regularly mixes 12 shows a year but I push boundaries and I'm seen a little bit as a renegade but by the same token I'm also seen as a mentor for a lot of the younger engineers" (ibid). He also recognises how all the parts of a theatre production need to be synched and that constant international touring experience has been fed back into his work with the Metropolitan Players.

One of the most ambitious companies in the region, Metropolitan Players, is a musical theatre company that has been operating for 40 years. Julie Black is Artistic Director of the company while Graeme Black is often Set Designer and Stage Manager for productions as well as being President of the player's committee. The company:

> first formed in 1977 and has been producing quality musicals ever since. We produce one major musical each year, although in the past there were sometimes two each year. . . . For many years we have used the 924-seat Griffith Duncan Theatre at Newcastle University. Our most recent productions have been at Newcastle's premier theatre, the 1400-seat Civic Theatre. The Company is run by a Committee that is elected each year at the Annual General Meeting in February. We used to rehearse at Broadmeadow Uniting Church Hall in Broadmeadow, but after 33 years have now moved to Glendale High School. Set construction is at our warehouse in Cardiff. Over the years our productions have received many

216 *Phillip McIntyre et al.*

City of Newcastle Drama Awards (the CONDAs). The most successful was *The Producers* in 2008 which won six Awards. However, this has now been beaten by our 2014 production of *The Phantom of the Opera* which won seven Awards. After *Wicked* in 2016, the Company has now won the CONDA Best Musical production five years in a row. We make all our own costumes for each show and many of these are for hire.

(MP 2018: online)

Metropolitan Players currently receive neither government nor corporate support. They have had some in-kind support from Newcastle City Council in the past but were unsuccessful in 2016 in their application for event funding, which offered up to $20,000. With budgets of approximately $400,000 per show, Graeme Black suggests:

It's a huge financial risk. It could be the last show every time. . . . Last year's production took nearly $500,000 at the box office but the costs are significant. Performing rights cost 16–18% of gross which was $80,000 last year, theatre hire was $140,000, $80,000 was spent on sound and lighting hire, and $8,000 on billboards.

(G. Black May 2017)

Metropolitan Players represents a working hybrid of professionalism and amateurism in that the quality of work, the budgets and the operational methods are of the highest industry standards, yet nearly everybody involved works on a voluntary basis. Graeme Black explains that this allows them to work to a scale and level that would otherwise be impossible. As Julie Black asserts, they all "do it for the love of it" (J. Black May 2017). Those who compete for roles with Metropolitan Players shows appear to be happy to work for nothing, attracted by the opportunity to be part of a successful, high-quality show where they can develop their experience, skills and profile in a positive atmosphere. Daniel Stoddart, who has performed in several Metropolitan Players shows, says that to ask for pay would be "pricing yourself out of the market" (Stoddart Oct 2015). He asks, "Why would Metropolitan Players pay you if there are ten other people lined up who are happy to do it for nothing?" (ibid). Indeed, roles with Metropolitan Players shows are hotly contested: in 2016, 207 people auditioned for 50 roles, only nine of which were leads. While Metropolitan Players shows do not pay performers, the economic value the shows generate is significant. For example, the production of *Mary Poppins* included a production crew alone of 100 plus a full cast of 56 actors, accompanied by a 17-piece orchestra:

Each of those people was going into town for up to two weeks. They were all putting money in the parking meters, they were all going into the little shop next door buying iceblocks. How much money did they spend on petrol to get their car into town? How much money was spent on buying stockings for that production from Lowes up the road, and costumes, fabric, wood from Bunnings to make sets and things? If there was some way of quantifying that in a really tangible, practical way and saying the arts contribute X amount of revenue to the local economy . . . comparing that to a packed-out Newcastle Knights stadium, I think we would probably give them a red hot run for their money.

(Stoddart Oct 2015)

Innovative television: taking advantage of shifts in a dynamic system

Sport has been the niche that Bar TV has occupied since they began by filming grassroots sports in a very cost-effective way and distributing it through a closed-circuit network of pubs and hotels. Bar TV began operations in Newcastle and initially offered a service to the Rugby League, which was to film their games for the local club, for the judiciary and for a subscription service that was available in local hotels:

> The luxury of us starting in Newcastle allowed us to really debug ourselves. We were hidden away, and it allowed us to, kind of, be a new business in a new market . . . by the time we did go to Sydney, we already had an established brand, we already had an established workflow, and we had a successful model. And then that allowed us to sit down with some of these bigger networks, bigger sporting associations, and then say to them – actually give them some real advice to say 'stop chasing this top tier coverage, because you're not going to get it . . . there's too many hoops to jump through and the profit margins aren't there', and things like that. So, for us, grassroots sport is where we're going to be based, really.

(McCormick Aug 2015)

In 2003, Brendan McCormick, working with Josh Mason, had created an SMS-based trivia game called Pubtriv, which has since been upgraded to a smartphone app. Bar TV grew from this idea. With McCormick and Mason using social media platforms like YouTube and Facebook, Bar TV Sports has now been able to stream sporting games from over 900 sporting fixtures across Australia, the UK and Europe. As a distributor of sporting content, Bar TV offers a variety of stakeholders, including supporters, sponsors and advertisers, a cost-effective way for sporting fans to view local competitions. As a content creator, Bar TV Sports offers pathways for production staff, commentators and camera operators to enter the sporting media market:

> We're at that new media side, so we can adapt quicker than the TV networks. And because of that, we can keep things under budget, you know, $60,000 to film at Fox for one game of football, and we can do the equivalent for, let's say, $5000. And it's mainly because of technology.

(McCormick Aug 2015)

218 *Phillip McIntyre et al.*

In 2017, the *Newcastle Herald* reported that "BarTV have attracted more than 1.04 million views for the first quarter of 2017 and are expected to reach four to five million by the end of the year" (Leeson 2017: online). In 2015, a typical weekend's sports coverage includes the logistical co-ordination of 40–45 staff, including commentators and producers, travelling to cover local sporting games:

> So, this weekend we had three sets of game days in the Illawarra and up to Wollongong. We had one game on the Gold Coast and two games in Sydney, so we covered all sports from Rugby Union, Rugby League, AFL, Soccer, to the point where we had our biggest viewership online which was the women's football Grand Final held on Sunday at Match Park here in Newcastle, and they had over 1200 viewers live. So that was quite good. And you might have one computer with a single IP address, but there might be three or four people watching on their smart TV or whatever device they use.
>
> (McCormick Aug 2015)

McCormick was contacted again in 2016 to provide an update on Bar TV sports activities:

> We have been commissioned to film and broadcast the Women's Domestic Twenty20 cricket tournament (Women's Big Bash League), which is a national competition, as well as filming and broadcasting all the Australian Women's cricket internationals versus South Africa. We are now Cricket Australia's exclusive Live Streaming provider (we film all the non-free-to-air matches including the Sheffield Shield Final).
>
> (McCormick Oct 2016)

Foxtel also made an offer to Bar TV Sports, who eventually became a subcontractor to them to cover the national Rugby Union and soccer as well as cricket. At the same time, they were managing a contract with FFA Cup soccer. These contracts have allowed Bar TV to alter their operating models. "It's allowed us to establish camera operators in the various capital cities, and we just literally send over producers" (Mason Aug 2015) using local crews on the ground in those cities.

In 2015, Bar TV was able to monitor IP addresses and could discern who was watching what content and for how long. This kind of extremely detailed data has been very valuable in monetising a very niche market. Bar TV continues to grow their brand throughout the UK and Europe. Indeed, they have found a gap in the market where there is an audience for mid-tier sport. As well as producing content, McCormick states, "being low level, we're really a marketing company, we're a promotions company, we're a live streaming company, you know, we wear many hats" (McCormick Aug 2015).

Conclusions

One factor that needs to be noted from the above is that the tangible structures of production that typify traditional industries, that is, "firms, labour, production network, industrial districts, and markets – that is the normal stock in trade of industrial investigation" (Hutton 2009: 139) are mutating. There are "shifting boundaries of function, evolving technical divisions of labour, and emergent product sectors" (ibid). However, the initial statistical analysis we used tended to replicate the industrial categories it was set up with. In ethnographically observing these increasing shifts from creative industries to creative systems, we also claim that current entrepreneurial approaches in the region are adapting innovatively to the pressures of globalisation and digitisation, but most are primarily employing extensions of more traditional business models. Furthermore, in an effort to maintain their productive output, companies and individuals working within the creative systems in the region have become increasingly diversified in generating income streams. With a rapidly growing trend toward outsourcing, freelancing and the casualisation of the workforce, many operatives have been forced to work cross-sectorally in order to gain an income: that is, for many of them, there is a need to undertake multiple tasks in order to gain one income. As a consequence, there is a great deal of mobility between professions, with a core set of skills needing to be maintained as they straddle different but related domains of knowledge, moving from sub-field to sub-field within this highly scaled creative system. As can also be seen from above, most operatives in the creative industries are also specialised vertically as well as multi-skilled horizontally. Additionally, many operatives are 'glocally' oriented: that is, many of them are locally rooted but globally active. Furthermore, many sectors, whether they are mature or emergent, have come to rely on amateurs and pro-amateurs to support their industrial structures.

It is readily apparent, from our broader study and the evidence above, that the gift economy is enormous in comparison to what the industrially oriented statistical analyses have revealed. In this case, we can conclude by claiming that the Hunter Region houses a set of complex and dynamic interactions where creative agents are both constrained and enabled by the arena of social contestation they work in, and they are equally dependent on an immersion in the necessary domains of knowledge that allow them to take part in those fields. It is the existence of these structures that affords their innovative activity. As we have seen, this regional creative system in the Hunter is itself part of a broader set of national and global systems. It is also composed of multiple local systems and sectors. The complexity of this scaled system survives and flourishes as it strives toward a dynamic equilibrium of inflows and outflows which are – at one and the same time – local, national and global. As such, the system is in constant flux. It is dependent on an active relationship being in place between choice-making agents, domains of knowledge and an arena of social contestation called a field – this is how the creative system in the Hunter works.

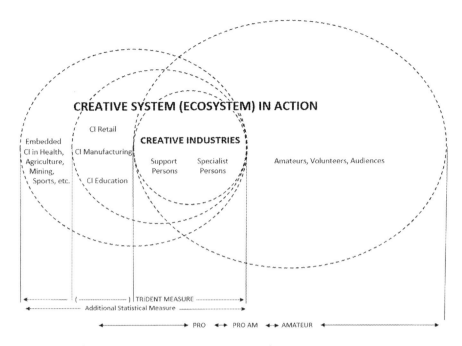

Figure 10.1 The creative system, or ecosystem, at work.

Source: Initially published in *Creativity and Cultural Production in the Hunter* final report

References

Andersen, J. 2011. "What Are Innovation Ecosystems and How to Build and Use Them." *Innovation Management*. Retrieved October 24, 2017 (www.innovationmanagement. se/2011/05/16/what-are-innovation-ecosystems-and-how-to-build-and-use-them/).
Bourdieu, P. 1977. *Outline of a Theory of Practice*. Cambridge: Cambridge University Press.
Bourdieu, P. 1990. *The Logic of Practice*. Cambridge: Polity Press.
Bourdieu, P. 1993. *Field of Cultural Production*, edited by Johnson, R. New York: Columbia University Press.
Bourdieu, P. 1996. *The Rules of Art: Genesis and Structure of the Literary Field*. Cambridge: Polity Press.
Braudel, F. 1990. *The Identity of France: Volume One: History and Environment*. San Francisco: Harper & Row.
CIIC. 2013. *Valuing Australia's Creative Industries: Final Report*. Pp. 1–95. Sydney: SGS Economics and Planning for the Creative Industries Innovation Centre.
Csikszentmihalyi, M. 1988. "Society, Culture and Person: A Systems View of Creativity." Pp. 325–329 in *The Nature of Creativity: Contemporary Psychological Perspectives*, edited by Sternberg, R. New York: Cambridge University Press.
Csikszentmihalyi, M. 1997. *Creativity: Flow and the Psychology of Discovery and Invention*. New York: Harper Collins.

Csikszentmihalyi, M. 1999. "Implications of a Systems Perspective for the Study of Creativity." Pp. 313–335 in *Handbook of Creativity*, edited by Sternberg, R. Cambridge: Cambridge University Press.

Csikszentmihalyi, M. 2014. *The Systems Model of Creativity: The Collected Works of Mihaly Csikszentmihalyi* (Vol III). Dordrecht: Springer.

Davies, R., and Sigthorsson, G. 2013. *Introducing the Creative Industries: From Theory to Practice*. London: Sage.

Evans, M. 2018. "Things That We Drink To: Morgan Evans' Debut Album Makes Global Impact." *News & Updates: Morgan Evans Music*. Retrieved December 1, 2018 (www.morganevansmusic.com/news/things-we-drink-morgan-evans-debut-album-makes-global-impact-23701).

Façon. 2017a. "Five Minutes with Lara Lupish." *Façon, Australia*. Retrieved August 12, 2017 (www.faconaustralia.com/5minuteswith-lara-lupish/).

Façon. 2017b. "The Release of Facon Book Two." *Façon, Australia*. Retrieved August 12, 2017 (www.faconaustralia.com/the-release-of-book-two/).

Facon. 2019. "Façon Magazine." *Façon, Australia*. Retrieved October 11, 2019 (https://www.faconaustralia.com/facon-magazine/).

Flew, T. 2012. *The Creative Industries: Culture and Policy*. Los Angeles: Sage.

Ford, J. 2017. "Bio." *Jaye Ford*. Retrieved August 6, 2017 (www.jayefordauthor.com/about-bio/).

Frenkel, A., and Maital, S. 2014. *Mapping National Innovation Ecosystems: Foundations for Policy Consensus*. Cheltenham, UK: Edward Elgar.

Goldstein, J. 1999. "Emergence as a Construct: History and Issues." *Emergence* 1(1): 49–72.

Green, P. 2015. "Pressing Style on the Runway." *The Newcastle Herald*. October 19, 2015. Retrieved August 12, 2017 (www.theherald.com.au/story/3433153/pressing-style-on-the-runway/).

Higgs, P., and Lennon. 2014. *Applying the NESTA Dynamic Mapping Definition Methodology to Australian Classification*. Brisbane Queensland: Queensland University of Technology Brisbane.

Hutton, T. 2009. "Cultural Production in the Transnational City." Pp. 139–160 in *Creativity, Innovation and the Cultural Economy*, edited by Pratt, A., and Jeffcutt, P. London: Routledge.

ILR. 2016. "Home." *Ison Live Radio*. Retrieved July 19, 2016 (http://www.isonliveradio.com/index.html).

Kerrigan, S. 2013. "Accommodating Creative Documentary Practice Within a Revised Systems Model of Creativity." *Journal of Media Practice* 14(2): 111–127.

Kerrigan, S., and Hutchinson, S. 2016. "Regional Creative Industries: Transforming the Steel City into a Creative City in Newcastle, Australia." *Creative Industries Journal* 9(2): 116–129.

Knox, P., and Marston, S. 2014. "Geography Matters." Pp. 9–41 in *Human Geography: Places and Regions in Global Context* (6th ed.), edited by Knox, P., and Marston, S. Harlow, Essex: Pearson.

Leeson, J. 2017. "Newcastle's BarTV Has Taken Local Sports to the World." *The Newcastle Herald*. March 31, 2017. Retrieved February 28, 2018 (www.theherald.com.au/story/4605537/sporting-field-of-streams/).

Lupish, L. 2011. "Bio." *Lara Lupish*. Retrieved August 12 2017 (http://laralupish.com/bio.html).

McIntyre, P. 2009. "Rethinking Communication, Creativity and Cultural Production: Outlining Issues for Media Practice." In *Communication, Creativity and Global Citizenship: Refereed Proceedings of the Australian and New Zealand Communications Association Annual Conference July 8–10*, edited by Flew, T. Brisbane: QUT. Retrieved April 4, 2012 (www.proceedings.anzca09.org).

McIntyre, P. 2011. "Bringing Novelty into Being: Exploring the Relationship Between 'Creativity' and 'Innovation.'" In *ANZCA 2011 – Communication on the Edge: Shifting Boundaries and Identities, 6–8 July*. Hamilton, New Zealand: The University of Waikato. Retrieved April 26, 2015 (www.anzca.net/conferences/anzca11-proceedings.html).

McIntyre, P. 2012. "Constraining and enabling creativity: The Theoretical Ideas Surrounding Creativity, Agency and Structure." *The International Journal of Creativity and Problem Solving* 22(1): 43–60.

McIntyre, P. 2013. "Creativity as a System at Work." Pp. 84–97 in *Handbook of Creativity Research*, edited by Chan. J., and Thomas, K. London: Edward Elgar.

McIntyre, P. 2015. "Creative Industries and Identity: From Older Conceptions to New Models of Creativity." Pp. 1–13 in *2015 ANZCA Conference, Rethinking Communication, Space and Identity, 8–10 July*. Queenstown NZ: University of Canterbury/University of Otago.

McIntyre, P. 2017. "What Is the Fifth Estate and Why Does It Matter? Digitisation, Globalization, and Neoliberalism and Their Part in the Creation of a Rapidly Changing World." *Communication Research and Practice* 2(4): 437–450.

McIntyre, P., Balnaves, M., Kerrigan, S., King, E., and Williams, C. 2019. "Creativity and Cultural Production in the Hunter: An Applied Ethnographic Study of New Entrepreneurial Systems in the Creative Industries." Report for ARC, University of Newcastle, Technica CPT, NBIA. Retrieved May 26, 2015 (https://soci.newcastle.edu.au/hci/final-report/).

McIntyre, P., Fulton, J., and Paton, E. (eds.). 2016. *The Creative System in Action: Understanding Cultural Production and Practice*. Basingstoke, UK: Palgrave Macmillan.

McManus, P., O'Neill, P., and Loughran, R. (eds.) [cartography by Lescure, O. R.]. 2000. *Journeys: The Making of the Hunter Region*. St Leonards, N. S. W: Allen & Unwin.

MP. 2018. "About Us – Metropolitan Players." *Metropolitan Players*. Retrieved September 15, 2018 (https://metropolitanplayers.com.au/about/).

NCC. 2016. "Economic Development Strategy 2016–2019." *Newcastle City Council*. Retrieved February 18, 2018 (www.newcastle.nsw.gov.au).

NSWSRD. 2009. *NSW Creative Industry Economic Fundamentals*. Report to the Department of State and Regional Development, February 2009.

Remplan. 2017. "City of Newcastle Economy Profile." *Remplan*. Retrieved February 16, 2018 (www.economyprofile.com.au/newcastle/industries/gross-regional-product).

Schulz, T. 2015. "Tomorrowland: How Silicon Valley Shapes Our Future." *Spiegel Online: International*. March 4, 2015–6.57pm. Retrieved April 21, 2015 (www.spiegel.de/international/germany/spiegel-cover-story-how-silicon-valley-shapes-our-future-a-1021557.html).

Tuan, Y. 1997. *Space and Place: The Perspective of Experience*. Minneapolis: University of Minnesota Press.

Westbury, M. 2015. *Creating Cities*. Melbourne: Niche Press.

Wilkinson, J. 2017. "The Hunter Region: An Economic Profile." *Parliament of NSW*. Retrieved July 10, 2017 (www.parliament.nsw.gov.au/researchpapers/Documents/the-hunter-region-an-economic-profile/Newcastle%20and%20the%20Hunter%20GG%202.pdf).

11 "Anything that's not in London"

Regions, mobility and spatial politics in contemporary visual art

Emma Coffield

Introduction

Discourses of modernist art history and contemporary creative practice tend to focus on the city. The modernist history of art, for example, relies on a linear narrative, or a "succession of artistic centres" (Joyeux-Prunel 2015: 41), which each come to dominate a particular period of time: Paris in the nineteenth century, New York in the twentieth and so forth. In such histories of art, each new cultural centre usurps the last to become the prime location for the production of contemporary art until it is usurped in turn by another. More recently, it has become possible to speak of a global network of such centres, all operating simultaneously and competing to establish the latest and greatest biennial, arts festival or grand museum project – biennials in particular being, as Paul O'Neill (2007: 17) puts it, "the global exhibition model [. . .] [and] the vehicle through which much art is validated and acquires value on the international circuit". In fact, so rapidly has what Charles Esche (2005) terms the "centre-first" model of global art expanded, that, he argues, those working on the "periphery" of a once tightly sanctioned art-world no longer need the permission of key institutions, but, through "the creation of significant biennials in places such as Kwangju, Havana, Tirana, Johannesburg (briefly) and Sharjah" can both "talk back – and, more significantly, talk amongst themselves". However, even in this rapidly expanding art world, with all its talk of centres and peripheries, it is still the city that holds sway. As Esche later put it, "almost without exception, these new events were and are defined in terms of the political and social mix of *the cities* that host them" (2011: 11 my emphasis). Indeed, it is telling that even the so-called "marginal" biennials are held in locations otherwise considered to be major, capital cities.

Further, bodies of work that focus on artists and the city are produced in, or at the intersection of, urban studies. For example, and perhaps most famously, notions of the "creative city" and the "creative class" (as per Landry and Bianchini 1995; Florida 2002 respectively) rely upon artists' attraction to, and their efforts within and upon, largely post-industrial or 'second-tier' cities. Then there is work that considers public art's relationship to "urban futures" (e.g. Miles 1997), artists as connected to urban regeneration and gentrification

224 *Emma Coffield*

(e.g. Miranda and Lane-McKinley 2017; Lees and Melhuish 2012; Ley 2003), as well as policy-led agendas that use the arts as a means by which to drive investment (e.g. Cameron and Coafee 2005) or where artists are positioned as "creative placemakers" (e.g. Courage and McKeown 2019). In fact, as Kate Oakley et al. (2017: 1510) put it, so frequently are artists depicted to as being "drawn" to the city that it can seem that there is "no choice for the ambitious or even the curious, but to go to the big city and try and make it".

There are, of course, exceptions. In art history, discussions concerning the representation of place in, and through, artwork are, geographically speaking, extremely wide ranging, as are studies of public, site-specific or site-orientated art (e.g. Kwon 2002). "Geohistories" (e.g. Kaufmann and Pilliod 2005) or "geobiographies" of artworks, artists and their varying schools and styles (Hawkins 2014: 3) tend to likewise cast a wider net, while pre-modernist histories of art are often arranged by the country of origin rather than the city (e.g. Gombrich's (1950) arrangement of *The Story of Art* into chapters dedicated to Holland in the seventeenth century, Italy in the later seventeenth and eighteenth century and so on). By and large however, the contemporary counterbalance to the city is largely held to be the rural, where the focus is on the interplay between art, the natural environment and a given community (as per Crawshaw and Gkartzios 2018), or the local, as in Lucy Lippard's (1997) landmark text, *The Lure of the Local*. Here, Lippard argues for lived experience, a connection to place and situated creative practices, although she notes that part of the allure of the local at the end of the twentieth century lay in "its absence or rather [. . .] the absence of value attached to specific place in contemporary cultural life, in the 'art world' and in postmodern paradoxes and paradigms" (ibid: 5). Having undergone something of a positive reclamation, "the local" no longer fails to signify in contemporary art practice to quite this extent today, offering instead a decidedly different way of working to that of the globe-trotting artist or curator.

The choice, however, is largely offered as a binary one, where the local is suggested to be "in constant dialogue" with the global (O'Neill 2007: 16), and the centre with the periphery – as though nothing lay between. For example, O'Neill (2007: 16–19) talks of biennials as "interfaces" between art and publics, where the exhibition model and market, artistic practices, "jet-set" curator(s), tourism generated and understanding of "culture" at play are global; the location, cultural context and supporting networks, local. This is the local as packaged largely for the benefit of global tourists, although O'Neill notes that the "larger publics" in question "are at once local and global" (ibid: 16). Elsewhere, there is similarly detailed discussion concerning the exact nature and extent of the terms "global" and "local" with occasional reference made to the "national" and "international" – albeit usually with the aim of arguing for the rise of the global art world as a separate category (e.g. Belting, Buddensieg and Weibel 2013; Charlesworth 2013; Steeds et al. 2013; Weiss et al. 2011; Elkins 2007). The "region" or the "regional," in contrast, are noticeable only by their absence.

"Anything that's not in London" 225

This is important, for local–global and centre–periphery dynamics act here as powerful framing devices. And, like all framing devices, they also occlude and obscure from view, with potentially significant consequences. In art history, for example, postcolonial scholars have long taken issue with the modernist centre–periphery narrative for constructing a "spatiotemporal idea of artistic progress" tied to Western understandings of, and control over, certain "centres", and the consequent dismissal of almost everything made anywhere else as "imitation, borrowing or influence" (Joyeux-Prunel 2015: 41). Attempts to decolonise the museum and resist such narratives, as L'Internationale (2015) do, are thus vital in the telling of other, and multiple, possibilities. There is also work that reassesses now familiar art centres and networks, as per Jo Applin, Spencer and Tobin's (2018: 3) work on London, which argues for "multiple and overlapping spheres, rather than a coherent system", or the "Glasgow Miracle: Materials for Alterative Histories" project (McKee 2012).

Similarly, work in cultural studies, urban studies, geography, and sociology has begun to complicate local–global and centre–periphery binaries. Here we find understandings of everyday creativity not as limited to any one "creative" location (e.g. Miles and Gibson 2017), as well as what Harriet Hawkins (2014: 1–3) describes as "creative geographies", or "spaces of co-operation between geography and art", where "geographers, art theorists, historians and practitioners are coming together in a range of practice-based ways" that work well beyond the confines of the city. Then there is work that explores and maps the geographies of the creative and cultural industries (e.g. Mateos-Garcia and Bakhshi 2016), including Ann Markusen's (2013: 482) analysis of the spatial distribution of artists in the US, which reported "artists actively moving among cities of all sizes as well as evidence of robust home growing". Such accounts still tend to focus on cities – of varying sizes – but they also include instances of "reverse migration" (*ibid*: 489) or what is known in the UK as the "boomerang effect", where artists and creative entrepreneurs return from the big city to their home region, seeking "the support of family, the availability of affordable housing and the ability to maintain a good standard of living" (Butt et al. 2017: 12). Indeed, Susan Luckman's (2012: 1) work has begun to address "rural, regional and remotely located creative practitioners", while Chris Gibson, Luckman and Willoughby-Smith (2010: 25) have argued that notions of "remoteness" and "proximity" can be understood both as geographical conditions and as metaphors "through which people understood themselves and their relationship with others". This last point is particularly important in the visual arts, where groups and individuals can self-identify as "peripheral" so as to place a critical distance between their practice and that perceived as more "mainstream", regardless of their geographic location.

It is further important to highlight that while understandings of the region may not be in vogue in discourses of visual art, artists and creative practitioners have nevertheless long actively contributed to, or resisted, the imagining of regions. There are bodies of artistic work made about, through or which bring into being regions; "Constable Country" in England is named after the work

226 *Emma Coffield*

of the Romantic painter John Constable, for instance. There are more complex claims too. Penny Fielding's (2014: 162) notion of the "curated region" – proposed in relation to both the literature of the "Scottish Border" in the late eighteenth and early nineteenth century and the 1998 Artstranspennine exhibition in the UK – explores how "the various claims of economy, geography, transport and the institutions of art and literature compete or collaborate to define a region". A key point here is understanding not only how "these acts of imagination take place" (ibid) but also who has the "right to define the region in terms of artistic value" (ibid: 159). Recent large-scale, one-off exhibitions attempting to use the arts to re-brand and re-define regions take this one step further. The Great Exhibition of the North, for example, was a £5 million government-funded event specifically devised to celebrate the North of England, attract investment and "rebuild a sense of pride and identity for those living in the North" (Great Exhibition of the North 2017). The idea that "the North" needed this kind of help, and help largely imposed from London, quickly drew claims of tokenism after years of austerity and cuts to local budgets, however (The Other Great Exhibition of the North 2018), proving that despite the involvement of numerous "Northern" artists and arts organisations, regional identities are not so easily performed. There are more permanent acts of display too, where understandings of the region are arranged and "housed" in archives, museums and galleries (as per "Northern Spirit: 300 Years of Art from the North East" at the Laing Art Gallery, Newcastle, UK).

Through all of the above, a far more expansive geography of art-making and display begins to emerge than that suggested by the local-global, and one that pays critical attention to all the many and varied "in-between" sites that hitherto have been deemed neither local nor global enough. This shift in focus is welcome, but it is also increasingly urgent, for understandings of place *matter* to creative practitioners, regardless of where they might be located. To give one brief example: all places, whether they be rural spots, world-renowned art centres or something else again, amass cultural and symbolic capital unequally. This capital in turn organises and positions artists so that being able to "place" oneself as a creative practitioner based in a "creative" city (e.g. London, Berlin, New York, Istanbul etc.) carries a far higher weight than an artist based in a small town in the North East of England – unless that artist's work relies upon a sense of their very localness. Or, as Francis McKee (2012) put it in relation to artists working across Scotland in the 1950s and 1960s:

> the consensus was that to be successful [. . .] it was necessary to move to a recognised centre, mainly London. If an artist chose to remain in Scotland then that choice came with an acknowledgement that it would be much more difficult to capture the world's attention.

Place, in this sense, helps to render a creative practice possible, and legible.

Yet while a global art world posits an infinitely mobile subject who can attend major art festivals around the world or relocate their practice with ease,

"*Anything that's not in London*" 227

not all creative practitioners are so fortunate. As Kim Allen and Sumi Hollingworth (2013: 500–502) point out, mobility is not "simply about the physical act of moving between places"; rather, it is a "social resource that is unequally distributed". Even more worryingly, as Allen and Hollingworth (ibid: 500, drawing on Skeggs 2004) continue, so infused with mobility is the figure of the artist that "immobility and attachment to place [. . .] [have] acquired connotations of defeat, fixity and failure" in the cultural and creative industries. Mobility and the spatial distribution of capital and other resources here become a matter of spatial justice; of who can become what, where and how, and who cannot.

It is with exactly these concerns in mind that this chapter proposes to explore understandings of "the region" – mutable as they are – in order to give purchase on mobile, complex and nuanced forms of creative practice that are not limited to the rural or the metropolitan, the countryside or the "creative" city. This is in part an effort to look beyond the traditional roster of cities involved in the "winning of mega events" (Sharp, Pollock and Paddison 2005: 1003) and to instead bring into view the cities, towns, conurbations and suburbs that are not thought of, or packaged, as especially "creative" in the understanding that artists and creative practitioners may yet live and work there. It is to consider what a creative practice might look like when situated "elsewhere", and how such places and their associated values are negotiated, arrived at and negotiated anew. For, as Markusen (2013: 481) puts it, "artists work everywhere".

Unlike the approaches to the region outlined above, however, this chapter considers how the region is brought into being as part of the seemingly mundane and everyday life-worlds of creative practitioners, and creative practitioners who did not set out to make work about place. It thus adopts a micro-focus and draws upon empirical data collected from a single artist-run initiative: Empty Shop in Durham, England. This focus on the ordinary – on artistic practices as they unfold day to day – it is argued, is vital to any fuller consideration of what and how the region means, for it allows for critical purchase on the textures and complexities that bring specific places into being as part of a life lived and not as bounded by the (time-specific) production of mega events or schemes or as limited to only those artists who make place the focus of their work. Following Gibson, Luckman and Willoughby-Smith (2010) and Nuala Morse, Rex and Harvey Richardson (2018), it is to focus not just on what might be considered "exceptional" moments in an artistic career, but on routine work of all kinds (i.e. administrative as well as creative), and the ways such routine practices nevertheless shape "the presentation of knowledge [and the] structuring [of] relationships" (ibid: 113). Finally, it is an appeal for nuanced, lived accounts in all their complexity, as a counter to the generic appeal of the creative city or centre-periphery binaries.

Understanding "the region" in arts discourse in the UK

Before turning to the discussion of empirical data, however, it is first necessary to very briefly set out a context for "the region" as it applies in the UK,

228 *Emma Coffield*

for there are a number of quirks that require explanation in an international volume. For example, the UK is habitually divided via the Nomenclature of Territorial Units for Statistics into twelve: the nine regions of England (Greater London, East Midlands, East of England, North East, North West, South East, South West, West Midlands, Yorkshire and Humber) plus Scotland, Wales and Northern Ireland (although Scotland claims eight further subdivisions as regions, Wales five and Northern Ireland six. These regions are an example of what Fielding (2014: 161) terms the "regulated region" – areas with defined, if not historically stable, boundaries; a larger whole subdivided for the purposes of administration. Indeed, the regulated region, as Fielding (ibid: 160) observes, tends to be "expressed in statistical form" – as per the abundance of arts policy documents that concern regional boundaries and their related statistics (i.e. the amounts of funding allocated, audience visits per area etc.).

However, an arguably more commonplace and straightforward application of the term "region" can be found even within such documents, whereby "the region" implies something non-metropolitan – or even more straightforwardly, something that is simply not based in England's capital city, London. Thus, for example, the independent report, *Rebalancing our Cultural Capital* (Stark, Gordon and Powell 2013) makes clear that "the London" referred to throughout the document is the *region* known as Greater London but simultaneously, and confusingly, separates this London from "the [other] regions" (ibid: 5). Similarly, a recent announcement by the Arts Council England that it would increase spending outside of London by £37 million (or 4%) in 2018–2022, was widely reported as a boost for "the regions" (e.g. Wilkinson 2016), while key figures in the art world are wont to describe as "regional" any and all arts organisations located "outside" the capital (as then Head of the Arts Council England Sir Peter Bazalgette does in Thorpe 2014).

In some respects this may be unsurprising: London, a profoundly cosmopolitan city and internationally renowned centre for the arts, rarely appears in its regional garb. Indeed, it is perhaps best known as a capital *city* (The City of London), and not as a *region* (Greater London), although the abbreviated "London" might equally refer to either area. Yet this use of the term has a peculiar consequence in the UK, for rather than seeking relation between multiple possible centres, the insistence on a London-and-the-regions perspective actively holds the capital, and only the capital, apart. As a result, major cities such as Birmingham, Leeds, Liverpool, Manchester, Glasgow and Newcastle – cities that might otherwise be reasonably claimed as metropolitan centres in their own right – become regional. Only London is at once a region and yet, through its very centrality, not regional.

This is important, because London tends to be constructed and produced in arts discourse not just as *a* centre, but *the* centre for the arts in the UK. Indeed, so strong is its allure that it is sometimes assumed that all creative practitioners must live, work and/or exhibit there at some point in their careers in order to be taken seriously. This reputational allure is seemingly combined with necessity; almost half of the workforce in the creative industries in the UK is based in London and the South East (Oakley 2006), with London's creative economy employing "one in six Londoners" (Khan 2018: 5) – so the chances of finding work, a studio or other "opportunities" might be deemed higher in the capital than anywhere else. Various other factors are at play here too, of course, including historical processes of regulation and administration that enmesh and fix the capital at the heart of political debate and decision-making in the arts, the active promotion of London as an international centre for the arts, and the size and scale of the city itself. As Robert Hollands and John Vail (2015: 175) point out, cities are not simply a background factor or setting but are capable of "asserting real effects", so that the physical form of a given location – its proximity to other places, the access provided (or withheld) to services and resources – can all impact upon the horizon of the possible. In this sense, we might view London as a self-fulfilling prophecy, a proclaimed "creative" city whose amassed resources, mechanisms and opportunities continue to attract new waves of creative practitioners and whose resources thus become further and further entrenched with the passage of time.

But while the attraction of the centre is not to be denied, there is a more complex story to be told. For example, the competition for land in London means that artists' studios and workspaces remain especially vulnerable to commercial developments, with as many as 30%, or 3,500 artists, deemed "likely to lose their places of work in the next 5 years" (Greater London Authority 2014: 5–7). Moreover, as Oakley et al. (2017: 1510–1511) demonstrate using pooled data from the UK's Labour Force Survey, "rather than acting as an 'engine room' of social mobility", the clustering of cultural and creative industries in the capital actually reinforces socioeconomic divides such as "gender, ethnicity and particularly class-based divides". This, combined with a comparatively high cost of living, the low average income for visual artists (a survey by a–n [2013: 18] found that 72% of artists earned less than £10,000 a year from their practice, a figure that later rose to 82% [Artfinder 2017]), changes to the UK welfare system and all the challenges associated with a freelance "creative career" – such as the lack of sick pay or maternity leave (see McRobbie 2016) – can render any move to the capital risky, even ruinous, for those without substantial support.

At the same time, a number of mainly post-industrial UK cities have re-branded and re-orientated themselves as centres of culture in their own right. Glasgow was named the European Capital of Culture in 1990, for instance; Liverpool won the same award in 2008; and a UK City of Culture has been awarded internally every four years since 2013 (to Derry-Londonderry in 2013, Hull in 2017 and Coventry in 2021), with the Labour MP Yvette Cooper (2018) recently suggesting that the UK also institute a yearly Town of Culture award. By 2016, in fact, Juan Mateos-Garcia and Hasan Bakhshi (2016: 5–6) mapped 47 "creative clusters" in the UK and argued that it was now possible to speak of "hip" creative cities (e.g. Brighton, Liverpool and Glasgow), "creative agglomerations" that encompass "more than one metropolitan area" (e.g. as found around Manchester, Leeds, Bristol, Cardiff, Brighton, Southampton and Bournemouth) as well as smaller "creative conurbations" (e.g. Slough, High

230   *Emma Coffield*

Wycombe, Peterborough and Guildford). As Mateos-Garcia and Bakhshi (ibid: 16) point out, this is a far richer picture than that painted by Richard Florida (2002) or even work that suggests that creative practitioners are likely to cluster in more affordable "second-tier" cities (e.g. Markusen and Schrock 2006). There are also widespread bottom-up or grassroots approaches to re-define locations as "cultural" and/or "creative", often as based on or around artist-run initiatives. Gavin Murphy (2016: 6), for instance, briefly charts a European history of artist-run spaces of the 1960s and 1970s, noting a tendency for this activity to lie "outside prescribed commercial or cultural zones – both ideologically and often literally – [by] situating themselves in run-down inner-city centre areas". Nor is it just the city that attracts this kind of self-organised activity; Lourdes Orozco, David Bell and Ben Walmsley (2018: 3) recently documented the "important cultural activity" taking place at three arts organisations located in "non-city centre areas" of Leeds, England; areas that were previously "perceived to be barren, undesirable places to live and not common destinations to engage in cultural activity" – together now known as the Donut Group.

This is not to say that all cities, towns and conurbations in the UK are equally renowned for the arts, however. Many of those locations listed by Mateos-Garcia and Bakhshi (2016: 19) are discipline specific; Oxford, Cambridge, Southampton, Norwich and Peterborough have "a strong publishing presence", for example. The scale and spread of the cultural and creative industries also remains deeply uneven: London overwhelmingly dominates and alone accounts for "four in ten UK creative industry employees, and a third of creative businesses" (ibid: 13). Artist-run or grassroots approaches, even in "creative cities" that rely upon such projects, can be precarious, reliant on short-term or "meanwhile" spaces that can be redeveloped at short notice, while longer term possibilities take many years to come to fruition (see Coffield et al. 2019). To this we might add that the re-branding of cities – and towns, conurbations, areas, hubs, clusters and zones – as "cultural", and similar notions of creative place-making or arts-led regeneration, requires caution, for artists are often positioned here, wittingly or otherwise, as agents of social change, even as a "tool for state-led gentrification" (Pritchard 2019). Magally Miranda and Kyle Lane-McKinley (2017), for example, in their writing about Los Angeles, are stark about the costs to long-term residents of a "booming arts industry" in terms of the displacement of working-class and/or black inhabitants and "the art which is already there" in favour of "formally trained semi-professional" artists and galleries. In the UK, similar work has focused on the role of public policy in gentrification (Cameron and Coafee 2005), the "limited and problematic evidence base" for arts-led regeneration (Lees and Melhuish 2012) and the perspectives of the artists involved (Whiting and Hannam 2017), although "creativity" and the arts continue to be used as a growth and investment strategy in UK policy by both central government and local councils alike.

Creative practitioners may thus be pulled in several directions at once. On the one hand, so overwhelming is the idea that artists must work in the largest and most cosmopolitan city they can reach that there can seem to be little

"*Anything that's not in London*" 231

choice or option but to move (Oakley et al. 2017), although relocation is not a strategy open or affordable to all, and the seemingly cosmopolitan and meritocratic capital can turn out to be anything but. On the other hand, to stay in a regional town or conurbation is to risk seeming stuck (Allen and Hollingworth 2013) and to contend with potentially far fewer opportunities and resources. To be an artist or creative practitioner in the UK is thus to contend with complex logics, narratives and positions, all concerning the "placing" of the visual arts.

Research background and methodology

The following draws upon qualitative data collected between 2010–14 as part of a wider study funded by the Arts and Humanities Research Council (AHRC) exploring the construction of culture(s) in artist-run initiatives. The term "cultures" here refers to the "maps of meaning" and value (Clarke et al. 1993 [1976]: 10) actively (re)constructed by members of three artist-run initiatives, which brought into being, and structured, thought, action, meaning and value. The case study presented in this chapter comprises a total of nine semi-structured interviews (from a total of twenty-four members presented); analysis of internal and self-published documents; and observation of key events (e.g. exhibition openings). Members were randomly sampled within three categories (e.g. core, active and non-active members) and included a range of positions over the lifespan of the group. Of the nine members interviewed two were female, seven were male, and all were aged between 20–35 at the time of interview. It was not possible or feasible to interview all members. Rather, attention was focused on presenting a necessarily partial but fine grained set of accounts for analysis.

Data was iteratively coded and analysed via key terms and "organising metaphors" (Hansen and Sørensen 2005), resulting in a constellation of linked practices, understandings, ideas, objects and persons, or "maps of meaning" (Clarke et al. 1993 [1976]: 10) as articulated by each individual. In what follows, the focus for analysis was upon the placed nature of artistic practice (e.g. the characterisation of certain places and locations, their boundaries, value and/or impact as well as the agency of the individual in contributing to, navigating or redefining such understandings). These maps were then compared to others in the same case study, through a critical and reflexive process. Care was further taken to analyse all data as produced and arranged via particular "communicative situation[s]" (Barker and Galasiński 2001: 65). Full ethical clearance was obtained from Newcastle University, and the research process was conducted with an ethics of respect for all those involved (BERA 2011). In what follows, participants are referred to by a codename.

At the time of research, Empty Shop was located in Durham, a relatively small cathedral city in the North East of England with a population of approximately 50,400 (Durham County Council 2016). Durham City is situated within the larger County Durham, an area that includes a number of ex-mining villages with a total population of around 523,600 (Office for National Statistics 2017). In 2013, 98.1% of the population of County Durham identified as "White" (Office for National Statistics 2013). Located a short distance from larger neighbouring cities (e.g. Sunderland, Newcastle, Hartlepool and Middlesbrough) and the coast, Durham is perhaps most famous for its UNESCO World Heritage listed cathedral and castle and a highly ranked university. In addition, the city hosts a large-scale festival of light art produced by the London-based company Artichoke as well as book, jazz and brass festivals, a small museum dedicated to African and Asian art and archaeology and a theatre with gallery space. In 2016, both the council-run Durham Light Infantry Museum and Durham Art Gallery (which occupied the top floor of the same building) were closed in the face of budget cuts. While the somewhat compact city centre caters to a large number of students, the university offers no fine art or creative practice degrees.

Empty Shop, Durham – "The Hole in the Doughnut for Art"

Founded in 2008 by two friends in an empty wine shop, Empty Shop had an explicit regeneration model from the start; the directors would locate an empty space, renovate that space so that it could be used to host exhibitions and events, and then move on when the building sold. Following some success in this endeavour (Empty Shops 1 and 2 were both let after a period of use) the pair

Image 11.1 The Directors outside Empty Shop 1.
Source: Empty Shop

"Anything that's not in London"   233

formed a Community Interest Company and established a central headquarters with studio, exhibition and workshop spaces, plus a fully licensed bar, in Durham city centre in 2010, although they continued to use a variety of additional temporary spaces throughout the city (to date they have used 41 spaces, the "semi-permanent" headquarters closing in 2018 (Empty Shop 2018)). Empty Shop is, by choice, "completely independent and unfunded", charging instead a "fee appropriate to the costs incur[red]" (Empty Shop 2013). The directors further routinely emphasise that "anyone can use the space for the arts, and it can be arts of any nature" (Empty Shop 2009a), describing the space as "accessible at every level" (Empty Shop 2010), and stressing that "there are no panels to please, no cliques to get involved with first" (Empty Shop 2009b). At the time of the research project, Empty Shop was run by the two founding directors and had a group of studio holders (known as the "Freebirds") who occupied part of the headquarters, as well as a wider network of artists, supporters and volunteers.

Understandings of the region loom large in even the earliest mission documents, forming an origin story based, in part, on the lack of suitable venues. For example, the directors originally described Empty Shop as "the North East's newest contemporary arts group, dedicated to giving artists in the region a much-needed platform to produce and exhibit their work" (Empty Shop 2009b), with ESD1 further noting that, "there was nothing in Durham that existed like that, even in the North East". The narrative of "lack" is one often adopted by artist-run initiatives (e.g. as per Murphy's (2016: 6) introduction to *Artist Run Europe*, where he states that the "common denominator among all these groups and spaces is that they arose out of a deficit") and something Hollands and Vail (2012) in their work with the Amber Collective identify as a key "justification frame" for social action. Importantly however, there is a clear placed element to the claims made above, so that it is not just that there is no space *like this* for artists, but that there is no space *like this here*.

To elaborate a little: prior to this moment, both directors had at a similar point in their lives moved to cities in the north of England better known for their cultural offer, in part because Durham did not seem like a viable option. Intriguingly however, both had then returned to their home city. ESD1, for example, remarked,

> I was definitely not satisfied with Durham [. . .] I moved to Manchester briefly just because Durham was shit [. . .] but I quickly realised [. . .] it doesn't solve that problem.

The articulated "problem" noted in the above (the lack of accessible venues for the arts in Durham) and the proposed solution (to start one) are particularly interesting, for while they adhere to the principles of a DIY artistic practice (see Daniels 2014), they nevertheless challenge contemporary understandings of the artist as a mobile individual drawn to ever more "creative" cities. Indeed, although both directors initially attempted this trajectory, their experiences had

234   *Emma Coffield*

been somewhat negative; the pair using terms such as "hierarchical", "sterile" and "monotonous" when describing arts spaces in those cities, noting a "pretentious atmosphere". Far from being readily assimilated into a new and welcoming arts scene then, the pair instead developed strong feelings about what they termed

> non-institutional gallery space and arts organisations that worked in buildings that were accessible, spaces that weren't white cubes [or] you know, the privileged kind of typical space that you are told to aspire to.
>
> (ESD2)

These strong feelings, it should be pointed out, were developed despite ESD1 and ESD2's ability to relocate in the first place and their being able to secure MA study, paid cultural work and a studio space. As such, the history they presented was not one of newcomers rebuffed at the first hurdle but of a growing certainty that the models they had been "told to aspire to" did not suit. When the pair found themselves back in Durham a little while later and began contemplating their next move, they therefore began to talk "about how we could do this differently, or in some cases better" and "create something really accessible, really democratic" (ESD1). The chance to use the old wine shop in Durham was seized upon "as a bit of an experiment" (ESD2), and, stripping it down and holding an open call for their first exhibition, which attracted 150 people on opening night, Empty Shop began in earnest – very quickly opening up vital opportunities for creative practitioners in the region to exhibit, make and see work.

Indeed, Empty Shop quickly drew interest from creative practitioners based throughout the region. ESF1, for example, who lived in Newcastle, noted that he attended the very first show, then later put forward an idea for an exhibition with friends, then a solo show, then rented a studio space for six months. ESF2, who was based in Sunderland, relocated to Durham on account of his gaining a studio space at Empty Shop. However, while ESF1 and ESF2 were able to move within the region in order to harness this new site of opportunity, a number of studio holders and volunteers were not so fortunate and either lacked the resources or were bound by family, employment or other commitments to Durham. Had Empty Shop not existed, these creative practitioners would have had recourse to little or no support.

The creation of a space in which to make, install, exhibit, curate and discuss work *in Durham* thus rendered creative practices possible, and visible, that might otherwise have floundered. Indeed, Empty Shop was regularly positioned in interviews as a site of transformation. In most cases this transformation was attached to what might be termed transitional exhibitions – the first show after graduation, for example, or the first solo exhibition – where those exhibitions work to consolidate and confirm an artist's practice and reputation at a crucial point in their careers. Many spoke of Empty Shop's "character" here, as "really friendly and open" to the extent that "anyone [might] show anything" (ES31), with ESV1, ESV2, ESF3 and ESLT1 likewise all using the word "open". Here then was an opportunity for anyone to test new ideas, make new work, and in so doing to evidence and call forth the position of "artist" (or illustrator, curator, arts worker etc.). ESF1 spoke at length of the Directors faith in him despite his being a "new person" in the area, saying: "they [. . .] believed in what I was doing enough to put to let me use their space [. . .] introducing me to people, helping me out with things [. . .] inviting me back". This, perhaps, was the kind of welcome the Directors had once expected to receive elsewhere and were now determined to provide for others.

For one member, however, this kind of professional transformation had an added geographical aspect:

> This is always what I wanted to do [. . .] I went to college and a particular artist from Belfast [. . .] encourage[d] me and said, 'You really can be a gallery exhibiting artist' [. . .] but you couldn't go to your mates in Northern Ireland and say 'I'm going to be an artist'. They would just laugh at you, it wasn't ok over here. [. . .] The lecturers [. . .] told me I should go to England, go to university, and be an artist.
>
> (ESF2)

The identity of "artist" is here not simply something one might select and work towards but something bound by place and the identities deemed socially acceptable in those places. As a result, ESF2 felt compelled to relocate, to undertake further study and to seek out resources that would allow him to establish and support an artistic practice. ESF2's account was singular amongst those interviewed, perhaps because Empty Shop tended to attract creative practitioners already based within the region, but it nevertheless fits the ideal "career pathway" pushed in the cultural and creative industries, in which "mobility is [. . .] a defining feature" (McRobbie 2016: 2). Indeed, it demonstrates both the lived impact of such narratives upon individuals (e.g. in being laughed at or being made to feel "out of place") and the considerable privileges required to move (e.g. having supportive tutors who might write references for future study as well as financial backing etc.).

Empty Shop further acted as a kind of hub for creative and cultural activities more closely associated with the city, running a "sign-up wall" during a short-lived attempt by Durham County Council to have Durham nominated as the first UK City of Culture in 2009, for example, or hosting events during festivals. Yet, at the same time, it was infused with a sense of cultural isolation. ESD2, for instance, described Durham as the "hole in the doughnut for art in the North East" – referring to the fact that neighbouring Newcastle, Gateshead, Middlesbrough and Sunderland all had high-profile galleries, whereas Durham did not. ESF2 was likewise scathing about Durham's UK City of Culture bid, responding, "it's like, how can you get it [the award] when the only thing there is here culture-wise is the cathedral [. . .] [except for Empty Shop] there's no arts going on".

236 *Emma Coffield*

Such concerns were seemingly well founded, for while Durham City boasted a famous castle and cathedral (together a UNESCO World Heritage Site), numerous festivals and a small art museum on the top floor of a military museum, nearby cities had a far richer cultural offer. Three major "destination" galleries all opened in the 2000s, for example, (the BALTIC Centre for Contemporary Art in Gateshead in 2002, the Northern Gallery for Contemporary Art (NGCA) in Sunderland in 2003, while Middlesbrough's art collection was consolidated into the Middlesbrough Institute of Modern Art (MIMA) in 2007). In addition, Newcastle in particular had a long history of artist-run practice, including Amber, a film and photography collective founded in 1968, the Basement Group (later Locus+) in 1979, Vane in 1997 and the Star and Shadow DIY cinema in 2001, alongside many others (see Tarbuck and Hearn 2007).

Yet these sites and organisations were regularly articulated as being out of reach despite their being relatively proximate. ESD1, for example, noted that before Empty Shop opened the idea of travelling the twenty or so miles from Durham to Newcastle to get a studio space felt like an "unachievable goal" or a "dizzy height"; something only open to those who "moved in the right circles". In part, this seemed to be due to the differing characteristics ascribed to the two art scenes; the "accessible" Durham crowd operating separately from the "cool" but potentially "intimidating [. . .] Newcastle circle" (ESF1). The sense of remoteness suggested by those working in Durham was thus perhaps remoteness as a "state of mind [as much as] geographical reality" (Gibson, Luckman and Willoughby-Smith 2010: 36).

To make matters worse, Newcastle and, a bit later again, Gateshead and Middlesbrough quickly began to capitalise on their "creative" potential. Thus, ESF2 joked that when he first found out about Empty Shop he "hadn't come across [anything similar] in the North East", but by the time of the interview, "in Newcastle [. . .] everyday of the week there's one". This regional competition, and the sudden abundance of opportunities in Newcastle, in particular, meant that for many artists the pull of Newcastle quickly became the stronger of the two. ESLT1, for example, who was based in Newcastle, remarked:

> a lot of people from Durham will travel to Newcastle to attend things in Newcastle [. . .] we're a little bit spoilt here and [. . .] don't tend to go to Durham as much.

ESF1, on the other hand, talked of his "making a point" to attend openings and events in Durham. The implication here of ESF1's making a special effort to stay in touch was not lost on those in Durham, and he was welcomed, along with other artists who had made the journey, extremely warmly. Yet there remained a palpable sense that the space between Durham and neighbouring cities did not allow for free and easy movement (as per Tuan 1977), but was thick and dense, encircling Durham and separating it from other art scenes.

That is not to say that feelings of isolation were trivial or easily dismissed. On the contrary, so deeply held were such convictions that they underpinned even mundane or routine choices, such as the wording used on labels and in promotional material. For example, regular events like "Really Good Friday" (an Easter-themed event that mixed art-making with music, quizzes and games) were felt to engage audiences in a light-hearted way, underlining that Empty Shop was "down to earth" and "part of a local community" (ESD2). Or, as ES31 put it: "it's very grassroots, no bullshit". But the "playful and casual" (ESD1) approach to language was also linked to the construction of those visiting Empty Shop as lacking any prior knowledge of art. ESV2, for instance, described the audience for Empty Shop as "people [. . .] that I think never would have come in to contact with art before", while ES31 spoke of "a big mix of all sorts of people you wouldn't ordinarily get in a white cube gallery". Similarly, the Directors talked of avoiding "big lists of arty words that people won't understand" or that might "put people off" in favour of being "very chatty and informal [. . .] let's just talk how we talk, how we would talk to anybody" (ESD1).

The strong preference for an accessible "local" voice over imported international "art-speak" (as described by Rule and Levine 2012) was thus premised on making visitors feel welcome – and there was much testimony to support this in practice. But there are other, equally possible, ways of imaging audiences in Durham: as highly visually literate students in no need of textual props or encouragement, for example, or as locals in full command of the knowledges and techniques that accompany exhibition-going. It was not just Durham that was brought into being as remote then, but its inhabitants too, and this understanding manifested itself in a range of pervasive effects and lived, everyday practices – right down to the choice of wording on a label or leaflet.

There was thus something of an animating tension. On the one hand, the collective imagining of Durham as culturally isolated worked to reinforce Empty Shop's continued existence and value as the only accessible art space in the city and the sole provider of vital opportunities for those based locally. On the other hand, there was a remoteness that contributed to the drawing away of potential collaborators and audiences, which artists had to navigate (e.g. as ESF1 did in his moving between multiple local art scenes).

Indeed, there appeared to be multiple possible "Durhams" as perceived, experienced and articulated during interviews. ES31, for example, considered Durham a "sleepy town [sic]" with "so many empty shops [. . .] wasting away", ESF2 considered it "beautiful", commenting on the "picturesque view of the cathedral" from his studio, while ESF3 spoke of his being "a County Durham person [who felt] patriotic to the mother county" despite living in a nearby city. The positions taken here are by no means incompatible, but they suggest, even within a small sample of creative practitioners (some of whom had spent long periods of time working together), understandings of place that are multiple, layered and nuanced.

Other factors should likewise be taken into consideration. For example, while the self-initiated activities of Empty Shop's members succeeded in transforming the opportunities available to artists in the region, this activity was nevertheless

238   *Emma Coffield*

reliant on there being available space(s) in the city over that period of time, a whole raft of regulations as applicable to Community Interest Companies, the availability of volunteers etc. The ability to "name" one of the directors as an artist, and both as "returning" to their home city, further meant that the pair could claim Empty Shop as artist-run and seek the benefits associated with this recognised form of practice (i.e. reduced rates) while avoiding, arguably, charges of gentrification. Moreover, while Empty Shop benefited from a regular influx of History of Art and Combined Arts students, the numbers of students taking such courses remained small in comparison to, for instance, those taking creative practice degrees in Newcastle. For all the ability of the group to reckon with existing infrastructures and discourses, they were thus unable to capitalise on a resource readily available elsewhere in the North East.

Conclusion

The case of Empty Shop highlights the complex interplay between the agency of a group of creative practitioners and a variety of factors, structures and affordances that worked to rank and order, compel and allow. Nuanced accounts of this kind are all too easily passed over as neither local nor global enough. The above thus concentrates not on "networked" curators or global artists as they move around the world, or on art made in and by rural communities, or even on a mega-events celebrating and performing the region anew, but on creative practitioners working day-to-day in a regional city not particularly well-known for visual or contemporary art. In so doing, it begins to bring into being the attachments and imaginings that animate creative practice in locations beyond local-global and centre-periphery binaries, or in what Markusen (2013: 482) might consider a "surprising place" for the making and display or artworks, so strong is the stereotype that artists must live and work either in the busy cosmopolitan city or a rural area known for its natural beauty.

The chapter further demonstrates how everyday artistic practices are animated and driven by the various meanings and understandings attached to the region over time. The region here acts as a kind of spatial imaginary, organising and shaping understandings of the world in the everyday, and as part of a process to which artists and creative practitioners actively contribute, albeit in at times fragmentary or contradictory ways and with varying degrees of power. The exploration of this infusion of geopolitics into the routine and lived practices of art-making and display is vital, for if we are to consider how creative practitioners understand and navigate the art-world, or art-worlds, we must pay attention to the ways in which places are characterised and imagined, ranked and experienced, made and re-made by artists and creative practitioners (e.g. as marginal, isolated, welcoming, or as a stepping stone to somewhere else). We need to interrogate the mechanisms and myths that draw artists, that can even compel them to relocate, and the consequences and options for those who are either less mobile, or who chose to remain. Indeed, it is important to remember that concerns over mobility in the arts are not restricted to international travel and that even relatively short distances between neighbouring regions can place resources, opportunities and longed-for identities and careers beyond reach. Collective understandings of regional art scenes and related notions of proximity (whether based on geography, or as imagined and lived, or both) *matter* here, as they work to welcome and enable, or intimidate and dissuade, potential members.

Doubtless there are many other stories that might have been told about Durham, and the account set out above is in no way intended as complete or static or as an essentialist claim to place and identity. Rather, specificity and multiplicity are very much the point, for it is in this attention to detail that the slippery and mutating in-between nature of places – whether they be small regional towns, metropolitan art centres, a bit of both or something else again – come into being for practitioners. Indeed, perhaps the key contribution of a focus on the region is to make plain that cosmopolitan art centres, rural landscapes and regional towns and cities are not always so distinct. As the above demonstrates, artist-run initiatives based in the regions might nevertheless allow for international quality artworks to be made and be made public, while "creative" cities can exclude, disappoint or fail to live up to their reputations. Creative practitioners may make and display work in one location while all the time placing themselves elsewhere. Creative work may equally be done in a city renowned for visual art or in a city, town, conurbation, zone, area or village, or a combination over time, and artists who live in one location may nevertheless maintain extensive networks elsewhere. Similarly, artists may move and make work in areas for reasons beyond that of having a creative career (e.g. to be with family, to live in a location considered home). The region can perhaps most usefully be employed as a caution against organising the creative landscape into too easily recognised patterns, bringing into view sticky, overlapping and lived understandings of places in all their specific textures instead.

Acknowledgements

The author would like to thank all those who gave up their time to participate in the project, for without their generosity none of the above would have been possible. Thanks are further due to the Arts and Humanities Research Council, UK (AHRC) for funding the research project as part of my doctoral study, and to the School of Arts and Cultures at Newcastle University for an Early Career Academic Fellowship that allowed me to develop the current chapter, as well as to Christopher Whitehead and Alex Deans for their insightful suggestions and unwavering guidance throughout the lifespan of this work, and to members of the Cultural Significance of Place research group at Newcastle University for providing feedback on a paper given in November 2015.

Interviews

Information correct at the time of interview.

ESD1 – Director of Empty Shop, male, aged 20–35, based in Durham
ESD2 – Director of Empty Shop, male, aged 20–35, based in Durham

240 *Emma Coffield*

ESF1 – Previous studio holder and practicing artist, male, aged 20–35, based in Newcastle

ESF2 – Studio holder and practicing artist, male, aged 20–35, based in Durham

ESF3 – Previous studio holder and arts professional, male, aged 20–35, based in Newcastle

ESLT1 – Illustrator and technician, exhibited at Empty Shop on multiple occasions, male, aged 20–35, based in Newcastle

ES31 – Student, exhibited at Empty Shop on multiple occasions, female, aged 20–35, based in Scotland

ESV1 – Student and volunteer at Empty Shop, male, aged 20–35, based in Durham

ESV2 – Student and volunteer at Empty Shop, female, aged 20–35, based in Durham

References

a-n. 2013. "Artists Information Company." Retrieved January 1, 2019 (www.payingartists. org.uk/wp-content/uploads/2015/04/Paying-Artists-Research-Phase-1-Findings.pdf).

Allen, K., and Hollingworth, S. 2013. "About: Everything You Need to Know." Retrieved June 8, 2019 (http://emptyshop.org/about/).

Applin, J., Spencer, C., and Tobin, A. (eds.). 2018. *London Art Worlds: Mobile, Contingent, and Ephemeral Networks, 1960–1980*. Pennsylvania: The Pennsylvania State University Press.

Artfinder. 2017. *The Artfinder Independent Art Market Report: 2017*. London: Artfinder.

Barker, C., and Galasiñski, D. 2001. *Cultural Studies and Discourse Analysis: A Dialogue on Language and Identity*. London: SAGE Publications Ltd.

Belting, H., Buddensieg, A., and Weibel, P. 2013. *The Global Contemporary and the Rise of New Art Worlds*. Cambridge, MA: MIT Press.

British Educational Research Association (BERA). 2011. "Ethical Guidelines for Educational Research." Retrieved July 25, 2017 (www.bera.ac.uk/wp-content/uploads/2014/02/BERA- Ethical-Guidelines-2011.pdf?noredirect=1).

Butt, M., Cross, E., Holliman, N., Kempton, L., Legget, J., Mackenzie, E., Ross, H., Sapsed, J., Swords, J., Vallance, P., and Whitehurst, F. 2017. *Creative Fuse North East: Initial Report*. Newcastle Upon Tyne: Newcastle University.

Cameron, S., and Coafee, J. 2005. "Art, Gentrification and Regeneration – From Artist as Pioneer to Public Arts." *European Journal of Housing Policy* 5(1): 39–58.

Charlesworth, J. J. 2013. "Global Versus Local." *Art Review* [November]. Retrieved January 1, 2019 (https://artreview.com/features/november_2013_feature_global_versus_local_by_jj_charlesworth_1/).

Clarke, J., Hall, S., Jefferson, T., and Roberts, B. 1993 [1976]. "Subcultures, Cultures and Class." Pp. 9–79 in *Resistance Through Rituals: Youth Subcultures in Post-War Britain*, edited by Hall, S., and Jefferson, T. London: Routledge.

Coffield, E., Markham, K., Richter, P., Huggan, R., Butler, D., Wainwright, E., and Prescott, R. 2018. *More Than Meanwhile Spaces*. Newcastle Upon Tyne: Newcastle University and The NewBridge Project. Retrieved January 24, 2019 (https://thenewbridgeproject.com/wp-content/uploads/2019/01/MTMS-Publication-2.pdf).

Cooper, Y. 2018. "'Town of Culture' Award Would Boost Arts and Investment." *The Guardian*. Retrieved January 1, 2019 (www.theguardian.com/politics/2018/dec/29/town-of-ulture-letter-to-jeremy-wright-yvette-cooper-labour-mps).

Courage, C., and McKeown, A. (eds.). 2019. *Creative Placemaking: Research, Theory and Practice*. Abingdon, OX: Routledge.

Crawshaw, J., and Gkartzios, M. 2018. "The Way Art Works: Insight for Community Development." Pp. 177–192 in *The Routledge Handbook of Community Development: Perspectives from Around the Globe*, edited by Kenny, S., McGrath, B., and Phillips, R. New York: Routledge.

Daniels, R. (ed.) 2014. *D.I.Y.* Chichester: University of Chichester.

Durham County Council. 2016. *Statistical Profile* (December 2016 Update). Durham County Council.

Elkins, J. (ed.) 2007. *Is Art History Global?* New York: Routledge.

Empty Shop. 2009a. "Northern Rock Foundation: Proposal for Eligibility" [draft application dated June 2009].

Empty Shop. 2009b. "January 2009: About Empty Shop" [draft text].

Empty Shop. 2010. "Empty Shop: About Us" [text from old webpage].

Empty Shop. 2013. "'Sticky Subjects' or 'Cosmopolitan Creatives'? Social Class, Place and Urban Young People's Aspirations for Work in the Knowledge Economy." *Urban Studies* 50(3): 499–517.

Empty Shop. 2018. "Goodbye Empty Shop HQ." Retrieved January 5, 2019 (https://medium.com/@emptyshop/goodbye-empty-shop-hq-b08543d2b077).

Esche, C. 2005. "Debate: Biennials." *Frieze* (92): 105.

Esche, C. 2011. "Introduction: Making Art Global." *Making Art Global (Part 1): The Third Havana Biennial 1989,* edited by Weiss, R. et al. London: University of the Arts, Afterall.

Fielding, P. 2014. "Curated Regions of the North: Art and Literature in the 'Scottish Border' and the 'Transpennine Corridor'." *Visual Culture in Britain* 15(2): 159–172.

Florida, R. 2002. *The Rise of the Creative Class*. New York: Basic Books.

Gibson, C., Luckman, S., and Willoughby-Smith, J. 2010. "Creativity Without Borders? Rethinking Remoteness and Proximity." *Australian Geographer* 41(1): 25–38.

Gombrich, E. H. 1950. *The History of Art*. London: Phaidon Press.

Great Exhibition of the North. 2017. *Aims and Objectives*. [print document].

Greater London Authority. 2014. *Artists' Workspace Study*. London: Greater London Authority.

Hansen, A. D., and Sørensen, E. 2005. "Polity as Politics: Studying the Shaping and Effects of Discursive Polities." Pp. 93–115 in *Discourse Theory in European Politics*, edited by Howarth, D., and Torfing, J. Hampshire: Palgrave Macmillan.

Hawkins, H. 2014. *For Creative Geographies: Geography, Visual Arts and the Making of Worlds*. Oxfordshire and New York: Routledge.

Hollands, R., and Vail, J. 2012. "The Art of Social Movement: Cultural Opportunity, Mobilisation, and Framing in the Early Formation of the Amber Collective." *Poetics* (40): 22–43.

Hollands, R., and Vail, J. 2015. "Place Imprinting and the Arts: A Case Study of the Amber Collective." *Local Economy* 30(2): 173–190.

Joyeux-Prunel, B. 2015. "Provincializing Paris: The Centre/Periphery Narrative of Modern Art in Light of Quantitative and Transformational Approaches." *Artl@s Bulletin* 4(1) Article 4: 40–64.

Kaufmann, T. D., and Pilliod, E. (eds.). 2005. *Time and Place: The Geohistory of Art*. Hants: Ashgate Publishing Limited.

242 *Emma Coffield*

Khan, S. 2018. "Mayor's Foreword." *Culture for All Londoners: Mayor of London's Draft Culture Strategy*. London: Greater London Authority: 4–9.

Kwon, M. 2002. *One Place After Another: Site Specific Art and Locational Identity*. London: The MIT Press.

Landry, C., and Bianchini, F. 1995. *The Creative City*. London: Demos.

Lees, L., and Melhuish, C. 2012. "Arts-led Regeneration in the UK: The Rhetoric and the Evidence on Urban Social Inclusion." *European Urban and Regional Studies* 22(3): 242–260.

Ley, D. 2003. "Artists, Aestheticisation and the Field of Gentrification." *Urban Studies* (40): 2527–2544.

L'Internationale. (eds.). 2015. "Decolonising Museums." *L'Internationale Online*. Retrieved July 26, 2018 (www.internationaleonline.org/media/files/02-decolonisingmuseums-1.pdf).

Lippard, L. 1997. *The Lure of the Local: Senses of Place in a Multicentred Society*. New York: The New Press.

Luckman, S. 2012. *Locating Cultural Work: The Politics and Poetics of Rural, Regional and Remote Creativity*. Hampshire: Palgrave Macmillan.

Markusen, A. 2013. "Artists Work Everywhere." *Work and Occupations* 40(4): 481–495.

Markusen, A., and Schrock, G. 2006. "The Artistic Dividend: Urban Artistic Specialization and Economic Development Implications." *Urban Studies* 43: 1661–1686.

Mateos-Garcia, J., and Bakhshi, H. 2016. "The Geography of Creativity in the UK: Creative Clusters, Creative People and Creative Networks." *Nesta*. Retrieved July 26, 2018 (www. nesta.org.uk/report/the-geography-of-creativity-in-the-uk/).

McKee, F. 2012. "What We Have Done." *Engage* (31). Retrieved January 21, 2019 (www. glasgowmiraclearchives.org/project-outputs/what-we-have-done/).

McRobbie, A. 2016. *Be Creative: Making a Living in the New Culture Industries*. Cambridge: Polity Press.

Miles, M. 1997. *Art, Space and the City; Public Art and Urban Futures*. London: Routledge.

Miles, A., and Gibson, L. 2017. "Everyday Participation and Cultural Value in Place." *Cultural Trends* 26(1): 1–3.

Miranda, M., and Lane-McKinley, K. 2017. "Artwashing, or, Between Social Practice and Reproduction." *A Blade of Grass, Fertile Ground*. Retrieved July 26, 2018 (www.abladeof grass.org/fertile-ground/artwashing-social-practice-social-reproduction/).

Morse, N., Rex, B., and Harvey Richardson, S. 2018. "Editorial: Methodologies for Researching the Museum as Organisation." *Museum & Society* 16(2): 112–123.

Murphy, G. 2016. "Introduction." Pp. 4–17 in *Artist Run Europe: Practice/Projects/Spaces*, edited by Murphy, G., and Cullen, M. Dublin: Pallas Projects Limited.

Oakley, K. 2006. "Include Us Out: Economic Development and Social Policy in the Creative Industries." *Cultural Trends*. 14: 283–302.

Oakley, K., Laurison, D., O'Brien, D., and Friedman, S. 2017. "Cultural Capital: Arts Graduates, Spatial Inequality, and London's Impact on Cultural Labour Markets." *American Behavioural Scientist* 61(12): 1510–1531.

Office for National Statistics (ONS). 2013. "2011 Census: Key Statistics and Quick Statistics for Local Authorities in the United Kingdom." Retrieved July 26, 2018 (www.ons.gov. uk/file?uri=/peoplepopulationandcommunity/populationandmigration/populationesti mates/datasets/2011censuskeystatisticsandquickstatisticsforlocalauthoritiesintheunitedkingdom part1/r21ukrttableks201ukladv1_tcm77-330436.xls).

Office for National Statistics (ONS). 2017. "Estimates of the Population for the UK, England and Wales, Scotland and Northern Ireland. Mid-2017." Retrieved July 26, 2018 (www.ons. gov.uk/peoplepopulationandcommunity/populationandmigration/populationestimates/ datasets/populationestimatesforukenglandandwalesscotlandandnorthernireland).

O'Neill, P. 2007. "The Curatorial Turn: From Practice to Discourse." Pp. 13–28 in *Issues in Curating Contemporary Art and Performance*, edited by Rugg, J., and Sedgwick, M. Bristol: Intellect Books.

Orozco, L., Bell, D., and Walmsley, B. 2018. "Donut Group: Donut Pilot Project." Retrieved January 1, 2019 (https://cloud.chapelfm.co.uk/wp-content/uploads/2018/08/1807-Donut-Pilot-Project-Report.pdf).

Other Great Exhibition of the North, The. 2018. [Flyer].

Pritchard, S. 2019. "Place Guarding: Activist Art Against Gentrification." In *Creative Placemaking: Research, Theory and Practice*, edited by Courage, C., and McKeown, A. Oxon: Routledge. Retrieved January 20, 2019 (http://colouringinculture.org/blog/placeguarding).

Rule, A., and Levine, D. 2012. "International Art English." *Triple Canopy*. Retrieved January 21, 2019 (www.canopycanopycanopy.com/contents/international_art_english).

Sharp, J., Pollock, V., and Paddison, R. 2005. "Just Art for a Just City: Public Art and Social Inclusion in Urban Regeneration." *Urban Studies* 42(5/6): 1001–1023.

Skeggs, B. 2004. *Class, Self, Culture*. London: Routledge.

Stark, P., Gordon, C., and Powell, D. 2013. "Rebalancing our Cultural Capital: A Contribution to the Debate on National Policy for the Arts and Culture in England." Retrieved July 26, 2018 (www.gpsculture.co.uk/rocc.php).

Steeds, L., and other authors. 2013. *Making Art Global (Part 2): "Magiciens de la Terre" 1989*. London; Afterall Books.

Tarbuck, J., and Hearn, M. 2007. *This Will Not Happen Without You: From the Collective Archive of The Basement Group, Projects UK and Locus + (1977–2007)*. Sunderland: University of Sunderland Press.

Thorpe, V. 2014. "Interview: Peter Bazalgette on Regional Arts Funding: 'The Blame Lies with Council Cuts'." *The Guardian*. Retrieved July 26, 2018 (www.theguardian.com/culture/2014/jun/14/peter-bazalgette-london-not-threat-regional-arts-funding).

Tuan, Y. 1977. *Space and Place: The Perspective of Experience*. Minneapolis: University of Minnesota Press.

Weiss, R. et al. 2011. *Making Art Global (Part 1): The Third Havana Biennial 1989*. London: Afterall Books in association with the Academy of fine Arts Vienna and Van Abbemuseum, Eindhoven.

Whiting, J., and Hannam, K. 2017. "'The Secret Garden': Artists, Bohemia and Gentrification in the Ouseburn Valley, Newcastle Upon Tyne, UK." *European Urban and Regional Studies* 24(3): 318–334.

Wilkinson, M. 2016. "Regional Arts Funding Boost as Arts Council Shifts Focus from London." *The Telegraph*. Retrieved July 26, 2018 (www.telegraph.co.uk/news/2016/10/04/regional-arts-funding-boost-as-arts-council-shifts-focus-from-lo/).

12 Sculptural coastlines
Site-specific artworks, beachscapes, and regional identities

Elizabeth Ellison and Michelle Thompson

Introduction

The beach is undeniably an important part of life for many coastal Australians and also plays a key role in our national and international identity. And yet the beach can be quite a complex site. The diversity of the landscape means it can be both regional and metropolitan, and the layout and structure of beach locations can differ dramatically. Regional beaches have their own distinct identities: many are isolated and private, almost impossible to access without a specialised vehicle; others border regional cities and centres. The use of these regional beaches then can vary across the country, and the interaction and engagement with these spaces can also change depending on location.

One way of investigating how the landscape emerges as a site of meaning-making for a region is to examine the emergence of curated, site-specific arts festivals in the location. These festivals are collections of temporary site-specific works, or art that is categorised by its place and situation (Kaye 2000). In regional Queensland, there are a number of public art festivals that are exhibited on beaches. Where the internationally renowned festival Sculpture by the Sea takes place on some of Australia's most iconic, urban beaches (Bondi Beach in Sydney and Cottesloe in Perth), similar festivals are occurring in regional beaches across Queensland. While more modest in size and scale, these festivals are important events that embody regional identity and sense of place, which is achieved by encouraging participants to engage with the artwork in-situ on the beachscape. Consequently, this chapter examines how the landscape (beachscape) is used to encourage participants' engagement with the artworks at three sculpture festivals based in regional Queensland: Currumbin's SWELL Sculpture Festival, Noosa's Floating Land festival, and Townsville's Strand Ephemera festival. Using a spatial analysis of the festivals and artworks, it is possible to see that the beach becomes more than a backdrop and is a site of meaning-making by enabling festival participants' to engage with both the artworks and the beachscape.

Literature review

Regional festivals occur within a specific and culturally relevant context. As such, the following discussion reviews a number of complementary themes that provide this context, including: regional beachscapes, public art in regional Queensland, and the connections between arts and tourism.

Regional beachscapes

It is possible to consider the Australian beach as a space that is at once wrapped up in concepts of Australian mythology and iconography while also being an everyday location with which many Australians are comfortably familiar. After all, the majority of the Australian population lives along the coastlines, gravitating around the metropolitan regions near Perth, Sydney, Melbourne, Adelaide, and the east coast of Queensland. There is a homogenising tendency to consider the Australian beach as a monolithic site in the popular imagination (see Ellison and Hawkes 2016); however, there is significant distinction in the way that Australia's over 30,000 individual beaches are accessed and used by visitors, both domestic and international.

Many regional areas along the Queensland coast have strong relationships with their local beaches. Some regions use the beaches as a drawcard, attracting tourists eager to experience, for example, the Great Barrier Reef, one of Queensland's iconic tourism sites. Foreshore and esplanade (re)developments also provide opportunities to engage with the landscape, capitalising on the desire of locals and tourists to walk, bathe, and swim along the beach. The development of the Townsville Strand is an example of how investment in coastal areas reimagines these spaces, providing opportunities for meaning making among locals and tourists engaging with the beachscape as well as with events and festivals such as Strand Ephemera, discussed in this chapter.

The beach in Australia has long been tied to concepts of democracy (Dutton 1985) and egalitarianism as 'the great leveller'. Ann Game suggests that "everyone, all Australians, own it [the beach]" (1990: 115). Where resorts have driven the development of coastlines in some countries, Australia has mostly maintained beaches that are managed by local councils and free to access. This has helped establish the longstanding idea that beaches are egalitarian spaces; certainly, popular representations of the beach as a freely accessible location for everyone regardless of class, gender, and ethnicity permeates cultural texts (consider, for instance, Debbie and Sue successfully – briefly – breaking down the barrier of gender at the end of the classic novel *Puberty Blues* [Lette and Carey 1979]). However, this has been challenged before (Ellison 2014), and it is worth noting that there are still complexities about how Australians use, describe, and access their beaches. This perhaps erroneous perception that the beach is open to everyone makes the inclusion of public art festivals on beach sites an interesting prospect. Game argues that the shared ethos of leisure is what unites beachgoers – "we all have the same fun" – unlike traditional discourses of egalitarianism that suggest "we all work" (1990: 115). Visiting the beach then is an experience of democratic inclusivity through leisure, and this is somewhat unique in cultural or artistic experiences. As Ryan and Picken (2017) have noted, galleries and museums can be considered exclusive and intimidating for certain audiences who believe themselves to be lacking cultural capital; in

246 *Elizabeth Ellison and Michelle Thompson*

comparison, the beach could be considered a more inviting, welcoming location for cultural experiences.

Public and site-specific art

Considering this shift towards public art happening outside of galleries and museums, local governments in Queensland are embracing the intersection of public art and design across the state. Public art strategies continue to be an important part of developing local identity in regions. Ryan and Picken (2017: 3) suggest that the "inclusion of art in everyday spaces [can lead to] unexpected encounters with visual forms that contribute to personal development, through invoking memories and pleasurable feelings". Perhaps most importantly, public art is considered a way of providing art experiences for the wider public in a way that is usually both free and accessible.

An important part of reading public art is considering the interwoven relationship the work has with its location. Most public art is fixed either specifically as a temporary work (as is the case for the festivals considered in this chapter) or as a permanent fixture. Regardless of its intended duration, there is a need for artists and/or curators to carefully consider how the artwork will contribute to and be part of the site in which it is erected. Nicholas Kaye (2000: 1), in *Site-Specific Art*, highlights the "exchange" between artworks and their sites and how "a work of art, too, will be defined in relation to its place and position" and that a strong relationship between site and artwork is integral for a successful installation (even if this means "troubling" or contesting the site through the work). Site-specific art can, in comparison to traditional gallery or museum settings, bring new meaning to the landscape in which the work is situated. There are also less-structured conventions for audiences approaching site-specific art works – they can be touched, climbed on, or ignored, all actions that would be considered inappropriate in a gallery. While much public art is located in urban environments, there is a growing recognition of public art that is embedded and incorporated within natural landscapes. Sculpture festivals like the ones discussed in this chapter are of course specifically and intentionally engaging with the beachscape in which they are situated.

The arts and tourism

Experiencing public arts and sculpture, whether in a gallery, at a festival, or in the surrounding landscape, is an activity that interests tourists as well as local community. As Derrett (2005: 5) suggests, "Tourism is one of the structured environments in which culture is embedded. Festivals are situated as attractions in the tourism literature". For tourists, regional arts festivals provide insights into, and opportunities to engage with, a community's creativity, its lifestyle, and the surrounding landscape unique to that region (in the context of this chapter, beachscapes) (Timothy 2011). In essence, arts festivals can tell the stories of a region's artists, its community and landscape, whereby the art draws inspiration from, and is an expression of, its cultural and geographic surroundings. From a tourism perspective, festivals are experiences that attract, engage, and create meaning for participants in interaction with the artworks as well as with the surrounding landscape.

Tourists are drawn to cultural tourism attractions because of the unfamiliar and unknown (Timothy 2011). It is this difference that frames how tourists look or gaze upon the landscape and appreciate it (Urry 1990, 2002). In the context of this discussion, arts and sculpture festivals provide a visual feast for participants, where they visually consume their surrounds – both artworks and landscape. However, tourists need to be provided with opportunities to move from simply gazing upon to engaging with festival artworks. Engagement can contribute to the long-term success and sustainability of festivals, including greater economic returns for festival organisers and regional communities. In addition, engagement also enables tourists to have more authentic, meaningful, and memorable experiences that contribute to their satisfaction with the festival as well as to their overall trip. Thompson et al. (2016) recognised the landscape as an integral part of developing experiences, describing how the landscape is comprised of three component spaces, which enables the development of immersive activities or experiences that allow tourists to engage with the landscape. Regional arts and sculpture festivals are activities which provide participants opportunities to engage with the artworks, but more importantly, with the beach (or landscape) in which the festival is located.

Methodology

This chapter provides a preliminary investigation into the three case studies: SWELL Sculpture Festival, Floating Land, and Strand Ephemera. Specifically, this will involve two main areas of focus: festival programming and aesthetics, and a spatial analysis of the festivals. In developing a methodological frame that incorporates both an arts and tourism perspective, there is scope to not only consider the festival as a whole but also analyse the individual pieces of artwork. In this approach, textual analysis becomes layered: it is used to consider the visual aesthetic of an individual artwork as well as the more nuanced context in which the artwork is displayed. Each piece in these festivals (with some exceptions) is created by different artists and then curated within an exhibition. Viewing them in isolation is restrictive, and considering them in context is essential; however, there is limited scope to investigate the overall festivals as texts in this chapter. As such, our analysis is informed by both ethnographic experience as well as associated, paratextual material, such as programs, websites, maps and photography of the festival.

It is important to note some key limitations to this investigation. SWELL Sculpture Festival, based in Currumbin on the Gold Coast, is the only festival of the three to run annually; both Floating Land and Strand Ephemera run bi-annually (each were active in 2017 and again in 2019). As such, we have primarily used 2017 data to provide a comparison. Importantly, this

248 *Elizabeth Ellison and Michelle Thompson*

chapter interrogates how these festivals work within the landscape; we have not approached the festivals through an artist/curator perspective in this instance. We have also primarily focused on the festivals as a whole, with some specific analysis of particular artworks as appropriate. Further research, including interviews with key festival personnel (artists, curators, arts workers, and so on) would provide different insights into the role of the landscape when developing, curating, and installing these artworks.

Spatial lens

The methodology of this chapter is framed through a reading of regional arts festivals from both an arts and tourism perspective. In particular, it is using a lens of spatial analysis that is informed by both cultural and tourism perspectives on space, place, and the use of zones in understanding meaning-making within landscapes.

It is important to identify the distinction between place and space, words that are often used interchangeably. Considering the trend of 'place activation' in regional arts and local government enthusiasm for rejuvenating or revitalising non-traditional or less desirable locations through arts and cultural activity, it is important to define these terms. Lawrence Buell's extensive work on spatial theory is useful in distinguishing between space and place. Inspired by E. V. Walter, he suggests that "place [is] by definition perceived or felt space, space humanized, rather than the material world taken on its own terms" (Buell 2008: 667). Space can be considered more ambiguous, more representative perhaps, of a bigger concept. As Walter identifies (1988: 142), "people do not experience abstract space; they experience places. A place is seen, heard, smelled, imagined, loved, hated, feared, revered, enjoyed, or avoided".

Cultural theorists Fiske, Hodge and Turner's (1987), in the first major work of academic research to specifically focus on the Australian beach, read the site as a place of zones (see Figure 12.1). For Fiske, Hodge, and Turner, people are assigned to certain areas based on their use of the space. Their reading of the beach appears to be mostly focused on metropolitan or more urbanised beaches; however, this is the only spatial analysis completed thus far on Australian beaches. These zones move from the urban-most part of the beach to the most natural: Zone 1 is the esplanade, featuring heavily human-built infrastructure. Zones 2 and 3 are both on the sand but still in the "central zone" – this is the place where most sunbaking activity happens. Zone 4, near the waterline, has a bit more activity – often walkers, but also sometimes children and parents. Zone 5 is in the water, the closest connection to the natural landscape. Fiske, Hodge, and Turner suggest there is a hierarchy to the usage of the space, where athleticism is usually more like to be found in Zones 3–5. Very young children, families, or those less comfortable with the landscape – such as those who are unable to swim – might be more likely found in Zones 1 and 2. It is worth noting that these zones are relevant for beaches designed for visitors: as such, these zoning conventions are not applicable to incredibly isolated beaches without any constructed amenities or access points. While there is nuance to these zones

Figure 12.1 Zones of the beach. This photograph is of Cottesloe Beach, in Perth (Western Australia). This image has been adapted to include Fiske, Hodge, and Turner zones (1987).

Source: Author

across the country, it is possible to use these zones as a methodological lens for the three specific regional beaches discussed in this chapter.

From a tourism perspective, these zones allow spatial considerations to be made in the development and management of attractions. As tourist spaces, beaches are linear in nature (Timothy 2011), bound by roads, carparks, and access points on one side, with the water on the other. Again, while there are specificities that challenge this generalisation (for example, a point), it is possible to read most Australian beaches in this way. Much like Fiske, Hodge, and Turner's (1987) zones, the beachscape directs how the space is enjoyed and where infrastructure, such as ancillary services and access points, is situated. Adopting this type of place-based approach enables a more holistic understanding of an activity, and people's engagement with it, within the context of its setting (or landscape) from two perspectives.

Findings

While there are distinctions between the three sculpture festivals discussed in this chapter, it is useful to undertake some comparative analysis to identify if there are significant trends in the way these festivals interact and engage with regional beach landscapes. Each case study considers brief contextual information about the artists, artworks, and festivals as identifiable, such as the numbers of artists showing work: their location – if they are from the region, or another state or country; visitor numbers; or other media information about the festival. This information is designed to provide an overview of each festival to contextualise the analysis of artworks and the festival in the second part of the case study.

Case study: SWELL Sculpture Festival (Gold Coast)

SWELL Sculpture Festival happens annually in September and is held at Currumbin Beach on the Gold Coast. The Gold Coast is near the very southern edge of Queensland, Australia, and is known to be a significant international tourist destination. Surfers Paradise is the hub of tourism activity for the region, hosts a number of key events throughout the year (Indy car racing event; schoolies week), and was also the home of the 2018 Commonwealth Games. Most notably, the beach landscape near Surfers Paradise is quite iconic because of the high-rise buildings lining the coast. Currumbin is a suburb south of Surfers Paradise and an area with stricter building regulation, which ensures a different visual profile along the beach.

2018 was the sixteenth year of SWELL after the festival began in 2003. And yet it is the youngest of the three case studies discussed in this chapter. Notably, as the only festival to run annually, there have been significantly more iterations of the festival than either Floating Land or Strand Ephemera. While the sculptural exhibition remains the main feature of the festival, there are a number of satellite components as well. These include workshops and masterclasses, as well as forums with invited keynote speakers.

The 2017 SWELL program opened with a welcome message from the Creative Director and Director/Curator, which included a statement that perhaps best captures the intentions of the festival: "There is strength in SWELL's temporary approach to public art. While its presence is short-lived, it leaves a lasting impression through the reverberations of the artists' voices and the echoes of memories and shared conversations" (SWELL Sculpture Festival 2017: 1). The curatorial policy, listed on the festival's website, is fairly generous in scope with a focus on the natural landscape (while maintaining awareness of safety and regulation). In particular, the policy encourages "large art forms or artworks that have a large footprint simply because the beach is a vast open space and lends itself to sculptures that are durable and built for permanent installation" (SWELL Sculpture Festival 2018).

In 2017, 51 artworks created by 51 different artists were exhibited as part of the festival. Of these, 28 were Queensland artists, a further 14 were national artists, and four were international. These numbers come from the programming material, in which each artist is identified with a location alongside their artwork entry. Of these artworks, at least three are recognisable as having

Sculptural coastlines 251

exhibited at other events, including *Strand Ephemera* and Sculpture by the Sea. From an artist's perspective, the transferability of work that occurs between festivals could be considered a useful opportunity. Unlike site-specific pieces that require significant reworking in new locations, many of the works exhibited in 2017's SWELL are not permanently installed and can be easily re-located to another similar beachscape in the future.

SWELL is a major event for the Currumbin region that attracts significant audience numbers each year. Considering the publicly available curatorial policy, with its focus on integration of works within the natural landscape and also the importance of scale, the works presented in 2017 were perhaps underwhelming in their size. Without speaking with the artists, it is impossible to know if this was a specific choice from the artists. However, in comparison to the significant and large-scale works presented in the more metropolitan Sculpture by the Sea, it was clear that the works included in *SWELL* are of smaller stature and therefore run the risk of being swamped by the sheer size of the linear landscape of the beach itself.

The works were curated in a linear fashion along the beach and up, reaching from what Fiske, Hodge, and Turner (1987) would consider Zone 3 (on the soft sand) into Zone 1 (the esplanade). The variety allowed for differences in accessibility for differing audience types. As the festival has been running for a long time, it is possible to presume the curators have expertise in working within this linear beach landscape and choose and place works accordingly. For instance, it is incredibly difficult to take prams onto the sand; as such, families are able to view the works on the sand from afar while also viewing some of the works more closely. Many of the works were free standing, a technique that makes the work transferable across festivals. Joy Heylen's *The Crab* was also included in Strand Ephemera, and yet in the SWELL setting, it found height and scale on the rock that provided a sense of significance to the work (see Figure 12.2).

Heylen's work was the winner of the major SWELL prize, the Neumann Family SWELL Sculpture Award, worth $15,000. It was one of the stronger works of the exhibition, and it is possible to consider this is in large part because of its scale. Another work that considered the importance of scale appropriately was *These Hands* by Michael Van Dam, which won the Bendigo Bank Tugun Artist Peer Award worth $1,000. These two works are strong examples of the significance of size when exhibiting on a long, vast space. The scale of the works suggest stronger engagement with the beach landscape – and an understanding of how these regional beaches border their regional centre. It is worth noting, for instance, that the Currumbin beach is starkly different from Surfers Paradise in which the beach is lined with skyscrapers.

The other distinguishing factor was the few works that incorporated elements of the site-specific location into their work, and others that were more transferable. As mentioned, *The Crab* was exhibited in a fixed location on the side of a rock face. However, the majority of the works were free standing, or indeed provided their own stand, as was the case with Phillip Piperides'

Figure 12.2 The Crab by Joy Heylen, exhibited at SWELL Sculpture Festival in 2017.
Source: Author

Conversations. This work depicted two figures in conversation, posed on a structure like the edge of a swimming pool.

Case study: Floating Land (Noosa)

Floating Land is a festival held biannually in Noosa since 2001 on the Sunshine Coast. In 2017, Floating Land was held along the Noosa River foreshore and into the Noosa Woods, a change from previous exhibitions on Lake Cootharaba. The festival usually runs in September through to October. Notably, in 2017, the budget announced for the festival was, for no publicly specified reason, significantly less than the 2015 offering (Gardiner 2017: para 2). The response to the 2017 festival was less enthusiastic than in previous years, and it is possible that the budget played a major part. As of 2019, renewed funding has been promised by Noosa Council to reinvigorate Floating Land.

In 2010, Susan Cochrane wrote about Floating Land and its role in tackling issues of climate change through the arts. She focused on the 2009 iteration of the festival, called Floating Land – Rising Seas, that specifically engaged with Pacific Islander artists to generate ephemeral artworks that challenged ideas around rising sea levels. This event was the first to take place at Lake Cootharaba. As Cochrane (2010: 93) states:

> Lake Cootharaba, located at the southern end of the Cooloola National Park and part of the Noosa Biosphere Reserve, was the setting for this exceptional environmental event. It was chosen because it is a significant feature of the Noosa Biosphere reserve with its many natural attributes, historical significance, capacity to provide a diversity of easily accessible sites for sculptural/performance works, close proximity to centres of population, and the enthusiasm of the Boreen Point community.

It is clear that this iteration of Floating Land had what Derrett (2003: 38–39) suggests are key success factors to festivals: a sense of community and sense of place. However, in 2017, Floating Land exhibited on the Noosa River and, as a result, may have lost some of that sense of community and place that was so apparent in Cochrane's discussions. While less than 20 kilometres apart, the identity of the Lake Cootharaba area is quite distinct from that of Noosa River. Lake Cootharaba is, obviously, a lake: although it still has a sandy shoreline, the lake water and surrounds are markedly different from the Noosa River area. For instance, the location of Floating Land on the Noosa River was much closer to the ocean (towards the mouth of the river) and also much closer to the busy tourist centre of Noosa and Main Beach. Notably, the 2019 festival, themed 'Point to Point' is scheduled to take place across both locations, "From the serene shores of Lake Cootharaba at Boreen Point to the rocky outcrops of Noosa National Park" (*Floating Land* 2018).

According to Floating Land's website, the aim is "to leave no mark on the environment but only to make an impression on the people who visit" (Noosa Regional Gallery 2017: para 1). The 2017 theme was 'Lost and Found' and encouraged audiences to "reconnect with the authenticity of nature through art" (Noosa Regional Gallery 2017). As in previous iterations, the importance of the environment and in the context of potential loss remained relevant.

Noosa Council (the organisers of the festival) opened an Expressions of Interest round for artists to submit proposals for commissioning. These were judged by an expert panel, and 15 proposals were selected. Of these, 11 were from Queensland, and the final one was from elsewhere in Australia. This is obviously a much lower number than SWELL Sculpture Festival, more locally focused, and immediately provides context to the scale of the exhibition overall.

Unlike the setting of previous festivals, there is no real beachscape on the Noosa River, and the artworks were instead exhibited amongst a forest area and therefore had the potential to be lost amidst the trees. This also challenges the very title of the festival – "Floating Land" – which speaks to the appearance of the artworks to be floating thanks to the shallow water in Lake Cootharaba. The loss of this impressive aesthetic in the 2017 festival highlights the importance of the landscape as a key and integral component of the exhibition's curation and appearance. When this identity of the location is lost, as appeared to be the case in 2017, the festival's artworks struggle to command attention. The 2017 festival appeared to have stepped away from some of the original intention of the festival; however, the emergence of the 'Point to Point' theme and the dual locations planned for the 2019 iteration suggests a major return to the more successful festivals of previous years.

Many of the works were too small in scope to really demand the audience attention. The artworks, as can be seen on the exhibition map, are in split locations – with the majority of works in the Noosa Woods and a few others in Noosaville along the main shore. This also differs from the linear curation of SWELL Sculpture Festival and provides less of an experience through the festival space. The lack of beachscape location for Floating Land makes it difficult to analyse the spatial zoning of the exhibition. Some of the works positioned in the Noosa Woods appeared to have been designed for viewing from the water, whereas others were more closely positioned to the pathways. As such, there is an unevenness to the experience for each artwork. This suggests a less successful curation of the exhibition that perhaps focused too closely on the individual works rather than the exhibition as a whole. Although more research needs to be considered to understand the motivations of artists and curators, it is expected in festival and exhibition curation that there is a thematic and/or aesthetic vision to the collected works as a whole. This speaks to the importance of the curator role.

Case study: Strand Ephemera (Townsville)

Strand Ephemera takes place in Townsville, in northern Queensland. It has a long history, beginning in 2001. According to their own reporting, they had "over 138,000 visitors" during the festival in 2015 (Townsville City Council 2018: para 4) and improved numbers of "155,000 visitors" in 2017 (Townsville City Council 2017: para 2). In 2017, the festival ran from 28 July until 6 August. After it finished, the local newspaper published an editorial suggesting there was enough momentum, enthusiasm, and success for the event to run annually instead of biannually (*Townsville Bulletin* 2017). It appears that Townsville's local council has prioritised Strand Ephemera as well as the Townsville Strand and beach as a necessary and significant part of its identity. This singular and continued presence of the festival on the Strand has enabled consistency in a way that appears to have been challenged in Noosa.

The festival invites artists to submit for consideration, and in 2017 those successful artists were granted a $5,000 Artist Fee and were eligible to compete for the major prize of $10,000. Alongside this, there were also key commissioned works. The curatorial policy is somewhat obscure, with no clear 'theme' identified. However, like both SWELL Sculpture Festival and Floating Land, the emphasis on temporary, ephemeral works has continued to play a role in the festival's history: "The focus on works being 'ephemeral' for the short-lived exhibition of around ten days encouraged artists to use inexpensive materials" (Townsville City Council 2018: para 2). This focus on the ephemeral speaks to the temporal nature of the beach – subject to the changing formations of sand as tides and winds erode and shift the site, as well as the danger of non-ephemeral material such as plastic packaging and straws. Many works – at Strand Ephemera and beyond – embrace these materials purposively to highlight the damage of these long-lasting, non-eroding materials.

In 2017, Strand Ephemera included 31 works in total. Of these, 25 were competing in the major prizes, and six were commissioned or non-competing works. There were 31 different artists or pairs/groups of artists. The majority of the artists were Queenslanders (20), with nine national and a final three international artists. The artworks themselves were exhibited along the Strand or major esplanade/foreshore location in Townsville across approximately 2.2 kilometres. Most of the works in this exhibition hug the esplanade and, as such, can be considered sticking closely to Zone 1 and 2 of the beachscape. The works of scale are arguably the most successful. For example, the work *Ancyent Marinere . . . Are those her sails?* by Marion Gaemers and Lynnette Griffiths are two large sails made out of ghost net, rope, and beach rubbish. The sails were dominant in their position along the esplanade, and the work was the winner of the People's Choice Award (Toll 2017).

The major award winner was Erica Grey's *Visceral Bodies*, a work intended to represent the colour of the deep ocean that is unusually hidden. The work appears strongly site-specific, relying on the irregular rocks that form its platform. This festival also included Heylen's *The Crab*, although this time in a different location right at the jetty on the foreshore. In this first showing, *The Crab* is still striking, yet not reliant on any landscape and instead is installed directly onto the grass. Of course, Heylen won the major prize at SWELL Sculpture Festival, when her work was positioned on the rocks. Despite the differences in location, the sculpture was powerfully commanding of the space. Interestingly, the extra height of the sculpture at SWELL Sculpture Festival (as seen in Figure 12.2) also helped elevate the sense of scale of the work and highlighted how the landscape could assist in scaffolding significance in the piece.

Discussion

From this analysis, it is possible to identify two main concepts that influence the overall impression of these festivals within the landscape: the importance of scale in the curation of the artworks, and the engagement of the festival within the beachscape.

It is clear that with a landscape as large, open, and linear as an Australian beach, the importance of scale when considering and curating sculptural works is incredibly important. This was apparent in the curatorial policies, through the analysis of the artworks, and also in the works that won major prizes at the festivals. When comparing to the premier national festival, Sculpture by the Sea, it is clear that scale is necessary to command attention in the landscape. While Heylen's *The Crab* (SWELL, Strand Ephemera) and Gaemers and Griffiths' *Ancyent Marinere . . . Are those her sails?* engaged with scale through their commanding and distinctive presence within the landscape, many of the works were overwhelmed by the vastness of the beach. It is worth noting here that SWELL Sculpture Festival included an inside gallery for small works, and this distinction for inside and outside works speaks to curatorial approaches that are aware of the limitations of smaller works in large, wide beach landscapes. The size of the sculptures is also linked with the spatial curation of the works within the landscape as well.

Both SWELL and Strand Ephemera strongly utilise the linear geography of the beachscape and curate along the 'strand' or esplanade components to capitalise on the walkthrough foot traffic in the region. They also access and activate Zones 1–3 of the beach successfully, if perhaps accidentally, allowing viewers to move between the accessible esplanade and the soft sand. In comparison, Floating Land in Noosa moved sites in the most recent iteration, and it is clear that this has had a detrimental effect on the aesthetic curation and interpretation of the works. The requirement for viewers to move between locations, and the way the artworks can be diminished by the forest landscape, all detract from the viewing experience. The linear homogeneity of the beachscape and the familiarity of its experience allow for transferability of these site-specific works and the translation of these works elsewhere. Sometimes, as is the case with Heylen's *The Crab*, this works to the sculpture's advantage, as the shift in location (from Townsville to Currumbin) brings new significance to the work.

Framing this research within a joint arts and tourism lens has highlighted the significance of the landscape, or beachscape, as an important contributor to the meaning-making of arts and sculpture festivals. In tourism terms, the landscape has a fundamental role in creating immersive and meaningful experiences (Thompson et al. 2016). The case studies have demonstrated that the role of the landscape is two-fold, as exemplified by *The Crab* sculpture. Not only does the landscape (beachscape) provide a broader context that enhances the meaning of the artworks, but the artworks provide a unique medium in which participants create new meaning from the landscape as they experience and appreciate it in a new way. Engaging with the festival and its artworks becomes a way of interpreting the surrounding landscape (beachscape), allowing participants to derive a greater sense of meaning from, and connection to, the landscape. This synergy reflects the distinct yet closely related concepts of place and space, whereby the beachscape provides a place in which to create more meaning spaces through the artworks and exhibits and, in tourism terms, providing a more meaningful and memorable experience for festival participants.

This chapter examined how the landscape (beachscape) is used to encourage participants' engagement with the artworks at three sculpture festivals based in regional Queensland: Currumbin's SWELL Sculpture Festival, Noosa's Floating Land festival, and Townsville's Strand Ephemera festival. Framed within a lens that considered arts and tourism perspectives, the landscape was found to be a significant contributor to the meaning-making derived from both the artworks and beachscape. The three case studies included in this chapter are, of course, not representative of a national or international reading of public art festivals on the beach. While the case studies provide valuable insights into the spatial considerations that influence the meaning-making of the beachscape as a site, there may be other factors that constrain the effectiveness of the landscape in enabling meaning-making. As discussed, a change in the site for Floating Land has had a negative impact on how meaning was drawn from the artworks within the context of a disrupted landscape, and it can be suggested other factors (such as budgeting and resourcing) played a role in this change. Therefore, future research is suggested to examine the administrative and financial infrastructure that not only determine if festivals will be held but, more importantly, shape decision-making about the size, scale, and location. Based on the methodological approach adopted in this chapter, these findings suggest there is room for further exploration in this under-represented field between tourism and the arts and the potential synergies and tensions encountered from leveraging regional arts and tourism priorities in the regions.

References

Buell, L. 2008. "Place, from the Environmental Education." Pp. 665–691 in *Modern Criticism and Theory: A Reader*, edited by Lodge, D., and Wood, N. Harlow, UK: Pearson Education Limited.

Cochrane, S. 2010. "Floating Land – Rising Sea: Arts and Minds on Climate Change." *LiNQ* 37(1): 93–103 (https://journals.jcu.edu.au/linq/article/view/3104/3058).

Derrett, R. 2003. "Festivals & Regional Destinations: How Festivals Demonstrate a Sense of Community & Place." *Rural Society* 13(1): 35–53 (https://doi.org/10.5172/rsj.351.13.1.35).

Derrett, R. 2005. "Why Do Regional Community Cultural Festivals Survive?" Pp. 1–23 in *The Impacts of Events: Triple Bottom Line Evaluation and Event Legacies: Third International Event Management Conference*, University of Technology Sydney, Sydney, New South Wales, July 13–15, 2005 (https://epubs.scu.edu.au/tourism_pubs/298/).

Dutton, G. 1985. *Sun, Sea, Surf and Sand: The Myth of the Beach*. Melbourne: Oxford University Press.

Ellison, E. 2014. 'On the Beach: Exploring the Complex Egalitarianism of the Australian Beach." Pp. 221–236 in *Navigating Cultural Spaces: Maritime Places*, edited by Horatschek, A., Rosenberg, Y., and Schaebler, D. Amsterdam, Netherlands: Rodopi.

Ellison, E., and Hawkes, L. 2016. "The Recurring Cure: The Australian Beachspace as a Healthy Tourist Destination." *Borderlands E-journal: New Spaces in the Humanities* 15(1): 1–20 (www.borderlands.net.au/vol15no1_2016/ellisonhawkes_beachspace.pdf).

Fiske, J., Hodge, B., and Turner, G. 1987. *Myths of Oz: Reading Australian Popular Culture*. Sydney, New South Wales: Allen & Unwin.

Floating Land. 2018. "SITE ANNOUNCEMENT: Floating Land: Point to Point." *Facebook*. November 29, 2018. Retrieved November 29, 2018 (www.facebook.com/FloatingLand2019/photos/a.465510863515491/2120003784732849).

Game, A. 1990. "Nation and Identity: Bondi." *New Formations* (11): 105–120.

Gardiner, P. 2017. "Plans Coming Together for Floating Land Festival." *Noosa News*. March 17, 2017. Retrieved July 18, 2018 (www.noosanews.com.au/news/floating-ideas-to-keep-us-creative/3155732/).

Kaye, N. 2000. *Site-Specific Art*. Abingdon, OX: Routledge.

Lette, K., and Carey, G. 1979. *Puberty Blues*. Sydney: Picador.

Noosa Regional Gallery. 2017. "Floating Land." Retrieved July 18, 2018 (www.noosa regionalgallery.com.au/floatingland).

Ryan, L., and Picken, F. 2017. "'Too Much to Look At – Sea, Seagulls, Art!': The Experiential Appeal of Art Exhibitions in Public Leisure Spaces." *Critical Tourism Studies Proceedings* (2017): 1: Article 138 (http://digitalcommons.library.tru.ca/cts-proceedings/vol2017/iss1/138).

SWELL Sculpture Festival. 2017. *Currumbin Beach, Gold Coast: SWELL Sculpture Festival*. Festival program.

SWELL Sculpture Festival. 2018. "*SWELL Sculpture Festival: People – Art – Place*." Retrieved July 26, 2018 (www.swellsculpture.com.au/).

Thompson, M., Prideaux, B., McShane, C., Dale, A., Turnour, J., and Atkinson, M. 2016. "Tourism Development in Agricultural Landscapes: The Case of the Atherton Tablelands, Australia." *Landscape Research* 41(7): 730–743 (doi:10.1080/01426397.2016.1174839).

Timothy, D. J. 2011. *Cultural Heritage and Tourism: An Introduction*. New York, USA: Channel View Publications.

Toll, N. 2017. "Ephemeral Artists Win People's Vote." *HUXLEY* (blog). August 10, 2017. Retrieved September 4, 2018 (http://huxley.press/2017/08/10/ephemeral-artists-win-peoples-vote/).

Townsville Bulletin. 2017. "Ephemera Can Stand Alone as Annual Event." *Townsville Bulletin*. August 7, 2017. Retrieved September 4, 2018 (www.townsvillebulletin.com.au/news/opinion/ephemera-can-stand-alone-as-annual-event/news-story/c8abae0832d004ffa03 18db4e77f89f7).

Townsville City Council. 2017. "Strand Ephemera 2017 Hailed an Overwhelming Success." (www.townsville.qld.gov.au/about-council/news-and-publications/media-releases/2017/august/strand-ephemera-2017-hailed-an-overwhelming-success, accessed August 4, 2018)).

Townsville City Council. 2018. "Strand Ephemera." Retrieved September 4, 2018 (www.townsville.qld.gov.au/facilities-and-recreation/theatres-and-galleries/strand-ephemera).

Urry, J. 1990. *The Tourist Gaze: Leisure and Travel in Contemporary Societies*. London: Sage.

Urry, J. 2002. *The Tourist Gaze* (2nd ed.). London: Sage.

Walter, E. V. 1988. *Placeways: A Theory of the Human Environment*. Chapel Hill, NC and London: University of North Carolina Press.

13 One piece blokes

On being a performing musician in regional Queensland

Andy Bennett, David Cashman and Natalie Lewandowski

Introduction

In summer 2016, Author David Cashman found himself recovering from the heat in a bar in Longreach in central western Queensland talking with the publican about music. Live music was "brilliant," said the publican. He'd have it every night if he could, it increased the bar takings that much. However, Longreach ran to cattle and sheep more than music, and he simply couldn't find the musicians. Those he could find he described as:

> just one piece blokes, you know, they're not going to blast the joint to pieces, which is good. It's just that sort of background music sort of stuff that play all the old classics and that sort of stuff which is what people like out in the bush, well, anyone likes, I think, so they're going to relate to it.

Such comments about the musicians and live music in regional areas are fascinating. However, there is little context to understand them. We know more about the urban music scenes such as those of Sydney, Melbourne, Brisbane, or Perth (see, for example, Homan 2000; Stratton 2008). Even satellite cities such as Wollongong, Lismore, and Newcastle have attracted their fair share of research (Gallan 2012; Threadgold 2018). But get into the real country, and it is often an open plain, void of both vegetation and research into popular music. And yet there are real questions that scholars cannot answer from the cosy confines of Newtown, St Kilda, or Fortitude Valley.

The creative industries in regional areas operate differently to those in urban areas. This point has been variously made, notably by Steven Threadgold (2018), who notes that regional areas are often characterised by small, more tightly knit networks of production and dissemination. In the case of music, production is also linked to performance, which is reliant upon the availability of hard and soft infrastructures (Stahl 2004) suited to this purpose. And in regional areas, the availability of such infrastructures is typically less evenly distributed. Thus, instead of having multiple venues scattered at small distances, a gig in the next town may be a four-hour drive. Musicians need to be more versatile, more flexible, and more willing to work as a solo act (hence the aforementioned publican's reference to "one-piece blokes"). However, little is known about music scenes in these areas because of the underrepresentation of this topic in the literature. We base this chapter on the results of an eight-month research project that interviewed musicians, venue owners, and music businesses in the Central Queensland area of Australia. It finds that there are some significant difficulties associated with being a performing musician in a regional area. Regional musicians travel more, perform for lower fees, and are more reliant on portfolio careers and solo performance than musicians in urban areas. They are also more vulnerable to an economic downturn in the area, such as the decline in the mining boom in Central Queensland. However, they may gig more regularly and with less competition than their urban counterparts. Their performances are more cost effective for pub owners than bringing in musicians from Brisbane to perform in the regions. In remote areas, a skilful musician is a valued commodity for the area. This chapter thus provides important insights regarding the socio-economic and spatial challenges confronting music scenes, and creative industries, in remote and regional areas.

A flourishing music industry is an indicator of a flourishing society. Music is central to every human society (Titon 2009: 2). Its continued flourishing within a modern commercial setting is socially and culturally important to a healthy society. While urban music scenes have issues – notably related to noise restrictions (Green and Bennett 2018), lockout laws (Homan 2017), and low wages for gigging musicians (Homan 2008) – because of a stronger infrastructure and a large and more stable audience, musicians in urban areas often find it easier to get gigs. Despite the globalising impact of the Internet, musicians in regional areas find it harder to make music than their urban counterparts. Because of the rise of social media and digital distribution, musicians have few physical constraints on their place of residence. Musicians with technical knowledge can record as easily in Mackay, Winton, or Longreach as they can in Sydney or Melbourne. On the other hand, the need for access to markets of consumers of live performances – a significant manner in which many musicians earn their living – requires them to embed themselves within a "scene." Because of lower populations in regional areas, performance opportunities are fewer. Along with that, talented musicians with whom to collaborate may be fewer. Rural musicians that wish to perform regularly have four options: a portfolio career where music may take a secondary role to earning a living (Bartleet et al. 2019), lots of travel and touring (Bennett 2010), embedding in a tourist destination such as Airlie Beach or Cairns (Gibson and Connell 2003), or relocation to an urban centre (Gibson 2008).

Music "scenes" are music-economic, geographical, and social phenomena. As musical entities, they provide employment to musicians and associated music industry workers, generate wealth, and create cultural "buzz" (Oakes and Warnaby 2011). The Live Music Office (2015) found that in 2014, live music contributed $15.7 billion to the national economy and employed 65,000 people. However, economic contribution tells only part of the story. Music, along with many arts, provides vitality to an urban centre. It also encourages a sense of community, an important aspect for regional towns. Rachel Healey, co-director of the Adelaide Festival, notes: "Among its many attributes, live music events build communities and social connections; provide economic value, employment and career paths; and help create vibrancy, buzz and atmosphere in a precinct" (Healy cited in Live Music Office 2015: 5). These attributes are even more important in economically depressed townships. As recent research has illustrated, going to see a live band at a local pub can be an important source of community connection in regional areas (see Bennett et al. 2018). Given the "value-add" role played by the local venue in regional locations, this suggests live music is at least one key driver for a strategy of ramping up local networks of cultural production. Given that culture is regarded as the "fourth pillar" of sustainable development (Hawkes 2001; Nurse 2006; Soini and Birkeland 2014), if rural areas want to develop sustainable and progressive development, they need to consider how to encourage and support the development of creative industries within regional areas.

This chapter discusses the musicians and music within the regional area of Central Queensland, Australia: how they generate a sustainable career, how they regard their music, and why they live in a regional area. We draw data from grounded theory analysis of forty-two interviews undertaken with musicians and industry personnel from the areas of Mackay and Rockhampton undertaken in 2015 and 2016. We posit that music scenes in this area contain features that are, to a greater or lesser extent, common in regional and remote areas around Australia.

Music and musicians in Central Queensland

Central Queensland might not be the first place that comes to mind when considering the Australian music industry. To be honest, it probably fails to make it into the top ten. If people think of the Queensland music industry at all, they will likely think of Brisbane's Fortitude Valley or maybe the party town of Cairns. Yet, this is a significant region in terms of its geographical size. Central Queensland is around the size of Austria, but with a population of 299,138 (3.4% of the Australian population). It is a region of mid-size towns spread hundreds of kilometres apart, of canefields and cattle; from Gladstone in the south to Airlie Beach in the north and west to the mining fields and beyond. It produces beef and sugar, mines for coal in the west, and in the extreme north, gets into the tourism scene of Far North Queensland. The area has produced well-known musicians. Country music star Graeme Connors comes from Mackay, as does young up-and-comer Tia Gostelow. Rock band Busby Marou hails from Rockhampton. Connors and Busby Marou are resident in the north, achieving their success through extensive touring. For many years, Mackay has had a traditional jazz program at CQUniversity, which is badged as "jazz and popular," but which does not engage strongly with industry. The regional music scenes of Central Queensland cater in most of the area to residents (temporary or otherwise) and to tourists in the north.

It is possible to earn a living from the music industry in regional central Queensland, as the success of Busby Marou, Tia Gostelow, and Graeme Connors demonstrates. However, being a performing musician in regional areas requires a different set of skills and different survival processes. Performers need to tour more. If they are not touring, for family or other reasons, they need a portfolio career or a day job in order to supplement their income and earn a living wage. The vast majority of performances in regional central Queensland occur on a Friday or Saturday night, and it is difficult to generate a survival income from two performances a week. Live music in this area places greater emphasis on covers rather than the creation of original and newly composed songs. Across the music industry, the accessibility of cover songs increases the profitability and lessens the risks of live performance. The process of boom and bust common in rural areas thus causes fluctuations in populations (and thus audiences), performance opportunities, choice of repertoire, and the sustained viability of venues.

Musicians choose to live in regional central Queensland for a variety of reasons. These include a perceived better, or more relaxed, lifestyle; family ties; opportunities for home ownership; and security. One now-established artist noted:

> We came back to Gladstone to find some secure work because we wanted to have a family and try and buy a home [. . .] I've always had ambitions to be a musician and, you know, pay the bills with it and then live that lifestyle. On the other hand, I've got commitments and there's other things that I want as well which are, you know, a secure family life for my children. And you know, for so long I've been told that it's one or the other, you cannot have both. And I guess right now I'm in the thick of it and learning what the reality of it is. And you know, for me, touch wood, so far so good. Things are moving forward and progressing.

Another observed:

> I've got family support, mine and my wife's parents are both here and I'm not tempted [to move to the city] one bit. Unless [my wife] actually said, "I've had enough I'm going," I'd go, "Right, I'm moving down south." But I mean I love it here purely because of the school system and our families are here. And because I'm travelling so much, I said, we could go and pick a place in Australia, we can live there. And you're going to have no support, we're not going to be able to dump the kids at the in-laws, if we want to go out on a bender.

Both these musicians were making a living from music while resident in regional central Queensland despite the perceived lack of opportunities. One informant noted that "It is possible [to earn a living as a musician in Central Queensland] but you really need to be open to touring or teaching, facilitating workshops and masterclasses to supplement your income". Another advised "Play gigs, play lots of them, play any gig you can get and don't worry about the money."

However, musicians also describe frustration with regional and rural scenes. Migration of talented performers from regional areas to the cities leaves fewer skilled musicians in the regions with whom to partner. Musicians describe rural areas as "a testing ground for many of the large acts just to go out and get some experience as they go through" in a form of artistic missionary work. Others describe migration of talented up-and-coming musicians to southern urban areas with their perceived greater opportunities.

Regional areas also have limited opportunities for relevant education. Educational opportunities in music are limited in Queensland to the extreme north and the south-eastern corner. The single major music program in regional Central Queensland is the jazz-focussed Bachelor of Music at Central Queensland University, which emphasises performance ability but places little emphasis on business aspects of the industry or on music technology. Further, distance education courses in popular and commercial music are expensive (such as the Berklee online courses) or unfocussed. One musician noted:

> we need a facility where we can actually study this music and be at the forefront of the music technology industry. There's so many musicians in this region and it's such a positive influence on so many peoples' lives, I don't understand why it hasn't been invested in earlier. There's lots of money actually going towards sports but as far as sort of providing a . . . I don't know, a base and an education for people that are passionate about music. It gives them an avenue to be successful.

This lack of technical and business education results in musicians that are not industry-ready. Few of the musicians interviewed, for example, have a web presence outside a Facebook page or a SoundCloud account. One musician noted:

> by our nature, creatives aren't necessarily that organised or au fait with the business side of things. So maybe partnering with someone who is or, you know, accessing . . . working together in different areas. So the musicians might have someone who helps them organise promoting themselves.

The Queensland educational system encourages music by their in-schools music program, and this extends to the regions whereby students attend instrumental lessons in primary school. However, this does not include industry education. Greater educational opportunities in music business and music technology is necessary in regional areas, whether delivered in person on TAFE or university campuses or via distance education.

Music in regional areas is covers-driven rather than derived from originals. In the wider popular music discourse, the creation and performance of original music is regarded as more authentic and real than covers. One artist noted that "originals are far more accepted in urban areas, whereas it really is very cover-driven here." Solis asserts that popular music:

> allows musicians the opportunity to produce work that is a direct expression of their true selves as individuals in a world that is otherwise alienating. In rock, musical authorship has come to represent self-authorship, the creation of authentic works as a symbol of the presence of an authentic subject.
>
> (Solis 2010: 301)

This belief in the primacy and authenticity of originals can be observed in regional Queensland. Musicians wish to perform and write original music; however, due to a perception among venue owners regarding audience familiarity with cover versions, covers are more commonly performed by local musicians and often mandated by venues as a conduction of securing a gig. One performer noted that he

> made a decision back then, it was either go left and playing all my original music, write original music, create a band, or go right, play covers, get paid for what we do accordingly and we get the regular work.

This is regarded as an economic necessity rather than an ideal state of affairs. A local booker noted that many acts play

> a couple of originals in amongst the cover things, which is the way to do it [. . .] it's coming together really well as far as original music, you know, we're starting to make headway with it, you know, and which is great to see. And we started doing stuff at the Glenmore Tavern with no covers allowed night and we were doing that.

Another musician noted that "you wouldn't make as much money [playing originals]; you probably wouldn't survive as much. It's just the culture where you go to the pub you want to hear." The perception is that musicians will not survive without performing covers.

This is not to imply that originals are not written. Many interviewed musicians write and perform originals. Sometimes these are generic songs of life and love that could emerge from any geographic region; however, regularly songs address rural issues. Busby Marou's 2017 "Living in a Town" discusses the experience of living in a rural town in economic decline, an experience familiar to many Central Queenslanders. Graeme Connors' "These Uncertain Times" discusses a similar concept. Busby Marou's "Paint This Land" talks of the experience of long road trips. Lloyd Saunders' video for "Head in the Clouds" uses Central Queensland imagery. Rural topics sit alongside universal themes in original music in regional central Queensland. As this account illustrates then, even while there is a strong market for covers artists in Central Queensland, like other places, regions produce original artists whose songs relate closely to the local physical and cultural environment and personal experience of having grown up in or relocated to the area. This provides further evidence of how, even in a time where much is increasingly made of the connections between music scenes due to trans-local and virtual (that is, digital connections) (see Peterson and Bennett 2004), music also remains a strong barometer of a local sense of place and local identity among musicians and their audiences.

Regional areas often exist in a cycle of boom and bust. Hajkowicz, Heyenga and Moffat (2011) observe the positive benefits of mining on regional areas such as Central Queensland; however, regional and remote areas are also at a disadvantage compared to urban areas (Bird et al. 2002) and can suffer from the "boomtown" cycle (Brown, Dorins and Krannich 2005). Mackay and, to an extent, Rockhampton, have been beneficiaries of the Australian mining boom but also have their own traditional industries, respectively sugar and beef. The decline in mining has had a significant impact on the number and size of music performances. One performer noted how it was once possible to

> be able to see six or seven live bands on any Friday night, but now that's dropped. All the pubs have dropped back to duos and solos with drum machines to cut back on costs. The days of five and six piece bands are gone.

Musicians observed that this was at least partially due to transient populations. A musician observed that Mackay had "gone down heaps. A lot of people just packed up and left. And unfortunately, it's the younger ones go with their families." This leads to problems with not only the music industry but also real estate and emptying communities. If the local pub is empty on the weekend, publicans are less likely to employ musicians.

However there seems to be a divide between regional urban centres and remote centres. One interviewed publican in a particularly decimated mining town two hours from Mackay noted: "We love local music here. We'll have it two, three times a week. Since the miners left, it's replaced our [topless barmaid] nights." Go another hour out to Winton, and one pub brought in a musician, accommodated, fed, and paid her for the winter tourist season. Combined with the comment of the Longreach publican, this evidence suggests that in small remote towns there is a dearth of musicians, whereas in regional urban areas such as Mackay, there is a dearth of musical opportunities.

To support themselves, many Central Queensland towns are attempting to promote themselves as tourist destinations, which has potential benefits for musicians. However, an oversupply of tourist destinations can cause problems, most obviously that these are then set in competition with each other for a share in the seasonal and relatively finite tourist market. Moreover, different places have different levels of tourist appeal. Thus, while Cairns is on the doorstep of the Great Barrier Reef, it is not accessible from towns in Central Queensland. Additionally, Mackay also suffers from a perception of being a mining town with an extremely politically conservative population. Consequently, the main street of Mackay is often deserted at 5 pm on a weeknight.

On the weekend, live music events occur at venues such as Maria's Donkey or the Seabreeze Tavern, but, as Bennett (2010) notes, rural musicians cannot make a living off one or two gigs a week.

Festivals and touring are regarded by musicians as staples of regional musicians and music industries (Bennett, Cashman and Lewandowski 2018). There are many opportunities to perform at the swath of annual festivals in regional central Queensland including Wintermoon (at Callum, north of Mackay), the Airlie Beach Festival of Music (Airlie Beach), the Palm Creek Folk Festival (north of Mackay), the Rockhampton River Festival (Rockhampton), the Village Festival (Yeppoon), the Grass is Greener (Mackay), and Mushroom Valley (Yalboroo, North West of Mackay). These typically volunteer-run festivals provide employment to local and touring musicians. Some musicians, such as the Appalachian music band Hillbilly Goats, make a living as itinerant musicians performing at music festivals all over the country. Respondents noted that, while annual festivals cannot replace regular work for musicians resident in a particular rural area, such performances are useful in two ways. First, they can add to the profile of musicians, bringing their work to the notice of audiences to whom they may not have been exposed. Second, between performance fees and merchandise, festivals can add a much-needed boost to the coffers of musicians. Because of this, festivals are often sought after by musicians. The organiser of the Airlie Beach Festival of Music describes musician interest in the festival:

> It was just going to be about 50 bands then it kept growing and growing then it got to 60 and then 65. And I just had . . . because people were, you know, ringing up, "Can we get on? Can we get on?" And, "Yeah, right, right, right." Got to 65 and I said, "That's enough, we cannot have any more bands, going to be too expensive." Then I went to Tamworth, sourced a number of bands down there and then I said yes to four more. So I said, "69, right, perfect number for Airlie Beach." Then I had a meeting with the tourism and they said, "Look, we don't want the number 69 for Airlie Beach Park, 74 bands and you can use our logo on everything, we'll be part of a sponsor." And I said, "Well, that's our number 74," so yeah.

Central Queensland musicians regard touring positively but acknowledge that it has had its own set of problems. An active touring circuit existed until the early 1990s but seems to have fallen by the wayside. Despite that, musicians still tour and respondents commented favourably on their experience of touring. One artist noted that

> Building a career as a musician doesn't necessarily have to mean that you're somewhere where there is a lot of gigs. Like you don't necessarily have to play a lot of gigs in your local area to become successful [. . .] a lot of the bands and stuff that do really well make sure they do a lot of touring, make themselves known around a few areas. So it doesn't matter where you're from.

However, touring comes with inherent issues. In remote areas, the distances between towns are greater, increasing the cost of moving from one town to another. Accommodation in remote or tourist areas can be expensive and is paid for by the venue. A publican in western central Queensland noted:

> Look, I believe, live music is something that out here we are starved of in country areas. And you do, you know, as a hotel owner, if you can pull it off it's good [. . .] but the added costs is, you know, your accommodation, which as you know, you can be paying 110 to a 100. So that's onto the cost and the travel, their meals, their drinks. So there's a lot of little added costs, there's just not, you know, which puts another five hundred on coming out here.

However, it is also perceived as worthwhile. One publican in far western Queensland employed and accommodated a saxophonist to play every night for two months during the high season. Another publican noted that live music added so much to the bar takings, he would have musicians several times a week if he could but find the players.

Implications

The live music industry exists and, to an extent, thrives in regional central Queensland. There are audiences and musicians earning a living from music. High-profile acts continue to emerge from the area. However, rural music scenes are different to urban music scenes in several respects: lack of industry knowledge, smaller audiences, and difficult logistics. Because of a lack of a business approach to the music industry, many musicians are unsure how to promote themselves. The state government music organisation, QMusic, is running workshops in rural areas, but this is yet to have a large impact. None of our informants mentioned attending these workshops. Audiences are smaller than in urban areas, more widely spaced, and more likely to demand covers over originals, limiting opportunities for the creation and performance of originals. The vast distances involved can make touring less profitable and musicians less willing to travel despite perceptions in country towns that it is financially and socially rewarding to support live music. The result is a strong pull to the cities. Two of the largest resident acts, Graeme Connors and Busby Marou, undertake large amounts of touring; many other musicians migrate to urban areas. Those who remain establish a portfolio career where they work a day job, or several day jobs, to play music at night.

While QMusic in Queensland (like WAM in Western Australia) has committed to regional music, similar organisations in other states are yet to embrace regional music with the same passion. There is a perception that regional music (as was pointed out to us recently) consists primarily of musicians playing in tourist areas to a pack of drunks and is not music industry. We strongly refute this and assert that musicians playing to audiences anywhere falls under the broad rubric of music industry activity. The regions are not "uncultured" and are worthy of the same attention, governmental and industry support, policy direction, and academic research as urban areas. Music scenes exist anywhere there are people, and the popular music industry exists anywhere there are commercial consumers and producers of music. This is as true of regional scenes as much as of urban scenes.

References

Bartleet, B., Ballico, C., Bennett, R., Draper, P., Tomlinson, V., and Harrison, S. 2019. "Building Sustainable Portfolio Careers in Music: Insights and Implications for Higher Education." *Music Education Research* 21(3): 1–13 (doi:10.1080/14613808.2019.1598348).

Bennett, A., Cashman, D., and Lewandowski, N. 2018. "'Twice the Size of Texas': Assessing the Importance of Regional Popular Music Scenes – A Case Study of Regional Queensland." *Popular Music & Society* 42(5): 561–575. (doi:10.1080/03007766.2018.1521714).

Bennett, D. 2010. "State of Play: Live Original Music Venues in Western Australia." *Perfect Beat* 11(1): 49–66 (doi:10.1558/prbt.v11i1.49).

Bird, K., Hulme, D., Moore, K., and Shepherd, A. 2002. Chronic Poverty and Remote Rural Areas. *Rural Sociology* 70(1): 28–49. (doi:10.1526/0036011053294673).

Brown, R. B., Dorins, S. F., and Krannich, R. S. 2005. "The Boom–Bust–Recovery Cycle: Dynamics of Change in Community Satisfaction and Social Integration in Delta, Utah." *Rural Sociology* 70(1): 28–49 (doi:10.1526/0036011053294673).

Gallan, B. 2012. "Gatekeeping Night Spaces: The Role of Booking Agents in Creating 'Local' Live Music Venues and Scenes." *Australian Geographer* 43(1): 35–50 (doi:10.1080/00049182.2012.649518).

Gibson, C. 2008. "Youthful Creativity in Regional Australia: Panacea for Unemployment and Out-Migration?" *Geographical Research* 46(2): 183–195 (doi:10.1111/j.1745-5871.2008.00509.x).

Gibson, C., and Connell, J. 2003. "'Bongo Fury': Tourism, Music and Cultural Economy at Byron Bay, Australia." *Tijdschrift Voor Economische En Sociale Geografie* 94(2): 164–187 (doi:10.1111/1467–9663.00247).

Green, B., and Bennett, A. 2018. "Gateways and Corridors: Spatial Challenges and Opportunities for Live Music on the Gold Coast." *City, Culture and Society* 17: 20–25. (doi:10.1016/j.ccs.2018.08.003).

Hajkowicz, S. A., Heyenga, S., and Moffat, K. 2011. "The Relationship Between Mining and Socio-economic Wellbeing in Australia's Regions." *Resources Policy* 36(1): 30–38 (doi:10.1016/j.resourpol.2010.08.007).

Hawkes, J. 2001. "The Fourth Pillar of Sustainability: Culture's Essential Role in Public Planning." *Common Ground* 80 (doi:uofrrheesHN28.H382001).

Homan, S. 2000. "Losing the Local: Sydney and the Oz Rock Tradition." *Popular Music* 19(1): 31–49.

Homan, S. 2008. "A Portrait of the Politician as a Young Pub Rocker: Live Music Venue Reform in Australia." *Popular Music* 27(2): 243–256 (doi:10.1017/S0261143008004030).

Homan, S. 2017. "'Lockout' Laws or 'Rock Out' Laws? Governing Sydney's Night-time Economy and Implications for the 'Music City.'" *International Journal of Cultural Policy* 25(4): 500–514 (doi:10.1080/10286632.2017.1317760).

Live Music Office. 2015. *The Economic & Cultural Value of Live Music*. Sydney.

Nurse, K. 2006. "Culture as the Fourth Pillar of Sustainable Development." *Small States: Economic Review and Basic Statistics* 11: 28–40. London (doi:10.1177/026327690007002004).

Oakes, S., and Warnaby, G. 2011. "Conceptualizing the Management and Consumption of Live Music in Urban Space." *Marketing Theory* 11(4): 405–418 (doi:10.1177/147059 3111418798).

Peterson, R. A., and Bennett, A. 2004. "Introducing Music Scenes." Pp. 1–15 in *Music Scenes: Local, Trans-local and Virtual*, edited by Bennett, A., and Peterson, R. A. Nashville, TN: Vanderbilt University Press.

Soini, K., and Birkeland, I. 2014. "Exploring the Scientific Discourse on Cultural Sustainability." *Geoforum* 51. January: 213–223 (doi:10.1016/j.geoforum.2013.12.001).

Solis, G. 2010. "I Did It My Way: Rock and the Logic of Covers." *Popular Music and Society* 33(3): 297–318 (doi:10.1080/03007760903523351).

Stahl, G. 2004. "'It's Like Canada Reduced': Setting the Scene in Montreal." pp. 51–64 in *After Subculture* edited by Bennett, A., and Kahn-Harris, K. London: Macmillan (doi:10.1007/978-0-230-21467-5_4).

Stratton, J. 2008. "The Difference of Perth Music: A Scene in Cultural and Historical Context." *Continuum: Journal of Media and Cultural Studies* 22(5): 613–622.

Threadgold, S. 2018. "Creativity, Precarity and Illusion: DIY Cultures and 'Choosing Poverty.'" *Cultural Sociology* 12(2): 156–173.

Titon, J. T. 2009. "The Music-Culture as a World of Music." Pp. 1–33 in *Worlds of Music* (5th ed.), edited by Titon, J. T. Belmont: Shirmer.

14 Positive deviance

Stories of regional social innovations from the *Big Stories, Small Towns* project

Martin Potter

Introduction

Big Stories, Small Towns is a collaborative, transmedia documentary project that has been evolving since 2008. The project facilitates the telling, recording, archiving and disseminating of autobiographical narratives from people living in small towns across South East Asia and Australia through face-to-face engagement of outside filmmakers with local people. The filmmaker-in-residence model around which the project is based has been delivered to 13 towns, with more than 500 stories produced over these residencies. As creative director and producer of the project and a filmmaker in residence, I defined the overarching focus of the project, described as "shining a light on people caring for and creating their community" (Potter 2014: 219). In each residency, we, the filmmakers, have operationalised an approach inspired by the synchronous ideas of "negative capability" (Unger 1987) and "positive deviance" (Zeitlin 1991). Unlike other theories of structure and agency, *positive deviance* (and by inference *negative capability*) does not delimit individuals or communities to either compliance or rebellion but rather portrays them as able to participate in a variety of activities of self-empowerment. Positive deviance explores how human beings both innovate and resist within confining social contexts. Within the context of the *Big Stories* project, operationalising positive deviance is the identification of behaviours or strategies that enable local people to find solutions to problems from other people in the same setting despite appearing to have no special resources or knowledge. This chapter reflects on members of small communities featured in *Big Stories* from across Australia and South East Asia who have created local social innovations and embody this concept of positive deviance.

Through the co-created stories produced during the *Big Stories* residencies, a range of local, social innovations have been highlighted. Across all sites, these innovations share key characteristics – they are relationship driven, require minimal external management and have been extensively replicated (often in both regional and urban communities). To illuminate these characteristics, the paper is underpinned by a case study of the Lepo Lorun Weavers Collective initiated in 1998 by Alfonsa Horeng in Sikka Regency on the island of Flores, Indonesia. This model has now been replicated in multiple towns across the island, engaging over 800 women. The case study of the weavers collective, one of many identified in the *Big Stories* project, exemplifies the notion of operationalising the concept of positive deviance by showing a focus on regional stories of local people caring for and creating their community.

Since 2008, the *Big Stories, Small Towns* documentary project has focussed on the co-creation and sharing of stories told with residents of small towns. The project is based around filmmakers living in residence in a small town making stories with, rather than about, local people. The stories and images created are then exhibited in each town and most are uploaded to the bigstories.com.au website. Stories from different towns have also been showcased at film festivals, exhibitions, events and broadcast television. The stories from the project exist online in the intimate space of people's homes and in the shared spaces of galleries, libraries and museums. This dynamic network of spaces creates a spatial assemblage specific to the ambitions of the broadcast itself. In each town, stories of everyday life in communities are re-mediated through the process and artefacts of conceiving of, creating and sharing stories. This generates a range of new and creative outcomes that include new methodologies and understandings of local cultures, language and history and ways of effectively disseminating under-represented cultures, languages and histories. *Big Stories* documents these multi-layered communities and explores complex relations between people, social backgrounds, technology and place. This shifts attention from individual stories towards practices of collective identification and action, creating acts of storymaking that offer a model of positive deviance that empowers individuals and communities to reject deficit discourses that marginalise them and their ways of life.

The project started in Port August, South Australia, in 2008, produced under the auspices of the Media Resource Centre, a community media organisation in South Australia. With financial support from Film Australia, the South Australian Film Corporation, Port Augusta City Council and Country Arts South Australia, I designed a participatory media project that could support local community members to speak back to external negative mainstream media reportage and to gain media and digital literacies that could support ongoing independent storytelling. I detail this work and the context from which it emerged in Potter (2014: Chapter 3), but key to this article are two points:

1   the project's participatory methods emerged as a reaction to mainstream media representations, and
2   the methods of production change according to local contexts in each residency.

During the first residency, with key collaborators in the project, Anna Grieve, Jeni Lee and Sieh Mchawala, we agreed on an approach to the stories and images that would subsequently define the project beyond Port Augusta, offering an overarching framing for the methods of production and the resulting stories. As noted in the introduction, this was described as "shining a light on

272 *Martin Potter*

those caring for and creating their community" (Potter 2014: 219). The stories that emerge from the *Big Stories* project are far from stories of rural dysfunction and decay. Rather, these are stories that speak to ideas around strengthening a sense of place, community and collective identity. The project's focus was to produce success stories that could work to enhance the image of communities in the eyes of both the advantaged and disadvantaged. This meant finding people or groups who had identified a problem, who had become concerned about it, and who were actively looking for ways to change (or had already begun to change). It could be about the search for solutions, as well as the solutions themselves, so it can refer to intent as well as to outcomes.

These approaches are underpinned by two assumptions on my behalf:

1   humans cast their identity in some narrative form in all cultures, and so storytelling is at the core of describing both individual and collective experience, and
2   participatory media have the potential to create a more nuanced, ethical, diverse and democratic media culture.

This speaks to the utopian and idealistic imaginings of the project and the hopefulness embedded within it. In the light of a mainstream media climate, which is often problem oriented and homogenising, the idealism underpinning these assumptions is vital and far from naïve. Rather, it is a critical and solutions-seeking approach to a highly problematised mediascape. McHenry (2011) observes that collaborative narrative activities strengthen a sense of place in regional communities and contribute to a collective sense of identity. In addition, stories can both remediate and re-imagine place, community and collective and individual identity. They are at once backward and forward-looking, individual and collective.

And, as with the idealistic construct of the *Big Stories*, formed through a reactive connection to mainstream media, so too have theories of deviancy – both positive and negative – emerged as a reaction to perceived norms. In their paper, "Positive Deviance in Theory and Practice: A Conceptual Review," Matthew Herington and Elske van de Fliert (2018) offer a synthesis and review of positive deviance literature. They trace deviant studies as emerging from American sociological theory from the early 1900s where the concept of "deviance" was defined as any transgression of norms; however, the concept was typically framed negatively (West 2004), a harmful, malicious or disruptive deviation. Herington and van de Fliert (2018: 665) draw on the work of Goode, who identifies Wilkins as an early thinker who conceived of deviance as also potentially positive. Wilkins (1964) illustrated the point by using a bell curve and drawing attention to both ends that represented acts regarded as sinful to the left and saintly to the right, with conforming behaviour in the middle.

However, even early theorists of deviance, including Durkheim (1964 [1895]) and Merton (1938), suggest deviance as an important function in the maintenance of social order and control, as it affirmed normative values and morals.

Positive deviance 273

This reactive bond of normativity to deviance suggests that all social change begins with forms of deviance. A positive deviance-oriented approach to social change echoes many thinkers from a tradition of radical pedagogy, including Dewey (1920, 1927), Buber (1958), Gramsci (1927–1935, 1988), Illich (1979, 1982, 1992) and Freire (1970). These thinkers emphasised critical awareness, the importance of everyday life, re-imagining social relations and the institutions that are the artefacts of these relations.

Positive deviance

Despite the connotations of negative qualities with deviance, a body of thought and practice has emerged that sees that "positive deviance" as a term in sociological studies was popularised by Marian Zeitlin et al. (1990) with the publication of *Positive Deviance in Child Nutrition: With Emphasis on Psychosocial and Behavioural Aspects and Implications for Development*. Zeitlin (1991) describes a positive deviance approach as identifying successful behaviours or strategies that enable people to find better solutions to problems despite having no special resources or knowledge. While sociological theorists such as Zeitlin et al. (1990) focus on the individual and family unit, organisational theorists Spreitzer and Sonenshein (2004) define positive deviance as not only an individual-level construct (as is the case with Warren's [2003] work) but as something that can also occur at the organisational and communal levels. They also provide a framework for operationalising positive deviance consisting of intentional behaviours that significantly depart from the norms of a referent group in "positive" ways. Positive deviance focuses on cases where groups and individuals change from the constraints of norms to conduct behaviours perceived by others as positive. Positive deviance is strengths-based and practice-driven. Much of the sociological positive deviance research emerges from the recognition that in every disadvantaged community there are individuals and families who are doing unexpectedly well. Individuals and families in situations of disadvantage, often characterised by systemic or structural disadvantage, have practices and strategies that are both positive and deviant in that they differ from most of their peers (Eastman et al. 2014). By answering the how and why questions for positively deviant behaviours, **Spreitzer and Sonenshein** claim that researchers can take an important step toward understanding and promoting additional positive behaviours.

Limitations for current theorising on positive deviance include a lack of critical inquiry on what constitutes "positive," especially when exploring values-based outcomes rather than more straightforward nutrition outcomes (nf: Zeitlin et al. 1990). To this end, my framework for operationalising positive deviance within the *Big Stories* project draws on Roberto Unger's thinking on formative contexts, false necessity and negative capability as outlined in *Social Theory: Its Situation and Its Task* (1987) and *False Necessity* (2004). Unger (1987: 89) notes that a formative context consists of imaginative assumptions about the possible and desirable forms of human association as well as in institutional arrangements or non-institutionalised social practices. Formative contexts of ideologies and institutions become fixed through the constraints of society, echoed, reinforced and amplified by the illusions of social thought. This, according to Unger, is the essence of the notion of false necessity. Unger proposes an anti-necessitarian social theory that helps form a social understanding that might free itself from institutional and structural fetishism – an imagined identification of "highly detailed and largely accidental institutional arrangements with comprehensive and vague ideals like freedom and equality" (1987: 200). Unger goes on to note that "an anti-necessitarian social theory does not strike down the constraints, but it dispels the illusions that prevent us from attacking them" (1987: 215).

To actualise this anti-necessitarian social theory, Unger (1987) describes the concept of *negative capability*, appropriating it from John Keats' use, which was focussed on the artist's capacity for uncertainty, mystery and doubt. A capacity, Keats' noted, was not constrained by "any irritable reaching after fact and reason" (cited in Li 2009: 1). For Keats, negative capability is framed by the artist's receptive openness to the world and rejection of those who tried to formulate theories or categorical knowledge. Unger's conception of negative capability explains how human beings innovate and resist within confining social contexts. Unger summarises this as "our power to defy formula and to transcend constraint" (2007: 104) and "not imprisoning insight in any particular structure of thought" (1987: 156). It is a "denial of whatever in our contexts delivers us over to a fixed scheme of division and hierarchy and to an enforced choice between routine and rebellion" (ibid). While recognising the constraints and influence of the formative contexts upon a person of social and institutional limitations, Unger finds that people (both individuals and groups) are able to resist, deny and transcend their context. The varieties of this resistance are negative capability.

Benkler (2006) describes Unger's work as central to the emergence of a "third way" literature that explores alternative production processes that do not depend on the displacement of individual agency by hierarchical systems. Unger (1987, 1998) emphasises transformation rather than dissolution of ideas of community and objectivity. He relates this change in the content of basic social ideals to certain efforts at human empowerment where both the conception of human solidarity and the practice of ascribing normative force to views of personality or society are reassessed. These efforts can be summarised as: we are not passive receivers of objective being. While we may be conditioned by formative contexts of institutions and ideologies, they do not determine us and we can rebel against this conditioning. Through dialogue, we can imagine and re-imagine reality and work to progress and transform it. Reality is constructed and negotiated in collective action rather than through an individual subject looking out at an objective world. Individual and collective emancipation and practical progress are both dependent on the transformation of access into agency. Practical, positive progress adheres to Unger's (1998: 5) definition as innovation or discovery resulting in the development of our power to "push back the constraints of scarcity, disease, weakness, and ignorance." Therefore, both practical progress and emancipation depend upon the capacity to transform social effort into collective learning and to act upon the lessons learned, undeterred by the need to respect a pre-established plan of social division and hierarchy or a confining allocation of social roles. Unger (1998: 7) observes:

> both practical experimentalism and individual emancipation require arrangements minimizing barriers to collective learning. This view is in turn connected with a thesis about our relation to the institutional and discursive structures we build and inhabit.

Unger (1987) positions his work between deep-structure social theory and what he describes as positive social science. He argues that deep-structure social theories, such as classical Marxism, privilege institutional routine practices and contexts. This limits the possibilities of human social development through privileging structural and contextual frameworks. It is social science adhering to a large-scale script of history. As a filmmaker, I drew parallels between this notion of deep-structure social theory and linear documentary films, especially those that emerge through broadcast or state-funding models. In Potter (2014: Chs. 2 and 3) I drawn on a body of literature and practice spanning 50 years of institutionally driven documentary practice and note that the necessity of foregrounded structural, institutional frameworks that define the commission-based funding model limit social development possibilities. Once produced, these standalone films are fixed objects, reflecting a particular moment in time and purporting to be of historical and archival value.

Unger (1987) describes positive social science as a practice that sees society and history as an endless series of episodes of problem solving. Unger argues this leads to denying explanation in favour of simply detailing conflict and resolution. This granular problematising of the world can be seen to be paralleled in the *Big Stories* project, and potentially more broadly in creative participatory practices, in two ways. The first is that of the subject of research as a problem that might be solved. The subject of research in this project is local people addressing local problems. The subjects of research are also the solution-seeking behaviours, the solution seekers themselves and the conceptualising and implementations of these solutions and the impact of this. The presentation of the research in the form of the participatory processes, transmedia artefacts and stories are multi-valent tools. The second way is critical reviews of the stories that emerge from the project which look to the artefacts produced (the stories) as texts to be read as if an essential truth will emerge from these small stories. The granular, individualistic reading of stories as texts that contain an entirety of truth or a granular focus on one episode of the multiple research subjects of the project is similarly reductive, dehumanising and anathema to understanding the practices of collective identification and action that are an essential part of the *Big Stories* project. The stories become multi-valent artefacts that can be data, artwork, story, educational resource and an embodiment of the relationship between facilitators and participants.

276 *Martin Potter*

Unger (1987: 50) concludes that both forms of social theory deny human ability to hope, resist and reshape the social and conceptual world and are inherently dehumanised and that a lack of vision of alternatives denies the human ability to hope, resist and reshape our social and conceptual worlds. Central to the *Big Stories* project, therefore, is the minimisation of barriers to collective learning and an attempt to re-imagine our relations to formative contexts (and encourage that re-imagination for others). It is therefore essential to engage with the task of embodying the assumption that real freedom is not an individualistic pursuit. Freedom is predicated on fostering a community where the ability of the mind to assess and act upon the reality of the world is a blessing rather than a source of repression.

In seeking to build a hopeful framework that works within the intersection of the three key conditions of individual expression, institutional and ideological contexts, and practical progress, I have chosen to use the phrase "positive deviance" when describing the approach to co-creation in place of "negative capability" despite the term lacking the depth of Unger's project. The term "positive deviance" reflects the fact that many of the tactics involved in challenging accepted codes of behaviour are characterised as deviant or abnormal, as determined by dominant discourses of knowledge and power. In addition, I used the term positive deviance from the outset of *Big Stories*, and its use in this context accurately reflects the historical language of the project. *Positive deviance* (and by inference *negative capability*) described the approach to community in *Big Stories*. The project's focus was to produce success stories that could work to enhance the image of communities in the eyes of both the advantaged and disadvantaged. The creative actions of making stories and images across a variety of mediums and contexts open up opportunities to re-imagine place and social relations. The act of making can embody personal and communal agency to transcend the formative contexts of institutions and ideologies. This act of transcendence as an expression of desire is a form of positive deviance. This deviancy, when accepted collectively, is subsequently reinterpreted as a process of "collective learning" that can allow those involved to escape on a "line of flight" from their particular hyper-controlled situation. Within the *Big Stories* project, the operationalisation of positive deviance has provided a way of capturing, through the artefacts of the stories that are told, the behaviours that traditional conceptualisations of deviance overlook.

Positive deviance in the *Big Stories, Small Towns* project

The combination of positive, local narratives and local solutions that emerge from the *Big Stories* project has constituted a powerful tool in strengthening a sense of place and contributing to a collective sense of identity. Placemaking requires sensitivity to local contexts. Rather than seeking external solutions to local problems, local solutions constitute another key element of creating place. The process and products of *Big Stories* have developed tools for high-impact advocacy on behalf of the community. Putland (2011), Potter (2014,

2017a, 2017b, 2017c) and Ryan (2015) have highlighted some of the project's impacts in some settings in Australia and Cambodia. To extend on these studies with further examples of impact, films from Strathewen, Victoria, Australia, co-created in 2013 about the community-led recovery from the Black Saturday bushfires have now been incorporated by the Victorian Bushfire Recovery Association as describing a model of best practice of community-led recovery and are used in training and support programs by the Red Cross and University of Melbourne. The stories from Indigenous people in Banlung, Cambodia, are held in the Bophana national archive in Cambodia and are archived by UNESCO as part of their collection of intangible cultural heritage. The stories were also used to foreground Indigenous voices in policy discussions of land and Indigenous rights and in fundraising endeavours for these communities.

Stories from the Men's Shed in Port Augusta, produced in 2008, were used as part of submissions to a Senate hearing into male health and to support other regional communities in replicating the program. The Port Augusta shed is widely acknowledged as one of the first Men's Sheds in Australia (Golding 2015). Golding also notes the rapid proliferation of sheds from around 30 in 2005 to 1,416 internationally by 2015 (Golding 2014). The stories were used by the Port Augusta Men's Shed in their winning submission to the SA Great Regional Awards, and the advocacy of Port Augusta shed founders and supporters was key in facilitating the spread of sheds to other communities across Australia and internationally. Similarly, in Beaudesert, stories of the Young Men's Indigenous Group have been used by the founders of that group to support the development of young Indigenous men's and women's groups in other Queensland areas.

A notable impact of the *Big Stories* project as a whole was its use as a model for the ABC Open project. ABC Open producers work with regional Australians to co-create stories through visual and written media. To date, according to the ABC Open website, almost 200,000 stories have been created, and dozens of Open producers are employed in residence in regional ABC radio stations across Australia. In addition to being a model for ABC Open, numerous *Big Stories* formats, such as the Dreams photo series, are replicated in the ABC Open site. This influence at institutional scale further reflects elements of an important theoretical underpinning that has shaped my approach to and reflections on the operationalising of concepts related to positive deviance within the Big Stories project. The potential for institutional transformation is not the essential goal; however, it is a profound possibility. Working with institutions can support development of individual and collective agency. Freire (1970) points out that institutions can be a creative act: "it is as transforming and creative beings that humans, in their permanent relations with reality, produce not only material goods – tangible objects – but also social institutions, ideas, and concepts." And as Unger (1998) has described, power can also be developed through revision of these structures, as well as resisting or transcending them. In the exercise and strengthening of our positive deviance – our capacity to defy the limits of our social and cultural contexts – Unger proposes that we

278 Martin Potter

may even make institutional and discursive structures more hospitable to this practice of deviance.

Over the course of a *Big Stories* residency on the island of Flores in Indonesia, there was a group of women who appeared to embody these ideas put forward by Freire (1970) and by Unger (1987, 1998). They have transformed and revised local social and cultural institutions through creative, collective actions and as a result have defied gendered limits of their formative context. The next section of the chapter will outline and review the *Big Stories* residency in Flores and reflect on elements of the creative transformation effected by the local operationalisation of practices, which will be framed as positive deviance.

Background to the *Big Stories* residency in Flores, Indonesia

In 2015, with the support of Screen Australia and the Department of Foreign Affairs and Trade (through the Australian International Cultural Council), the *Big Stories, Small Towns* team (consisting of me and documentary filmmaker Charlie Hill-Smith) worked on the island of Flores with the Lepo Lorun Weavers Collective in Nita Village, near the capital of Maumere in the Sikka Regency, and a team of Indonesian filmmakers, led by Dodid Wijanarko, to create films, photo essays and a range of other media including a feature-length documentary, *Au Lorun (I Am Weaving)* Wijanarko and Potter (2016). A website (Potter and Wijanarko 2016) was created on the *Big Stories, Small Towns* platform, and a range of social media outputs showcased the production and stories produced. Workshops on filmmaking and photography were also run in the community, and local screenings and performances supported extensive local participation by members of the Weavers Collective and wider community.

Dodid Wijanarko had worked in Flores previously and had met the founder of the Lepo Lorun weaving collective, Alfonsa Horeng. I had previously undertaken a West Papua-based *Big Stories* project with filmmaker Enrico "Rico" Aditjondro. Rico introduced me to Dodid, and we began to discuss another Big Stories project in the region. Central to this discussion was the approach of positive deviance in terms of shaping the overarching tone of the project. I suggested that the *Big Stories* project in Flores could offer stories and images that might re-mediate mainstream media representations in Indonesian media that portray Flores as a backward place. Based on this, Dodid identified Alfonsa and the local weaver community in Nita town (the Indonesian naming of this is place is "Nitakluang." This can be translated as Nita town or Nita village, with the suffix -kluang more commonly translated as town) as a possible story thread for the project. Dodid described Alfonsa's experience returning from the city of Surabaya following tertiary study and starting up a weaving collective in the village in 2002, the subsequent growth of that collective and the replication of the collective model to other communities. This model of local, social innovation that builds on the pre-existing creative capacities in new and surprising ways fit well with the *Big Stories* framework. I was able to raise funding through grants

Positive deviance   279

from the Department of Foreign Affairs and Trade (Australian International Cultural Council) and Screen Australia to support the project. After confirming funding, Dodid and I put together a production team, including Frengky "FX" Making, a West Papuan filmmaker who had been mentored during the *Big Stories* West Papua project.

Lepo Lorun Weaver's Collective

The history and cultural significance of weaving across Flores has been well documented (e.g. Barnes 1987; Hamilton 1994; deJong 1994; Buckley 2012). These are ancient traditions, and Buckley (2012) notes that many Southeast Asian weaving traditions are related and share common ancestry that can be traced back to Neolithic cultures on the Asian mainland. Alfonsa Horeng observes in the documentary produced as part of the *Big Stories* residency, *Au Lorun (I Am Weaving)*, that there is strong evidence that weaving practice has been in existence in the region for over 2,000 years (Wijanarko and Potter 2016). Alfonsa notes there is a bronze statue of a traditional weaver in the National Gallery of Australia dating to around 600 BC. Alfonsa reflects that only now do people in Flores and in Indonesia more broadly realise the historic value of the statue and the practices represented.

In the Sikka Regency, the Tenun Ikat weaving tradition has long been an instrumental part of everyday life. The cloths are still exchanged on a relational level – notably as part of a marriage dowry (deJong 1994) and for building relationships between family groups and village communities. Weavings are exchanged for goods and services including food, stock and equipment. The weavings themselves represent a complex connection to place, tradition and environment. The cloth that weavers use was once made of cotton grown in the region, and rare cloths still use this Flores cotton. Dyes used in the process are sometimes made in the traditional way, with local indigo creating the iconic blue shades on the cloth. The pictorial and geometric motifs tell stories and indicate social status such as whether the wearer is married. Weavings are created for different purposes, from everyday use to sacred, ceremonial wear. The acts and products of traditional weaving are a complex system. However, according to Alfonsa, despite the acknowledged social-cultural and historical importance of weaving in Flores, the women weavers have not been perceived as equals in local society. Alfonsa's goals for the standing of the weaving women in society are high. She says, "It is sad to hear people refer to them as artisans instead of maestros. . . . The women weavers of Flores are maestros from the time they are very young until the day they die." All of the work emerging from the *Big Stories* residency, from the *Au Lorun* documentary to the web series, sought to reflect on and elevate the cultural and social standing of the weavers. In a support letter to the project, Alfonsa observed that the *Big Stories* project (spanning films, website and the activity of making the works) offers a unique opportunity to support the Sikka region to create a lasting archive for both the local community and for those interested in the region and Flores culture.

280   *Martin Potter*

In the documentary *Au Lorun (I Am Weaving)*, Alfonsa notes there are a lot of things she set out to change locally when she returned to Flores from Surabaya. Alfonsa notes that she had made a decision to return to her parent's town rather than stay in Surabaya or another big city. Alfonsa (in Wijanarko and Potter 2016) recalls,

> My father always said: 'Never leave the land your great grandfathers inherited to you, and develop it for a good cause.' That wisdom was what convinced me to leave my career in the big city of Surabaya and return home to develop Flores.

On her return in 2002, Alfonsa's parents, who are teachers, gifted her a small piece of land on the outskirts of Nita village. Nita is a small village tucked away in the lush tropical hills some 12 kilometres from Maumere, the capital of Flores. This hilly region dominated by Catholic seminaries and small villages is well-known for its weaving, known as *Tenun Ikat*, a traditional weaving method using pre-dyed threads and motifs that are individually hand-tied in the yarns. In the portrait film produced on Alfonsa as part of the *Big Stories* project (Potter and Wijanarko 2016), she says, "I wasn't a leader with some kind of powerful influence over people. I was considered a young adult. I was 27 years old, a young person who had recently returned from Java from my education." Despite her youth and inexperience, she had a vision and so, on her new land, Alfonsa started a weaving group, Lepo Lorun (the House of Weaving), with 14 women in 2002. As Alfonsa observes in the portrait film, "I wanted to develop what we already have with the 'kain tenun ikat' [both the traditional weaving practice and the artefact of the 'Sarong' produced according to this practice] without taking away the traditional values."

Each village in Flores that has a weaving tradition has its characteristic motifs, either icons or geometric patterns or symbols (Buckley 2012). In one of the *Big Stories* portraits of other Lepo Lorun weavers (Potter and Wijanarko 2016), Memi states that "Maumere sarong and other woven fabrics is the pattern – Sikka sarongs have big patterns, patterns from Kio are much smaller than those from Maumere." In the documentary film *Au Lorun*, Alfonsa observes that the motifs geo-locate the cloths and notes that every village not only has its own designs, it has its own philosophy and its own weaving style, often based on each traditional root used in the dyeing process. Not only do the motifs carry meaning, the dyes carry meaning in terms of the type of dyes used, the process of dyeing and the understanding of what that dye root and the resulting colour means. The colour wash also carries meaning: for example, the indigo plant is extensively used across areas. In one of the shorter *Big Stories* films, *Indigo Colour*, Alfonsa details the process of making the indigo colour from the indigo plant and the process of dyeing and setting the colour using lime (Potter and Wijanarko 2016). Alfonsa reflects in *Au Lorun* (in Wijanarko and Potter 2016),

> I had heard so much about how our great grandmothers used to make natural dyes from plants such as mango, mengkudu [noni], indigo and turmeric.

Positive deviance   281

So, I thought, why not revive this knowledge? We can benefit from what we already have around us and contribute to the environment at the same time.

As cheaper, imported cotton and synthetic, more vibrant dyes came to dominate Flores weavings, the traditional processes and materials became less time- and cost-effective. Part of the process of bringing the collective together was to revive these traditional processes and to frame this work of growing and making both cotton and dye as instrumental to the creation of authentic weavings that would embody the ideal of weaving as works of art and significant cultural and historical artefacts. In the *Indigo Colour* film, Alfonsa notes that "there are 11 primary dyes in Flores." Alfonsa displays a visual chart that shows formulas for mixing colours using natural dyes and says, "We've also tried to standardised the colours that weavers used as part of trying to create clear classifications and recipes for the dyes and for the colours. We make up formulas to create consistent colours." Professionalism, consistency and cultural and historical awareness are recurring themes in how Alfonsa conceives of the work of the collective. This awareness feeds into a broader informal pedagogical program focussed on empowerment. In the *Au Lorun* documentary, Alfonsa outlines this program. She says, "for this community we would like to create a good educational system and for it to be a learning centre that serves everyone here." In order to do this, she wants to focus on one thing (weaving) and do it seriously while at the same time be an agent to develop the women's education. Alfonsa notes that this understanding of education doesn't necessarily refer to formal education; rather, this is about building on natural talents and developing relationships with other "stakeholders," with the weaving practice as multi-modal means to foster agencies of self-expression, historical and cultural standing, economic value and independence. This reflects the radical pedagogical thought highlighted earlier in this chapter that emphasises the importance of everyday life from thinkers such as Antonio Gramsci, who describes a notion of the "organic intellectual." Alfonsa goes on to say in *Au Lorun* that the women in the collectives have to create what she calls "an educational package" in order to "deliver their talents in order the women of Flores to be able to live independently and better."

As part of the *Big Stories* project and the *Au Lorun* documentary, many members of the Lepo Lorun collective were interviewed. Questions centred on their perception and experience of the collective, their understandings of the Tenun Ikat and personal reflections. One of the collective members, Memi, comments that they didn't see "Kain Tenun Ikat" as having economic value in the past. However, there has always been perceived cultural value. Memi goes on to observe that now the traditional sarongs have value both economically and culturally. The use of traditional processes, natural fabrics and dyes has become a selling point. Other members note that the weaving is an economic driver for local families. Theodora Elizabeth (Beth) provides administrative support for her husband Yanto in his construction business. Beth's work in the weaving collective provides additional income that pays for their children's education. In her *Big Stories* portrait film, Beth also reflects on a profound connection to ancestors and culture in her practice of the weaving. Beth describes how her weaving has been

282 *Martin Potter*

informed by her deceased aunt's legacy. Beth's aunt was from Lembata Island. On her death, she willed her most sacred and precious Ikat to Beth. These Ikat incorporate motifs, dyes and cloth unique to Beth's aunt as well as being emblematic of the Lembata Tenun Ikat style and form. For Beth, the legacy Ikat are a tangible memorial of her aunt as well as a script for her to learn from as she incorporates the patterns, dyes and materials into her own weaving. The result is a Sikka/Lembata fusion that is a new expression drawing on recognisable weaving motifs from both regions but filtered through Beth's connection to her aunt.

By 2016, the Lepo Lorun collective in Nita town had grown to 56 people. In addition to this high impact in Nita, there were a further 42 weaving collectives with 1,026 active members spread across the rest of the island. Each collective was set up around a similar profit-share model. However, the economic arrangements are a basic functional operational principle. The methods of weaving and the valuing of local knowledges – as embodied in the local motifs, dyes and cloth – were the key framing principles of the collectives. The women would come together and practice their art and ensure they maintained their cultural expression and became masters of the cloth. This aspiration to mastery and the positioning of the weavers as artists has been central to the success of the collectives. The groups are artists' collectives that offer economic, historic, cultural and social benefit for those involved. In order to activate this benefit at a local level, Alfonsa has engaged globally, visiting more than 30 countries to promote the practice and history. Alfonsa states that the weaving is "the integrity of our culture. And if we go somewhere and wear kain tenun ikat it means our pride stays with us." The traditional value of weaving fulfils cultural and traditional needs. Alfonsa observes that because the weaver's work has not been given credit in the past, "many people perceive these women as nobodies, and what they do as nothing, but our traditions, in the hands of these women, have been preserved." Alfonsa goes on to state that, "through weaving we're able to preserve culture, heritage and raise economic status of women."

Conclusion

As part of the ongoing Dreams photo series that has been part of the *Big Stories* project since the first residency in Port Augusta in 2008, many of the Lepo Lorun collective shared their dream. Alfonsa's dream (Image 14.1) indicates both her ambition for Flores as a whole and her role now as a leader and advocate for local rights and empowerment. She says:

> I wish my homeland of Flores to be a model island, to showcase the role of cultural and environmental preservation and sustainability. The Indonesian Government's task must be to care/protect local land rights and governance.

Alfonsa's collective weaving model realises this dream as it taps into deep cultural, social, historical and gender practices. The collective model has transformed

Positive deviance 283

Image 14.1 Alfonsa's Dream: "I wish my homeland of Flores to be a model island to showcase the value of cultural and environmental preservation and sustainability. Indonesian Government task must be to care/protect local lands and governance."

Source: Photo by Martin Potter

local, national and international perceptions of Tenun Ikat. Key ideas from Alfonsa's local innovation can also be generalised. The collective represents an amplification of women as key economic and cultural drivers. Through the collectivised model of income sharing and subsequent replication of the model in other areas – resulting in over 1,000 women creating and working within collectives across Flores – this has echoes of other local social innovations that have emerged in other sites in small towns that have been observed in the *Big Stories* project such as the Men's Shed movement.

All across the world, people spend much of their lives at work, engaged in practical economic activities. It matters whether people's workaday lives are shaped so as to tap and sustain the common element in democracy and experimentalism. To have an understanding that the production of tangible, everyday objects can also result in the production of ideas, concepts and even institutions might result in operationalising positive deviance towards practical progress and emancipatory outcomes. Central to all aspects of material progress is the relation between cooperation and innovation. Innovation requires cooperation.

284 Martin Potter

Nevertheless, every real form of cooperation remains embedded in arrangements generating settled expectations and vested rights of different groups relative to one another. People regularly resist innovation because they correctly believe it to threaten such rights and expectations. However, this proposal risks moving towards abstract declarations. Through exploration of the Lepo Lorun weavers case study, we might see elements of this transformative ideal.

Emerging from the *Big Stories* project, the artefacts of videos and photos produced are multi-valent works. They are the material embodiment of the production of these new forms of local knowledge and transformative ideals. They are a creative co-construction in and of themselves. Traditional stories of everyday life of this community are re-mediated through the process of the participatory media – generating new and creative outcomes, methodologies and understanding of Flores culture, language and history as well as informing broader Flores culture, language and history. The resulting stories illuminate characteristics of positive deviance, identifying behaviours or strategies that enable people to find solutions to problems despite having no apparent special resources or knowledge. Through the participatory, inter-cultural process of co-creativity the variety of media (films, photos, websites etc.) produced constitutes a reflexive interplay between participants and filmmakers in residence. As a result, this media can be viewed not only as texts that can be read that describe, to some extent, the social, historical and cultural context out of which the Lepo Lorun collective emerged; the media can also be understood as enacting a shift away from a centralised vision of storymaking, defined by a single author or documenter, toward a collectivised storytelling practice. The result is a "living," participatory, transmedia work that moves attention from the rhetoric of texts to be read to practices of community organisation and the technological and embodied material relations, which aspire to produce a collectively enacted sense of place and identity.

Throughout the *Big Stories* project, with the application of new technologies, new ways of learning and new critical theories, there is a utopian attempt to radicalise institutions and social practice in order to enable space in everyday life for a community to articulate and reaffirm progressive tendencies. This process was conceptualised as "reconstruction" by progressive educators like Dewey (1920) and philosophers such as Gramsci (1929–1935, 1971), who noted that every critical juncture offers a possibility of re-imagining in which "the normal functioning of the old economic, social, cultural order provides the opportunity to reorganize it in new ways" (Hall 1987: 19). As much as we acknowledge the agency of an institution upon humans, we must also consider the possibility of human agency upon the institution. In every case there is a formative context that can be transformed, and in every case there is a productive tension between realism and imagination. Unger (1987) states:

> we must be realists in order to become visionaries and we need an understanding of social life to criticize and enlarge our view of social reality and social possibility.

References

Barnes, R. 1987. "Weaving and Non-Weaving Among the Lamaholot." *Indonesia Circle* 15(42): 17–31.

Benkler, Y. 2006. *Wealth of Networks: How Social Production Transforms Markets and Freedom.* New Haven and London: Yale University Press.

Buber, M. 1958. *I and Thou.* New York: Scribner.

Buckley, C. D. 2012. "Investigating Cultural Evolution Using Phylogenetic Analysis: The Origins and Descent of the Southeast Asian Tradition of Warp Ikat Weaving." *PLOS One* 7(12): e52064 (https://doi.org/10.1371/journal.pone.0052064).

de Jong, W. 1994. "Cloth Production and Change in a Lio Village." Pp. 210–227 in *Gift of the Cotton Maiden. Textiles of Flores and the Solor Islands,* edited by Hamilton, R. W. Los Angeles: Fowler Museum of Cultural History.

Dewey, J. 1920. "Reconstruction in Philosophy." *The Project Gutenberg eBook.* Retrieved September 2018 (www.gutenberg.org/files/40089/40089-h/40089-h.htm#).

Dewey, J. 1927. *The Public and Its Problems.* New York: Holt.

Durkheim, E. 1964 [1895]. *The Rules of Sociological Method.* Vol. 8, edited by Catlin, G. E. G. and translated by Solovay, S. A. and Mueller, J. H. New York: The Free Press.

Eastman, C., Hill, T., Newland, J., Smyth, C., and Valentine, K. 2014. *Thriving in Adversity: A Positive Deviance Study of Safe Communities for Children* (SPRC Report 30/2014). Sydney: Social Policy Research Centre, UNSW Australia.

Freire, P. 1990 [1970]. *Pedagogy of the Oppressed.* Harmondsworth, Penguin: Continuum Publishing Company.

Golding, B. 2014. "The Men's Shed Movement: The Company of Men, Book Detail." Retrieved December, 2018 (https://barrygoanna.com/2014/05/29/new-and-forthcoming-books/).

Golding, B. 2015. *The Men's Shed Movement: The Company of Men.* Champaign, Illinois: Common Ground Publishing.

Gramsci, A. 1929–1935, 1971. *Selections from the Prison Notebooks,* edited and translated Hoare, Q., and Smith, G. London: ElecBook.

Gramsci, A. 1988. *An Antonio Gramsci Reader: Selected Writings, 1916–1935,* edited by Forgacs, D. New York: Schocken.

Hall, S. 1987. "Gramsci and Us." *Marxism Today.* June 1987, pp. 16–21.

Hamilton, R. W. (ed.). 1994. *Gift of the Cotton Maiden: Textiles of Flores and the Solor Islands.* Los Angeles, CA: Fowler Museum of Cultural History, University of California.

Herington, M., and Van de Fliert, E. 2018. "Positive Deviance in Theory and Practice: A Conceptual Review." *Deviant Behaviour* 39(5): 664–678 (doi:10.1080/01639625.2017.1286194).

Illich, I. 1979. *Tools for Conviviality* (2nd ed). London: Fontana.

Illich, I. 1982. "Silence is a Commons." Speech Presented at *Asahi Symposium Science and Man: The Computer-Managed Society,* Tokyo, Japan." Retrieved September 12, 2018 (www.preservenet.com/theory/Illich/Silence.html).

Illich, I. 1992. *In the Mirror of the Past: Lectures and Addresses 1978–1990.* London: Marion Boyars.

Li, O. 2009. *Keats and Negative Capability.* London: Continuum International Publishing Group.

McHenry, J. A. 2011. "Rural Empowerment Through the Arts: The Role of the Arts in Civic and Social Participation in the Mid-West Region of Western Australia." *Journal of Rural Studies* 27(3), 245–253.

Merton, R. K. 1938. "Social Structure and Anomie." *American Sociological Review* 3(5): 672–682.

286 *Martin Potter*

Potter, M. 2014. *Big Stories, Small Towns: A Participatory and Web-based Documentary*. Unpublished PhD Thesis, Flinders University (www.academia. edu/11786257/Big_Stories_Small_Towns_a_participatory_and_web-based_do-cumentary_and_exegesis_www.bigstories.com.au_).

Potter, M. 2017a. "Critical Junctures: Place-based Storytelling in the Big Stories, Small Towns Participatory Documentary Project." *Media International Australia* 164(1): 117–127.

Potter, M. 2017b. "The Tarob and the Sacred Oath. Liminal Spirits and Stories Creating Heterotopic Spaces in Dusun Culture." *Etropic: Electronic Journal of Studies in the Tropics* 16(1): 112–124 (http://dx.doi.org/10.25120/etropic.16.1.2017.3569).

Potter, M. 2017c. "Story Systems: The Potential of Transmedia Storytelling as Material Embodiment of a Collective Enactment of Place and Identity." In *Con La Red/En La Red*. Granada: University of Granada Press.

Putland, C. 2011. *Ripples Murray Bridge SA Regional Centre of Culture 2010, Country Arts SA, Program Evaluation Report*. Country Arts SA, June 2011.

Ryan, S. 2015. "Co-creative Processes in the Big Stories, Small Towns Project." *WACC*. Retrieved September 2018 (www.waccglobal.org/articles/co-creative-processes-in-the-big-stories-small-towns-film-project).

Spreitzer, G. M., and Sonenshein, S. 2004. "Toward the Construct Definition of Positive Deviance." *American Behavioral Scientist* 47(6): 828–847.

Unger, R. 1987. *Social Theory, Its Situation and Its Task*. Cambridge: Cambridge University Press.

Unger, R. 1998. *Democracy Realized*. London: Verso.

Unger, R. 2004. *False Necessity: Anti-Necessitarian Social Theory in the Service of Radical Democracy* (Revised Ed.). London: Verso.

Unger, R. 2007. *The Self Awakened: Pragmatism Unbound*. Cambridge Massachusetts: Harvard University Press.

Warren, D. 2003. "Constructive and Destructive Deviance in Organizations." *Academy of Management Review* 28: 622–632.

West, Brad. 2004. "Synergies in Deviance: Revisiting the Positive Deviance Debate." *Electronic Journal of Sociology* 7(4):19.

Zeitlin, M. 1991. "Positive Deviance in Nutrition." *Nutrition Review* 49(9): 259–268.

Zeitlin, M., Ghassemi, H., Mansour, M., and Levine, R. 1990. *Positive Deviance in Child Nutrition: With Emphasis on Psychosocial and Behavioural Aspects and Implications for Development*. Japan: United Nations University Press.

Filmography

Potter, M. 2009. "Big Stories, Small Towns: Version 1." [website]. Media Resource Centre, South Australia (v1.www.bigstories.com.au).

Wijanarko, D., and Potter, M. 2016. *Au Lorun (I Am Weaving)* [documentary]. Big Stories Co., VIC, Australia.

Index

3 Ds (Digitisation, Disintermediation and Deterritorialisation) 138

ABC Open Project 277
Aboriginal Australians 46; chefs 60; and European settlers 47–49, 50–51, 52; hunter-gatherer stereotype 49; land management 47–48
adaptation, to climate change 40
Adelaide Festival 261
Advance Queensland initiative 177
aesthetics 69, 247
Ager, W. 52
agglomeration 11, 124, 175
agriculture: Bioregion Food System Design and Study 37–38; *see also* food production
Allen, Kim 227
Amber Collective 233
Ambo, The 182–183
analytical knowledge work 148
anchor institutions 134–135
Andes, S. 131–132
Aquarius festival 55
ARC Centre of Excellence in Creative Industries and Innovation 4, 6
architectural design 102, 111, 112; deck-chair innovation 108; place-responsive 103
architecture: dongas 110; place-responsive 110; regional 107, 108; *see also* deck-chair innovation
art history: centre-periphery narrative 224; local-global narrative 223, 226
arts, the 11; biennials 223, 224; music scene in Central Queensland 261–267; regional 160, 162–164; Regional Arts Services Network (RASN) 166–167; and regions 227–231; and tourism 246–247; *see also* creative practice; festivals

Arts and Humanities Research Council (AHRC) 231
artwork: place in 224; site-specific 246
Au Lorun documentary 279–280, 281
'aura' 78
Australia 1, 103, 105; beach sculpture festivals 12–13; "Black War in Queensland" 48; Census of Population and Housing 151–152; Commonwealth Film Unit 70; creative economies 3; *Creative Nation* 3; Crown Land Acts 50–51; European settlement 48–49; festival culture 75; identity 102; knowledge cities 155; Landed Histories Project 47; macadamia nuts 59, 62; measurement of knowledge across 143–144, 145, 147–148; Outback 76–77; regional 103, 135, 177; regional beachscapes 245–246; service sectors 145; Uluru 106; wine regions 31; *see also* Blue Mountains; Brisbane; Katoomba; Northern Rivers; Queensland; Winton
Australia Council for the Arts, *Connecting Australians: Results of the National Arts Participation Survey* 163, 164
Australian Age of Dinosaurs 73
Australian Agricultural Company 26, 27
Australian Centre for Cultures, Environments, Society and Spaces (ACCESS) 4
Australian Native Food Industry 59
Australian Research Council, Linkage Projects: *Vines, Wine & Identity: the Hunter Valley NSW and Changing Australian Taste* 35; *Creativity and Cultural Production in the Hunter: An Applied Ethnographic Study of New Entrepreneurial Systems in the Creative Industries* 203
authenticity regime 98
automation 145

288　*Index*

Bakhshi, H. 160, 230
Bannerman, Colin 54
Bar TV 217–218
Barthes, Roland, *Mythologies* 89–90
Bayley, Bobbie 9, 103
BC Wine Institute (BCWI) 34
beach sculpture festivals 12–13
beaches: regional 244, 245–246; SWELL
　Sculpture Festival 250–251, 252; zones
　248, 249
Bell, David 1, 128, 129, 230
Benjamin, Walter 78
Benkler, Y. 274
Bennett, Andy 13, 266
Berry, Wendell 61
biennials 223, 224; Floating Land Festival
　252–254
Big Stories, Small Towns 13, 270, 272, 273,
　275, 278, 284; Lepo Lorun Weavers
　Collective 270–271; positive deviance
　276–278; residency in Flores, Indonesia
　278–279
Bilandzic, Ana 4, 11
Bioregion Food System Design and
　Study 38
Birch, E. 134
Black, Graeme 215
Black, Julie 216
"Black War in Queensland" 48
Blackwood, Matt 165
Blair, Tony 3, 123
Blakely, Edward 10
Blue Mountains 8, 82, 83, 84, 100; branding
　86, 87, 95–96; controlling "messaging"
　about 86, 87; craft breweries 96–97;
　Echo Point 82, 87, 90, 92; elevation
　theme 86, 87; Federal Pass 95; food
　tourism 97; foraging 97, 98, 99;
　Katoomba 91–93; nonrepresentational
　imagery 95–96; panoramas 88–89;
　tourism 84, 89–90; UNESCO World
　Heritage listing 85; as visual landscape
　87, 88–91; walking in 95–96
Blue Mountains Economic Enterprise
　(BMEE) 96
Blume Illustrated 93
Bonifacio, G. 133
"boomerang effect" 225
Bourdieu, Pierre 12, 202, 207; fields 5
Brabazon, Tara 10, 14, 134; *Unique
　Urbanity* 133
branding, of the Blue Mountains 86, 87,
　95–96
Braudel, Fernand 203

Breitbart, M. 163
Brisbane 177
British Columbia 34; climate 34; wine
　industry 33
British Council, *Mutual Influence?
　Universities, Cities and the Future of
　Internationalisation* 135
Brownscombe, Ross 87
Brunderlin, Christine 211
Buell, Lawrence 248
Bundjalung Country 46
Bundjalung people 49, 58, 60, 62; Clayton
　Donovan 60; Mark Olive 60
Burke, A. 84, 95
Busby Marou 261, 262, 264, 267
buzz 176, 261

Callon, M. 97
Canada 7; British Columbia 33; college
　towns 129–130; Grape Marketing Board
　34; *see also* Okanagan Valley
Canadian Pacific Railway 32
Cashman, David 13, 259
Casual Creative Environments (CCEs)
　175–176, 177, 179, 191, 192; digital
　technologies 189–190; iNQ 181, 182,
　186, 187–188; Old Ambulance Station
　180, 181, 182–183, 186, 188–189; people
　185–187; Substation33 183, 184, 187,
　189; use of space 187–189
Catchfire Press 211
celebrity authors/consultants 2
Census of Population and Housing
　151–152
Central Queensland, music scene in
　261–267
Central Queensland University, partnership
　with Creative Regions 167–170
certification: *Cittaslow* 38, 39; eco- 36
Cervone, John, *Corporatizing Rural
　Education: Neoliberal Globalisation and
　Reaction in the United States* 136
Chambers, Robert 137
chefs 59–60
cities 122, 123, 142, 162, 163, 179, 203,
　223; buzzing 176; development 123;
　downtown 131; four-stage modelling
　128; global 124, 132; as hybrid space 187;
　large 124; layers 179; London 228–229;
　people 185; small 127; temporal
　dimension 124; third-tier 127, 128, 130;
　see also creative cities; knowledge cities;
　Knowledge City Index (KCI); small
　cities; third-tier cities

Cittaslow 38, 39
climate: British Columbia 34; of Hunter Valley 23; of Okanagan Valley 26
climate change 40, 252
clusters 1, 2, 99, 127, 167, 229, 230; temporary 176; *see also* creative clusters
Cochrane, Susan 252–253
Coffield, Emma 3, 11, 12, 14
collaboration 161, 162, 175; in the university-industry-government (UIG) sector 164–166; *Writing the Digital Futures* project 166
Collectivist-Mass tourist gaze 89–90
college towns 129–130, 159; ranking 132–133
Collet-Sera, Jaume, *The Shallows* 68, 71
Collins, Felicity 76
colonialism 2, 7, 62
common opinion regime 98
community capital 22, 38
complex systems 201, 202
Connors, Graeme 261, 262, 264, 267
consumption of food 58–60
Coutts, Thomas 50
craft breweries 96–97
Craven, Allison 8
Craw, Charlotte 45, 57, 59
creative cities 1; London 228–229
"creative class" 163
creative clusters, and universities 160
creative economies 2, 3, 9; Australian 3; and regional arts 162–164; small cities 3
creative industries 4, 12, 161, 232–238; collaboration 161–162; Hunter Valley 205–207; place-sensitive research 5; in regional areas 259–260; in the United Kingdom 159
creative practice: "boomerang effect" 225; Empty Shop 232, 233–238; mobility 227; and "the region" in UK arts discourse 227–231
creative processes, and place 5
Creative Regions 11; partnership with Central Queensland University 167–170
creative systems 12, 201, 202, 203; *see also* Hunter Valley
creativity 15
Crown Land Acts 50–51
Csikszentmihalyi, Mihaly 12, 201–202, 207
Cultural Asset Mapping Project in Regional Australia (CAMRA) 67
cultural capital 245–246
culture 6, 106, 107, 161, 162, 231; cities of 229–230

Cummins, Marlene 75
Cunningham, Stuart 4, 161

dairy industry, Northern Rivers 54–55, 57
Darwin, Charles 89
Davidson, Robyn 106
Davidson's plum 58, 60, 61
Davis, Therese 76
day-trip tourism 92
de la Fuente, Eduardo 8
deck-chair innovation 9, 15, 102, 103, 106, 107, 108, 112, 114
Delmas, A. 36
Dena, Christy 165
design foraging 110, 115
Destination Marketing Organisation (DMO) 34
development 123, 131; regional 174–175; rural 137; urban regeneration 124; urbanisation 132
"deviance" 272, 273
digital access 10, 150
Digital Doctorate project 138
digital innovation 10; in filmmaking 67; "image phenomena" 70–71
Discover Naramata 38
Dolgopolov, Greg 74–75
Dominion Experimental Farm 31–32
Doneman, Michael 185–186
dongas 110
Donovan, Clayton 60
Donut Group 230
downtown 131
Drolet, J. 133
Duif, Lian, *Small Cities with Big Dreams* 129
Durham 12, 231–232; Empty Shop 232, 233–238
Durkheim, E. 272

"e-change" 176
Echo Point 82, 87, 90, 92
eco-certification 36
ecologies of creativity 5
economics of singularity 97–98, 99
Edible Garden Trail 99, 100
education cities 129, 137–138; 3 Ds (Digitisation, Disintermediation and Deterritorialisation) 138
Ellison, Liz 12, 167
emergence 201, 202
employment, university 126, 131
Empty Shop 227, 231, 232, 233–238
Engels, Friedrich 123

290 *Index*

entrepreneurship 161; Casual Creative Environments (CCEs) 175–176, 177, 179; *see also* Casual Creative Environments (CCEs)
Entwine accreditation 39
environmental affordances 5
Erickcek, G. 127
Esche, Charles 223
European land management 47–48
Evans, James 123
Evans, Morgan 210–211
everyday creativity 225
exhibitions 57, 226, 232, 234, 252, 271
expert opinion regime 98

Fab Labs 4, 11, 175
face-to-face interaction 142
Façon Australia 212–215, 213–215
Falconer, Delia 82, 91
fashion sector, Hunter Valley 212–215
fast policy 2, 9
festivals 244, 247, 248, 261; Aquarius 55; Floating Land 252–254, 256; grape harvest 29–30; music 266–267; Outback Writers Festival 75; regional 244–245; Sculpture by the Sea 244; Story Plus 165; Strand Ephemera 254–255, 256; SWELL Sculpture Festival 250–251, 252, 256; Vision Splendid Film Festival 74, 75; Way Out West Music Festival 75
fields 5, 12, 202, 207
filmmaking 13, 14, 15, 67; 'aura' 78; *Big Stories, Small Towns* 270, 272, 275, 276–278, 278, 278–279, 284; Gold Coast 78; Great Barrier Reef 70, 72; hybridity 72; "image phenomena" 70–71; Lepo Lorun Weavers Collective 271; Outback landscapes 76–77; regional landscapes 69; taxation offsets 68, 71, 72; *terra nullius* 68–69, 76, 78; terraforming 68, 70–72; the tropics 70; Village Roadshow Studios 67; Vision Splendid Film Festival 74–75; in Winton 68–69, 69, 74
finger limes 58
Fiske, J. 248, 249
Fitzgerald, David 215–217
Flew, Terry 4, 11, 161
Floating Land Festival 244, 247, 252–254, 256
"Floating Land" festival 13
Flores, Indonesia 14, 278–279, 283; Lepo Lorun Weavers Collective 270–271, 279–282

Florida, Richard 1, 2, 6, 123, 127, 142, 147, 156, 157, 163, 230
food consumption: chefs 59–60; macadamia nuts 59
food production 56–57; and expositions 57; and food consumption 58–60; Landed Histories Project 47; Northern Rivers 46; slow food movement 38; *see also* Northern Rivers
food tourism, Blue Mountains 96–97
foraging 97, 98, 99; architectural 102, 110; design 115
Ford, Adam 83
Foth, Marcus 4, 11
four-stage city modelling 128
fourth industrial revolution 143
Free Trade Agreement 34
Freeland, Max 103
Frenkel, A. 201
Full Fat Jazz 215
Funkhouser, Mark 135

Gammage, Bill 7, 46–47
Gehry, Frank 9, 103
geography 142; Hunter Valley 23; Northern Rivers 46; Okanagan Valley 25, 26
Gergaud, Oliver 36
Gibson, Chris 1, 5, 224, 227
Gibson, Ross 5, 6, 67, 69, 73, 76, 78
global cities 132, 162
Global Financial Crisis 126–127, 138
global financial crisis 124
globalisation 15, 124, 136, 163
Gold Coast 8, 70, 78; SWELL Sculpture Festival 250–251, 252; *see also* Village Roadshow Studios
Goldsmith, Ben 67
Gostelow, Tia 261, 262
Grady, Sean 134
Gramsci, Antonio 281, 284
Grand Section 103, 107, 114
Grape Marketing Board 34
grassroots organisations 38; Organic Okanagan 36–37
Great Barrier Reef 70, 72
Great Exhibition of the North 226
Greater Blue Mountains, UNESCO World Heritage listing 85
Grieve, Anna 271
gross domestic product (GDP) 144

habitus 12
Hancox, Donna 4, 11, 14, 212

Index   291

Hankinson, Janette 211
Harper, Andrew 106
Harrison, Rodney 50
Hartley, John 4
Hawkins, Harriet 225
Healey, Rachel 261
Hearn, Greg 4, 11
Herington, Matthew 272
Heylen, Joy, *The Crab* 251
Higgs, Peter 207
Higher Education Relations Officer (HERO) 135
Hillcoat, John 69; *The Proposition* 68
Hodge, B. 248, 249
Hogan, John 126
Hollands, Robert 229, 233
Hollingworth, Sumi 227
Holt-Giménez, Eric 57
Horeng, Alfonsa 270, 279, 280, 281
Horne, Julia, *The Pursuit of Wonder* 84
Howell, M. 124
Howitt, Richie 2
Hu, Richard 10
Huat, Chua Beng 70
Hughes, J.W. 32
Hull, John 7
human capital 11, 134
Hume, Lindy, *Restless Giant* 163
Hunter River Vineyard Association (HRVA) 27
Hunter Valley 7, 12, 21, 40, 201, 203; Aboriginal population 27; climate 23; creative industries 205, 206, 207; family wine businesses 35; fashion sector 212–215; fine dining culture 29–30; geography 23; grape harvest festivals 30; Gunn and Gollan report 29; Hunter Valley Vineyard Association (HVVA) 30; Hunter Valley Wine & Tourism Association (HVWTA) 30; industries 204; irrigation 30; land use 26–27, 28; Lovedale subregion 39; Morgan Evans 210–211; musical theatre 215–217; Newcastle 205, 206; organic wine firms 39; publishing sector 211–212; radio sector 208–210; soil 23; subregions 23, 25; television sector 217–218; tourism 30; urban areas 205; waterways 23; winegrowing 21–22, 27, 27–28
Hunter Valley Heritage Vineyards Study 36
Hunter Valley Vineyard Association (HVVA) 30

Hunter Valley Wine & Tourism Association (HVWTA) 30, 39; Hunter Valley Heritage Vineyards Study 36
Hunter Wine Industry Association (HWIA) 30
Hunter-Mooki Tectonic Fault Thrust system 23
Hurley, Frank 70
Hutchinson, S. 205

identity 6, 272; of "artist" 235; of Australia 102; of regions 69–70
"image phenomena" 70–71
inclusive communities 6
Independent Australian Radio Broadcasters Association 208
Indigenous knowledge 60, 62; *see also* Aboriginal Australians
industrialisation 123
information technologies 142–143, 144
innovation 10, 11, 15, 82, 174, 175, 283–284; architectural 103; Casual Creative Environments (CCEs) 175–176, 177, 179; *Cittaslow* 38–39; in filmmaking 67; in the university-industry-government (UIG) sector 161; *see also* Casual Creative Environments (CCEs); deck-chair innovation; digital innovation
iNQ 181, 182, 186, 188, 191
iNQ Central 187–188
Institute for Sustainable Agriculture 38
interaction 161
inter-firm regime 98
irrigation, Hunter Valley 30
Ison, Sean 208
Ison Live Radio (ILR) 208–209

James, Thelma 49–50
Janke, Terri 60
Jayne, Mark 1, 128, 129
Jones, Phil 123

Karpik, L. 97–98
Katoomba 91–92, 93; craft breweries 96–97; *kitschification* 94
Kaye, Nicholas, *Site-Specific Art* 246
Keane, Michael 4
Keats, John 274
Kelly, Owen 9, 103
Kerrigan, Susan 11, 205
Kettle Valley Railway 32
King, James 27
Kirby, James 49

292 *Index*

kitschification 94
Klocker, Natasha 1
knowledge 9, 10, 137, 142; Indigenous 60,
    62; measuring 143–144, 145, 147–148
knowledge capital 10, 150, 152
knowledge cities 155
Knowledge City Index (KCI) 10, 143,
    148, 149, 150–152, 156; knowledge
    capital 150; knowledge economy 151;
    as measure of proportion and raw size
    154, 155; by proportion 153, 154; by raw
    size 154
knowledge economy 10, 14, 22, 143, 156
knowledge industries 151
knowledge mobility 10, 150
Knowledge Transfer Partnerships
    (KTPs) 164
knowledge work 147, 148
Knox, Paul, *Human Geography: Places and
    Regions in Global Context* 202–203
Kotkin, Joel 126
Kowalski, A. 85

land use: European 47–48; Northern
    Rivers 56
Landed Histories Project 47
Landry, Charles 69, 123
landscape(s) 15, 22, 67, 91, 163; Blue
    Mountains 83; cultural nature of 85–86;
    The English and Australian Cookery Book
    53; Katoomba 91–92; mountain 83–84,
    84; nonrepresentational 99; Okanagan
    Valley 32; Outback 76–77; plateau
    83–84; as tension 82; value of 84–85;
    visual, Blue Mountains as 87, 88–91
Lane-McKinley, Kyle 230
Lang, John Dunmore 49
large cities 124
Laurie, Arthur 48
Lawson, William, *Wasteland, Wilderness,
    Wonderland* 83
Leadbeater, Charles 123
Ledwidge, Ringan, *Gone* 68
Lee, John 271
lemon myrtle 60–61
Lepo Lorun Weavers Collective 13, 14, 270,
    279–282, 284
Lewandowski, Natalie 13
Lindeman & Sons 28, 30
Lippard, Lucy, *The Lure of the Local* 224
Living Labs 175
living labs 11
local buzz 176

Local Government Areas (LGAs) 177,
    179, 192
local-global narrative 223, 226
locavore movement 21
London 228–229
Lovedale subregion of Hunter Valley 39
Luckman, Sue 3, 5, 69, 73, 88, 224, 227
Lupish, Lara 212, 213

Mabo Native Title act 76–77
macadamia nuts 58, 59, 62
Mackay, Sasha 4, 11, 13
Mackenzie, E. 148
MacLean, Mark 211
Macpherson, Emma, *Recollections of a Visit to
    the Australian Colonies in 1856–7* 53
Maital, S. 201
manufacturing 128; in third-tier cities 130
Markusen, Ann 225, 238
Marston, Sallie, *Human Geography: Places and
    Regions in Global Context* 202–203
Marx, Karl 123
Mason, Josh 217
Massey, Doreen 61
Mateos-Garcia, J. 160, 230
Mayes, Christopher 61
Mayes, Robin 76
McCormick, Brendan 217, 218
McFarlane, John 48
McGrath, Simon 131
Mchawala, Sieh 271
McHenry, J. A. 272
McIntyre, Julie 7
McIntyre, Philip 11
McKinney, H. 127
Meadel, C. 97
measurement of knowledge across Australia
    143–144, 145, 147–148
mega regime 98
Melchior, Americo 55
Men's Shed movement 283
Merton, R. K. 272
metropolitan creative industries
    imaginaries 2
metropolitan imaginary 3
Metropolitan Players 216–217
Milson, J., *Will the Great Barrier Reef Cure
    Claude Clough?* 70
mining in regional areas 265
Miranda, Magally 230
mobility 227
modernisation 136
modernist art history 223

Index 293

Modi, Narendra 191
Morse, Nuala 227
Morton 162
mountain landscapes 83–84; walking in 95–96
Mt Perry 105
Murphy, Peter 93
music festivals 266–267
music industry 13, 15; Morgan Evans 210–211; in Queensland 261–267; in regional areas 260; touring 267
music "scenes" 260–261
musical theatre, Hunter Valley 215–217

Naramata 38
Naramata Bench Winery Association 38, 39
native foods 45, 62; Australian Native Food Industry 59; chefs 59–60; consumption of in Northern Rivers 58–60; Davidson's plum 58, 60, 61; finger limes 58; growing 60, 61; lemon myrtle 60–61; macadamia nuts 58, 59, 62; 'Noma effect' 60; Northern Rivers 53–54, 57; Orana Foundation 60
natural landscapes 22
nature 67, 69; and culture 106, 107; walking in 95–96
negative capability 274
New South Wales: European settlement 50–52; *see also* Northern Rivers
Newton, John 62
'Noma effect' 60
non-premium wines 22
Noosa 13; Floating Land Festival 252–254
North America: Free Trade Agreement 34; wine industry 32–33
Northern Rivers 7, 45, 62; agricultural industry 54–55, 56; Aquarius festival 55; consumption of native foods 58–60; Crown Land Acts 50–51; dairy industry 54–55, 57; Davidson's plum 58, 60–61; environmental preservation 55–56; European settlement 48–50, 51, 52; finger limes 58; food production 56–57; geography 46; land-use conflicts 56; lemon myrtle 60–61; macadamia nuts 58, 59; massacres 50; native foods 53–54, 57; riberry 54; Robertson Land Acts 50–51; tourism 55; waterbirds 52–53; waterways 46; zircon mining 55; *see also* native foods

Oakley, Kate 224
O'Connor, Justin 4

offsets 68, 71, 72
Okanagan Valley 7, 21, 40; adaptive change 36; agricultural economy 32; Bioregion Food System Design and Study 37–38; Bioregion Food System Design and Study project 37–38; climate 26; community capital 38; Dominion Experimental Farm 31–32; eco-certification 36; *Embracing our potential, 2012–2022* 34–35; forest fires 40; geography 25, 26; grassroots organisations 38; Kettle Valley Railway 32; landscapes 32; Naramata Bench Winery Association 38–39; rural tourism 35; settler agriculture 31; steamboats 32; sustainability 38; Thompson Okanagan Tourism Association (TOTA) 34; tourism 33–34; winegrowing 22; wineries 34
Old Ambulance Station 180, 182–183, 186, 188–189
Olive, Mark 60
O'Neill, Phillip 30
Orana Foundation 60
O'Regan, Tom 67
Organic Okanagan 36–37
organic wine firms, Hunter Valley 39
Orozco, Lourdes 230
O'Shea, Maurice 29
Outback, the 76–77
Outback Writers Festival 75

Paisley 121, 122
Pandosy, Charles 31
Pascoe, Bruce 7, 49, 62; *Dark Emu Black Seeds: Agriculture or Accident* 46
Patterson, Banjo 73
Peck, Jamie 2
Pederson, Aaron 77
Peppercorne, Frederick Septimus 51
Perkins, Rachel, *Black Panther Woman* 75
Petrie, Tom 48
Pholedros, Paul 106
phylloxera 28
Picken, F. 245, 246
Pike, Andy 71
place 1, 3, 5, 6, 13, 14, 15, 21, 47, 106, 142, 143, 249, 272; in artwork 224; and creative processes 5; deck-chair innovation 102, 103, 107, 108; design foraging 115; local-global narrative 226; and region 69–70; remoteness 73–74; and space 248; tropics 72; *see also* regions
plateaus 83–84

294 *Index*

Pokolbin and District Vinegrowers
  Association (PDVGA) 28–29
policy, fast 2, 9
Porter, Michael 1, 5
positive deviance 13, 14, 270, 273–276; in
  Big Stories, Small Towns project 276–278
Potter, Martin 13, 276
Potts, Jason 4
Powell, Michael, *Age of Consent* 70
Prachett, Lawrence 10, 11
premium wine-growing 22–23, 40
Private Irrigated District (PID) 30
Producer Offset 68
professional regime 98
public art 246
publishing 15; Hunter Valley 211–212
push bikes 106
Putland, C. 276

Queensland 67, 70, 177–178; Casual
  Creative Environments (CCEs) 179;
  film industry 68; Mt Perry 105; music
  scene in 261–267; public arts festivals
  244; Regional Arts Services Network
  (RASN) 166–167; regional beachscapes
  245–246; SWELL Sculpture Festival 244;
  Village Roadshow Studios 67, 68; *see also*
  Casual Creative Environments (CCEs);
  Winton
Queensland University of Technology
  (QUT) 4

Rabeharisoa, V. 97
radio sector of Hunter Region's creative
  system 208–210
Rafferty, Gerry 121, 138
ranking college towns 132–133
Rawson, Mina, *Antipodean Cookery Book* 54
Redhead, Steve 131
Redzepi, Rene 60
regeneration 123
regional architecture 107, 108
regional areas 22, 69–70, 78, 177; in arts
  discourse in the United Kingdom
  227–231; creative industries in
  259–260; "curated" 226; landscapes 244;
  local-global narrative 226; mining in 265;
  music scene in 260, 263–264; regulated
  228; *see also* wine regions; Winton
regional arts 162–164, 248
Regional Arts Services Network (RASN)
  11, 166–167
regional beaches 244

regional creativity 14, 22, 69
regional development 174–175
regional economies 11
regional landscapes 8, 67; in filmmaking 69
regional locations 14, 15
regional universities 122, 131
regulated regions 228
remoteness 73–74
Rendall, Kimball, *Guardians of the Tomb* 71
reticular regime 98
reverse migration 225
riberry 54
Richards, Greg, *Small Cities with Big
  Dreams* 129
Richardson, Harvey 227
Robertson Land Acts 50–51
Robinson, William 96; *Creation* 95
Rous, Henry 46
Rozin, P. 53
rural areas 33, 40, 46, 135–136, 224;
  development 137; and opportunities
  136–137; urbanisation 132
Rush, Gary 133
Ryan, Lyndall 77, 245, 246, 277

Salt, Bernard 176
Saunders, Lloyd 264
scalability 202
Schulz, T. 204
Scott, Allen 1
Screen Australia 68
Screen Queensland 74
sculpture 13; SWELL Sculpture Festival
  250–251, 252
Sculpture by the Sea 244
seaside festivals 13
second-tier cities 223
self-organisation in complex systems 201
Sen, Ivan 69, 75, 77; *Goldstone* 68, 77;
  Mystery Road 68, 77
Senese, Donna 7
sensescapes 9
service sectors 145
settler agriculture, Okanagan Valley 31
significant urban areas (SUAs) 149
site-specific art 246
slow food movement 7, 38; *Cittaslow*
  38–39; Thompson Okanagan Slow Food
  convivium 38
small cities 10, 122, 127, 133, 135;
  invisibility of 135; and opportunities
  136–137; Paisley 121; types of 127; and
  universities 126; universities 125

Index   295

Smart Work 151
smart work 10
Smith, Adam 52
Snapshot of Poverty in Rural and Regional Australia, A 162
soil, of Hunter Valley 23
Solitary-Romantic tourist gaze 89–90
Sonenshein, S. 273
space, and place 248
spatial imaginaries 12
Spearritt, Peter, *Syney's Century* 92
Spreitzer, G. M. 273
Standing, Guy 126
Stanford Innovation Survey 161
Story Plus 165
Strand Ephemera festival 244, 247, 254–255, 256
studios: Village Roadshow Studios 67, 68; *see also* filmmaking
Substation33 183, 184, 187, 189
Surfer's Paradise 250
sustainability 124, 134; Bioregion Food System Design and Study 37–38; eco-certification 36; of the Hunter Valley 36
SWELL Sculpture Festival 244, 247, 250–251, 252, 256
symbolic knowledge work 147
synthetic knowledge work 147
systems 207–208; *see also* complex systems; creative systems

tastescapes 7, 8, 60; *see also* food consumption; food production; native foods
taxation offsets 68, 71, 72
Taylor, Thomas Griffith 83–84, 134
technology 189
television sector, Hunter Valley 217–218
temporary clusters 176
terra firma 8; in the Winton Region 72–76
terra incognita 51
terra nullius 68–69, 76, 78
terraforming 8, 68, 70–71; 'Wet tropics' 72
terroir 38, 39
third-tier cities 121–122, 127, 128, 130, 131, 132, 135, 137; community engagement 131–132; development 131; diversity 138; manufacturing 130; and opportunities 136–137; and universities 126, 129; urbanisation 132
Thomas, Martin, *The Artificial Horizon* 85–86

Thompson, Michelle 12
Thompson Okanagan Slow Food convivium 38
Thompson Okanagan Tourism Association (TOTA) 34; *Embracing our potential, 2012–2022* 34–35
Threadgold, Steven 259
tourism 15, 40, 128; and the arts 246–247; Blue Mountains 84, 89–90; day-trip 92; Embracing our potential, 2012–2022 34–35; Hunter Valley 30; Katoomba 91–93; *kitschification* 94; Northern Rivers 55; Okanagan Valley 33–34; rural areas 33; zones 249
tourist gaze 89–90, 91, 95
Townsville, Strand Ephemera festival 254–255
Tredinnick, Mark, *The Blue Plateau* 92
Trident Methodology 206–207
Triple Helix framework 161
tropics, the 70
Trump, Donald 136
Tuli, Sajeda 10
Turner, G. 248, 249
types of small cities 127

Uluru 106, 107
Unger, Robert 273–274, 275, 276, 277, 278
United Kingdom 3; cities of culture 229–230; creative clusters 160; creative industries 159; Durham 12; Great Exhibition of the North 226; Knowledge Transfer Partnerships (KTPs) 164; "the region" in arts discourse 227–231
universities 10, 121, 122, 124, 125, 159; as anchor institutions 134–135; Central Queensland University, partnership with Creative Regions 167–170; and creative clusters 160; employment 126, 131; entrepreneurship 161; regional 122, 131, 160; Regional Arts Services Network (RASN) 166–167; and small cities 126; "spillover effect" 135; staff 130; in third-tier cities 129, 130
university cities 130, 133; community engagement 131–132; diversity 138; Finnish 132; Higher Education Relations Officer (HERO) 135; human capital 134; invisibility of 135; and opportunities 136–137; sustainability 134
university-industry-government (UIG) sector 161; knowledge exchange 161, 162, 164–166

296 *Index*

urban agglomeration 175
urban informatics 178, 179, 187, 189
urban regeneration 124
urbanisation 132
urbanity 123
Urry, John 89, 91

Vail, John 229, 233
value of landscape 83–84, 85
Van Dam, Michael, *These Hands* 251
van de Fliert, Elske, "Positive Deviance
    in Theory and Practice: A Conceptual
    Review" 272
van Heur, Ban 2
Village Roadshow Studios 67, 68, 70,
    70–71
"Vines, Wine & Identity: the Hunter Valley
    NSW and Changing Australian Taste" 35
Vision Splendid Film Festival 74, 75
visual arts, centre-periphery narrative
    15, 225
visual landscape, Blue Mountains as 87,
    88–91
viticulture, eco-certification 36
Vogt-Roberts, Jordan, *Kong: Skull Island*
    68, 71
von Guerard, Eugene, *Weatherboard Creek
    Falls* 89

Waitt, Gordon 5
walking in mountain landscapes 95–96
Walmsley, Ben 230
Walsh, Michael 10
Walter, E.V. 248
Waltzing Matilda Centre 73, 75
Wan, James, *Aquaman* 71
Ward, Susan 67
Warden, Rebecca 134
waterbirds, Northern Rivers 52–53
waterways, Northern Rivers 46
Watson, Sophie 93

Way Out West Music Festival 75
Wentworth, William Charles, *Wasteland,
    Wilderness, Wonderland* 83
Wessel, Adele 7
Westbury, Marcus, *Creating Cities* 204–205
Wilkins, L. 272
Willoughby-Smith, J. 224, 227
Wilson, Faye 93
wine production 7, 21, 22; British
    Columbia 33; Hunter Valley 27–28;
    non-premium 22; premium 22–23
wine regions 22, 23, 40; in Australia 31;
    natural landscapes 22; *terroir* 38, 39; *see
    also* Hunter Valley; Okanagan Valley
wine tourism 7, 21, 22, 23
winegrowing, eco-certification 36
Winton 8, 68, 68–69, 69, 72, 74–75, 78;
    Evert family 76; festivals 75–76; film
    industry 74, 76; Outback Writers Festival
    75; regional landscapes 69; remoteness
    of 73–74; *terra firma* 72–76; Waltzing
    Matilda Centre 73, 75; Way Out West
    Music Festival 75
Winton Shire Council 74
Wollogong School of Cultural Geography
    4, 12
work 175
Wotherspoon, James 58
Writing the Digital Futures project 164–165,
    166, 170
Wylie, John 82, 95

Yi, Wang 4, 11

Zeitlin, Marian, *Positive Deviance in Child
    Nutrition: With Emphasis on Psychosocial
    and Behavioural Aspects and Implications for
    Development* 273
zircon mining 55
zones 248, 249
Zonfrillo, Jock 60

Printed in the United States
By Bookmasters